Subversive Spirituality

Princeton Theological Monograph Series

K. C. Hanson, Charles M. Collier, and D. Christopher Spinks,
Series Editors

Recent volumes in the series:

Richard Valantasis et al., editors
The Subjective Eye: Essays in Honor of Margaret Miles

Anette Ejsing
A Theology of Anticipation: A Constructive Study of C. S. Peirce

Caryn Riswold
Coram Deo: Human Life in the Vision of God

Paul O. Ingram, editor
Constructing a Relational Cosmology

Michael G. Cartwright
Practices, Politics, and Performance: Toward a Communal Hermeneutic for Christian Ethics

David A. Ackerman
Lo, I Tell You a Mystery: Cross, Resurrection, and Paraenesis in the Rhetoric of 1 Corinthians

Lloyd Kim
Polemic in the Book of Hebrews: Anti-Judaism, Anti-Semitism, Supersessionism?

At the very outset, one can see that Jensen has taken on an ambitious project. It not only covers a wide range of thinkers that span more than two millennia, but addresses a complex array of ideas. And yet, what could be more pertinent and to the point in this age, with all the challenges it portends, than an analysis that connects time and space to devotion to God and mission? Jensen's research is consistently rigorous and his powers of comparison and analysis superior. I highly recommend this provocative and important study.

—JAMES BRADLEY, Geoffrey W. Bromiley Professor of Church History,
Fuller Theological Seminary

Some thinkers teach us by digging deeply into a specialized area and discovering new facts and insights. Others change us by explaining new connections and relationships that not only enlighten our minds, but also change what we do. Jensen's book is of the latter type. Backed by a sweeping panorama of historical and biblical material, he urges us to change our lives and our world by connecting the spiritual life and mission in a holistic, fresh way. I hope and pray many will listen—and change.

—JON L. DYBDAHL, Professor of Mission, Andrews University,
and former president of Walla Walla University

Jesus was frequently heard saying, "If a person has ears, let him hear!" *Subversive Spirituality* attests to the fact that Paul Jensen "hears." It affirms that he has one ear to the ground of the postmodern generations, hearing the painful results that the energy-sapping disintegration of space and time produces in their lives, while his other ear is tuned to the life-generating pulse of our Creator and to the rhythms he has designed for our renewal and for empowerment in mission. I first saw the transformed lives of those who practiced what Paul suggests in this work, and now as I read the concepts in print, I realize the magnitude of the mission that could be ignited by the Spirit in the hearts of those who read and "hear."

—JULIE A. GORMAN, Professor of Christian Formation and
Discipleship, Fuller Theological Seminary

For so many people today, life is busy and full, and only picking up steam. This is true for ministers as well. We have a great need for time and space to meet with God. Jensen presents an integrative model for spirituality and mission that can help the church engage the generation of this age in ways that deepen their inner life with God and move people to participate in God's kingdom mission. Grounded in grace, Jensen offers both critique and hope for how spiritual practices can bring about the transformational work of redemption in our lives and the world today. This is a solid work that speaks to the longings of a postmodern generation to know God and to engage in meaningful, redemptive work in the world.

—EVAN HUNTER, director of the Ivy Jungle Network

With careful research, analysis, and diagnosis, Paul shows us what Gen X and Y most need (particularly their "mentor deficit") and how helping them implement the timeless practices of Christians throughout history will help them be formed into disciples of Jesus.

—JAN JOHNSON, speaker and author of many books on spirituality, including *Invitation to the Jesus Life*

Subversive Spirituality

Transforming Mission through the Collapse of Space and Time

L. PAUL JENSEN

☙PICKWICK *Publications* · Eugene, Oregon

SUBVERSIVE SPIRITUALITY
Transforming Mission through the Collapse of Space and Time

Princeton Theological Monograph Series 113

Copyright © 2009 L. Paul Jensen. All rights reserved. Except for brief quotations in critical publications or reviews, no part of this book may be reproduced in any manner without prior written permission from the publisher. Write: Permissions, Wipf and Stock Publishers, 199 W. 8th Ave., Suite 3, Eugene, OR 97401.

Table 5 "Living in the Ecotone: A Continuum of Worldview Change" by Jonathan Campbell, used by permission

Pickwick Publications
A Division of Wipf and Stock Publishers
199 W. 8th Ave., Suite 3
Eugene, OR 97401

www.wipfandstock.com

ISBN 13: 978-1-60608-154-9

Cataloging-in-Publication data:

Jensen, L. Paul

    Subversive spirituality : transforming mission through the collapse of space and time / L. Paul Jensen.

    xxiv + 370 p. ; 23 cm. Includes bibliographical references and index.

    Princeton Theological Monograph Series 113

    ISBN 13: 978-1-60608-154-9

    1. Spirituality. 2. Mission of the church. 3. Christian leadership. 4. Postmodernity—Religious aspects—Christianity. I. Title. II. Series.

BV4501.2 J53 2009

Manufactured in the U.S.A.

Dedicated to

my wife, Cheris,

whose grace and love led me to become a follower of Jesus

and has sustained me ever since,

and to the memory of

Josh Turville, a Generation X martyr,

whose radical love for Jesus

helped ignite the spiritual journeys of many in his generation

including our three children.

Contents

List of Illustrations / xi

Acknowledgements / xiii

Foreword / xix

Preface / xxiii

1. Introduction / 1
2. The Collapse of Time and Space / 31
3. Jesus's Rhythms of Spirituality and Mission / 70
4. The Early Church's Rhythms of Spirituality and Mission / 112
5. Rhythms of Spirituality and Mission in the Modern Age / 153
6. Rhythms of Spirituality and Mission in the Postmodern Age / 213
7. Conclusion / 258

Appendices:

    A Some Contemporary Definitions of Spirituality / 291
    B What Is a Spiritual Discipline? / 293
    C Physical Symptoms, Psychological Signs, and Underlying Beliefs of Time Pathologies / 295
    D Luke's Gospel, Part A: Jesus's Rhythms of Spirituality and Mission / 297
    E Luke's Gospel, Part B: Jesus's Rhythms of Spirituality and Mission / 299
    F Three Branches of Spiritual Theology / 301
    G Summary of Rhythms of Spirituality and Mission in the *Devotio Moderna* / 302
    H Summary of Rhythms of Spirituality and Mission in Ignatius and the Early Jesuits / 304

I Journey to Reach the Next Generations: Project Questionnaire / 306
J Suggestions for Extended Personal Communion with God / 309

References Cited / 311

Scripture Index / 345

Subject Index / 350

Illustrations

Figures

1. Effects of REST Treatment on Smoking Addiction / 60
2. Youth Leaders Concerned over Sacrificing Devotional Time / 231
3. Correlation of Verbal Witness with Frequency and Duration of Solitude and Duration of Solitude and Bible Reading / 248
4. A Model for Christian Spirituality and Mission / 271
5. Effects of the Collapse of Space and Time / 276
6. Jensen's Integrative Model for Studying Spirituality and Mission in the Academy / 285

Tables

1. Comparisons of Pre-Modern, Modern, and Postmodern Eras / 4
2. Classifications of the Disciplines / 6
3. Classifications of Spiritual Practices / 8
4. Characteristics of Authentic Christian Spirituality / 11
5. Living in the Ecotone: A Continuum of Worldview Change / 16
6. Definitions and Descriptions of Christian Mission/Theology / 20
7. Sheldrake's Earmarks of a Spiritual Classic / 29
8. The Development of Universal Clock Time / 41
9. Time and Social Capital: Some Findings and Recommendations / 47
10. Where Millennials Lost Free Time Compared with Xers / 51
11. Descriptions of the Time Pathologies and Their Effects / 63
12. Plotting My Approach to Studying New Testament Spirituality / 72
13. Israel's Spiritual Practices and Jesus's Redefinition of Them / 82
14. Jesus's Withdrawals from the Crowds in the Synoptics / 86
15. Mark's Gospel, Part A: Jesus's Rhythms of Spirituality and Mission / 87

16	Mark's Gospel, Part B: Jesus's Rhythms of Spirituality and Mission / 89	
17	Summary of Jesus's Practices of Spirituality and Mission in the Synoptics / 92	
18	Summary of Jesus's Teaching on Spirituality and Mission / 102	
19	Contrasts in Jesus's Teaching on Spirituality and Mission: The Sermon on the Mount Compared with John 15 / 106	
20	Keeping Spiritual Practices from Becoming a New Legalism / 109	
21	Acts, Part A / 117	
22	Acts, Part B / 123	
23	Rhythms of Prayer and Mission: Parallels and Contrasts Between Luke and Acts / 127	
24	Church Fathers Who Read the Apostolic Fathers / 130	
25	Solitary Prayer and Mission in the *Shepherd of Hermas* / 137	
26	Space, Time, Spirituality, and Mission in the Apostolic Fathers / 142	
27	Sheldrake's Three Stages of a Spiritual Tradition / 164	
28	The New Devout's Emerging Spiritual and Mission Practices / 170	
29	New Devotion Quotes on Empowering Grace / 174	
30	Ignatius Discovers the Need for Spiritual Discernment and Direction / 180	
31	Ignatius on Empowering Grace for Spirituality and Mission / 188	
32	Spiritual and Mission Practices Taught in the *Constitutions* / 191	
33	Early Jesuit's Emerging Practices of Spirituality and Mission / 194	
34	Summary of Brainerd's Rhythms of Spirituality and Mission in His *Life and Diary* / 208	
35	Summary of Generation X Spirituality and Time-Space Collapse / 232	
36	Classifications of Three Kinds of Practices in a Model for Spirituality and Mission / 273	

Acknowledgements

THIS BOOK IS THE CULMINATION OF YEARS OF RESEARCH AND WRITING done during my PhD studies at Fuller Theological Seminary's School of Intercultural Studies. I owe a debt of gratitude to many people. Wilbert R. Shenk, the chairperson of my committee, wrote the foreword. During my doctoral program, I leaned heavily on his teaching and vast knowledge of contemporary culture and mission history. His mentorship, wise counsel, prayers, and unflagging encouragement were invaluable. The rationale for this study comes from his penetrating analysis of contemporary culture, which introduced me to the notion of "the collapse of space and time."

At the dawn of the new millennium, I was stunned by the implications of this newfound idea and its relationship to something I had heard Henri Nouwen preach about seven years before. "A spiritual discipline," Nouwen had said, "is the human effort to create open space to listen to the voice of the One who calls us the beloved." Nouwen's definition of a spiritual discipline implies both grace and a reversal of the cultural collapse of space and time. This suggested that I look for the presence or absence of a *graced link* between *spiritual discipline*—in terms of space and time—and *mission practice*—in terms of deed and word. I not only wanted to explore this linkage culturally in twenty-first century North America, but also historically, as well as biblically and theologically. Wilbert Shenk enthusiastically embraced this line of inquiry, as did Richard V. Peace, who gently guided me through the biblical and historical study of spirituality, so needed at a time when our culture is fascinated by all things spiritual. Peace's scholarly work on conversion and his integration of spirituality with evangelism are imaginative and compelling, and helped shape this book. Often, his comments were "prophetic" or proved to be spiritual direction at critical junctures along the way. James E. Bradley's oversight of my historical research on second-millennial spiritual classics and his input on historical methods have proven invaluable to the historical parts of the book, found in chapters 3–5. These chapters also drew upon Paul E. Pierson's course and personal consultation on the history of the Christian mission. Jerry W. Lee's many years of experience and encyclopedic knowledge of quantitative research on religious practice and faith maturity proved indispensable to the design and implementation of my field research reported in chapter 6. He offered helpful comments on this part of the chapter, which is based on his extensive statistical analysis of data collected from two samples comprising more than 2,700 respondents to a questionnaire. Simon Chan, a systematic theologian who has written on spiritual and liturgical theology, served as the outside reader for this work at the dissertation stage. A number of his suggestions and critiques are reflected in the book. I thank him for these.

As the preceding makes clear, this study is multi-disciplinary, drawing from a wide range of scholars in at least seven academic fields that often have little overlap with each other. I am grateful for the multifaceted research and writing of the more than 350 scholars and writers cited in this book. Doing research in such diverse fields offers the opportunity to be more holistic and less atomized than is sometimes the case in research limited to a narrow set of questions in one particular field. The risk, however, in multi-disciplinary work (typical of the fields of spirituality and missiology) is that such research may miss some relevant findings that are already available in the various fields being probed, because the mastery of all the relevant literature in various fields will necessarily be less than the mastery of the literature in a single field. This undoubtedly is one of the many weaknesses of this book. Readers from the various disciplines in which this study is done can judge for themselves the extent to which it overcomes the risk and maximizes the opportunity.

I must also mention other important influences on my life and thinking that have affected this book. Betsy Glanville, Julie A. Gorman, and J. Robert Clinton have contributed profoundly to my understanding of and approach to integrating spirituality with academic work. Bobby Clinton and Julie Gorman first showed me that formation could find a place in the academy when I took masters level courses from them in the late 1980s. Julie Gorman opened the door for me to begin teaching formationally as an adjunct in her Department of Christian Formation and Discipleship at Fuller Seminary in 1990, which I have done ever since. Beginning in 2004, Betsy Glanville gave me the opportunity to lead retreats for doctoral students. The influence of these three is largely implicit in this book, but crucial nonetheless. Additionally, my mid-career journey into graduate academic work would be unthinkable without the mentorship, encouragement, gracious friendship, and towering scholarship of Nicholas Thomas (N. T.) Wright. His massive work as a historian and New Testament theologian is evident in chapters 3 and 4. Upon hearing about the initial findings in the research I was doing on the spirituality of leaders and members of Generations X and Y under Lee's supervision in the mid 1990s, Tom Wright said, "You must write!" The next morning I heard Francis Bacon cited in a sermon by David Mitchell: "Reading maketh a ready man, conference a full man, and writing an exact man." At that moment, I was unmistakably called to read and write about spirituality and mission. That October day in 1996 set in motion a series of processes that have resulted in the publication of this book.

I shall always be grateful to the editorial committee at Pickwick Publications and Wipf & Stock, which gave me the opportunity to publish this work as my first book, and to Chris Spinks, my editor at Pickwick, for his advocacy for this project with the other members of the committee. Chris's patience, experience, wisdom, and prompt answers to my questions have demystified the learning curve for an author preparing the manuscript of his first book. Since this work was originally written in the bibliographic style of the American Anthropological Association (AAA) at the dissertation phase, I appreciate Pickwick's special permission to publish it according to AAA conventions rather than Pickwick's standard style used in its Princeton Theological Monograph Series. Their gracious exception saved considerable time and expense. I also thank Rob Johnston for first suggesting Wipf & Stock and for connecting me to Chris Spinks. I am likewise grateful to my wife, Cheris, for reading the manuscript in its entirety before sending it to Pickwick, and for her questions, comments, corrections, and suggestions, which have made the text more readable and accurate.

During the dissertation stage, Michael Evans devoted hours of meticulous work to this manuscript, which elevated its style and saved it from a myriad of mistakes. His suggestions added enormously to the book's clarity and readability. Oksana Bevs, the acting research librarian at Fuller Theological Seminary, also made important criticisms and gave timely help. All remaining errors and omissions are solely my own and in no way reflect upon those who have contributed so richly to this study.

These acknowledgments would be incomplete without thanking the many who made this book possible through generous financial gifts and prayer over the years. The faithful prayers and love of my wife, Cheris, enabled me to stay with this project in its hardest hours as did the prayers of our three children and their spouses, Erika and David Carlson, Kirk and Wanda Jensen, and Kristoffer and Erin Jensen. These couples have also helped paint a picture of their generation's relationship to Jesus, which plays a prominent role in this book. I am grateful to them, to my parents, Lyle and Mildred Jensen, and to my mother-in-law, Marjory Martin, for their prayers and generous support. Many thanks to my family and the scores of friends who have prayed for and financially supported my life's mission since 1968, and to those who stood with me in my academic journey over these years. I especially think of Douglas R. Ayres, whom I mentored through his conversion and subsequent journey of spiritual formation. I thank him for prayerfully encouraging me throughout my research and writing and for his generosity, which continued even through the greatest tragedy of his life, the loss of his son Dylan, in an automobile accident in 2006. I also thank the members of the Global Ministries Scholarship Committee at Fuller Seminary for awarding me several grants, which funded a significant portion of my PhD studies.

Finally, I thank my colleagues at The Leadership Institute for their contributions to the development of this book. The extraordinary service of Alan J. Fadling, the Institute's associate director, helped it flourish while I completed my research and writing, which required that I devote less time to my responsibilities as executive director. He also helped develop the concluding chapter's figures, which capture graphically the message of the book. I also thank my other remarkable colleagues at the Institute: Charles R. Miller, for his modeling and teaching on how to integrate spirituality and leadership; the late Wayne Anderson, for introducing me to the contemplative tradition of spirituality and the biblical idea of grace as "God's enabling power"; Joy Mosbarger, for sharing her taxonomy of New Testament approaches to the study of spirituality and her copies of numerous articles on spirituality; Willy Hernandez, for his unfailing encouragement to finish this project even as he completed and published his own work on Henri Nouwen; and Jon Byron, Craig

Babb, Paul Kaak, David Montzingo, and Jon Ciccarelli, for their prayers and encouragement. The Leadership Institute board members have my undying gratitude for their approval and wholehearted support of my course of research and writing. They are Don Barkley, Jeff Immel, Gary Jones, Sandy Roberts, Don Sprenger, and Gary Tabor. I also acknowledge Lynn F. Mallery, who as much as any single person outside the immediate Institute family contributed to its birth and growth. He provided the design, conceptual framework, and opportunity to start the Institute's most important extensive non-formal training—the *Journey to Reach the Next Generations*. His passing on November 7, 2007 was an immense loss personally and organizationally. He opened many doors of teaching and training for the Institute and for me personally, without which both the Institute and this book would not be what they are. Within a year, two others, who have been acknowledged above, died suddenly. My father, Lyle H. Jensen, a world-class x-ray crystallographer whose integration of Christian spirituality and scholarship left an indelible mark on my own work, died on October 16, 2008. Three days after his memorial service came shocking news of the October 23 passing of my spiritual director, Wayne Anderson, whose emphasis on solitude, silence, and extended communion with God became a feature of The Leadership Institute. Our organizational structure is unthinkable without the Institute's legal counsel and my close lifetime friend, Ernest F. Ching, and my long-time friends and colleagues in campus ministry, Joe and Nancy Jerus, who helped establish the non-profit apparatus in which the Institute has functioned. The courage to pioneer, risk, and start The Leadership Institute would have been inconceivable without the encouragement and spiritual support over many years of: my beloved mother, Mildred Jensen, a woman of great prayer, hospitality, and compassion; Norman and Dottie Versteeg who pastored us with unconditional love providing freedom and significant ministry opportunities; and another lifetime friend, Paul Johnson, my spiritual father and early mentor, along with his parents, Genevieve and the late Paul A. Johnson whose optimistic belief in me even amidst great difficulty never wavered since my conversion to Jesus. May the contributions of so many bear fruit to the glory of God.

Foreword

"It is the black hole of the digital age," declare Matt Richtel and Ashlee Vance.[1] This "black hole" is the three minutes it takes for a PC to boot up when it is turned on. "To an information-addicted society" that cannot tolerate "even a moment of downtime," these three minutes have been the focus of intense frustration for millions of people.

What is the source of this frustration? It has been created by the technology industry with its constant drumbeat for ever-faster response. Each innovation raises our expectations, setting the stage for another round of innovation that will shave a few more seconds off the time it takes to do a task. "Our brains have become impatient with the boot-up process," according to Dr. Gary Small at UCLA.[2] "We have been spoiled by the hand-held devices." These technological changes have penetrated our culture deeply and pervasively.

The PC manufacturers have been hard at work to solve this problem, and in 2008 new technology was introduced that promised to reduce the boot up process to a matter of seconds. Millions of people are poised to purchase the new technology promising to get rid of this "black hole."

This parable throws light on a defining dynamic of modern culture. Late modernity has become a culture obsessed with abolishing anything that stands in the way of instant gratification. It can be traced back to the emergence of modern technology. Initially, the focus was on tools that would help lighten the load of backbreaking work. Later, a new selling point was introduced. New products were touted as "labor-saving devices." Now we praise those who are able to multi-task.

The irony is that we are so bedazzled by each new technology that we fail to reflect on what all these "labor-saving" devices have actually

1. "In a New Age of Impatience, Cutting Computer Start Time," *The New York Times*, October 26, 2008: A1. Online: http://www.nytimes.com/2008/10/26/technology/26boot.html.

2. Ibid.

done to the pace and quality of life. For several decades therapists have been noticing psychological disorders that stem from the stress people living in technological culture must cope with. One term for this syndrome is "hurry sickness." Modern scientific culture continues to impress with its ability to produce a range of new technologies. While we struggle to cope with our "nano-second" lifestyle, we cannot face the prospect of technological obsolescence. We are reluctant to face up to this paradox.

For more than three decades Dr. Paul Jensen has been working with students, pastors, missionaries, and lay people to help them cultivate spiritual practices. He has observed that unless we pay attention to the cultural forces that shape and determine how we live, we will not understand which practices are appropriate and how or why they are effective. Traditional cultures had a strong sense of time and space. The one supported the other, thereby providing a structure for the way people lived.

Modernity has collapsed space and time. Each is nothing more than a factor of production—something to be exploited, consumed, and discarded. Our hurried lifestyle represents a heroic effort to get rid of both time and space, for these represent resistances to instant self-gratification.

In this book Dr. Jensen breaks new ground in three important ways. *First, he relates the theme of spirituality in a fundamental way to modernity/postmodernity. Second, he canvasses the history of culture and the spiritual practices of Jesus Christ, the early church, and contemporary Christians, to establish patterns and models from which we can learn.* Much can be gleaned from the spiritual practices developed in other ages and cultures. *Third, this book offers a challenging proposal to Christian disciples committed to living faithfully in contemporary culture.* If we are to think clearly and constructively about how we can avoid being co-opted by the powers that work against our total wellbeing—physical, psychological, social, and spiritual—we must understand the powerful dynamics of modernity. The goal of this subversive action is nothing less than to create time and space for the disciple to be in God's presence in solitude and community, as modeled by Jesus Christ, and there be ministered to by God's Spirit. This is urgently needed not only to sustain our personal discipleship but as the foundation for our engagement with the world.

Every generation needs to hear the ancient command, "Be still, and know that I am God!" (Ps 46:10a). This seems to be an especially desperate need in the over-stressed culture of late modernity. Paul Jensen invites—indeed urges—us to live against the grain of the world for the sake of the world.

—Wilbert R. Shenk
Professor Emeritus of Mission History
and Contemporary Culture
Fuller Theological Seminary

Preface

ALL IS NOT WELL UNDER THE HOOD OF CHRISTIAN FAITH IN WESTERN culture. This study represents but one attempt to look underneath and examine our current condition to see what might be needed to make our vehicle more travel ready. In short, I will argue that various complex factors have conspired in disconnecting the transmission of our vehicle (mission) from its engine (spirituality). But this has not been so in periods of expansion of the church fueled by a robust spirituality. Hopefully, what I write will help us see more clearly what God has done in the past and is doing now to connect our vehicle to a "spirituality for the road," to use missiologist David J. Bosch's term (1979). Thus, this work attempts to link Christian spirituality with Christian mission and to integrate the academic study of spirituality with that of missiology.

These are crucial tasks in light of various phenomena that have arisen in Western societies over the past half century, including: (1) a pervasive postmodern fascination with the para-natural and with spiritualities not usually associated with modern forms of Christianity; (2) the opportunity to be instantaneously connected to any kind of spirituality anywhere on the globe through the Internet; (3) widespread recognition that Western culture now represents a cross-cultural missional challenge to the church; (4) our culture's increasingly hurried pace of life, which has tended to separate outward mission practice from its inward spiritual roots; and (5) the disappearance of spaces and places conducive to intensive relationships, mentoring, and community.

The loss of the sense of place and our addictive hurry sickness have drained spiritual vitality and power for mission from the church in North America. We often focus on outward ministry to the exclusion of spirituality amidst the pressures of maintaining organizational structures infected with collapsed spatial and temporal codes and devoid of sufficient time and space for relationships. A spiritual discipline or practice, according to Henri J. M. Nouwen, is the creation of "space for God to be active" or "the human effort to create open space to listen to the voice of the one who calls us the beloved" (1993b). The practice of a discipline, then, requires a reversal of what Wilbert R. Shenk has termed the cultural "collapse of space and time" (2000), which explains why it feels like we are swimming cross-current when engaging in spiritual practices. This study provides windows into this milieu as to how God might want to renew us and his mission in the world he loves. I pray it may nudge us further in renewing our practices of spirituality and mission for God's glory.

1

Introduction

> What could be more pertinent in a new age, with all the challenges the age portends, than an analysis that connects time and space to devotion to God and mission!
>
> —James E. Bradley (2006)

TIME AND SPACE. THE TWO GO TOGETHER. IT IS HARD TO THINK OF ONE without the other. In Western cultures we usually do not plan or attend an event without knowing a time and location. Relationships between people cannot occur without some kind of shared space and time. Yet, the way that we spend time and share space with each other has been radically changed since the beginning of the modern age. Even a century ago we lived in a different world of time and space.

Movies containing time warps typically contrast the high-speed pace of contemporary society with those of earlier historical eras. A case in point is the movie *Kate & Leopold*; the main character Leopold, a duke, had immigrated with his family from Europe to New York City. One day in 1876, Leopold happens upon a stranger named Stuart who had just arrived from the year 2001 having discovered a "crack in time" through which he had jumped. Upon being detected, a startled Stuart flees with Leopold in close pursuit and jumps back through the crack (a leap off the Brooklyn Bridge) back to the year 2001. Instantaneously, the two are transported through 125 years of monumental cultural change to the Manhattan of 2001. Leopold is bewildered and amazed by the strange technology and culture into which he is immersed (Miramax 2001).

Much of the movie's humor and tension revolves around a romance, which develops between Leopold and Stuart's ex-girlfriend Kate, who are befuddled by clashes between their radically different worldviews and values. The clashes often center around Leopold's difficulty in adjusting to the hectic tempo of his new environs. In high English he protests one-minute microwave meal preparations: "The culinary arts demand reflection and study." Elsewhere he reacts, "Life cannot be reduced to tasks. It must be tasted." Like all love stories, *Kate & Leopold* reflects something of the sacred romance—the story of God's passionate love and costly pursuit of us in our temporal and spatial world—what we call the Incarnation.[1] Once the movie resolves Kate's disbelief that Leopold has indeed come from another era, it portrays her attempts to comprehend his sense of space and time, so different from her own. While spending a leisurely day with him at a park away from her high-powered advertising job, she asks Leopold if he misses where he is from. "Yes," he answers, "I miss the rhythm. It's slower" (Miramax 2001).

The Rationale for this Book: The Collapse of Space and Time

Since the beginning of the Industrial Revolution, our relationship to time and space, like Leopold's, has accelerated and changed especially in the last fifty years. Social theorists and other scientists have variously described these transformations and their effects as "the collapse of space and time" (Shenk 2000), "time-space compression" (Harvey 1990:vii), fragmentation of the "sense of place" (Sack 1988:642), "future shock" (Toffler 1970), "hurry sickness" (Ulmer and Schwartzburd 1996:331–32), "the juggernaut . . . rush[ing] out of control" (Giddens 1990:139), "the annihilation of time" (Castells 1997:126), "the emancipation of time from space," and "the conquest of space" (Bauman 2000:112–13). Lyle H. Jensen decried the accelerating tempo of recent years in a lecture given after he received a prestigious award from the American Crystallographic Association for his pioneering work in that

---

1. This point was repeatedly made in a long tradition of spiritual writers, more recently by Brent Curtis and John Eldredge in *The Sacred Romance* (1997). They argue that God has created the human heart with two universal longings—for romance and for adventure—which can ultimately be quenched only by the grand story of God's passionate and seeking love. A Christianity that has been enculturated by Enlightenment rationalism, however, has robbed this drama of its power by reducing it to propositions and ideas (1997:38–46). Having lost touch with its own matchless narrative and the capacity to tell and live it well, the Western church has become impotent in the face of postmodernity's paradoxical love of story and suspicion of meta-narratives.

field. "So now we live in a technological age, computers of unprecedented capacity and speed, and almost instantaneous communication with colleagues anywhere in the world. But I have a question: 'When do you have time to think?'" He voiced the concern that "the frenetic pace of so much research today results in undue stress that can be detrimental in human terms" (2000). His remarks elicited a standing ovation rarely accorded by this group and numerous conversations initiated by colleagues. He tapped into a growing discontent linked to an accelerating pace of life and a loss of discretionary time, which by some accounts decreased by ten percent in the decade of the 1990s (Lingenfelter 2000).

Cramming more tasks requiring greater speed into a given measure of time and packing more into less space eventually leads to a point of collapse. Theorists argue that we have reached or are reaching that point now. "Space-time implosion" is how Charles Jencks describes this radical new spatial-temporal phenomena produced by the historic changes of the past fifty years (1996:56)—a period usually called the postmodern era.[2] This collapse, centered in the information revolution, is the culmination of long historical processes associated with the modern age, including the Industrial Revolution, the routinization of factory work, the invention of the mechanical clock, and the separation of time from place or space. The latter resulted from the rise of standard time zones, which allowed for fixed railroad schedules and the demise of local time—flexibly set by customs of particular places, seasons, and the varying length of the day. Jencks dates the modern era from the invention of the printing press in 1450 to the end of the Baby Boom generation in 1960, and the pre-modern era from 10,000 BC to AD 1450 (1996:56). Perceptions of space and time and the social and economic structures in each of these eras are summarized and compared in Table 1 below.

---

2. But increasingly, theorists view the cultural shifts of the last fifty years not as a postmodern phenomenon but as a new and perhaps final phase of modernity. Alternate terms used include liquid modernity (Bauman 2000), the third wave (A. and H. Toffler 1995), late modernity (Bogler 2000), the networked society (Castells 1997), and high modernity (Giddens 1990). Whatever term is used, all theorists agree that fundamental worldview changes have occurred since World War II. Though, in my opinion, the current phase constitutes a very different type of modernity—perhaps a transitional period preparing us to move out of the modern age—I will use the commonly accepted term postmodern to refer to this era. Until our culture has a less dependent relationship to technology—a favorite child of modernity—I fail to see how we can yet be beyond the modern age.

Table 1: Comparisons of Pre-modern, Modern, and Postmodern Eras (Adapted from Cassells 1997; Jencks 1996; Giddens 1990)

	Social/Economic Structures	Space/Time
Pre-Modern (10,000 BC –AD 1450)	Feudal-City-Empire/ Agricultural Revolution	Cyclical, elastic, local
	Agrarian/Handwork	Social tied to place/Slow, seasonal time
	Peasants/Dispersed	Local space/Place determines time
Modern (1450–1960)	Nation-state/ Industrial Revolution	Linear, standardized, universal
	Factory/Mass production	Relationships dis-embedded from place/Clock time-sequential, fixed
	Workers/Centralized	Space-time separation, compression
Postmodern (1960–)	Global/Information revolution	Linear and non-sequential
	Office/Segmented production	Instantaneous, segmented, reversible
	Office workers/decentralized	Space-time implosion

The Book's Purpose and Thesis

This book seeks to show a correlation between inward spirituality and outward mission in the historical context of space and time and the current cultural collapse of these. Findings from my cultural, Biblical/theological, historical, and field research will demonstrate this correlation. My thesis is twofold: (1) that empowered inward spirituality—expressed in creating time and space for God through solitary and communal spiritual practices—correlates with transforming outward mission—expressed in word and deed; and (2) that because of the cultural collapse of space and time, postmodern mission requires the church to subvert these temporal-spatial codes by devoting more plentiful space and time to spiritual practices in her structures of mission, church, and leadership development.

Definitions and Descriptions of Spiritual Terms

This section covers some definitions and descriptions of key terms gleaned from the field of spirituality, which are used in the research questions for this study.[3] I will say more about the field of spirituality in the concluding chapter when drawing out the implications of this study.

Spiritual Discipline and Spiritual Practice

As was mentioned in the preface, a spiritual discipline or practice, according to Henri Nouwen, is "the human effort to create open space to listen to the voice of the one who calls us the beloved" (1993b) or the creation of space "for God to be active." I would add that a discipline creates unhurried time to listen to God and to notice ways he is already active (see Table 2 below for some classifications of the disciplines).[4] These definitions play a key role in this study. Culturally, they require a reversal of the collapse of space and time. Theologically, they entail various dimensions of grace. Though Nouwen's definitions do involve human effort, the primary focus is not the discipline itself but God, especially what God says in intimate love and what God does that we cannot—both aspects of grace. Spiritual disciplines or practices can subtly usurp the center

---

3. Since the late 1970s, the scholarly study of spirituality has forged a place in the broader academy through the work of scholars such as Sandra M. Schneiders, one of its early pioneers, who helped legitimize this field outside the confines of theological institutions. In North America this field is distinguished from the older field known as spiritual theology, which had been limited to seminaries and schools of theology focusing primarily on the spiritual formation of its seminarians. Historically, spiritual theology originated in monasticism and developed in Catholic institutions over centuries. Protestant seminaries have only recently begun fostering the spiritual formation of their seminarians. For an excellent overview of classical spiritual theology and its branches of ascetic and mystical theology by a mainline Protestant scholar, see Diogenes Allen (1997:7–20, Appendix F). For an early attempt at an evangelical spiritual theology, see Richard Lovelace (1975).

4. Here I am adding the notion of time to Nouwen's use of space and the concept of noticing God, which Richard Peace classifies as a spiritual discipline in its own right (1998b).

Table 2: Classifications of the Disciplines
(Adapted from Foster 1988:v; C. Miller 2007:77–95; Nouwen 1993;
Peace 1998b:89–103; Peterson 1992:105–10; Willard 1988:156–92)

Foster	*Willard*	*Peterson*
Inward Disciplines	*Disciplines of Abstinence*	*The Regula (rule)*
Meditation: "the ability to hear God's voice" (1988:17)	Solitude	Weekly common worship
	Silence	Daily praying the Psalms
Prayer: listening, asking, believing, thanking	Fasting	Recollected prayer: short prayers throughout the day that help recall God's presence
Fasting: the voluntary setting aside of normal functions for the purpose of uninterrupted concentration	Frugality: "frees us from a multitude of desires" (1988:169)	
	Chastity: total focus on a goal	*Disciplines: when needed*
		Spiritual reading
Study	Secrecy: "ceasing to make one's good deeds and qualities known" (1988:72)	Spiritual direction
		Meditation
Outward Disciplines:		Confession
Simplicity: "joyful unconcern about possessions … [in order] to seek His kingdom first" (1988:86–87)	Sacrifice: abstain from "what is necessary" (1988:174)	Fasting
		Sabbath-keeping
	Watchings: "abstaining from sleep in order to attend to prayer" (1988:51)	Dream interpretation
Solitude		Retreats
Submission		Pilgrimage
Service: "many little deaths of going beyond ourselves" in care for others (1988:126)	*Disciplines of Engagement:*	Almsgiving/tithing
	Study: particularly of the Word	Bodily exercise
		Journaling
	Worship: ascribing worth to God	Sabbaticals
Corporate Disciplines:		Small groups
	Celebration	
Confession	Service	
Worship	Prayer	
Guidance	Fellowship	
Celebration	Confession	
	Submission	

Other Classifications	Nouwen's Classifications	C. Miller's Classifications
Noticing God	Communion/solitude	Abiding/solitude
(Peace 1998b:89–103)	Community	Loving one another
Spiritual friendship	Ministry	Bearing witness
Celibacy		
Poverty		
Feasting		

of attention, becoming ends in themselves drawing us away from God and what God says and does. In such case, spiritual disciplines lose their function as "God's means of grace," which is how Richard J. Foster (1988:7) and his mentor in the spiritual life, Dallas Willard (1988:33, 156), understand them. Eugene H. Peterson insists that *askesis* (Greek for discipline) is "not a spiritual technology at our beck and call but is rather immersion in an environment in which our capacities are reduced to nothing or nearly nothing and we are at the mercy of God to shape his will in us" (1992:90).[5]

Robert Wuthnow (1998), Dorothy C. Bass (1997, 2000), Kenda Creasy Dean (2006), and others prefer the term spiritual practice over spiritual discipline.[6] As with the disciplines, spiritual practices are de-

---

5. For a comparison of definitions for spiritual disciplines offered by various theorists, see Appendix B. See Table 2 for classifications of spiritual disciplines given by Foster (1998), Willard (1988), Peterson (1992), Nouwen (1993b), and C. Miller (2007).

6. See Table 3 for various classifications of spiritual practices given by Dean and Foster, and Bass. These scholars, and those such as Stanley Hauerwas, draw upon a lengthy discussion about the nature of practices in a profession, vocation, trade, or game, and their role in forming virtue and personal or group identity. Wuthnow's discussion draws from the work of William James, Alasdair Macintyre, and Jeffrey Stout. The latter two have written about practices and virtue in the field of ethics (Wuthnow 1998:170–71).

Table 3: Classifications of Spiritual Practices[7] (Adapted from Bass 2003; Dean and Foster 1998:107)

Bass	Dean and Foster
Honoring the body	Baptism
Hospitality[8]	Eucharist
Household economics	Catechesis
Saying yes, saying no*[9]	Christian conference*
Keeping Sabbath*	Christian marriage
*Testimony**	Confirmation
*Discernment**	Covenanting
Shaping communities*	*Discernment*
Forgiveness*	*Dying well*
Healing	*Healing*
Dying well	Hospitality and care
Singing our lives*	Justice
	Preaching
	Reconciliation
	Speaking truth in love*
	Spiritual resistance
	Testimony

---

7. Descriptions of spiritual disciplines given by Foster (1988:7), Peterson (1992:90), and Willard (1998:353) are roughly similar to those given for spiritual practices by Wuthnow (1998:170), Bass (2000:vi), and Dean and Foster (1998:107). The primary differences lie in that spiritual disciplines as conceived by the former are more inward or solitary and less corporate than are the spiritual practices identified by Bass and Dean, and Foster. From the descriptions of both groups of authors, 87 percent of the spiritual disciplines and 75 percent of spiritual practices can or must be done in solitude. Eighty-two percent of the practices, but only 44 percent of spiritual disciplines, can or must be done in community.

8. I have italicized those spiritual practices that appear in both columns of Table 3.

9. The asterisk indicates those practices that appear in the classifications of spiritual disciplines in Table 2, but often under another name. For example, the practice of saying yes and saying no has a lot of overlap with Richard Foster's simplicity.

scribed in terms of intentional sustained human behavior and effort, as well they must, and in terms of the collapse of space/time.[10] Likewise, spiritual practices are "vessels of grace" (Dean 2006:145–75) and should not become ends in themselves. Wuthnow's extensive research of North American spirituality since 1950, reported in his seminal work *After Heaven*, has shown of his interviewees that "the center of their spirituality was neither a group nor themselves but their relationship with God" (1998:181). Yet, the language writers use to describe a spiritual practice or discipline risks focusing predominantly on human activity rather than on divine action—that is, grace.

Spirituality

Most people intuitively understand what spirituality[11] is, but their efforts to define it have proven illusive. It is little surprise, then, that the nature of spirituality has been much debated in the academy. Appendix A gives various definitions on offer. Though not much agreement exists as to the precise definition of the term, scholars have tended to describe spirituality in terms of human response and behavior, rather than emphasizing divine activity and initiative. Important facets of grace often disappear. British scholar Gordon S. Wakefield, editor of *A Dictionary of Christian Spirituality*, wrote that spirituality is "those attitudes, beliefs, practices which animate people's lives and help them to reach out towards super-sensible realities" (1983:361).[12] I call this defining spirituality from below, which tends to hide God; his intervening and

---

10. See Wuthnow (1998:16–17, 21–23, 27, 38, 42–44, 49–50, 177–78, 197), Bass (2000:1–14), and Dean and Foster (1998:105–23, 185–94) as to how these authors see practices addressing the collapse of space and time.

11. For an etymology of the term "spirituality," starting with the New Testament, see Sheldrake (1992:34–37), Schneiders (1986:255–60), Wakefield (1983:361–63), and McGinn (1993:3–4).

12. Other descriptions of spirituality emphasizing human response, discipline, practice, or ritual offered to some reality or god include: "the human subjective response" (Chan 1998:15); "prayer, worship and whatever other practices are associated with the development of the spiritual life" (Macquarrie 2000:63); "those aspects of a person's living a faith or commitment that concern his or her striving to attain" (Principe 1983:139); and "the combination of praying and living" (Wainwright 1986:592). See Appendix A for a more extensive collection of definitions, some of which include the notion of grace.

enabling power, and his unconditional embrace of us—also key aspects of grace.[13]

The definition most widely accepted and used in the academic study of spirituality in North America since the early 1990s is that of Sandra M. Schneiders, who defines the term solely from below. She says that spirituality refers to "(1) a fundamental dimension of the human being, (2) the lived experience which actualizes that dimension, and (3) the academic discipline which studies that experience" (2000:250).[14]

One advantage of this definition is its breadth, which has helped the field gain a birth in the wider academy outside of seminaries and theological schools. A glaring weakness is the absence of grace—God's initiative, transforming activity, and embrace. In my view, describing spirituality from below is legitimate, but incomplete at best or misleading at worst if it dominates the description. This study, however, deals with Christian spirituality. If Christianity is anything, it is the story of God coming to do for human beings what they cannot do for themselves. Even a Christian's human response to God should be enabled and empowered by divine activity. Unfortunately, definitions such as "striving for an ever more intense union with the Father through Jesus Christ by living in the Spirit" (Principe 1983:139) mislead us without including a description from above. Spiritual practices can become a means of manipulating or currying favor with God just as pagans use rituals to control, cajole, buy off, or placate their deities. What then characterizes authentic Christian spirituality? Elsewhere, I have proposed that Christian spirituality has at least four pairs of distinctive characteristics, shown below in Table 4 (2003:8).

---

13. See Anderson (2006) and Chan (1998:79–101) for approaches that ground spirituality in grace. The reader may access the late Wayne Anderson's teaching on grace at http://www.tli.cc/grace/ in both audio and printed form.

14. Kenneth J. Collins uses Schneider's definition to develop a taxonomy of spiritualities divided into two broad categories: (1) spirituality as the nature of human beings; and (2) spirituality as lived experience. The former category is broad enough to include Twelve Step spirituality and secular ethics. The latter is divided into naturalistic (e.g., Samuel Colleridge), monistic (as in Eastern religions), and theistic spiritualities (2000:9–14).

Table 4: Characteristics of Authentic Christian Spirituality

---

1. *Grace-centered/Spirit-initiated, shaped, and empowered*: Christian spirituality is initiated, directed, empowered by grace—God's embracing love and enabling power. Grace results in human response and participation in various spiritual disciplines, but those disciplines ought to be initiated, shaped, empowered, and guided by God's Spirit.

---

2. *Christo-centric/Kingdom-in breaking*: Christian spirituality centers on the person of Jesus Christ through whom God's reign comes to all who know and obey him. In his name and authority, Jesus's followers displace the reign of evil principalities and powers with the coming of God's reign in their inward and outward spheres.

---

3. *Biblically-shaped/Gospel-rooted*: Anticipated and portrayed in Old and New Testaments, Christian spirituality flows from the gospel of Jesus's death, burial, resurrection, and ascension through which God offers his salvation and redeeming love freely to all who respond in repentance and trust. Those who follow Jesus will experience his patterns of death and resurrection, suffering and joy.

---

4. *Trinitarian/Transformative*: Repentant and believing people are brought into the intimate communion and community of Father, Son, and Holy Spirit by the power of God, which transforms them over time from the character of the culture into the compassionate character of Christ.

Meye's Definition of Christian Spirituality

The finest and most comprehensive definition of Christian spirituality I have read to date is offered by Robert P. Meye:[15]

> Above all else, grace—God's grace—and gratitude—our response to the grace of God—are the two most essential components of an authentic Christian spirituality which, patterned in the imitation of Christ, and empowered by the Spirit of Jesus Christ, will ever bear fruit in love, joy and peace. All of this will happen only within the framework of our privileged response of faith in God in Christ and in the power of the Spirit, especially expressed in our life in prayer, in the Word, and in the commu-

---

15. In the early 1970s, Meye helped instigate a group of professors who discussed and prayed for a rebirth of teaching, study, and practice of spirituality in theological education. The centrality of grace in Meye's definition reflects the influence of Karl Barth, under whom he studied.

nity of faith. Such life ever rises to the true worship of God and flows out into witness and service to the world. (1993:11)

Meye defines spirituality from above and from below. His definition, at least implicitly, includes most, if not all, of my distinctives of Christian spirituality. Though other definitions are explicitly rooted in grace, I have yet to find a definition for Christian spirituality that so comprehensively describes spirituality from above and from below as does Meye's.[16] My one criticism is his omission of explicit mention of the role of suffering in spirituality, which is only implied in his reference to the "imitation of Christ."

Meye's definition describes mission—"witness and service to the world"—as an overflow of Christian spirituality involving the spiritual disciplines of prayer, the word, worship, and community, practiced "in the power of the Spirit" (1993:11). Thus, Meye explicitly links spirituality and mission with grace. In this study, I will examine the degree and nature of the correlation between inward spirituality—expressed in solitary and corporate disciplines—and the outward expression of mission in classic spiritual texts and the groups these texts influenced.[17]

Grace and Subversive Spirituality

Thus far in the discussion, grace has played an important role in the definitions for spiritual disciplines, spirituality, and particularly Christian spirituality. In this study I do not intend to discuss the many debates and views concerning grace, except as they may be important to my research questions. Rather, I want to detect in the spiritual texts under consideration the presence of the notion of grace in three senses—initiating (prevenient) grace, empowering (transforming) grace, and embracing (accepting) grace—in connection with the practice of both spirituality and mission. As we will discover throughout this study, grace-centered spiritualities overflowing into missions that transform are deeply subversive of the status quo. *Webster's Dictionary* defines subversion as "a systematic attempt to overthrow or undermine a gov-

---

16. For example, see Marjorie Thompson's description of spirituality as a divine-human dance (2001).

17. Adrian Thatcher rejects the inner/outer distinction as a false dualism (1993). He argues for "between-ness" or relationality at the core of spirituality. My use of "inward" subsumes relationality.

ernment or political system by persons working secretly from within" (1987:1177). Applied to spirituality, it means creating sustained time and space for secret and corporate prayer practiced in fresh ways in the Spirit to undermine the status quo and de-construct the deadening effects of the principalities of darkness. Eugene H. Peterson argues that Christian leaders who follow Jesus's way will be subversive:

> I believe that the kingdoms of this world . . . will become the kingdom of our God and Christ, and I believe this new kingdom is already among us. The methods that make America strong—economic, military, technological, information—are not suited to making the kingdom of God strong. I have to use a new methodology: truth telling, love making, prayer and parable. These are not . . . very well adapted to raising the standard of living in suburbia or massaging the ego . . . . I am undermining the kingdom of self and establishing the kingdom of God. (1989:38)

Motivation for the Book

My interest in spirituality became more passionate when my two sons were transformed during the 1995–96 spiritual awakening that touched their generation in North America.[18] Through prayer and other disciplines, our youngest was delivered from a severe drug addiction, which nearly took his life. A key figure in our two sons' spiritual transformations during the awakening was Josh Turville, an Xer, who was later shot and killed by a troubled teen he was mentoring and providing a place to live. The adolescent murdered Josh and two others during a drug-induced psychotic break after having served time in the juvenile justice system. As Jesus said, "No one has greater love than this, to lay down one's life for one's friends" (John 15:13). The more than eight hundred people who attended Josh's funeral heard moving tributes from those he had influenced. Eric Williams spoke of Josh's sacrificial love, noting especially how he lavished time on others. "Time is love," Williams said (1996). Partly because Josh created time and space for God and others in a culture in which these have been compressed, my

---

18. My two sons, born in 1975 and in 1977, are part of the age cohort referred to as Generation X. Various boundaries for this generation abound: 1961–81 (Howe and Strauss 1993:13; Mahedy and Bernardi 1994:10; Miller and Miller 2000); 1965–85 (Crouch 1997:31); and 1965–77 (Hornblower 1997:58).

sons' lives were turned around. For good reason, the spiritual journeys of my three children motivate much of this study. Will their generation be as fortunate in finding within Christian institutions plentiful space and unhurried time devoted to communion with God and community with one another, in which transparent relationships are nurtured by costly mentoring love? Perhaps they will, but only as God brings about new forms of community that support the radical transformation of Christian leaders and the structures in which they serve.

Significance: Challenges and Opportunities for Mission

Anecdotal evidence from Christian leaders taking training from The Leadership Institute, the organization I direct, indicates that time needed to tend these leaders' relationships with God and others is often given to maintaining ministry structures or tending to urgent needs. This compression has resulted in diminished spirituality and a lack of depth in relationships among these leaders and their followers alike. As Ronald Rolheiser writes,

> A number of historical circumstances are blindly flowing together and accidentally conspiring to produce a climate within which it is difficult not just to think about God or to pray, but simply to have any interior depth whatsoever. The air we breathe today is generally not conducive to interiority and depth. (1999:31–32)

Like Rollheiser, Dallas Willard believes that the collapse of space and time is a serious spiritual problem (2001). At the same time, the spiritual hunger emerging amidst recent postmodern cultural shifts[19] constitutes what pollster George Gallup Jr. sees as a "quiet revolution" representing a major opportunity for the church in our age (Feuerherd 2001).[20] Generations X (b. 1964–81) and Y (b. 1982–2000), the first generations born in the postmodern era, are playing a central role in this revolution.

In the new cultural landscape, summarized by Jonathan Campbell in Table 5 below, many are surprised by the spirituality of the post-

---

19. For an excellent discussion of the cultural shifts between the modern and postmodern ages, see Campbell (1996). For Campbell's summary of these shifts see Table 5 below.

20. See article based on interview of Gallup by Peter Feuerherd (2001:7–9).

modern generations in light of their suspicion of religious institutions, their immersion in relativism, and their epistemology that rejects the idea that truth has an objective dimension. Each of these poses a fresh challenge to the church's mission. The barriers and bridges to the transmission of the Christian faith in the new context are "taking on a new shape" (Shenk 2000). Spiritual hunger is being expressed in the desire for mystery, healing, mentors, community, relationships, authenticity, story, a sense of history, ecological concern, and rising volunteerism. These bridges require costly investments of unhurried time. The great missiologist David F. Bosch gives six essentials that missiology in Western culture must include (1995:55–59):

1. An ecological concern;
2. It must be counter-cultural;
3. It must be ecumenical;
4. It must be contextualized;
5. It must be primarily focused on the ministry of the laity;
6. It will not be authentic unless it "flows from a worshiping community." (1995:59)

Bosch gave these six essentials before his untimely death in 1992 (Shenk 1995b:ix–x), and they are largely confirmed by my research in this study. In the concluding chapter, I will synthesize my findings into a model for spirituality and mission from which I will draw implications and make recommendations for mission in North America.

Table 5: Living in the Ecotone: A Continuum of Worldview Change (Campbell 1996)

	(From) Modernity	*(To)* Postmodernity
Worldview	Either / Or Microscope Bipolar / Separated Left Brain / Conceptual Mechanical / Organized Deterministic / Linear Reductive / Analyze	Both / And Kaleidoscope Double Helix / Interrelated Right Brain / Perceptual / Intuition Ecological / Organic Creative / Open / Non-linear Holistic / Synthesize
Philosophy	Reason & Scientific Empiricism Aristotle (Western Perspective) Optimism Toward Knowledge Singular Causation Pluralism Knowledge May Be Certain	Emotion & Intuition Confucius (Eastern Perspective) Pessimism Toward Knowledge Multi-Causation Relativism Rejects Certainty of Knowledge
Society	Era of Certainty / Steady Incremental Changes Progress Inevitable Verbal / Written Communication National / National Economy Value Autonomy / Do It Yourself Strive for Security & Success	Era of Change / Unpredictable Accelerated Change Progress Questionable Visual / Virtual Communication Supranational / Global Economy Value Interdependence / Network Strive for Pleasure & Identity

Organization	Establishment / Centralized / Pyramid Classroom Training Rigid Structures Authoritarian / Bureaucratic Centralized / Control / Hierarchy Policies & Procedures Reactionary—Built on Past Serve the Institution	Movement / Decentralized / Lattice Field Education (Lifelong Learning) Flexible Structures Cooperative / Charismatic Decentralized / Freedom / Anarchy Vision & Values Anticipatory—Oriented toward Future Institution Serves Me
Strategy	PERT Charts Rational / Empirical Linear / Sequential Static—Plan Before Action Systematic / Organized Independence / Separateness Top-Down Focus on Product	Mind Mapping Intuitive / Imaginative Non-Linear Dynamic—Plan on the Move Systemic / Organic Interdependence / Interconnectedness Bottom-Up (Grass Roots) Focus on Process
Religion	Religious / Institutional Disenchantment Atheism Dogmatism "Is there a God?" / "God is Dead" Truth Evidence / Apologetic Transcendence / God the Father Orthodoxy	Spiritual / Relational Re-Enchantment Panentheism / Pantheism Pluralism / Syncretism "Which God?" / "We are God'" Beliefs Experience / Incarnational Immanence / The Holy Spirit Paradoxy

Definitions and Descriptions of Missiological Terms

In this section, I give definitions and descriptions of key terms gleaned from the field of missiology, which are used in my research questions and their subsidiaries.[21] I will say more about the field when I summarize the implications of my research in the concluding chapter.

21. Missiology originated as a branch of practical theology and dogmatics in the nineteenth century and emerged as a discipline in its own right in the early twentieth

Indigenizing and Pilgrim Mission Practices (Walls)

Andrew Walls, eminent missionary to Africa, articulates two principles that bear on all situations in which the gospel crosses cultural boundaries, including mission to a postmodern context. First, the indigenizing principle holds that whenever the gospel penetrates a culture, it becomes enfleshed (John 1:14) through appropriate cultural forms and language. Every culture has within it traces of initiating grace, bridges over which the gospel and God's people may travel, which allow them to be at home and be understood in that culture.[22] By this principle, in the practice of mission people and their cultures are loved, served, and affirmed as they are.

Second, the pilgrim principle holds that every culture into which the gospel is transmitted possesses barriers to God's reign. God's people are aliens belonging to "a holy nation" (1 Pet 2:9), called not to "be conformed to this world but [to] be transformed" (Rom 12:2). By this principle, people and their cultures are loved as they are but not left as they are. Unconditional acceptance precedes deep transformation—two sides of grace—both central to God's mission. Yes, the gospel and God's people must be incarnated in the culture, but by the Spirit, they also free God's creation from captivity to cultural idols. As Walls argues, these twin principles will always be in tension but are not opposed to each other in the practice of mission (1996:53–54). Both accepting and transforming grace, then, are foundational to mission. But so is initiating (prevenient) grace. The indigenous principle assumes that God has already worked within a culture to provide forms and language that reflect something of his image and contain what Don Richardson termed "redemptive analogies" of his saving work (2000:812–23).[23] So grace in all three senses is embedded in the definitions of both spiritual and mission practices that I will use in this study.

---

century. J. Verkyl discusses the etymology of the term "missiology"—the generally accepted name for the academic discipline, which studies mission—and gives a historical overview of the field up until the late 1970s (1978:1–16). Also, see Alan Neely's article on missiology (2000:633–35).

22. The indigenizing principle is summarized in Paul's stated modus operandi (1 Cor 9:19–26).

23. Don Richardson popularized the idea of redemptive analogy in his book *Peace Child* (1975).

Mission

As in the field of spirituality, no single commonly accepted definition of mission has been accepted by missiologists—a necessary condition given the complexity and fluidity of the missionary task, according to Bosch (1991:1–11). I have displayed some definitions offered by various scholars in Table 6 below. Charles Van Engen argues that scholars have tended to broaden the definition of mission in recent years (1997a:47). Some definitions lie outside the meaning of Christian mission,[24] which is the case to an even greater degree for the definitions of spirituality noted above.[25]

Absent from Table 6 are any definitions from Eastern Orthodox missiologists. According to Charles Van Engen, missiology in this tradition emphasizes the glory of God and the sacramental presence of God in his people through liturgy (1997a:38). Also missing are Roman Catholic missiological perspectives arising after Vatican II.[26] However, despite the limited sample, the definitions exhibit a lot of variety, but with one constant: explicit or implicit references to the kingdom of God figure prominently in all the definitions.

---

24. Bosch argues that, despite the danger of slipping into a non-Christian definition of mission as in some in inter-religious dialogue, we need a broader definition for Christian mission, which is always changing and always in need of reformation depending on the new cultural contexts facing the gospel (1991:1–11).

25. The tendency to broaden the meaning of missiology has evolved partly in the reaction to the complicity of Western mission with the colonial power of the nations in which they originated. Mission expansion accompanied Western imperialistic expansion, which is rightfully seen in the academy as an unholy alliance that subjugated and exploited indigenous peoples and their cultures. Sadly, history is replete with examples of arrogant ethnocentrism exhibited by Western governments and mission agencies alike.

26. Louis J. Luzbetak says recent Catholic missiology is: (1) more practical than theoretical; (2) more ecumenical with cross-denominational implications, which reflect the theological pluralism in most missiological associations; and (3) more advanced than previous Catholic literature in its pastoral concern (1995:19–20).

Table 6: Definitions and Descriptions of Christian Mission/Theology

Missiologist/ Theologian	Definition or Description
Oscar Cullman	"The missionary work of the Church is the eschatological foretaste of the kingdom of God, and the Biblical hope of the end constitutes the keenest incentive to action." (1961:43)
Jerald D. Gort	"[Christian mission from a Reformed perspective] is the liberating coming of God in Christ through his disciples to people who no longer know or have never known him." (1979:37)
Leslie Newbigin	"The mission of the Church to all the nations, to all human communities in all their diversity and in all their particularity, is itself the mighty work of God, the sign of the inbreaking of the kingdom. The Church is not so much the agent of the mission as the locus of the mission. It is God who acts in the power of his Spirit, doing mighty works, creating signs of a new age, working secretly in the hearts of men and women to draw them to Christ. When they are so drawn, they become part of a community which claims no masterful control of history, but continues to bear witness to the real meaning and goal of history by a life which—in Paul's words—by always bearing about in the body the dying of Jesus becomes the place where the risen life of Jesus is made available for others (2 Cor 4:10)." (1989:119)
Charles Van Engen	"Mission is the intentional crossing of barriers from Church to non-church, faith to non-faith, to proclaim the coming of the Kingdom of God in word and deed through the Church's participation in God's mission of reconciling people to God, to themselves, to each other, and to the world and gathering them into the Church through faith in Jesus Christ with a view to the transformation of the world as a sign of the coming of the Kingdom of God in Jesus Christ." (1997a:176)

J. Verkuyl	"Missiology is the study of the salvation activities of the Father, Son, and Holy Spirit throughout the world geared toward bringing the kingdom of God into existence. Seen in this perspective missiology is the study of the church's divine mandate to be ready to serve this God who is aiming his saving acts toward this world. In dependence on the Holy Spirit and by word and deed the church is to communicate the total gospel and the total divine law to all mankind." (1978:5)

Mission from Above and Below

These definitions with their inclusion of kingdom language describe mission both from above—God's action—and from below—human activity. This parallels my observations regarding how spirituality and spiritual disciplines have been described. I hold that Christian mission, along with Christian spirituality, should be described both from above and from below. In my view, mission, like spirituality, is best defined primarily from above and secondarily from below, as in Newbigin's definition (see Table 6). His definition is further strengthened by including the notion of suffering love: "always bearing about in the body the dying of Jesus" (1989:119).

Unlike the field of spirituality, the field of missiology has developed terminology to distinguish between mission from above and mission from below. For scholars like Newbigin, to think of "mission from above" is to conceive of God as being on mission to redeem the world he loves from slavery and the reign of evil. This is referred to as *missio Dei*, or "the mission of God," and is differentiated from both *missiones ecclesiae*, which refers to programs and structures of mission in ecclesiastical organizations, and *missio hominum*, the mission of human instrumentality and practice (Van Engen 1997b:28).[27]

Mission: Duty or Gospel? (Newbigin)

The human practices and activities associated with mission (i.e., mission from below), like those human practices associated with spirituality, can

---

27. For a survey of these distinctions and terms, see Van Engen (2000a:951) and Verkuyl (1978:4).

easily uproot us from gospel soil and become a new legalism, as Leslie Newbigin, the late Anglican missionary to India, has written:

> There has been a long tradition which sees the mission of the Church primarily as obedience to a command. . . . [This] tends to make mission a burden rather than a joy, to make it part of the law rather than part of the gospel. If one looks at the New Testament evidence one gets another impression. Mission begins with a kind of explosion of joy. The news that the rejected and crucified Jesus is alive is something that cannot possibly be suppressed. . . . One searches in vain through the letters of St. Paul to find any suggestion that he anywhere lays it on the conscience of his readers that they ought to be active in mission. For himself it is inconceivable that he should keep silent. (1989:116)

Paul writes, "Of the gospel I have become a servant according to the gift of God's grace that was given me by the working of his power" (Eph 3:7). This calls us to ground *missio homonum* and *missiones ecclesiea* in *missio Dei* so that God's mission activity is the focus, not our activity or mission structures. This requires a robust spirituality that listens to the Good Shepherd calling and seeking his beloved sheep. As J. Verkuyl puts it, "the *missiones ecclesiarum* are connected with the *missio Dei* only when, in union with Christ the true vine and under the guidance of the Holy Spirit, they display the fruits of love for God and neighbor in countless ways" (1978:4).

The fundamental nature of mission, then, is theocentric and grace based. It originates in God and is carried out by God as he seeks to redeem the world he loves, but it involves human response, cooperation, and participation. Neither our practice of spiritual disciplines nor our mission practice is duty. Newbigin argues that, like the law, particular practices and structures of spiritual life and mission are given by God, but they are not to be absolutized in the new creation. If they become written in stone they cut us off from grace, the power of the Spirit, and relationality in our experience with God. They are the elementary things (*stoichei*) Paul mentions in Colossians (2:8, 14–15, 20), which may be good but must not supplant the supremacy of Christ in all things (1989:198–206).

Bosch's Contours of Christian Mission

In his magisterial work *Transforming Mission*—a classic text in mission theology worldwide—David Bosch argues that the shape and nature of mission has gone through six major paradigm shifts corresponding to the six major epochs in church history formulated by Hans Kung.[28] Bosch holds that in each epoch there existed various theologies and definitions of mission.[29] Instead of arguing for a single static view of mission, he develops a more fluid plural understanding. "Ultimately, mission remains undefinable; it should never be incarcerated in the narrow confines of our own predilections. The most we can hope for is to formulate some *approximations* of what mission is all about" (1991:9). Yet Bosch does argue that any authentic view of Christian mission should possess three specific contours.

First, "mission is God's 'yes' to the world," his activity to restore justice and alleviate oppression and human need in the world. Mission brings the church into participation with this divine activity through deeds of compassion, liberation, and justice (1991:10).

Second, mission includes evangelism—"the proclamation of salvation in Christ to those who do not believe in him, calling them to repentance and conversion, announcing forgiveness of sin and inviting them to become living members of Christ's earthly community and to begin a life of service to others in the power of the Holy Spirit" (1991:10–11).

Third, "mission is also God's 'no' to the world." Mission cannot be limited to the "human progress on the horizontal plane," which resulted from evangelism and social action. Bosh writes that "neither a secularized church (that is, a church which concerns itself only with this-worldly activities and interests) nor a separatist church (that is, a church which involves itself only in soul-saving and preparation of converts for the hereafter) can faithfully articulate the *missio Dei*" (1991:11). For

---

28. Bosch draws on Hans Kung's six paradigms of church history: "1. The apocalyptic paradigm of primitive Christianity. 2. The Hellenistic paradigm of the patristic period. 3. The medieval Roman Catholic paradigm. 4. The Protestant (Reformation) paradigm. 5. The modern Enlightenment paradigm. 6. The emerging ecumenical paradigm" (Bosch 1991:181–82).

29. Bosch asserts that "at no time in the past two millennia was there only one single 'theology of mission'. This was true even for the church in its pristine state.... However, different theologies of mission do not necessarily exclude each other; they form a multicolored mosaic of complementary and mutually enriching as well as mutually challenging frames of reference" (1991:8).

him, authentic Christian mission in every age will always include word, deed, and evangelism.[30]

Centrifugal and Centripetal Mission

Missiologists have developed terminology to distinguish between two basic directions in the movement of mission. *Centrifugal* indicates outward movement of the missionary or mission community towards and into the population of those being reached. Any people group that has not been exposed to Christian faith will require centrifugal movement on the part of someone who will cross a cultural boundary to enter that group if it is to be reached. As we will see in chapter 3, in the beginning of Jesus's public ministry his mission was first centrifugal; he took the initiative and went to the synagogues of Galilee to announce the coming of God's reign in his own words and actions. The doctrine of the Incarnation teaches us that *missio Dei* is supremely centrifugal, in that the God of grace takes initiative towards us and comes to be with us in our world.

Centripetal indicates the movement of individuals or groups towards the missionary or mission community, often in response to the transformation of those who have been touched by the missionary and the mission. From the earliest days of Jesus's ministry, people heard of his healings and powerful teaching and they came repeatedly to wherever he and his disciples were. Much of Jesus's mission was centripetal.

---

30. The relationship between word and deed in mission caused heated debate among Protestants in much of the twentieth century, when conservatives viewed mission mainly as proclaiming the gospel and liberals viewed it primarily as social action. During the past thirty years, however, mainline Protestants have increasingly included evangelism in their understanding (c.f. Junkin 1996:311). Coming from the other direction, most evangelicals now include social action, with evangelism having primacy. Some evangelicals see social action as an equal partner with evangelism, such as Samuel Escobar, Rene Padilla, and Ron Sider (c.f. Moreau 2000:637–38). My view as to whether social action or evangelism should take priority depends if the question is asked theologically or methodologically. Theologically, I believe that the Great Commission implies love to God as a higher priority than love to neighbor and thus the word of the gospel has priority. Methodologically, I believe scriptural patterns as well as the current cultural realities of a postmodern world suggest that the priority be given to compassionate social action as the starting point.

Research Questions

Having described the most important terms in my research questions, I am now ready to state these questions along with the chapters that will address them:

1. What characterizes the collapse of space and time and the spirituality of the postmodern generations (chapters 2 and 6)?
2. How does space and time with God relate to mission in selected texts from the New Testament (chapters 3 and 4)?
3. How does space and time with God relate to mission in selected spiritual classics and their authors' movements from the first and second millennia (chapters 4 and 5)?
4. How does space and time with God relate to the mission and faith maturity of the postmodern generations (chapter 6)?

Elements of Spirituality and Mission to Be Examined

Throughout this study I will examine secondary questions when they appear to be important, promising in themselves, or relevant to my research questions. However, at this point, I can generally say that this study of selected classic spiritual texts and the movements they influenced will examine spirituality in terms of (1) time and space devoted to solitary and communal spiritual practices; (2) what these practices were; (3) the presence of Scripture, silence, fasting, and prayer in these practices; (4) whether grace (prevenient, accepting, transforming) was associated with these practices; and (5) whether the practices were culture affirming or culture denying.

Likewise, I will examine mission in terms of (1) word: proclamation of the gospel, which includes manifold expressions of evangelism as Bosh has described it; (2) deed: suffering love, compassion, justice, and social transformation to alleviate human suffering and need; (3) whether the mission was centrifugal or centripetal in its movement; (4) the extent to which grace (prevenient, accepting, transforming) was associated with the practice of mission; and (5) whether the indigenous or pilgrim principle was being expressed in the mission practice.

The work closest to the historical part of this study is Jesuit missionary Michael Collins Reilly's *Spirituality for Mission: Historical, Theo-*

logical, and Cultural Factors for a Present-Day Missionary Spirituality (1978).[31] Like Reilly, I select various spiritual classics and certain leaders who contributed to the expansion of the Christian faith, examine their spiritualities, and draw inferences for mission today.[32] Though he wrote almost thirty years ago, some of his insights can inform spirituality for mission in our contemporary context, and I do emulate his approach in parts of this study. However, I do not wish to emulate other elements of his work. Unlike Reilly, I draw heavily upon Jesus as a missionary— in my opinion, the omission of this resource constitutes an important deficiency in Reilly's work. Also, I do an extensive cultural analysis and a field study of contemporary groups, which he does not. As his title suggests, Reilly argues that spirituality is formed by the interplay of Scripture, theology, tradition, and culture, resulting in particular constants and variables. The constants occur in various traditions and across different eras and cultural situations. I too am looking for constants from which to form a model of spirituality and mission that can be valid in a variety of cultures, traditions, and eras. In David A. Shank's helpful review of Reilly's book, he succinctly summarizes Reilly's constants and variables:

> These constants he discovered are: a love for Christ; union with God and personal holiness; trust in God, with accompanying boldness, courage, perseverance and joy; and loving service and humility. These are seen to be appropriate in the context of every theology, every ecclesiology, every culture and every time. But Father Reilly also perceived variables: the consciousness of the sinfulness of man and his need of Christ; the awareness of the damnation of non-believers, and those of other religions; an

---

31. Reilly's work is not a PhD dissertation, as far as I know, and some might think I have bitten off more than I should chew in this study, which was originally a dissertation. Christine Pohl's work on the history of hospitality is also an example of a study similar in scope to mine (1999). As Sandra Schneiders notes, the historical study of spirituality involving various themes and motifs (such as the role of Scripture or the place of women in spirituality) across various periods and eras of spiritual history has become increasingly acceptable in the academy (1995:213–14).

32. Reilly's work includes case studies from the pre-modern era (1978:46–84)—the patristic mission before Constantine, the medieval mission, Celtic monasticism, Boniface, Ramon Lull, Francis Xavier, and the early Jesuit missionaries—and from the modern era (1978:85–115)—Ludwig Zinzendorf, William Carey, Hudson Taylor, and Charles de Foucauld. I deal with the early Jesuits as part of the modern era since I view this era as starting earlier than does Reilly.

exclusiveness about salvation being only within the institutional church, itself identified with the kingdom of God, a pilgrim-consciousness of travel through and out of this world into eternity; a world-denying, self-denying asceticism. (1980:231)

I strongly protest Reilly's reduction of the pilgrim impulse of past spiritualities to a variable that can and should disappear from contemporary mission, a critique seemingly echoed by Shank.[33] Perhaps if Reilly had included Jesus's spirituality in his study, he would have seen it as deeply subversive to the status quo while at the same time being incarnational and indigenous. Maybe he would then have been less willing to relegate the pilgrim principle to a variable that can be discarded without peril. Every culture contains barriers to God's reign.

The Limits for this Study

I have narrowed my study of spirituality and mission to soundings from biblical and church history. From the New Testament I have selected passages in Matthew, Mark, Luke, John, and Acts.[34] After the death of the twelve apostles, only nine Christian texts from 90 to 120 have survived. Known as the writings of the apostolic fathers, they give us our only sources for studying spirituality and mission during these crucial years of Christian expansion. I will also look briefly at Origen and his influence on Antony and St. Benedict. These selections leave out volumes of New Testament data (e.g., Paul's epistles from which can be detected his spirituality) and a vast array of patristic sources. Having said that, this selection of first millennium texts places us at the very fountainhead of Christian spirituality and mission, from which subsequent spiritualities and missions can trace their origins.

My study of second millennium spiritual classics is limited to (1) texts of the *Devotio Moderna*, which includes *The Imitation of Christ* by Thomas à Kempis, writings by the movement's founder Geert Groote, and others; (2) Ignatius of Loyola's *Spiritual Exercises*, *Autobiography*,

33. Shank writes that "if a proposed spirituality is demonstrated to be appropriate because of its harmony with cultural presuppositions, the author owes his readers parallel evidence that previous spiritualities were specifically appropriate to their times. ... The author [Reilly] simply assumes it to be so. Many ... were indeed out of harmony with their times; they were not . . seeking to be 'attuned to the rhythms' of their times" (1980:233).

34. Unless otherwise noted, I use the NRSV in this study.

his *Diary*, and excerpts from his *Constitutions of the Society of Jesus;* and (3) *The Diary of David Brainerd* (edited by Jonathan Edwards) and its influence upon William Carey, Adoniah Judson, and women like Mary Lyon who made such a great contribution to Protestant missions during the nineteenth century. I used two criteria for selecting these spiritual classics. First, does the text exhibit earmarks of a spiritual classic? Phillip Sheldrake has identified these earmarks, given in Table 7 below. Second, has the text contributed in crucial ways to the development of mission and spirituality?

I should mention one thing about my historical treatment of these texts. Except for my work on Jesus in chapter 3, I do not develop much of the historical context of each classic or era because of the constraints of this study's length—an obvious limitation. James E. Bradley's comparative study of spiritual texts comprising a course on the history of Western spirituality is much longer than, but similar to the historical parts of this study. Bradley concedes that one hazard in this type of study is the insufficient time to build an in-depth historical backdrop for each period treated (1997). Similarly, N. T. Wright's massive work *The Resurrection of the Son of God* compares early Christian texts on the subject without providing a backdrop of the church's historical rise during the second century—"a huge and sprawling story, too vast even to summarize here," says Wright. "Others have laboured and I have entered into their labour" (2003:480). Then, in a footnote, he refers to four leading scholars who have provided such a backdrop. I will only refer to some of the important secondary literature on my selected classics and their historical contexts, usually in footnotes.

In the cultural analysis and field research I do, I will discuss the boundaries and methods of my inquiry as I introduce them in the discussion. In fact, I will clarify all my methods in the appropriate sections rather than attempt to describe them all here. Since missiology and spirituality are both *multi-disciplinary fields,* this study is also multi-disciplinary, drawing from the disciplines of spirituality, missiology, theology, history, sociology, psychology, and the scientific study of religion—each of which has its own unique methods. Therefore, it will be less confusing to introduce methods as I go, in footnotes whenever possible.

Table 7: Sheldrake's Earmarks of a Spiritual Classic (Adapted from Sheldrake 1992:164–65)

What Characteristics Help Us Recognize a Spiritual Classic?	
Brings "us into transforming contact with what is enduring" in Christianity	Can challenge and surprise us
	Gives practical help while avoiding technical language
Wisdom document	"Effectively translates Christian ideas into lifestyle so that connection between theory and practice are made explicit"
Makes "divine truth accessible in our world"	
Not only teaches us but moves us to response	
Draws on author's own values and experience	"Gives accessible map for charting life's depths through verbal images or pictures that stimulate the imagination"
Personal, intimate, and pastoral rather than just objective spiritual theology	

Overview of the Book

Chapter 2 provides a brief history of space and time through the premodern and modern eras. It examines some fundamental mechanisms and four manifestations or traces of this collapse and how these were derived from modernity. One of the primary characteristics of the collapse is that it functions like an addicting virus, which can be effectively treated by periods of extended solitude and transparent community. My cultural analysis shows significant hunger for time intensive spiritual practices associated with ancient traditions.

Chapter 3 examines how Jesus practiced his spirituality and mission, and what he taught his followers in the Sermon on the Mount, John 15, and Matthew 28:16–20. Though he drew his spiritual disciplines primarily from those of first century Judaism, he radically critiqued and subverted these and aimed to fulfill in his own mission what Israel failed to do in hers. To what better source in antiquity can we turn for spiritual practices than Jesus himself? The most important finding in this chapter is that solitary and communal spiritual practices were inseparably linked to mission in deed and in word, in what Jesus modeled and in what he taught.

Chapter 4 looks at what the early church practiced and taught concerning spirituality and mission. To what extent did they follow what Jesus taught and modeled? Though communal spiritual practices played a bigger role in the early church than in the life and ministry of Jesus, solitary practices still were crucial at least in Acts, the apostolic fathers, and Origen. As with Jesus, spiritual and missional practices were inseparably linked in the teaching and practice of the early church.

Chapter 5 examines the rhythms of spirituality and mission in three movements. The first is from the pre-Reformation era, which subsequently influenced both Catholic and Protestant spiritualities. The second is from the Catholic Reformation, which influenced modern Catholic missions. The third is from the Protestant Puritan movement in eighteenth century America, which heavily influenced the Protestant expansion of missions in the following century. As with Jesus and the early church, I find similar correlations between spirituality and mission in these examples from the modern age.

Chapter 6 profiles the spirituality of the postmodern generations and argues that they need to be mentored in habitual daily, weekly, monthly, and occasional rhythms that become life-giving. My field research on these generations also shows a clear linkage between spirituality and mission. It also suggests the possibility that twenty to thirty minutes in prayer and Scripture could be a minimal daily threshold beyond which the warmth of a group moves from moderate towards strong. Further research on this is needed. Monthly extended times such as those practiced in the *Devotio Moderna* also appears to be crucial. Annual and extended solitude from the *eremitic* tradition and Ignatius's *Spiritual Exercises* might well be fostered also.

Chapter 7, the conclusion, summarizes this study's key arguments and findings and proposes a model for spirituality and mission. Based on these, the chapter concludes with recommendations for (1) making spirituality the ethos for structures of mission, church, and leadership development; (2) mission practices to engage our contemporary culture; (3) further study and research; and (4) studying and teaching spirituality in the academy.

2
The Collapse of Time and Space

> The world suddenly feels much smaller and the time horizons much shorter.
> —David Harvey (2001:123)

THIS CHAPTER ANALYZES THE CULTURAL CHANGES IN THE EXPERIENCE of space and time during the postmodern era.[1] I deal with a number of theorists who address various aspects of this collapse. Interestingly, they

---

1. My method in this cultural analysis is twofold: (1) a review of selected literature dealing directly or indirectly with space and time and their collapse written by sociologists, geographers, generational theorists, economists, psychologists, marriage and family therapists, journalists, and secular ethicists; and (2) a survey of empirical research projects that touch on some aspect of the issue in fields such as public policy (Putnam 1999), environmental psychology (Seudfeld 1980), cardiac psychology (Ulmer and Schwartzburd 1996), and social psychology (Levine 1997). My cultural analysis in Chapter 6 will be further developed when I analyze the spirituality that has arisen among the postmodern generations in light of the collapse of space and time. This will include my analysis of data collected from a field sample of Xers and Millennials. Because many volumes have been written on space and time, I will limit my survey to theorists from the fields mentioned above, which leaves totally unrepresented some disciplines that have participated significantly in the discussion. Contemporary architects and physicists, for example, have contributed extensively to current discussions on space and time. In an interview with Tim Folger, physicist Julian Barbour argues for an unusual theory of the universe in which time and motion do not exist at all. Nor does speech occur, only stillness. There is no past or future, only moments that are frozen eternally much like the still frames of a movie film. A movie's movements are illusionary since no movement occurs within each frame. Similarly, each stage of life is eternal—frozen in an unchanging universe. Humans live in many eternal moments and many universes. In this sense humans are immortal, not in the traditional sense of an afterlife. Obviously, Barbour's view does not allow for a compression of time since time does not exist in the first place (Barbour 1999). His theory purportedly resolves mathematical difficulties between the logical implications of the theory of relativity on a cosmic level and quantum physics at the atomic level (see Folger 2000:54–51).

each call for efforts to minimize its harmful effects. Cardiac psychologists, for example, have found effective treatment for hurry sickness, which is an addictive relationship to time and a potentially harmful pathology implicated as one factor in heart disease. In the last section of this chapter, I look at various proven means for directly or indirectly resisting and subverting the spatial-temporal compression in North America. Many of these include some form of spirituality. To begin, I will sketch the historical development of this collapse and some major factors behind it, such as the receptacle view of space, the mechanical clock, and the separation of space from time.

A Short History of Space and Time: From Pre-Modern through Modern Eras

In 1961 G. J. Whitrow, a mathematician and historian of natural science, wrote *The Natural Philosophy of Time*, the first comprehensive work on the scientific study of time. He and others claim that the ancient world generally considered space to be a more important reality than time (1980:v).[2] This can be seen in the fact that the scholarly study of space dates all the way back to ancient Greece, while the academic study of time was not recognized until 1966.[3]

More recently, Robert Levine, a social psychologist, has made a lifetime study of time in various cultures.[4] In *A Geography of Time*, he traces the earliest method of time measurement to the sun dial, which came into existence around 3,500 BC. Also called shadow clocks, these depended on the movement of heavenly bodies and seasonal changes. Eventually, more uniform ways to measure time emerged. Within five hundred years of the earliest sundials, water clocks were invented,

2. Agreeing with Whitrow's claim are Thomas Torrance (1969:56), Bruce Chilton (2002:8–12), Thorleif Boman (1960:39,128), and H. C. Hahn (1980:841–45). In Western thought, the natural sciences have generally followed this bias.

3. The International Society for the Study of Time, an interdisciplinary group established in 1966, was the first of its kind, with Whitrow as its first president. In a 1959 article in the *New Scientist*, J. L. Synge argued that time, not space, was the most important measurement of physics. He thought that Euclid, the father of geometry, had it wrong in positing space, not time, as the primary idea in science. Synge argued for a subspecialty of physics devoted to the study of time and suggested the field be called "chronometry" (Whitrow 1980:v–vi).

4. Levine is motivated in part by his Jewish heritage, which is known for its preoccupation with the concept of time (1997:208–10).

which employed the steady dripping of water through a small hole in a vase or container. These were used by Egyptians, Romans, and others to measure the passage of time in cloudy weather or at night. Utilizing the same principle, other methods evolved using materials that flowed or could be consumed. Examples include sand hour glasses, candles, and Chinese incense clocks (1997:54–56).

The Judeo-Christian Preoccupation with Time

In the ancient world, the Judeo-Christian tradition was unique in elevating the idea of time to a more equal footing with space. The God of the Hebrews created the world with days and seasons, and moved within history to save his people in the exodus, the giving of the Torah, the conquest, and the return from exile. These acts were celebrated in weekly Sabbaths, monthly new moons, annual festivals, fasts, and other celebrations such as the Sabbatical and Jubilee Years, each involving rituals demarcated by specific time boundaries. YHWH's creative, saving, and covenantal acts gave the Hebrews a higher view of time than other cultures.[5] But it was the expansion of Christianity that proved most helpful in lifting the notion of time in the West. According to Thomas F. Torrance, "It is largely to Christianity that we owe the important place given to *time* in the development of Western thought" (1969:56).

Until recently, scholars generally thought that Judaism and Christianity exclusively held a linear view of time while the rest of the ancient world had only cyclical views of time.[6] It was thought that the doctrines of the Incarnation and atonement and the Christian expectation of the final consummation of God's kingdom inserted a linear-teleological sense of time into the Greco-Roman world. For example, Whitrow wrote that "the rise of Christianity, with its central doctrine of the Crucifixion as a *unique* event in time, was the cardinal factor causing men to think of time as linear progression rather than cyclical repetition" (1980:27). Though this view holds some truth, as Bruce Chilton has pointed out, Greek thought was not completely devoid of a linear view of time (2002:8–10). Nor was the Judeo-Christian tradi-

---

5. Thorleif Boman, for example, says the "Hebrew's thinking moves in time" while Greek thinking is rooted spatially (1960:123). For a Jewish perspective on time, I have drawn on Levine (1997:208–10). For Jewish origins of set prayers, I am indebted to Donin (1980:11–12) and Steinsaltz (2000:47–49).

6. Oscar Cullman, for example, reflects this view (1964:51–60).

tion without cyclical notions of time, but its eschatological expectations were unique among the ancients.

Torrance's Receptacle and Relational Views of Space

If space was more important than time in late antiquity, how did ancients understand it? In *Space, Time and Incarnation*, Thomas Torrance says that the Greeks predominantly held a "receptacle or container notion of space" (1969:4). Various forms of this view conceived space as containing bodies within it. For Aristotle, space not only contained things but also exercised a force over them, exerting limits that defined and constituted their boundaries and places. Torrance contends that Aristotle's view separated and isolated "the notion of space from that of time," introducing a "rigidity into the concept of space" (1969:7–9), a notion to which I will return later. This view of space, he says, appeared later in Newtonian physics and various eras of Christian history, proving problematic for Christian theology (1969:22).

Indeed, the receptacle view of space posed a theological challenge to the early church as it penetrated Greek culture with the gospel. Simply put, how could the space occupied by the finite body of Jesus contain an infinite God?[7] If God could not be contained in temples made with hands (Acts 17:24) nor by the world God made, how could Deity be contained in the physical body of Jesus of Nazareth? Arius resolved the problem by denying Jesus's divinity. But the Nicene Fathers rejected Arius's view of Jesus and the receptacle idea of space implicit in his Christology. Instead, they fashioned what Torrance calls a relational view of space in response to inadequate Greek categories (1969:4). Space in this view is a relational medium by and through which bodies and beings relate to each other over time. Relationships between created bodies or persons dynamically interact, develop, unfold, and change as time passes. In this view, time and space are inseparably linked as finite created realities, which are elastic, not fixed; relative, not absolute.

Space and place conceived in this way better accounts for how an incarnate God provides a dynamic relational bridge into finite space and time through which humans can be welcomed into the intimate communion between Father, Son, and Holy Spirit—an idea known

---

7. The Latin phrase for this idea is *finitum non capax infinite* (the finite cannot contain the infinite) (Lilburne 1989:104).

as the doctrine of *perichoresis* (Torrance 1969:15–18, 58). Though the Nicene Creed affirms that God stands apart from space and time since he created them both, it equally affirms that God the Son takes on space and time through the Incarnation. Torrance elaborates:

> Thus while the Incarnation does not mean that God is limited by space and time, it [the Creed] asserts the reality of space and time for God in the actuality of his relations with us, and at the same time binds us to space and time in all our relations with him. We can no more contract out of space and time than we can contract out of the creature-Creator relationship and God *"can"* no more contract out of space and time than He *"can"* go back on the Incarnation of His Son or retreat from the love in which He made the world, with which He loves it, through which he redeems it, and by which He is pledged to uphold it. (1969:67)

This view of the Incarnation has furnished a theological foundation for the ecological concern of Geoffrey R. Lilburne, who believes that Western society's disregard for the environment flows out of "the loss of the sense of place" (1989:110).[8] Following Torrance, Walter Brueggemann (1977), and W. D. Davies (1974), and in opposition to Harvey Cox (1965),[9] Lilburne argues that the sense of place is regained in the Incarnation since God has entered space in the One who cared intimately about the land and especially for those living there. By so doing, God made sacred first century Palestine and all places where Jesus's followers live and gather. As believers congregate in particular places and spaces, they sacralize them by turning them into localities of intimacy with the one who created them. Such a relationship to a particular place will result in Christian attempts to resist forces that threaten the environment in order to preserve it as a sanctuary where people can encounter the one true and living God in worship and thanksgiving for his creative power.

With the revival of Aristotelian philosophy in the medieval church beginning in the twelfth century, the receptacle view of space again

---

8. Sociologists generally agree that what Lilburne calls the "loss of the sense of place" is caused by uprooting relationships from localities in the modern and especially postmodern eras. See for example, Gidden's discussion on the dis-embedding of social relationships (1990:16–17) and Castells's discussion on the disembodiment of the cultural and historical meaning of locality in the information age (1996:375).

9. See Lilburne's discussion of Cox's argument that Christianity desacralized space, nature, and place (1988:20–34).

regained prominence, according to Torrance (1969:25). It manifested itself in the view that Christ's presence was contained in particular fixed spaces such as bread, wine, holy relics, and places. God's presence came to be understood in spatial terms without reference to time, which removed the sense of dynamism from the experience of God (1969:27).[10]

The Separation of Time from Space

The pre-modern isolation of space from time in ancient and medieval eras prefigured the modern separation of time from space as articulated by Antony Giddens (1990). But, the modern separation introduced rigidity into the concept of time. Giddens uses the term "separation of time from space" to mean that time was gradually removed from the flexible and indefinite ways in which particular localities marked it. Time-keeping became less and less determined by seasonal changes, agricultural rhythms, and people's varying customs specific to the places where they lived.[11] Giddens thinks that this separation constitutes a primary factor in the dynamic quality of modernity (1990:16–17). In other words, the efficiency, speed, rapid change, and devaluation of the past characteristic of modernity accompanied the separation of time from space.

This has resulted in the second main feature of modernity, what Giddens calls the dis-embedding of relationships from place and the re-embedding of them in ways that are less tied to place. In other words, people have increasingly formed and nurtured relationships across

---

10. Torrance thinks the Reformed and Anglican branches of the Reformation returned to a relational view of space (1969:28–29) while Martin Luther and Sir Isaac Newton each viewed space as an infinite attribute of God. Thus, space for Newton was an absolute, fixed container in which the laws of physics governed and determined nature (1969:34–39). As Colin Brown notes, Newton's ideas generated a mechanistic view of the universe, which replaced God's activity in the world with the operation of natural law (1990:218), which provided fertile soil for deism. Certainly not deists themselves, Luther and Newton would have been appalled by deist assumptions, which left no room for either the miraculous nor intimacy with God. The idea of a mechanistic universe existing in absolute space and time dominated modern science until Einstein's theory of relativity held that time and the mass of objects vary relative to their speed (Torrance 1969:28–35). J. B. Jackson (1979) thinks Newton's concept of fixed, infinite, and undifferentiated space was reflected in the development of America's landscape through the use of a rectangular grid system in the late 1700s—an idea James Bradley finds unconvincing (2006).

11. The duration of an hour changed depending on the season, for example.

greater and greater distances, which has generally eroded the depth of social bonds and community.

The separation of time from space developed gradually from the thirteenth to the twentieth centuries through twin phenomena. First, the emergence of mechanical clocks changed time-measuring devices from being a means to call a community to prayer into instruments of control for financial gain. Second, time was commercialized by its standardization inside of factories, and then in surrounding communities through new modes of transportation, especially the expansion of railroads across North America in the late nineteenth century.

The Mechanical Clock and the Commercialization of Time

The first mechanical time devices appeared in late medieval monasteries. Bells driven by weights called monks to the hours of prayer (Levine 1997:56).[12] Levine dates the first mechanical clocks to the fourteenth century. Judith Middleton-Stewart dates public clocks to the same period.[13]

> The modern system of hour reckoning and the public clock originated in the Italian cities, Milan the first ... in 1336 .... At York in about 1360, during the building of the cathedral, one clock called the people to prayer, another got the workforce on the job: God's time and merchant's time. (2002:135–36)[14]

Mechanical clocks and time pieces gradually introduced various monetary conceptions of time, including:

1. *Merchant Time.* Richard Fox (1448–1528) introduced "merchant time" into England's religious, political, and educational spheres, in which he exerted national influence according to church historian

---

12. The monastic motivation for keeping time was to ensure regular timely prayer during the divine offices—a stark contrast to the economic rationale of modern societies. Though some pre-moderns kept time for commercial reasons, modernity's monetary motivation became dominant in the nineteenth and twentieth centuries.

13. Middleton-Stewart's article on the concept of time in European late medieval wills is part of a collection of papers entitled *The Use and Abuse of Time in Christian History* (2002).

14. Merchant time is the term used by Jacques Le Goff in his book on time in the Middle Ages (1960:29–42).

Barry Collett (2002). Working seventy hours per week, Fox emphasized the efficient use of time[15] and his stress on efficiency was admired a century later by Francis Bacon. Fox adapted the Rule of St. Benedict for English nuns, including many references to time (2002:145–46). The introduction of clock time in Europe with the consequent increase in efficiency eventually reduced the amount of leisure time people enjoyed, which previously had been plentiful. "In Europe through the Middle Ages, the average number of holidays per year was around 115 days" (Levine 1997:12). Surprisingly, time saved is used for yet more work under the pressures of modernity.

2. *Uniform Time.* The construction of town clocks in the fourteenth century and the use of portable spring-loaded clocks among aristocracy in the fifteenth century spread a uniform sense of time among the aristocracy in urban areas, says Christopher B. Kaiser.

> Before the nineteenth century . . . only urban populations had access to clocks of any sort, and the time discipline of town life was still understood as an enclave within the variable, diurnal cycle of day and night. In fact the operation (or reading) of clocks was often adjusted to the seasonal duration of the day so that daytime hours were longer in the summer and shorter in the winter. The time of day at any given location was also specific to its meridian or longitude. In other words, time was still fairly elastic and relational. (1996:93)

Except for the urban elite, in the fourteenth through seventeenth centuries time was still flexible, determined by solar or lunar movements and the environment over which humans had little control.

3. *Labor Time.* Medieval scholar Jacques Le Goff pointed out that for laborers in the fourteenth century the basic "unit of labor time in the medieval West" was the day, which began at sunrise and lasted until sunset (1980:44). As Le Goff shows, the demarcation and definition of labor time became a point of conflict and change reflecting tensions between the labor and ruling classes. In the same century the half-day, ending at noon, was established as a unit of labor time (1980:44–45).

---

15. Fox served as the bishop of the dioceses of Exeter, Durham, Winchester, and Bath, and Wells and he held various positions in the government of Henry VII, including responsibility for foreign affairs. He also founded Corpus Christi College at Oxford (Collett 2002:145–46).

Finally, "the sixty minute hour was firmly established as ... the fundamental unit of labor time" (1980:49).

4. *Factory Time.* Beginning in the 1740s, the Industrial Revolution brought about the control of time to a new level through the routinization of work in factories. Workers' output per unit time became an important idea. Mass production required careful time coordination of assembly lines and work schedules. The sense of time in factories became rigid and dehumanizing (Levine 1997:12–15). Time came to be defined economically, as Ben Franklin ostensibly said, "Time is money."[16] In the factories of the Industrial Revolution, then, time became rigidly uniform, even though outside the factory work environment time remained flexible at least until the nineteenth century.

Expansion of the Railroad and Universal Standard Time

Historian Stephen Kern writes that "the most momentous development in the history of uniform public time since the invention of the mechanical clock in the fourteenth century was the introduction of standard time at the end of the nineteenth century" (1983:11). The latter was accomplished by the expansion of railroad interests assisted by the telegraph (Ventura 1995:20). The completion of the first American transcontinental railroad in 1869 created a need to standardize time from coast to coast. Kern estimates that a rail passenger traveling from one coast to the other would have had to set her watch more than two hundred times in order to match the various local times of towns through which she passed (Kern 1983:12).[17] The movement of trains required precise scheduling, which would be made easier by a nationally uniform way to keep time. Journalist Michael Ventura describes how railroad companies began urging the government to create time zones in the early 1880s when a given time in San Francisco corresponded to no precise

---

16. A number of scholars have written that Ben Franklin said "Time is money," but they include no citation. For example, see Levine (1997:90) and Bauman (2000:112).

17. Kern also writes that in 1870 there were still some 80 different railroad times that railroad companies themselves maintained in the United States. Levine estimates this number in the 1860s to be about seventy, which dropped to about fifty in 1880. Each railroad line developed its own times. In Buffalo, New York, the train station had three clocks each showing a different time—one for Buffalo time and the other two for the different times kept by the two railroad companies using the station (1997:65). This pressure to standardize time was repeated in many countries (Kern 1983:12–13).

time in New York or anywhere in between. During these years time was still fairly flexible, as there was no such thing as being twenty or thirty minutes late except in factories. "Coordination was largely a matter of bells and whistles," Ventura writes. "The factory whistle would blow, the town-hall clock would chime, and if they felt like it, people would set their house clocks and pocket watches accordingly. Absolute precision wasn't expected, nor, for most endeavors, was it needed" (1995:20).

In 1883 the railroads established four time zones for their own operation—the same ones that were enacted into federal law in 1918 and are still in use today (Levine 1997:67). Stiff opposition emerged as railroad schedules began to change the temporal practices of farmers and businessmen to allow the production of goods to be coordinated with their distribution to markets.[18] It was argued that standardizing time invaded privacy, threatened to centralize excessive power in the federal government, and assaulted states rights and local control (1997:72–73). In spite of the opposition, the separation of time from local definition and custom spread from factories to other urban commercial ventures as well as to farming communities in late nineteenth century America.

With the standardization of time, the inventions of the telegraph, telephone, light bulb, automobile, airplane, and radio could be coordinated with precision across great distances between 1880 and 1920—a period T. J. Jackson Lears calls the second industrial revolution (1981:8). Universal standard time fueled the rapid acceleration of life. Yet, of these years Kern says,

> If a man travels to work on a horse for twenty years and then an automobile is invented and he travels in it, the effect is both an acceleration and a slowing. In an unmistakable way the new journey is faster, and the man's sense of it is as such. But that very acceleration transforms his former means of traveling into something it had never been—slow—whereas before it was the fastest way to go.... As quickly as people responded to the new technology, the pace of their former lives seemed like slow motion. The tension between a speeding reality and a slower past

---

18. The city of Cincinnati took strong exception to a discrepancy of twenty-two minutes between its time and the new railroad time: "The proposition that we should put ourselves out of the way nearly half an hour from the facts so as to harmonize with an imaginary line through Pittsburgh is simply preposterous . . . let the people of Cincinnati stick to the truth as it is written by the sun, moon and stars" (quoted in Levine 1997:73).

generated sentimental elegies about the good old days before the rush. It was an age of speed but, like the cinema, not always uniformly accelerated. The pace was unpredictable, and the world, like the early audiences, alternately overwhelmed and inspired, horrified and enchanted. (1983:129-30)

The sense of time changed unevenly with ebbs and flows in these years, as well as throughout the modern age as a whole. Though occasionally leisure time increased following technological advances—even though technologically advanced societies have the least discretionary time compared with agrarian and hunter-gatherer societies (Lingenfelter 2000)—the general pattern was a loss of free time. The next major round of time-space compression came after World War II with the dawn of the postmodern era. It is to that discussion we now turn. Table 8 below summarizes the historical development of universal standard clock time during the pre-modern and modern ages, which laid the groundwork for the radical new temporal and spatial realities of postmodernity.

Table 8: The Development of Universal Clock Time (Adapted from Levine 1997:53–63; Kaiser 1996:80–93; Kern 1983; Whitrow 1980:54–59; Ventura 1995:21–23)

3500 BC	Sundial
3000 BC	Water clocks, hour glasses, Chinese incense clocks
13th–14th century	First mechanical clocks developed in monasteries in Western Europe
14th century	Jean Buridan and Nicoloe Oresme developed the idea of the universe as clock-like mechanism running without God's intervention
	Town clocks introduced/sense of time gradually became more uniform
15th century	Portable, spring-loaded clocks used by the aristocracy
18th–19th century	Industrial Revolution: routinization and precision of time in factories
19th–20th century	Standardization of time and the coming of the railroad-Transportation revolution
20th century	Commercialization of time is completed

Lamenting the Collapse of Space and Time in the Postmodern Era

"The world suddenly feels much smaller and the time horizons much shorter." So writes geographer David Harvey referring to the recent round of time-space compression (2001:123). I will begin this section with a review of Harvey's theory of the key mechanisms in this collapse, and that of sociologists Anthony Giddens (1990:14–17, 53) and Zygmunt Bauman (2000:91–129). All three scholars view space-time compression as the defining characteristic of the modern and postmodern eras. Each laments it, though Giddens is the most muted of the three. Each thinks something must be done.

Next, I will survey prime manifestations of the collapse. Lamenting the loss of the sense of place, sociologist Ray Oldenburg (1997) wants to reestablish public places devoted to informal social connections. Robert D. Putnam (2000) decries the loss of social capital, which he attributes in part to the loss of time that has occurred in many segments of society. Then I will look at the effects of space-time compression on the generations. Christopher Lasch (1978) tells how many narcissistic Boomers raised Xers without spending much time with them, and Howe and Strauss (2000), Wendy Zoba (1999), and Tom Beaudoin (1998) describe the temporal-spatial experience of Xers, who had more free time, and Millennials, who had less time. Both generations were greatly molded by the Internet, which can be addictive and isolating. The most extensive sociological treatment of the information age is the three-volume work by Manuel Castells (1996, 1997, 1998). He protests the spatial-temporal codes imbedded in the Internet and calls for resistance communities to work within cyberspace to subvert these codes into slower time rooted in place.

More Flexible Modes of Capital Accumulation (Harvey)

David Harvey proposes several key mechanisms of the "tiger of time-space compression" (1990:351) in *The Condition of Postmodernity*, where he devotes an entire section to the new spatial-temporal realities in the cultural sea changes that began around 1972 (1990:201–326). These changes are economically based and associated with late capitalism, not with a post-capitalist or post-industrialist economy. They represent surface phenomena, not fundamental changes in economic structures. He sees a "relationship between the rise of postmodernist cultural forms, the emergence of more flexible modes of capital accumulation, and a new round of 'time–space compression'" (1990:vii). In a later work, *The Spaces of Capital: Towards a Critical Geography*, Harvey links this compression to computerization, telecommunications, and transport containerization, each an integral part of recent capital accumulation. Ironically for Harvey, postmodernity presents the opportunity for a radical critique of capitalism and its resultant pace of life about which he is highly critical. As he laments, "Capitalism has transformed the face of the earth at an accelerating pace the past 200 years. It cannot possibly continue on that trajectory for another 200 years. Someone somewhere has to think about what kind of social system should replace it" (2001:126–27).

Time-Space Separation, Dis-embedding, Reflexivity (Giddens)

Anthony Gidden thinks the key mechanisms for the collapse of space-time in the postmodern era are the same as those that dominated the modern age. In fact, "postmodernity" has not yet arrived, claims Giddens, only "high modernity" or "radicalized modernity." The same mechanisms are bringing "the consequences of modernity" to roost more universally in this period (1990:3).[19] In contrast to Harvey, Giddens sees this phase and its acceleration as both positive—creating security and human accomplishment—as well as negative because of the "degrading nature of modern industrial work, the growth of totalitarianism, the threat of environmental destruction, and the alarming development of military power and weaponry" (1990:cover). As already mentioned, Giddens sees the main sources of modernity's dynamism as the separation of time from space and dis-embedding mechanisms, which have uprooted social ties from place and re-embedded them across great distances. To these he adds a third source, "the reflexive

19. Giddens contends, "Beyond modernity, I shall claim, we can perceive the contours of a new and different order, which is 'post-modern'; but this is quite distinct from what is at the moment called by many 'post-modernity'" (1990:3). He does not look at modernity primarily from an epistemological perspective, as does Jean-Francois Lyotard, who argues against grand narratives and a unified field of knowledge, or Jurgen Habbermas, who argues for "a coherent epistemology." Instead he develops "an institutional analysis of modernity with cultural and epistemological overtones" (1990:1–2). For an excellent comparison of postmodernity as conceived by de-constructionists with Giddens's "radicalized modernity" see (1990:150).

appropriation of knowledge," which is modernity's capacity to accumulate information about its institutions and reflect and act critically upon them. Summing up the effect of these factors, he writes, "These features of modern institutions help to explain why living in the modern world is more like being aboard a careening juggernaut rather than being in a carefully controlled and well-driven motor car" (1990:53).

Nomadic Existence of the Ruling Elite and Dissolving Social Commitments (Bauman)

Sociologist Zygmunt Bauman devotes a full chapter to recent space-time changes in his book *Liquid Modernity*—his term for late twentieth century culture (2000:91–129). Like Giddens, he thinks we are in a new phase of modernity, not postmodernity. He argues that during most of the modern age space was solid while time was variable. In other words, speed, a function of time, accelerated while space and place remained more stable entities, as evidenced by large industrial plants, heavy machinery, and large hierarchal organizations, each still tied to fixed places. In this milieu, entire careers were often lived out within a single organization, which nurtured loyalty and strengthened social bonds. As speed increased exponentially, space ceased to be a barrier to transportation, communication, and commerce, thus dissolving the solid state of modernity. So, time conquered space (2000:2–10). In the following section, Bauman implicates the nomadic elites' role in dissolving space.

> Throughout the solid stage of the modern era, nomadic habits remained out of favor. Citizenship went hand in hand with settlement, and the absence of "fixed address".... In the fluid stage of modernity, the settled majority is ruled by the nomadic and exterritorial elite....The contemporary global elite is shaped after the pattern of old-style "absentee landlords". It can rule without burdening itself with the chores of administration, management, welfare concerns, or for that matter, with the mission of "bringing light," "reforming the ways," morally uplifting, "civilizing" and cultural crusades. Active engagement in the life of subordinate populations is no longer needed (on the contrary, it is actively avoided as unnecessarily costly and ineffective).... Traveling light, rather than holding tightly to things deemed attractive for their reliability and solidity... is now the asset of power.

Holding to the ground is not that important if the ground can be reached and abandoned at whim, in a short time or no time. On the other hand, holding too fast, burdening one's bond with mutually binding commitments, may prove positively harmful. (2000:13)

Manifestation #1: Loss of the Sense of Place (Oldenburg)

In *The Great Good Place*, sociologist Ray Oldenburg warns that America has been losing its "informal public places," which he also calls "third places." Home and work constitute people's first and second places respectively. Third places are within walking distance from home, continuously available, and inclusive. They serve no particular function other than to provide people a setting in which to enjoy conversation and social interaction with others from their community. Motivation to frequent such places is fun, not personal gain or civic duty. In fact, other agencies of society do not and cannot fulfill the function of these informal places according to Oldenburg (1997:ix).[20]

Formerly, front verandas and porches of houses overlooking neighborhood streets have served such purposes. More recently, Starbucks explicitly identifies itself and functions as a third place. At some Starbucks outlets, interactional and conversational games are sold. Current examples of third places mentioned by Oldenburg include coffee shops, cafes, drug stores, community centers, as well as "beauty parlors, general stores, bars, hangouts . . . [and places that] get you through the day" (1997:cover). He attributes to current zoning and

---

20. According to Oldenburg, third places serve to: (1) unite the neighborhood by helping everybody to know everybody; (2) relieve stress and produce laughter—"the competitive successes and the enervating stresses of the mundane world are 'put on hold'" (1997:xxii); (3) provide mixers in which everybody is at ease with everybody even if they do not like them; (4) assimilate newcomers via "ports of entry"—the more transitory the society the harder it is for newcomers to feel welcome, especially in suburbia; (5) provide "'neutral ground'—space upon which one is not burdened by the role of host or guest . . . People may come and go as they please and are beholden to no one" (1997:xviii); (6) function as a "sorting area" by bringing together those who may develop other forms of association; (7) provide a staging area for community disasters or crises; (8) bring generations together in a relaxed setting rather than separating them; (9) provide a place for retirees to stay connected to the workforce instead of being confined to retirement places; (10) allow people to do for one another—not just a program; (11) provide participatory entertainment instead of the detachment of most entertainment; (12) foster political activity and intellectual life; (13) provide "office space" for the poor (1997:xvii–xxxii).

architectural practices the disappearance of these places—the loss of which he believes is having a devastating impact on our society.

Manifestation #2: Loss of Social Capital and Time (Putnam)

In *Bowling Alone*, Harvard professor of public policy Robert Putnam urges Americans to reconnect with each other and reverse the nation's alarming loss of social capital, which has occurred since the late 1960s. Social capital is the benefit derived from the activity in various communal entities such as families, small groups, groups committed to grassroots political or community endeavor, churches, clubs, and bowling leagues.[21] Putnam shows that Americans have become increasingly disconnected from group involvement over the past three decades.[22] This loss even extends to informal connections such as card playing, visiting or entertaining friends or neighbors at home, and eating together as a family (2000:93–115). Over this period, attendance at club meetings declined 58 percent; family dinners dropped 38 percent; and those reporting having friends over dropped 45 percent (2002:1). A falling percentage of Americans spend time in informal connecting activities, epitomized by a drop in the number of participants in bowling leagues.[23] This loss threatens both our societal and personal health, as suggested by the surprising finding that joining a group cuts in half the odds of dying in the next year (2002:1).

21. Putnam builds his case from the massive amounts of empirical data that he and his team have gathered from the Roper Social and Political Trends survey, the DDB Needham Lifestyle survey, other established research efforts, and records from scores of political, religious, and social organizations.

22. Putnam has amassed an impressive array of empirical data, which he has displayed in ninety-six figures, nine tables, and three appendices. The last appendix contains forty graphs showing the membership patterns for forty civic and professional associations during the twentieth century. He has controlled the data for standard demographic variations such as gender, marital status, employment status, home ownership, age, region, income, parental status, birth date, date when the survey was taken, average commuting time in the county where the respondent lives, financial worries, etc.

23. Figures from the American Bowling Congress show that league bowling among men peaked in 1964 at about 83 per 1,000, dropping to about 23 per 1,000 in 1997. The figures for women peaked in 1978 at 54 per 1,000, dropping to 18 per 1,000 in 1997 (Putnam 2000:112). Though the number of Americans bowling remains unchanged due to increased numbers of those bowling alone, bowling lane operators are alarmed at the decline in league bowling because league bowlers consume three times more concessions as do those who bowl alone (2000:113).

This loss in social capital has reversed the trends of the first two thirds of the twentieth century, when a higher percentage of Americans voted, attended church, participated in political and civic organizations, and had greater trust in the honesty of others.[24] Even so, Putnam thinks that "we are still more civically engaged than citizens in many other countries, but compared with our own recent past, we are less connected" (2000:183). He also finds hope in countercurrents where social capital is not eroding but may actually be growing: (1) an increase in youth volunteering, (2) the rise of the Internet, (3) grassroots evangelical activism, and (4) the growth of self-help and recovery groups (2000:180).

Table 9: Time and Social Capital: Some Findings and Recommendations (Adapted from Putnam 2000:195–233, 402–14)

Putnam's Findings			
1. *Full time employment among women (who exhibit greater social capital than men) leaves less time for social involvements and apparently reduces* (2000:195):			
Entertaining	10%	Visiting friends	25%
Club and church attendance	15%	Volunteering	50%
More women in the workforce in past thirty years is related mostly to financial necessity, not choice (2000:195–200).			
Most socially involved:	women who work part time by choice		
Next most involved:	homemakers		
Least socially involved	women who work full time out of necessity		
"One practical way to increase community engagement in America would be to make it easier for women (and men too) to work part-time if they wished." (2000:201)			

---

24. Putnam surveys the unabated declines reported during the past twenty-five years in political activity (chap. 2), civic participation (chap. 3), religious involvement (chap. 4), connections at work (chap. 5), informal social contact (chap. 6), altruism as demonstrated by volunteerism and philanthropy (chap. 7), and reciprocity, honesty, and trust (chap. 8). This data clearly supports Putnam's basic thesis concerning the loss of social capital. However, when he looks at small groups, social movements, and the Internet (chap. 9), Putnam finds that the patterns of civil disengagement are more ambiguous.

2. Men over fifty-five, who represent a growing percentage of the population, have more free time than any other segment of the population, whereas working single parents have the least. (2000:189–90)
3. Between 1983 and 1995, time spent commuting grew by fourteen percent, while every ten minutes of commuting reduced social capital by ten percent. (2000:213)
4. *TV has become more habitual with each generation.* In a typical evening eighty-one percent of Americans watch TV, fifty-six percent talk with their family, and twenty-seven percent do chores (2000:227). Writing friends, club meetings, and church attendance is negatively related to TV watching (2000:232–33).

Putnam's Recommendations

1. Spirituality	"Let us spur a new, pluralistic, socially responsible 'great awakening,' so that by 2010 Americans will be more deeply engaged than we are today in one or another spiritual community of meaning, while at the same time becoming more tolerant of the faiths and practices of other Americans." (2000:409)
2. Work / family / community	"America's workplace will be substantially more family-friendly and community-congenial, so that American workers will be enabled to replenish our stocks of social capital both within and outside the workplace." (2000:406)
3. Leisure time / participatory entertainment	"Americans will spend less leisure time sitting passively alone in front of glowing screens and more time in active connection with our fellow citizens. Let us foster new forms of electronic entertainment and communication that reinforce community engagement rather than forestalling it." (2000:410)
4. Time and space for neighbors / community	"American's will spend less time traveling and more time connecting with our neighbors than we do today, that we will live in more integrated and pedestrian-friendly areas, and that the design of our communities and the availability of public space will encourage more casual socializing with friends and neighbors." (2000:408)
5. Participatory arts / community	"Significantly more Americans will participate in (not merely consume or 'appreciate') cultural activities from group dancing to songfests to community theater to rap festivals. Let us discover new ways to use the arts as a vehicle for convening diverse groups of fellow citizens." (2000:411)

What accounts for the loss of social capital? The most obvious reasons include the twin factors of time and money pressures, to which Putnam devotes a full chapter (see Table 9 above). Though leading social theorists see time-space compression as a defining characteristic of modernity and postmodernity, some actually argue that per capita free time has actually increased in the last thirty years.[25] Putnam points out that, whether leisure time per capita has increased or remained unchanged, neither trend is mirrored in many parts of society. All researchers, whatever their position in the debate, agree that compared to the late sixties some segments of the population have lost free time, while others have gained it. While earlier retirement ages and an increased percentage of retirees have resulted in men over fifty-five having far more free time than thirty years ago, single mothers and working women in general have vastly less leisure time. Married couples worked fourteen more hours per week in 1998 than in 1969. While poorer working people have gained free time, educated wealthier people have lost leisure time (2000:190–91). Surprisingly, Putnam attributes only ten percent of the erosion of social capital to time-money pressures and the rest to other factors.[26] Though I think Putnam underestimates the effect of time-money pressures, he does give his findings and make recommendations about social capital in terms of time (see Table 9 above).

---

25. Their conclusions derive from time use studies at the Universities of Michigan and Maryland, which indicate a drop in work and a doubling of free time. A 6.2 hour-per-week gain in leisure time between 1965 and 1995 was reported by John Robinson and Geoffrey Godby in *Time for Life* (1997:339), while Harvard economist Juliet B. Schor holds that closer data analyses show a decline in free time (1992:167–74). Manuel Castells sees a 37 percent decline between 1973 and 1994 (1996:369). Other research, such as the Harris Polling data, shows leisure time remaining steady at twenty hours per week over the past quarter century—findings that Putnam seems to favor (2000:190).

26. Other factors responsible for the loss in social capital and the relative contribution of each to the problem estimated by Putnam are: (1) mobility and sprawl–ten percent; (2) technology and media–twenty-five percent; (3) generational change–fifty percent; and (4) roughly fifteen to twenty-nine percent is attributed to other mysterious sources, which are not yet understood (2000:277–84).

Manifestation #3: Generations X and Y and the Loss of Time-Space

Twenty years before Putnam urged the nation to renew its lost social capital, American historian Christopher Lasch called for a similar reform in the face of widespread political disengagement following Watergate. In *The Culture of Narcissism* he called for a "new politics, new discipline, [and] new love to replace the narcissistic self absorption" of our culture (1978: cover). Lasch writes:

> Because the narcissist has so few inner resources, he looks to others to validate his sense of self. He needs to be admired for his beauty, charm, celebrity, or power—attributes that usually fade with time. Unable to achieve satisfying sublimations in the form of love and work, he finds little to sustain him when youth passes him by. He takes no interest in the future and does nothing to provide himself with the traditional consolations of old age, the most important of which is the belief that future generations will in some sense carry on his life's work. (1978:211)

Nowhere has a narcissistic character, a lack of "interest in the future," and an inability "to equip the younger generation to carry on the tasks of the older" been more evident than in the way many Baby Boomers (born 1946–64) raised their children. Their offspring, primarily Xers, became known as latchkey kids because so many of them returned from school to empty residences. Since so many Boomers were absentee parents sacrificing their children on the altars of career and pleasure, typical Xers had little time invested in them, and thus entered young adulthood with a huge mentoring deficit. The media, more than their parents, shaped their character and worldview. Large numbers from this abandoned generation have been deeply wounded by the narcissistic character of their Boomer parents—a generation for which Lasch's book is a primer (Peace 2002).

Generational theorists Neil Howe and William Strauss have co-written seminal works on Generation X (1993) and Generation Y, also called the Millennials (2000). They compare how much free time both generations had growing up based on time use data from 1981 and 1997 surveys conducted by the University of Michigan's Institute for Social Research—considered the best source for such studies. The 1981 survey showed the amount of free time was fifty-two hours per week for children ages three to twelve years old (born 1969-78), these considered Xers by most definitions. According to Howe and Strauss, the 1997 survey of Millennials in the same age range showed their average free time was only thirty-three hours per week, a nineteen hours per week—or thirty-seven percent—loss of free time (2000:171). This loss was distributed among changes in time devoted to the activities shown in Table 10 below. Xer free time, a by-product of being abandoned, manifested itself in a widespread "whatever, whenever" attitude when they reached young adulthood—an attitude much less evident among the Millennials, who began coming of age around 2000. In contrast to Boomers who lived to work, Xers work to live.[27] In the early 1990s, researchers encountered Xer rage towards their Boomer parents over abandonment issues and the lack of time spent with them. As twenty-year-old Myra Brock said, "I don't want my kids to go through what my parents put me through." Xers want to spend more time with their children than their parents did (Gross and Scott 1990:58).

Table 10: Where Millennials Lost Free Time Compared with Xers[28] (Adapted from Howe and Strauss 2000:158–74)

Some Time Usage Changes among Children Ages 3–12 between 1981 and 1997. 19 Hours Net Free Time Lost

Discretionary activities showing a *decrease* in hours per week:	Required or structured activities showing an *increase* in hours per week:	Discretionary activity showing an *increase* in hours per week:
• 4.5 in unorganized activity • 2 in TV watching • 1.7 in eating/conversation • 1.2 in church attendance	• 8.3 in school/day care • 3.5 in household chores • 3 in grooming/personal care • 1 in study/reading • 2 in organized sports • 2.5 in traveling/visiting	• 2.5 in passive leisure

27. Margo Hornblower holds that this is also true of entrepreneurial Xers (1990:58–68), who desire to find "opportunities that will free them from the career imprisonment that confined their parents" (1990:58).

28. The figure of nineteen hours per week loss of free time apparently was based on Howe and Strauss's criteria for determining which activities should be classified as using free time. Researchers with somewhat different criteria have arrived at different figures. For example, Sandra J. Hofferth and John F. Sandberg show a drop of 7.5 hours of free time per week (2000:22). Despite these differences, researchers generally agree that a significant loss of free time occurred, except among poor children and those engaged in at-risk behaviors.

And so they have. They and younger Boomers became soccer parents, supervising their Millennial kids in endless rounds of homework and extracurricular activities to enrich them and keep them out of trouble, and to pursue their future success. But these kids are paying a high price. The 1999 Nickelodeon/Yankelovich Youth Monitor Survey shows 50 percent of girls between twelve and seventeen report feeling "too tired" (as quoted in Howe and Strauss 2000:170). Children and teens burn out in a society where "achievement begins with the first breath of life" (Brooks 2001:44).[29] The hectic pace of Millennials only increases once they enter college, according to David Brooks' *Atlantic Monthly* article on the "meritocratic elite"—the accomplished Millennials who attend prestigious academic institutions. Many pack their days so full that they must get by on only a few hours of sleep each night. On a visit to Princeton University in late 2000, Brooks interviewed a few dozen articulate students recommended by faculty. When asked to describe their schedules, the students sounded like a meeting of "Future Workaholics of America" (2000:40). They have little time for dating, reading newspapers, politics, or involvement in bigger causes. None spent several hours with classmates just to "shoot the breeze"—typical of Brooks' college experience in the late 1970s and early 1980s (2001:40). The Millennial time press is typical of students at schools across the board, not just elite institutions.[30] An abandoned generation, which had free time but without intimacy, is being followed by a pressured generation, which needs love not tied to performance.

Manifestation #4: The Internet's Timeless Time and the Space of Flows (Castells)

Xers, and to a greater extent Millennials, have been molded by the information revolution, which has compressed their sense of time and space with a logic and rhythm all its own. As Wendy Murray Zoba wrote, "The way young people receive and process information has been influenced by shock and speed" (1999:59). Media executives responded by reducing

---

29. See also Noonan (2001:54–55) and Rosenfeld, Wise, and Coles (2001), who urge parents to protect family time, let children be kids, and resist trends for pre-school stimulation and the undue pressure for kids to excel.

30. The annual UCLA national study of college freshman shows the percentage of freshmen feeling overwhelmed growing from eighteen percent in 1985 to twenty-eight percent in 2000 (Brooks 2001:42).

the length of sound bites and the duration of any single image. "Channel surfing has created a demand for quicker and more affecting images to capture the viewer" (Zoba 1999:51). The demand is even more evident on the Internet, where time is instantaneous, segmented, and reversible, and successive images correspond to no chronological order (Beaudoin 1998:127–29). Past generations were "small players in a large universe" (Zoba 1999:34), but technology has made the world smaller (Harvey 1990:241).

The spatial-temporal compression of the Internet can also be addictive and isolating. Hours spent sifting through information attained at blazing speeds can have a numbing impact on feelings. Blocked feelings are a part of all addictions. The Internet can also have an insulating effect on people, who replace real interactions with virtual ones. Though it has created vast networks in which virtual community occurs through Web sites like MySpace and Facebook, concerns have been voiced over the isolating potential of information technology. Michael Ventura warns about the effects of family members using personal computers at the home, where "people occupying the same quarters aren't necessarily sharing their lives." He argues that virtual reality "will become a substitute for both inner life and human interaction—much more seductive and transformative than television" (1995:24–25). Bringing virtual reality into the home, Ventura reasoned, would further pull family members away from sharing meals and communicating with each other (1995:25).

Sociologist Manual Castells echoes similar concerns over the effects of the Internet in his seminal three volume work on the information age (1996, 1997, 1998). He argues that the dominant conception of space on the Internet—what he calls "the space of flows"—differs radically from the logic and patterns associated with the places we actually live. Moreover, this threatens our culture's social cohesion because, as Castells notes,

> People do still live in places. But because function and power in our societies are organized in the space of flows ... its logic essentially alters the meaning and dynamic of places.... It follows [that] a structural schizophrenia between two spatial logics ... threatens to break down communication channels in society. The dominant tendency is toward a horizon of networked, ahistorical space of flows aiming at imposing its logic over scat-

tered, segmented places, increasingly unrelated to each other, less and less able to share cultural codes. (1996:428)

In other words, the Internet may be creating a parallel universe that undermines the meaning people derive from the places they live. Castells fears a technologically challenged class being exploited by the elite and a Tower-of-Babel-type breakdown (Gen 11:1–11) in which the culture and language used in the space of flows becomes incomprehensible to that used in the space of places.

Castells believes that space in the networked society annihilates time, rendering it instantaneous or timeless (1997:126).[31] He distinguishes between timeless time, which is non-sequential and segmented—typical of postmodernity—and clock time, which is chronological—typical of modernity. He advocates glacial time—typical of environmentalism—in which the slower rhythms of nature are lauded (1997:125–26).[32] To slow time, Castells calls for groups rooted in place to navigate the space of flows while subverting the dominance of the information culture elites and the spatial-temporal codes embedded in the Internet. He thinks environmental groups offer the most effective such resistance communities. Putnam, however, shows that recent dramatic membership increases in the environmental movement reflect financial, not grassroots participation, which remains small at the local level.[33] Based on the unexpected growth in evangelical activism, Putnam thinks the social networks of religious groups have greater potential for social capital and resistance (2000:161). Castells, too, sees the potential of religious groups as resistance communities.

> When networks dissolve time and space, people anchor themselves in places, and recall their historic memory.... God, nation, family, and community will provide unbreakable, eternal codes, around which a counter-offensive will be mounted against the

---

31. Castells argues that in the networked society space "organizes time," unlike most social theories in which time dominates space, as argued by Bauman, Harvey, and Giddens above (1996:376).

32. Castells (1997:125–26) credits the idea of glacial time to Scott Lash and John Urry (1994).

33. Analyzing active participation at the local level, Putnam finds "no hard evidence that grassroots environmentalism in general has grown." Instead, the figures suggest a decline in the 1990s (2000:160–61).

culture of real virtuality. Eternal truth cannot be virtualized. It is embodied in us. (1997:66)

Counter-offensive: Effective Means of Resisting the Collapse of Space and Time

We have listened to various voices analyzing the mechanisms and manifestations of the collapse of space-time, each lamenting directly or indirectly some of its aspects. Each calls for some response. I will look at proven means of resisting and subverting this collapse along with its harmful effects. These include the recovery movement, environmental psychology, cardiac psychology, marriage and family therapy, social psychology, and those working to reverse our culture's corrosion of character. In this survey I will discuss the question of how a fast-paced life becomes addictive and whether it is always harmful. Effective treatment of hurry sickness and other addictions include solitude, silence, and transparent community.

The Recovery Movement: Addictions and a Higher Power

The recovery movement is among the fastest growing movements in the U.S. (Putnam 2000:150–52). It is built upon practicing the Twelve Steps, whose biblical origins were altered so that any deity or power could be called upon for assistance in the battle against addiction.[34] Addictions of all kinds have been a growing concern among medical and therapeutic professionals, and their support for the recovery movement has been widespread, if not universal.

Busyness has become an addiction for many in our culture according to James Houston, and those suffering from its hold are "increasingly referred to as 'workaholics'" (1989:17). In a study conducted by the Families and Work Institute, nearly a third of employees report chronic feelings of being overworked and overwhelmed (Galinsky, Kim, and Bond 2001:6). Houston puts his finger on the inner emotional

---

34. Alcoholics Anonymous founder Bill W. took the Twelve Steps directly from the twelve spiritual traditions practiced by a lay renewal group called the Oxford Group (not to be confused with the Oxford Movement in nineteenth century England). Bill W. replaced the scriptural references to God and Jesus Christ with "higher power as you understand it" for the benefit of agnostic and atheistic alcoholics (see Stafford 1992:14–19).

dynamics that feed workaholism: "Busyness acts to repress our inner fears and personal anxieties, as we scramble to achieve an enviable image to display to others. We become 'outward' people obsessed with how we appear, rather than 'inward' people, reflecting on the meaning of our lives" (1989:17). As Joan Chittister says, "I become a cardboard cutout that breathes.... I go through life on fast speed but numb" (1990:157). The inability to stop keeps workaholics running from the feelings and thoughts of their hearts, and when they do stop, the Internet provides instant opportunities to feed gambling and sexual and shopping addictions, which cover over depression, anxiety, and pain with artificial feelings.[35]

An addiction can be described as a disease of the feelings according to F. Scott and Jean Cassidy. It requires the use of a substance, behavior, or relationship that is mood altering and progressive,[36] but eventually physically harmful or life threatening (1995). As the potential addiction exceeds casual use, a dependency sets in, which becomes impossible to break by the addict's effort or that of family and friends. In fact, such efforts generally result in the addiction becoming more entrenched. Recovery becomes impossible without the intervention of an outside power. The addict is a slave and captive, which is why Step One of the Twelve Steps begins with the honest confession, "We admitted we were powerless over alcohol and drugs—that our lives have become unmanageable" (Cassidy n.d.:15).[37]

---

35. Seminary students have approached me concerning sexual addictions they have struggled with, involving Internet pornography and in one case homosexual pornography. In the latter, the student had begun to visit gay bars and bathhouses while attending seminary. One student reported that when he began to practice the disciplines required for my course, his addiction was arrested until the end of the quarter, after which the addiction again took over as the practice of the disciplines diminished. For an overview of various kinds of pornography addictions and resources to address them, see Christine J. Gardner (2001:42–49).

36. I.e., it takes more of the substance, behavior, or relationship over time to reach the same altered mood. The body's capacity to require increasing amounts of a substance or behavior to reach the same effect is called tolerance (see Stone n.d.:2).

37. I am indebted to Scotty and Jean Cassidy, who founded and directed Second Chance Ministries, for permission to use materials that they developed for this program, where one of our sons received drug treatment in 1994–95. I am grateful to them for much of my knowledge of addictions, which is summarized in this section. The Cassidys developed a Christ-centered version of the Twelve Steps complete with biblical references. For another Christian-based Twelve Step resource, see J. Keith Miller (1991). For a theological treatment of addiction, see Cornelius Plantinga (1995:129–49).

Tragically, at first addicts do not know they are addicted. They live in denial and deceit often until life spirals out of control through the loss of a job or an accident, overdose, arrest, or physical and emotional burnout. Close friends and relatives often feed the addiction with coping behaviors that cover up the problem or deny that it exists. These behaviors often restore surface harmony and apparently help the addict by giving emotional or material support in ways that enable the addiction. This behavior on the part of family or friends is called codependency.[38] The addictive system is a form of insanity, fueled by a sense of invincibility and the lie that behaviors lack consequences. Addicts and codependents are incapable of open and truly caring relationships. From a biblical perspective, Satan, the father of lies, rules this system. No wonder Jean Cassidy says that "without spirituality, there can be no recovery" (1995). If God does not come to the addict and "create space or room in his life" for God (Torrance 1969:10), healing will not occur. Space and time to commune with God are essential to recovery. In Step Eleven the addict says, "[We] sought through prayer and meditation to improve our conscious contact with God praying only for knowledge of his will for us and the power to carry that out" (Miller 1991:193).

Virtually all medical and therapeutic treatment centers include the Twelve Steps in their programs. Follow-up care and outpatient programs generally require regular participation in lay-led Alcoholics Anonymous groups or Twelve Step groups for other addictions. Because of the space and time devoted to unhurried meditation, self-examination, and mutual burden bearing practiced in Twelve Step programs, the recovery movement, in both its lay and professional aspects, is a major force in resisting the addictive tempo of the information age. Treatment for ad-

---

38. I define codependency as the attempt to show love to an addicted friend or family member in ways that fail to trust God for their healing or salvation and actually feed their addiction(s) while depriving oneself of biblical self-care. Self-care and sacrificial love are not mutually exclusive. Codependency prevents one from truly loving and trusting God and from genuinely loving the addict as oneself. Unfortunately, codependent attempts to love are often mistaken for biblical love. In place of the widely accepted view of a codependent as "a partner in dependency" (Beattie 1937:27), leading theorist Melody Beattie offers her definition: "one who has let another person's behavior affect him or her, and who is obsessed with controlling that person's behavior" (1987:31). Regrettably, much of the codependency literature, including this definition, so emphasizes self-care and personal boundaries that costly love for others—desperately needed in our individualistic culture—can be mistaken as codependency—a criticism Bauman levels at Beattie (2000:65).

diction requires stopping and paying attention to one's inner life—living in the moment "one day at a time" (Cassidy n.d.:17).

The collapse of space and time, then, can be viewed as a part of an addictive disease that has infected postmodern society and its institutions, including the church, much as a virus infects a computer hard drive. When the virus sufficiently infects church and mission structures, its addictive pace leaves insufficient time and space for God in its operations, especially its leadership structures. Organizations with schedules crowded in God's name leave people empty of his fullness. God's activity and fullness get frozen out. Though the machine continues its active pace, the organism of the Spirit becomes paralyzed. Like a workaholic, the organization becomes powerless over its addictive pace and needs God to free it from sick patterns. It needs treatment. This is precisely the view of organizational consultants Ann Wilson Schaef and Diane Fassel, who wrote *The Addictive Organization* (1990) and who have developed Twelve Step treatment processes for organizations and the individuals working in them.[39] This is an approach that should be welcomed by those who believe in both personal and corporate evil, as well as both demonic and human fallenness (Eph 6:12, 4:22).

Environmental Psychology: REST and Solitude (Suedfeld)

Environments with reduced stimulation have been found to effectively enhance the treatment of addictions and other mental, emotional, and physical conditions. Psychologist Peter Suedfeld, a leading theorist in the field, has studied environments such as prisons, submarines, and polar expeditions, in which people undergo prolonged sensory deprivation. He does not advocate such extreme levels, but thinks that reducing stimulation would be healthy for our over-bombarded culture.

---

39. Schaef and Fassel classify four types or stages of addiction in organizations and have developed treatment processes for each: (1) key leaders who suffer from destructive addictions like alcoholism or workaholism; (2) the replication of one's addiction in the organization's culture—e.g., denial and deceit spread; (3) the organization as the addictive substance—e.g., the bottom line is more important than people; (4) the organization as an addict—e.g., rampant deceit and denial threaten the organization's life. Each stage grows from the previous stages. Schaef and Fassel recommend treatments that create space and time within the organization's structure for reflection, self-examination, communion with a higher power, and community through Twelve Step groups (1990:77–202).

In *Restricted Environmental Stimulation, Research and Clinical Applications*, Suedfeld reviews more than thirty years of his own and others' research on the effects of what he calls Restricted Environmental Stimulation Technique (REST).[40] This technique requires a limited period of silence and solitude in a dark room with food, water, a bed, and a toilet (1980:7–11). What are the effects of REST? For one, Suedfeld's experiments showed dramatic reductions in smoking for those with chronic nicotine addiction, which is among the most difficult to treat.[41] In a study reported in 1974 (see Figure 1 below), Suedfeld and his colleagues studied seventy-seven subjects who had smoked twenty or more cigarettes a day (the average was thirty-two) for a minimum of three years (the mean was fifteen). All scored pre-addicted or psychologically addicted on the Tomkins-Ikard Smoking Scale. These are shown to be the type least likely to quit (1980:261). Most stop in the days immediately following a treatment, but they have high attrition rates, returning to pre-treatment smoking levels over time (1980:257).[42] Figure 1 below shows the contrasts between those receiving REST as part of their smoking cessation treatment with those not receiving REST as part of theirs. A year after treatment, smoking levels for those receiving REST fell to 50 percent of pre-treatment levels, while smoking levels of those treated without REST only fell to 84 percent. Two years after treatment, smoking levels fell further to 45 percent for REST recipients but 82 percent for those not treated with REST. Twenty-seven percent of the REST groups were totally abstinent after a year, compared to only 11 percent of groups not receiving REST. After two years these figures increased to 37 and 16 percent, respectively (Suedfeld 1980:260–61). REST more than doubled the rates of recovery from nicotine addiction.

40. Suedfeld prefers the term "restricted environmental stimulation" to sensory deprivation. He feels the latter term is misleading because it implies totally removing all stimuli whatsoever—a clinical impossibility—and because of its negative "connotation of disturbance, threat, and aversiveness" (1980:2–3).

41. See Suedfeld (1980:261, 264–265). Our son had an easier time kicking his addictions to alcohol, crystal meth, and other drugs than he did breaking free from nicotine, a gateway drug. Nicotine users are eleven times more likely to use illicit drugs than those not using nicotine (Cassidy and Cassidy 1995).

42. The addicted participants were assigned to four groups on a random basis, except that gender distribution was roughly equal. Each group received various treatments—two groups had REST sessions of twenty-four hours in a light and soundproof room, and two groups received smoking-cessation treatments without REST sessions (1980:259).

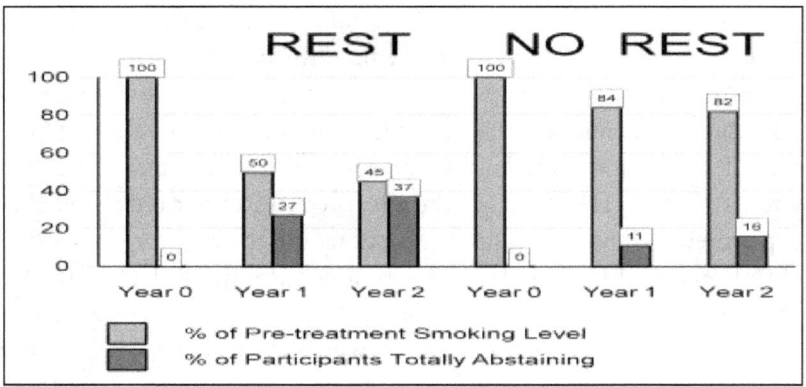

Figure 1: Effects of REST Treatment on Smoking Addiction (Adapted from Suedfeld 1980:259–61)

Henry B. Adam's review of research on REST used in treating severe drug abuse has shown its positive effects on PCP and LSD psychosis, though these studies did not meet the clinical criteria of Seudfeld's lab for legal and ethical reasons (1980:338–47). Adam's review also showed that REST sessions helped in treating other psychiatric symptomology requiring institutionalization.[43] Why then has REST not emerged as a leading mode of treatment? Adams gives his explanation:

> I was struck by the discrepancy between the actual research findings, which were generally positive, and the widespread negative beliefs about "sensory deprivation" research.... These negative beliefs originated with the sensationalized and confusing early reports which erroneously linked "sensory deprivation" or restricted environmental stimulation with dissimilar psychological phenomena such as "brainwashing," coercive persuasion, mind control, torture and the like. These erroneous beliefs were subsequently perpetuated by psychology textbooks,

---

43. Of twenty studies in which REST was used in the treatment of adults institutionalized for psychiatric symptomatology, six used control groups, which were compared with the study groups using pre- and post-testing with analysis of the data for statistical significance. Adam found that all six groups undergoing REST experienced greater improvement in symptomatology than did the control groups. Twelve studies (not using controls) reported a majority had positive changes, a minority experienced no change, and a few actually got worse after the session. Two studies showed no improvement at all (Adams 1980:360–61).

despite the fact that there was never any empirical evidence to support them. (1980:320)[44]

On the contrary, REST's effectiveness has neuropsychological, cognitive, and environmental explanations (Suedfeld 1980:382–404). Another explanation for REST's efficacy is that a day of solitude and silence in a REST session removes participants from the culture's addictive tempo, providing them opportunity to pay attention to their inner life—the very thing addictive processes avoid. In solitude and silence people become aware of what is actually occurring in their hearts—without incessant external stimuli, they discover who they are. As Anna Quindlen writes, "Downtime is where we become ourselves.... I don't believe that you can write poetry, or compose music, or become an actor without downtime, and plenty of it, a hiatus that passes for boredom but is really the quiet moving of the wheels inside that fuel creativity" (2002:76).

Developing Synchronicity (Ritterman)

Not only does downtime help us pay attention to our inner feelings, discover who we are, and become creative, it can also foster community by creating what marriage and family therapist Michele Ritterman calls synchronicity—a crucial aspect of loving interpersonal communication. This involves shifting out of cyber-time or clock time into a slower communal sense of time in which our natural rhythms become adjusted to those we are with.[45] This requires a more attentive and serving posture toward others (1995:45–49).[46] She cites the example of a time-stressed couple, who

---

44. Also, for Suedfeld's defense against critics of REST, see 1980:404–23.

45. See R. Todd Erkel's article "Time Shifting," which deals with the work of Stephen Rechtschaffen and the Omega Institute for Holistic Studies (1995:33–39). A well-known example of synchronicity is the fact that women who live in the same physical environs over time develop the same menstrual cycles.

46. And Ritterman illustrates the concept from the experience of couples who have come to her for marriage counseling. She instructs them to break their constant stream of high speed activity when arriving home with a few minutes together on a couch sharing a kiss and listening to each other's days before launching into the activities awaiting them at home. But "if there is no change in the inner sense of the time taken for the kiss, it will be perfunctory without any vital current of compassion or empathy" (1995:49).

had become so physically and psychologically habituated, if not addicted, to the rush of their time, that they had to learn to *tolerate* slowness before they could enjoy it. The assignments were active forms of meditation, reminding them to approach their relationship, even the most pedestrian daily moments, with mindfulness, savoring each second. (1995:50)

Synchronicity is also essential to the therapeutic relationship. Ritterman argues that unless the therapist slows the sense of time in the therapy session so that clients do not feel rushed, much that needs healing will be missed. She criticizes brief therapy, a symptom of managed healthcare's demand for efficiency, for leaving too little unhurried time for the synchronicity needed to address the serious pathologies abounding today. Therapy, she writes,

> requires a sense of temporal spaciousness. . . . As technological time breaks temporal experience down into smaller and smaller, disjunctive increments—each day a long, draining sequence of interruptions and unconnected time bytes—it destroys our capacity to concentrate, to take full advantage of the sustained, unsegmented time needed for the unfolding understanding, the possibility of healing. (1995:47)

Treating Time Pathologies: Cardiac Psychology

Cardiac psychology is a subspecialty concerned with physiological damage associated with time compression. The rapid pace of life has been implicated as a risk factor in coronary artery disease (CAD) in Diane K. Ulmer and Leonard Schwartzburd's review of clinical research on the treatment of cardiac patients who have developed a pathological relationship to time. Time pathologies lie along "a toxic continuum of disordered behaviors, perceptions and states running the gamut from mild time urgency to severe hurry sickness" (1996:332).

Table 11: Descriptions of the Time Pathologies and Their Effects (Adapted from Ulmer and Schwartzburd 1996:330–35)

Time Pressure	The sense that there is not enough time for a task or tasks. (1996:331)
Time Urgency	"The frequent experience of time pressure with the corresponding conviction that one needs to hurry or speed up the rate at which one is doing things..." (1996:331) *Symptoms:* <ul><li>Behaviors are more rapid (examples include faster eating, speaking, walking, and thinking).</li><li>Multi-tasking—doing many things at once (polyphasic activity).</li><li>Becomes chronic when feelings and behaviors are habitual even without actual time constraints.</li></ul>
Hurry Sickness	"Severe and chronic feelings of time urgency that have brought about changes affecting personality and lifestyle." (1996:331) *Symptoms:* <ul><li>Personality deterioration marked by losing interest in the being aspects of life and becoming exclusively focused on numbers, achieving goals, evaluating life in terms of quantity not quality.</li><li>Racing mind syndrome—rapidly shifting thoughts, which cause a growing inability to concentrate or focus and to disrupt sleep.</li><li>Inability to compile pleasant memories due to preoccupation with past or future events and fleeting attention to the present. Focus on the present becomes limited to crises and problems.</li></ul>

Time Pathologies' Detrimental Effects in Three Areas:

1. *Intrapersonal*: They write that a busy "lifestyle can lead to a decreased sense of self-esteem, largely, we believe, because in the long run, quantitative accomplishments are not as self-esteem enhancing as nourishing relationships. Our clinical experience also supports the observation that . . . a rapid-paced lifestyle significantly erodes one's spiritual sense of self." (1996:330)

> 2. *Interpersonal*: It takes time to build and sustain healthy relationships. Time pressures can erode the quality of relationships and create fragmentation and isolation. Research from the past twenty years (they cite seven studies) shows a clear correlation between poor systems of support, social isolation, and higher rates of mortality and morbidity due to all causes including heart disease (Ulmer and Schwartzburd 1996:330). This is consistent with Putnam's research finding that joining a group reduces mortality rates (Putnam 2000:331).

> 3. *Physical health*: Their review of the research shows that many time urgent patients develop a physiologically reactive response to time stressors. These responses include increased blood pressure and higher cholesterol counts, which are both known risk factors for CAD (1996:332–34).[47] Their review of the research and their clinical experience also links time pathologies, exhaustion, and coronary episodes (1996:335). For the physical symptoms, psychological signs, and underlying beliefs of time pathologies, especially hurry sickness, see Appendix C.

Three major types of time pathologies in this taxonomy, listed in increasing severity, are time pressure, time urgency, and hurry sickness—the latter being equivalent to workaholism. See Table 11 above.

> The way people progress from experiencing time pressure to more severe states of chronic time urgency and hurry sickness leading to exhaustion seems to be a complex interaction among physiological, psychological, and sociological processes. We believe that it begins with the adoption of a belief system that is almost a cultural imperative in this country: the belief that one's worth as a person is dependent on one's accomplishments. (1996:335)[48]

In biblical terms, a life crammed with activity can crowd the Spirit's activity, leaving the soul empty.[49] Programs have been developed

---

47. While writing this section, my sister Ann C. White, suffered a cardiac episode requiring the insertion of a stent in a partially-blocked artery. Her cardiologist identified five major risk factors for heart attacks: family history, high cholesterol, hypertension, diabetes, and smoking (2002).

48. In addition to the belief that self-worth is established by accomplishment, see Appendix C for other beliefs that feed time pathologies.

49. Ulmer and Schwartzburd suggest that busyness is often substituted for lack of inner peace and that severe time pathologies function as a defense against underlying emotional problems such as anxiety or depression. Hurry sickness may be understood as an addiction to one's stress hormones. One health professional resisted treatment

to rehabilitate cardiac patients' relationships to time. These have demonstrated that permanent changes in the life patterns of cardiac patients are best achieved through participation in groups of six to twelve that meet weekly for the first two or three months, and then twice a month for at least one or preferably two years (Ulmer and Schwartzburd 1996:341–52) Heart disease is the number one killer in the United States. Cardiac psychology is a potentially sizeable resistance community against the temporal codes ruling the postmodern era.

Developing Middle Time: Is a Rapid Tempo Always Harmful? (Levine)

Surprise! Hurry is not necessarily harmful, say Ulmer and Schartzburd (1996:330). Some fastpaced people do not work to exhaustion or have high blood pressure and elevated cholesterol, and thus are not at higher risk for CAD.[50] Social psychologist Robert Levine agrees that a fast tempo is not necessarily harmful. He cites research showing that its destructiveness depends on whether a person's temperament is slow- or fast-paced (1997:215).[51] This finding is further supported.

First, though time pathologies, with their harmful effects, always involve a rapid pace of life, the converse is not necessarily true, if Schartzburd, Ulmer, and Levine are correct. This contention would be strengthened by counter examples of fast-paced populations with low heart failure death rates. Japan and Salt Lake City are two such examples, which Levine and his researchers found in studying the relationships between pace of life, wealth, health, and charity in different countries and in U.S. cities. Japan's overall pace of life ranked fourth fastest among

---

until he saw his pace of life as an addiction that he did not have the power to change. He entered treatment and now "avoids giving himself a 'fix' about ninety percent of the time" (1996:330).

50. The negative effects depend partially on the extent to which a person's reactivity to time stressors is pathological. Ulmer and Schartzburd write that "we cannot say that a rapid-paced life-style with its attendant time pressure is always harmful. But we can say that such a lifestyle has the potential to erode health and well-being, and for many people it has done so" (1996:330).

51. Levine cites a University of Michigan Institute for Social Research study on two thousand men from twenty-three occupations. "By far the best predictor of work stress turnout out to be the fit between workers' personal temperament and the characteristics of their jobs" (1997:215).

the countries studied,⁵² but it also has the lowest coronary death rate of all industrialized nations according to the World Health Organization (Levine 1997:174).⁵³ In comparing the pace of life in thirty-six U.S. cities,⁵⁴ Levine found that faster places also had higher coronary death rates, except for Salt Lake City, which had a low coronary death rate even though it was the fourth fastest city.⁵⁵ The cases of Japan and Salt Lake City suggest that a fast-paced life may not always be harmful, at least in terms of cardio-vascular disease.

Second, Levine also found that people in faster places were more satisfied with their lives. For these reasons, he concludes, "A rapid pace is neither inherently better nor worse than a slow one" (1997:153–59). Levine suggests people develop what is called "middle time," which is the flexibility to adapt to either slow time or fast time depending on the need (1997:211–15).⁵⁶

Third, the most important evidence for the conclusion that fast-paced living may have either harmful or positive effects, or both, was Levine's finding that slower places do not necessarily translate into time and money spent helping strangers in need.⁵⁷ He found that people in

52. Levine's research shows Switzerland with the fastest overall pace of life, followed by Ireland, Germany, and then Japan. The U.S. was sixteenth and Mexico thirty-first (1997:131–32).

53. Levine is citing the *World Health Statistics Annual, 1980: Vital Statistics and Causes of Death*. Japan has a low coronary death rate in spite of the fact that the Japanese work more per capita than their counterparts in other countries. Their average annual working time is estimated at 2,159 hours, compared to 1,957 paid hours in the U.S., 1,646 hours for the French, and 1,638 in Germany (1997:140).

54. Cities in the Northeast had the fastest overall pace of life, followed by cities in the Midwest, the South, and the West. Boston was the fastest and Los Angeles the slowest (Levine 1997:146–15).

55. Levine suggests that Mormon spiritual values and health practices act as a buffer against its pace of life (1997:157).

56. Levine calls this "multitemporality . . . the ability to move quickly when the occasion demands it, to let go when the pressure stops, and to understand the many temporal shades of grey may be the answer to the question of 'Which pace of life is best?'" (1997:219).

57. Levine's team recorded the frequency with which strangers in the cities studied offered assistance to an undercover researcher by: (1) picking up an "accidentally dropped" pen, (2) helping a person in a cast with a dropped pile of magazines, (3) helping a blind person to cross a street, (4) giving change for a quarter, and (5) mailing a "lost" stamped addressed to the experimenter's home. Finally, the cities' per capita giving to United Way was ranked. After statistically combining each city's scores on

eleven California cities—the slowest places compared with these other regions of the country—were less likely to help strangers than were urban residents of these same regions. He concludes, "These Western cities demonstrate that having the time to lend a helping hand does not mean that hand will be offered. Beliefs about the allocation of time and appropriate social behavior must be linked together by a moral code" (1997:163).

Responses to the Loss of Duration and the Corrosion of Character

As Levine's research demonstrates, having leisure time and a slower pace of life does not in itself mean that people will care for others. However, I hold that unhurried time is necessary, though not sufficient, for developing compassionate character. In particular, diminished time in solitude and community deforms the self and erodes compassionate character. It is in solitude and self-giving community that the self is formed and responsibility towards others is cultivated.

But this has become increasingly unlikely in the workplaces of late capitalism, according to Richard Sennett. In *The Corrosion of Character: The Personal Consequences of Work in the New Capitalism,* he argues that capitalism's recent increased flexibility has restructured time in ways that have corroded character. Workers who stay in one company or career, typical in early capitalism, are now rare. Echoing Bauman's critique of modernity's fluid state, Sennett laments that economic realities are robbing U.S. and European workplaces of long-term relationships that foster loyalty, fidelity, and duration. "The conditions of time in the new capitalism have created a conflict between character and experience, the experience of disjointed time threatening the ability of people to form their characters into sustained narratives" (1998:31).[58]

---

these six measures, the overall score was computed for each city, which allowed for ranking (1997:161–63).

58. A marked shift from a "character ethic" to a "personality ethic" over the past seventy-five years has been detected by business consultant and leadership theorist Stephen R. Covey in his review of the success literature since the republic's founding. Before the beginning of the twentieth century, the literature assumed that to be successful, persons needed to be honest, caring, and loyal. Character and the time necessary to cultivate it were deemed fundamental to success. Since then, personality, method, and image have progressively replaced character as key (1989:18–21).

The collapses of Enron, Worldcom, and other publically owned companies have underscored the crisis of character in many of society's leaders and the consequent loss of public trust in "faceless experts" and the erosion of "trust in systems" on which our society functions (Giddens 1990:87–88).[59] How many of the leaders and accountants responsible for corporate scandals took time to reflect upon the destructive impact of their actions on themselves and others, or to discuss these in an unhurried way with colleagues in authority? According to journalist Lee Green, it was to create such dialogue and self-critical reflection that Michael Josephson founded and now directs the Joseph and Edna Josephson Institute of Ethics, whose clients have included Pacific Bell, the Los Angeles Times, 3M, the American Heart Association, the CIA, and the 3,000–4,000 who are certified each year to teach their Character Counts curriculum to children in 2,500 schools (Green 2002:11–12). Josephson questions how parents can teach children morals when they so seldom sit down anymore around the dinner table where time might be spent discussing ethical issues. Rushworth Kidder, founder of Global Ethics, and others worry that technology is outpacing virtue (1994:7–9). How can we reflect seriously on the ethical issues raised by exponential advances in technology when the pace it involves is producing a growing backlog of questions society has not yet begun to resolve? Kidder argues that

> Ethics is absolutely essential to our survival. We probably won't survive the 21st century with the ethics of the 20th century. Something profound has got to change, and unless we begin thinking very hard and very systematically about this, we run the risk of having the technology get so far ahead of the ethics that there really is no restraint on it. (Green 2002:13)

Josephson and Kidder are among a growing number of secular ethicists calling us to take time to "begin thinking very hard and very systematically" about three decades of social and moral decay (Green 2002:13).

---

59. These are Gidden's terms describing the results of what he calls "space-time distanciation," or the separation of time from space. The result is public "commitments to expert systems" (1997:87–88).

Summary

Thus far, I have discussed some of the historical factors that led to the collapse of space and time in the modern and postmodern eras. I have considered several sociological, economic, and cultural theories for the space-time implosion that has occurred since the mid-twentieth century, which was fueled by a further separating time from space and dis-embedding relationships from place in radically new ways in the networked society. Manifestations of this implosion include a widespread loss of social capital and the disappearance of neighborhood places that serve as hubs for pleasurable association. The accelerating pace of life in this period has left less leisure time for many segments of society, especially the Millennials, and most parts of the working force; yet retirees, the poor, and Xers in their childhood gained time. Theorists have lamented this collapse and have called for action. This hurried tempo in our time has become addictive for a large part of the population, for which the medical and therapeutic communities have developed treatment processes involving solitude, transparent community, and spirituality. These treatments have proven remarkably effective in healing addictions and time pathologies and providing the opportunity to recover love and compassion. The collapse has also contributed to the corrosion of character, the loss of community, and the erosion of self identity, which, from our survey of effective means of resistance, develops best in the context of communal commitment to (1) spiritual and character formation centered in divine power and accepting grace, and (2) the spiritual practices of solitude, mutual confession, meditation, and the prayer of relinquishment. We have also observed that there is a sense of mission that flows from these practices. Where can we go to find resources for building such resistance communities? Alasdair MacIntyre points to Western monasticism after the fall of the Roman Empire (1984:263). Robert Wuthnow suggests various historical spiritual traditions, especially the Rule of Benedict, as a prime source (1998:5–6, 16). Robert Webber commends the traditions of the early church as providing the resources we need (2003:14, 18–25, 36). But what better source is there for building such communities than Jesus himself—his spiritual practices, his compassion, his identity, his ethics, and his model for building community in a small group? To a discussion of Jesus's spirituality and mission I now turn.

3

Jesus's Rhythms of Spirituality and Mission

> Get away with me . . . I'll show you how to take a real rest. Walk with me . . . Learn the unforced rhythms of grace.
>
> —Jesus, Matt 11:28 (*The Message*)

IN THIS CHAPTER, I ANALYZE JESUS'S PRACTICES OF SPIRITUALITY AND mission and what he taught his followers about them. Having examined the collapse of space and time in the last chapter, which addressed part of my first research question, I will now address how space and time with God relate to mission in selected New Testament texts—my second research question—along with related subsidiary questions. After investigating first century Jewish spiritual practices and Jesus's subversion of them, I will analyze the close ties between Jesus's mission and his withdrawing from the crowds for the practice of spiritual disciplines, including rest as described in the Synoptic Gospels.[1] Next, I will survey Jesus's teaching on the relation between spirituality and mission in Matthew 5–7, John 15, and Matthew 28:16–20. My findings are displayed in Tables 11–18. This chapter and part of the next constitute the theological and biblical part of this study.

Considering theologians' growing interest in spirituality and its newness as a field relative to others, I will cite the tried approaches to the study of New Testament spirituality I am employing. Using Joy Mosbarger's survey of the approaches adopted by New Testament scholars who have studied spirituality (2004a)[2]—the only such survey

---

1. Sleep and rest are explicitly viewed as spiritual disciplines by Willard (1998a) and implicitly by Peterson (1987:68–69). See Luke 9:32 and Mark 6:30–32.

2. Mosbarger surveys the history of the term spirituality (2004a:2–4) and various definitions offered by New Testament scholars. From them she identifies seven

I know—I was able to locate the approach I am utilizing. Mosbarger found that various approaches to this kind of study fall into three broad categories: topical,[3] historical,[4] and biblical.[5] To varying degrees, each approach encompasses several levels of a study: (1) its scope—the whole New Testament, a particular book or books, smaller passages; (2) its perspective—i.e., whose spirituality is being examined; and (3) its method—i.e., which biblical, historical, or topical methods are used. Mosbarger's taxonomy can help locate and clarify one's approach, scope, perspective, and methodology, and identify those scholars being consulted (2004a:17–31). I have plotted these for my work in this chapter in Table 12 below.

In the historical part of this chapter, I draw on secondary sources by scholars specializing in first century Jewish spiritual life and that of Jesus. In the late 1980s, the Society of Biblical Literature (SBL) convened a consultation (later elevated to a working group) to study prayer from

---

characteristics of spirituality—derived from the New Testament—common to two or more scholars. From these she synthesizes her own definition (2004a:5–15). Mosbarger, following Edward Kinnert (1981:3–19) and Kenneth J. Collins (2000:10), argues that a precise definition of spirituality helps limit the study and create boundaries necessary for academic inquiry (2004a:12).

3. Joseph F. Wimmer's *Fasting in the New Testament* (1982) is a topical approach also using the tools of biblical theology. Though one approach is dominant, a scholar may use aspects of other approaches. C. F. D. Moule's topical study on worship (1961) also has a historical element (Mosbarger 2004a:19).

4. For example, Mosbarger cites Louis Bouyer's *The Spirituality of the New Testament and the Fathers* (1963) as a historical approach (2004a:20).

5. A biblical approach is more comprehensive than a topical one since the researcher must plum all the data of a New Testament book to arrive at a full understanding of the book's or author's spirituality or that desired for the community to which it was written (Mosbarger 2004b). My examination of spirituality from the perspective of specific practices employed by Jesus during selected retreats is a more limited inquiry. In *The Spirituality of Mark* (1996), Mitzi Minor uses a biblical approach with a definitional method—she also utilizes the tools of narrative, social, and redaction criticism, according to Mosbarger (2004a:30–31). Minor defines Christian spirituality as "the expression of the experience of God through Jesus Christ, which calls believers to dialectical personal growth moving from inauthentic responses to God's initiatives toward authentic responses to God's initiatives" (1996:6). From this definition flow questions that guide Minor's study (cf. 1996:7–12). She also asks what images for spirituality Mark's Gospel suggests, so her definitional method is wedded to one that looks for metaphors or images. She found the phrases "the way of the Lord" (Mark 1:2–3) and "the way" (8:27, 9:34, 10:32, 10:52) to suggest a journey motif as an important way to understand Mark's spirituality (1996:10).

the time of Alexander until Constantine. From this group came *The Lord's Prayer and Other Prayer Texts from the Greco Roman Era*, edited by James H. Charlesworth, Mark Harding, and Mark Kiley (1994). Bonnie Thurston's accessible *Spiritual Life in the Early Church* (1993) was another helpful study by a member of the working group (Charlesworth 1994:ix). Also helpful is the massive historical reconstruction of first century Israel by N. T. Wright (1992, 1996). He sees Jewish practices (or *praxis*, as he prefers) as the means of preserving the central symbols and stories of Israel, which comprised her worldview (1992:233–43).[6] These and other scholars emphasize the Jewishness of both Jesus and early Christianity,[7] reflecting Moule's contention that Israel was "The Rock Whence Ye Were Hewn" (1961:9). Through their work I look at the daily, weekly, and annual spiritual practices of first century Judaism, which were carried on but subversively redefined by Jesus.

Table 12: Plotting My Approach to Studying New Testament Spirituality (Adapted from Mosbarger 2004a)

Approach	*Primarily topical:* The relationship between spiritual and mission practices. Studying spiritual practices in a text is more limited than a biblical approach looking at spirituality in a text (see n. 5).
	Secondarily historical: I give a historical survey of first century Jewish spiritual practices by drawing on secondary sources.
	Secondarily biblical: I will relate my findings to others who are studying the spirituality of the Gospels where appropriate.
Scope	*Selected smaller passages* in which Jesus and/or his followers withdrew for prayer and other practices and where he/they taught others concerning these. Various narrative texts in the Synoptics describe these withdrawals. I will use Mark's Gospel to control the discussion, drawing from Matthew and Luke as needed. Though the Gospels are primarily narrative in genre, they contain teaching blocks dealing with prayer and other spiritual practices, including their time/place—most notably the Sermon on the Mount (Matt 5–7) and the upper room discourse in John 15.

6. Without praxis (both inner and outer practices), Israel's stories, symbols, and questions that make up her worldview would fade from memory. Israel's weakened worldview would lose its grip on YHWH's people and be replaced by deviant ones (see Wright 1992:233–43; 1996:245).

7. See also Charlesworth's "Jewish Prayer in the Time of Jesus" (1994) and "How Did Jesus Pray? The Spirituality of Jesus in the Apostolic Church" (1992) by Markus Bockmuehl. Larry W. Hurtado emphasizes the radical difference between Jewish-Christian practices and those of first century paganism (1999:28–38).

Perspective	*Primarily* the spirituality of Jesus and his disciples, and *secondarily* that of four New Testament authors and their audiences.
Methods	*Definitional methodology:* Nouwen's definition of a spiritual discipline as "the creation of open space" for God, as mentioned above, has shaped not only my research questions but also their subsidiaries in this chapter:
	When, where, and for how long did Jesus and/or his followers withdraw from others to create space and time for God in solitude or community?
	What were the disciplines that he/they practiced in these withdrawals?
	Did mission occur in word and/or deed subsequent to the creation of time and space for God by Jesus and/or his disciples? Was it centrifugal or centripetal?
	The centrality of grace to Nouwen's definition suggests another question
	Is God's grace, initiative, or power associated with the narrative passages in which Jesus and/or his disciples created space for God followed by subsequent mission?
	Metaphorical methodology: I include a metaphorical approach to Matt 5–7 and John 15.
Scholars Engaged	To narrow my study of secondary literature, scholars with whom I will dialogue in this chapter are limited to writers in the following categories:
	1. Theologians who have studied the spirituality of the New Testament books that contain the passages I am analyzing or who have commented on these passages.
	2. Spiritual writers, many of whom have commented on these passages.
	3. Scholars who have written about space or time and the historical background to spiritual practice in the ancient world.
	4. Several missiologists who have written about mission and spirituality in the New Testament or who have commented on these passages.

Historical Backdrop of Jewish Spiritual Practices and Jesus's Subversion of Them

Bruce Chilton, who has studied the development of festal calendars in Judaism and the early church,[8] thinks the rhythms built into these calendars are highly relevant to the current collapse of time and space. He holds that our culture's problem with time is "the dominance of time as interval [linear time] over time as rhythm [cyclical time]" (2002:111). Healthy rhythms are destroyed by progressively demanding goals and ever-increasing tasks typical of linear time, without periodic respite from these. On the other hand, when we do have plenty of time, we are often bored, not knowing what to do while struggling to find meaning. "Time is either scarce or vacant," writes Chilton and "the constraints of time—both as too occupied and as too empty—are not endurable" (2001:6). He thinks that the recurring spiritual practices in Jewish and Christian calendars could help recover a healthy experience of "time's rhythm" with stretches of linear time in between—that is "time's interval."[9] What, then, were Israel's spiritual rhythms and how did Jesus transform them?

Daily Rhythms

1. *Shema*. The Shema was Israel's central confession, given by Moses to the Israelites near the end of their forty years of wilderness wander-

---

8. Wright identifies Chilton among twenty contemporary scholars who, as of 1996, had attempted serious historical reconstructions of the emergence of Christianity that emphasize its roots in first century Judaism based in apocalyptic Jewish eschatology (1996:84). He calls this approach the "Third Quest." The Third Quest scholars (as identified by Wright) whom I cite in this study are Chilton, Moule, S. F. G. Brandon, Borg, and Charlesworth. Wright considers any biblical or topical approach not grounded in serious historical reconstruction of first century Judaism as lacking.

9. More than fifty years ago S. G. F. Brandon used the terms "ritual perpetuation of the past" and "basic teleology" to portray these two senses of time—cyclical and linear (1951:xiii). Brandon argued that the "ritual perpetuation of the past" in the ancient world dealt with the threat of time's eventual annihilation of the lives and achievements of individuals and their societies. For Brandon, teleological thinking "concerns Man's attempts to understand, amid the phenomena of change, his own significance and that of the society, which he recognizes himself to be a member" (1951:xiii). Though he argued that the Christian teleological view of time was essential to the dynamism of Western civilization, unlike Chilton, he felt that Christianity's ritual perpetuation of the past death of Christ and it's teleological hope and purpose are now inadequate (1951:i–xiii, 177–96).

ings. "Hear O Israel, the Lord our God is one Lord. . . . Love the Lord your God with all your heart, with all your soul and with all your strength" (Deut 6:4–5). It has been prayed by Jews three times daily ever since (Wright 2006:169). Bonnie Thurston says that from the age of twelve devout Jewish boys recited or prayed the Shema when they awoke and before they went to bed (1993:8). She notes that the Shema was Israel's thanksgiving for God's deliverance from slavery in the Exodus and also "an act of dedication" to the Lord. Shema means "to hear" (1993:8), suggesting that silence and attentiveness to God's voice were part of the prayer.

In silence, thanksgiving, and dedication, Jesus undoubtedly prayed the Shema throughout his life. In response to a young lawyer's question, Jesus amended the Shema to include loving the Lord with one's mind, and significantly, he added the command to love one's neighbor as oneself (Mark 12:29–31). Elsewhere, he redefined the concept of neighbor to include "all the wrong people,"[10] such as Samaritans,[11] which was totally new to Jewish religious groups of all stripes (Wright 1996:305). His amendment of the Shema to include the command regarding love of neighbor is but one indication that Jesus's spirituality and mission were shaped by and reformulated from within Judaism and that the two could not be separated in his daily prayer life.

2. *Eighteen Benedictions*. In addition to praying the Shema, devout Jews practiced fixed hours of daily prayer, which emerged in post-exilic Judaism and originated in Daniel's and King David's practices of praying three times a day (Dan 6:10, Ps 55:17) as well as in the prayer patterns of Abraham, Isaac, and Jacob.[12] Israel's worship at home and in the temple involved set hours of prayer in the morning, afternoon, and evening, during which the Eighteen Benedictions, or Tephillah, were recited.[13] The Tephillah, "from a word that means 'prayer,' sometimes

10. Wright's phrase for Jewish exclusion of sinners, tax collectors, the poor, and Gentiles (2005).

11. See Luke 10:25–37. In his Gospel, Luke places the parable of the Good Samaritan right after the Greatest Commandment given by Jesus in response to the lawyer's question.

12. For Jewish origins of set prayers, see Donin (1980:11–12) and Steinsaltz (2000:47–49).

13. Charlesworth writes, "Worship, especially the *Shema* and Amidah, provided a heart and essence to Judaism. . . ." He says that the most important dimensions of Jewish

called *amidah* in reference to the standing position in which the prayers are recited.... is a great petitionary prayer asking the blessing of God on various activities" (Thurston 1993:9). Marcus Bockmuehl thinks Jesus may have prayed an early form of the Eighteen Benedictions three times daily (1992:59). This prayer contains *berakah*, a blessing-thanksgiving, which could "make every activity of the devout Jew a sacred, liturgical action" (Thurston 1993:9).[14] The Lord's Prayer implicitly includes *berakah* in the form of invoking God's kingdom on earth and forgiving our debtors, which requires that we bless those who do us harm. According to Jesus, the idea of forgiving those who harm or persecute us is central to prayer if we are to follow him. N. T. Wright's spiritual director suggested he pray the Lord's Prayer for a particularly difficult colleague—a form of blessing one's adversaries (Wright 2006:170–71). However, this idea was not a part of first century Judaism nor any major religion since. In fact, forgiving one's enemies and blessing them as an expression of prayer constituted a radical redefinition of spiritual practice by Jesus, which has remained part of Christianity's uniqueness.[15]

3. *The Temple—Worship, Prayer, and Forgiveness.* In their daily prayers, first century Jews faced towards Jerusalem and the temple, which was considered to be the special place of Yahweh's presence.[16] There, regular hours of prayer were kept and impressive worship occurred (Charlesworth 1993:49–50). Wright refers to the temple in Jesus's day as "the central symbol of Judaism, the location of Israel's most characteristic praxis, the topic of some of her most vital stories, the answer to her deepest questions, the subject of her most beautiful songs" (1996:406).[17]

---

prayer were their corporate nature, the way they reinforced Israel's identity as the people of God, and the way they brought "cosmic and calenderic harmony" (1993:53–54).

14. For an accessible contemporary version of the *berakah*, see Richard Peace's fine chapter on the prayer of blessing, which includes instructions for its practice in small groups and in solitude (1998c:25–34).

15. In a phone conversation with Wright the subject of forgiveness came up. He agreed with my contention that the belief in the physical resurrection of Jesus and the command to forgive and bless one's enemies are unique to Christianity among world religions (2000).

16. By the first century, some Jews saw the temple as a symbol of moral, economic, and spiritual corruption or oppression. The Qumran community was one such group, and John the Baptist's followers another.

17. In Wright's historical reconstruction, the primary symbols in Israel's worldview are: (1) temple; (2) land; (3) torah; and (4) racial identity. The praxes are: (1) worship and the feasts, including fasts and monthly days; (2) teaching and study; and (3) torah

Most importantly, only there could her guilt be cleansed through daily and annual sacrifices. But Jesus's words and actions "took forgiveness to the streets" and he gave his disciples the power of absolution (Wright 2005). Wright argues that Jesus's mission constituted a counter-temple movement.[18] In offering forgiveness and restoration to the lame man (Mark 2:5)[19] and Zacchaeus (Luke 19:1–10), Jesus was claiming to be and to do for them what the temple was supposed to be and do. Because Israel had failed to obey God's call to repent and become God's instrument to bless the nations, Jesus predicted the temple's destruction and proclaimed that it was being rebuilt in and through his own person and mission. What Israel's God had done for his people in the temple, Jesus now was doing in his own person.[20] Jesus's reconstitution of the temple around himself remained the greatest discontinuity between the spiritualities practiced by Jews[21] and those practiced by Jesus, his disciples, and eventually the early Christian church. After the resurrection, his followers recognized Jesus as the true temple through whom Israel's God was fully present to forgive, purify, and restore anywhere and anytime.

in practice—Sabbath, circumcision, and food and purity laws. The most vital themes in all the various renditions of Israel's story include: creation by one God (monotheism); fall; call and election of Abraham and his descendants to undo Adam's sin and bless the nations; slavery of Abraham's descendants in Egypt; God's rescue of them in the Exodus; God covenanting with his people through the Torah and making them a nation; conquest of the land promised to Abraham; God establishing a monarchy through David; the monarchy's unfaithfulness to the covenant; exile to Babylon; and return from exile, which proved to be partial because the land was again occupied by pagan powers who defiled it with various gods and pagan practices. Thus, the story remained unfinished and the plot needed resolution. The various groups in first century Palestine each provided their own endings, which they claimed either had happened already in some way or would happen through the coming of some sort of Messiah through which God would in various ways defeat the pagan powers, purify the land, and rule the nations. Jesus and Paul, of course, reconstituted these symbols, praxes, and stories around Jesus, in whom God's reign is realized. The importance of praxis in Wright's scheme cannot be overstated: "Judaism gives 'theology' a lower place in its regular discussions than it does to the question: what ought one to do? If one is to keep the symbols alive, one must quite simply live by them" (1992:233).

18. Wright notes the almost universal agreement among scholars that Jesus was crucified in part for his action in and against the temple (1996:405).

19. See also parallels in Matt 9:2–6 and Luke 5:20.

20. See Wright 1996:102, 108, 130, 338, 343, 362.

21. Except for groups like the Essenes.

4. *Prayer Anywhere.* As suggested by the prayer of blessing in the Tephillah, any action anywhere could be made holy by prayer. Prayer occurred in Jewish homes. Jews prayed daily at meals and on special occasions. So did Jesus (Wright 1992:233). Regularly during his public ministry—perhaps daily—he withdrew to solitary places to pray (Mark 1:35; Luke 5:16); places such as mountains (Luke 7:12; 9:28) and the Garden of Gethsemane (Mark 14:32–42). The pattern of regular retreat from the people and their customary places of prayer to these solitary places was part of his implicit critique of Israel's spirituality.

The daily spiritual rhythms of Judaism were both personal and corporate. Indeed, Jesus and his disciples emerged from a culture saturated in prayer on both levels. Jesus used these practices and the symbols they represented, modifying and subverting them for his mission to be and do for Israel what she had failed to be and do for the sake of the world.

Weekly Rhythms

The weekly Sabbath service, whether in a synagogue or the temple, was important socially and as a "sign of loyalty to Israel" (Wright 1992:233).[22] Synagogues typically conducted four services of prayer each Sabbath: "morning prayer; additional prayer; afternoon prayer; and evening prayer, at each of which the Tephillah was used. Three hours correspond to hours of daily prayer for individuals . . . and two seemed to be linked to the daily hours of sacrifice in the Temple" (Thurston 1993:8). Jesus attended weekly Sabbath services in the synagogue at Nazareth as he grew up, and in his public ministry he frequented synagogues in Galilee and Judah, as well as the temple when he was in Jerusalem. But Jesus redefined Sabbath around himself by claiming to be its Lord (Mark 2:28). He was accused of desecrating the day by performing a healing (3:1–6) and picking grain with his disciples on the Sabbath (2:23–26). Jesus said that the Sabbath was made for people, not the other way around (2:27).

---

22. Moule suggests that some more sacramentally-oriented circles in the early church may have drawn more on the temple's ritual of sacrifice in the celebration of the Lord's Supper, while other more word-centered circles reflected the synagogue's stronger emphasis on teaching and prayer (1961:12–13). But, as Moule himself observes, both Christianity and Judaism cannot be stylized according to a simplistic schemata into which the variety of beliefs and practices of the many groups in first century can neatly fit (1961:12).

Monthly Rhythms

Jewish calendars were based on lunar as well as solar cycles (Chilton 2002:45–58). Monthly New Moon festivals were a regular part of the calendar of Israel's holy days. At these festivals, the light of the new moon followed a time of darkness and pointed to the hope and expectation that God would restore the fortunes of his people, bringing them light after the darkness of exile and judgment (Wright 1992:234). Festivals on the fourth, fifth, seventh, and tenth months required fasting to recall incidents of God's judgment on Israel (Zech 8.19). One fast commemorated the destruction of the temple and another recalled the capture of Jerusalem by Babylonians.[23] The Law had commanded only one day of fasting each year—the Day of Atonement, but "by the close of the prophetic period other occasions of fasting had become traditional, and these observances continued into the first century" (Lane 1974:108–9).

However, Zechariah predicted that these fasts would be turned into "seasons of joy ... and cheerful festivals" (8:19), which Wright interprets as a prophecy of the complete return from exile that was yet to be fully realized (1992:234–35).[24] Though Jesus probably celebrated Israel's monthly New Moon festivals, he did not observe the four monthly fasts because God's reign was now being realized in and through him, and Israel's judgment would finally be lifted. Except for his pilgrimage to the wilderness, Jesus did not fast during his public ministry, but he feasted and ate with sinners, welcoming all. He was a happy, joyous, humorous[25] person accused of keeping company with people who would defile him, thus disqualifying him as a prophet in the mind of the religious leaders of his day. Though Jesus did not fast, he left his followers with instructions that "when you fast" not to practice fasting like those who put on a dour appearance to draw attention to their practice (Matt 6:16–18).

---

23. According to William Lane these two fasts occurred on the fifth month (recalling the temple's destruction) and tenth month (recalled the capture of Jerusalem). The fasts on the fourth and seventh months commemorated the breaking of the tablets of stone (Exod 32:19) and the murder of Gedaliah (2 Kgs 25:25), respectively (1974:108 n. 57).

24. Wright's view that the return from exile had not yet been complete by the first century has been a matter of dispute. Craig Evans agrees (1999:77–100) while Richard Hays dissents (1999:147–48).

25. See, among others, Elton Trueblood's *The Humor of Christ* (1964).

Annual Rhythms

As a boy, Jesus went with his parents to the temple in Jerusalem for the Passover festival (Luke 2:41). Devout Galilean Jews who could afford to do so went on pilgrimage to all three main annual festivals centered in Jerusalem. In addition to Passover in the spring, which celebrated the exodus, was Pentecost in early summer—celebrating the giving of the Torah—and the Feast of Tabernacles in the fall—celebrating God's provisions in the wilderness. The latter was preceded by the Day of Atonement five days earlier. These three festivals signified Israel as a redeemed people, as a commanded people, and as a people who were provided for by Yahweh (Peterson 1980:14–15). Wright makes similar theological observations and also notes that these festivals were tied to various annual harvests bringing together two symbols of Yahweh's blessing—land and temple. Two other annual feasts had no connection to agriculture: Hanukkah, the Festival of Lights, which celebrated the victory of Judas Maccabees over the pagan occupiers in 166 BCE; and the Feast of Purim, which remembered the deliverance of the Jews through Queen Esther (1992:234). Estimates of the temporary population in Jerusalem during these occasions have ranged from 150,000 to 3 million.[26] Whatever the numbers, the scene must have been impressive. "Apparently, the temple cult was especially brilliant at the major festivals, Pentecost and Tabernacles" (Thurston 1993:8). During his public ministry, according to the Gospels, Jesus frequented these festivals,[27] which were filled with music, psalms, and prayer. Scholars who have studied ancient prayer have difficulty differentiating between prayer and hymns (Harding 1994:104). The prayers of first century Judaism derived from the Psalms—"the hymnbook of the Second Temple . . . [which] could be heard not only when read in study groups but also in chants accompanied by music" (Charlesworth 1994:49). The grandeur of the temple worship and prayer at these festivals was breathtaking.

> All human senses were aroused in the Temple. The smell of the burning incense was intoxicating. The cavalcade of sounds was overwhelming: the melodious tones of Levites singing, the blast of trumpet and shofar, the chanting of priests (sometimes

---

26. See R. A. Stewart (1982:882), who favors lower estimates in this range.

27. For example, Jesus celebrated the Passover (John 2:23; 13:1; Matt 26:17; Mark 14:12; Luke 22:8) and the Feast of Tabernacles (John 7:2–37).

> numbering into the thousands), the cries of animals about to
> be sacrificed, and humming voices of prayers being offered and
> of sacred texts being read aloud. The eye was mesmerized by
> ... the majestic size of the Temple mount, the porticoes, espla-
> nades, and the Temple itself with its massive and intricate doors.
> (Charlesworth 1993:49–50)

Though no independent evidence exists, a long tradition among Christian and Jewish scholars holds that pilgrims sang the Psalms of Ascent (Pss 120–134) on their way to the annual festivals as they ascended to Jerusalem the highest city in Israel (Peterson 1980:14,193).[28] In any event, to be a devout Jew meant that prayer and worship were saturated with praise and lament offered to God in hymns and spiritual songs.

Jesus both sang and prayed the psalms. During the Passover meal, the Hallel (Pss 113–118) was sung and/or recited, and it is thought that the last half of the Hallel (Pss 116–18) is the hymn that Jesus and his disciples sang at the end of the Last Supper (Bockmuehl 1992:59).[29] On that occasion Jesus instituted the Eucharist, which would call his followers to recollect his saving work on the cross, from which he would shortly pray the opening words of Psalm 22 as he hung shrouded in darkness and the despair of God-forsaken solitude (Mark 15:34). For Jesus's disciples, then, the Passover meal was reconstituted as the Lord's Supper, or Communion, by which they would celebrate the new exodus from slavery to the power of sin and evil.

Though Jesus participated in Israel's annual festivals and their spiritual practices, he drew from and reformulated some of them. However, he began his ministry in a deeply symbolic and prophetic act of judgment—his journey to the Jordan to be baptized, which was rare in the ancient world (Wright 1992:361), and to the wilderness beyond. Rather than beginning his public ministry with a community of fellow Jews on a typical pilgrimage to Jerusalem, the center of religious, political, and economic life, he went instead to the Jordan and to the solitude of the desert—an implicit critique of the inner spiritual practices of first century Judaism and her oppressive practices towards the poor, sinners,

---

28. Nevertheless, there may be valid reasons for the tradition (see Peterson 1980:193 n. 5).

29. See Mark 14:26.

Table 13: Israel's Spiritual Practices and Jesus's Redefinition of Them

Rhythms	Israel's Spiritual Practices: Time / Place	Jesus's Redefinition
Daily	Shema (Deut 6:4–5): morning and evening / home and in travel. Shema means "hear"—implies the discipline of silence.	Added the love of neighbor to the Shema and radically redefined neighbor to include the marginalized (Mark 12:28–31). The Shema became the great commandment, likely part of Jesus's daily prayers.
Daily	Eighteen Benedictions, also called Tephillah, *Amidah*. These benedictions contained *barakah* ("blessing"): prayed 3 times per day / home and vocation	Incorporated the blessing of the Tephillah and directed it towards enemies in the Lord's Prayer, which by the second century was prayed three times each day as instructed in the *Didache* (8.3). He called on followers to bless those who persecuted them.
Daily	Daily sacrifices offered in Jerusalem at set hours of prayer: morning, afternoon, evening / the temple	Claimed to be and to do for Israel what only YHWH did in Israel's temple. Jesus practiced absolution and gave his followers authority to do the same.
Weekly	Worship services—4 hours of corporate prayer and teaching: on Sabbath / synagogues and the temple	Redefined the Sabbath around himself as the Lord of the day. It was made for us, not us for it. It set the pattern for weekly gatherings of the early church both on the first and seventh days of the week during the first several centuries.
Monthly	New Moon festivals: fasts on 4th, 5th, 7th, 10th months (Zech 8:18–19), on feast day early in each month / synagogues and the temple	Did not fast except during his wilderness temptation in solitude. He left his followers with the instructions that "when you fast" not to do so as those who desired notice for their dour appearance (Matt 6:16).

Annually Psalms of Ascent (Pss 120–134) may have been sung by pilgrims on the way to annual festivals in Jerusalem	Passover (Hallel, Psalm 113–118 recited and sung at Sader feast; Mark 14:26); 1 week in spring / Jerusalem	Transformed the Passover meal into the Lord's Supper, or Eucharist.
	Feast of Harvest or Pentecost: 1 week in summer / temple in Jerusalem	Trek to the Jordan to be baptized (unique in the ancient world) and to the wilderness to be tempted was an implicit critique of the inner spiritual practices of first century Judaism. His frequent withdrawals from the crowds continued this pattern (Luke 5:16).
	Feast of Tabernacles: 1week in fall / Jerusalem	
	Day of Atonement: 5 days before the Feast of Tabernacles / temple in Jerusalem	
	Feasts of Lights and Purim: winter / synagogues and the temple	

and outcasts.[30] His journey probably took about fifty days—roughly the cumulative time needed to journey from Galilee to Jerusalem for the three annual feasts.

Table 13 above summarizes Israel's rhythms of spiritual practice in the first century and Jesus's redefinition of them. It clearly shows that Jesus subverted the status quo, and that his prophetic judgment of Israel's failed mission contained a critique and reformulation of her spiritual practices. His role as prophet flowed from these, but he reconstituted them in new ways. Nourished by these practices, Jesus brought God's reign to a climax through his redeeming death and resurrection for Israel and the world as the rightful Messiah.

Jesus's Practices of Spirituality and Mission

Having examined Jesus's spiritual practices—drawn and reformulated from within Judaism—we turn to the question of how these related to his mission in the Synoptic Gospels (Matthew, Mark, and Luke). One way to examine this question is to look at how the synoptic writers portray the withdrawals of Jesus from the crowds for rest, solitude, communion with his Father, and the practice of other spiritual disciplines. In

---

30. For an excellent interpretation of Mark's Gospel that emphasizes the social dimension of Jesus's ministry to the poor and oppressed against the backdrop of religious-political-economic power and oppression, see Myers et al. (1997).

this section, I will examine synoptic descriptions of these withdrawals to see how time and space are demarcated for God in these episodes; what disciplines were practiced; how God's initiative, power, and acceptance were exhibited; how these relate to subsequent mission in deed and word; and whether the mission was centrifugal or centripetal.

Mark and the Synoptic Gospels

Many scholars hold that Mark's was the earliest of the Synoptic Gospels to be written, and that Matthew and Luke drew from it and/or that all three drew from a common oral or written source—the so-called Q source.[31] Most of the withdrawals of Jesus and his disciples that I selected are recorded by Matthew, Mark, and Luke, while several are included by only one or two Gospels (see Table 14 below). In addition to the similarities between the various accounts of these withdrawals, there are important differences.[32] Obviously, each synoptic writer selected his material and organized it for his intended hearers, which accounts for many of the differences. An important explanation of these is suggested by Jesuit New Testament scholar Robert Doherty, who views the gospel writer as a "spiritual formulator" of the community for which he wrote. Thus, the challenges and opportunities for the spiritual formation of those for whom he wrote constituted the primary criteria for his selection and organization of material (2003).[33] As noted in this chapter, spirituality is also thought to be a central concern of Mark (Mitzi Minor [1996]—see n. 5; see also Karen Barta [1988]). Indeed, Peterson refers to Mark as "the basic text for Christian spirituality" (2002:328). But Mark is also considered to be a text focused on mission. Chilton thinks that Mark and the other Synoptic Gospels are "curriculum for catechisms," for the purpose of preparing and screening candidates seeking baptism

31. See Marcus Borg and N. T. Wright's friendly debate expressing their differing views on Q (1999:11–24).

32. See, for example, *Gospel Parallels* (1992) by Burton H. Throckmorton Jr. Here the famous synoptic question can be easily visualized by seeing the parallel synoptic texts laid side-by-side.

33. For example, Mark's Gospel has been understood as a confessional manual encouraging those facing persecution to stay loyal to Jesus as Lord under threat of martyrdom; thus, the organizing principle for Mark's writing would be the imitation of Christ, especially in his suffering and death. See Lane's commentary on Mark, in which he holds that Mark was written for Christians in Rome who were suffering persecution under Nero (1974:12–17). Robert Gundry views Mark as an apology for the cross (1993:1).

in the late first century, when the church often had to meet secretly under persecution (2002:94–95). Richard V. Peace considers Mark a key text for understanding biblical conversion primarily as a process and secondarily as an event (1999:106).[34] His helpful outline of the Gospel shows the gradual progression of the disciples' conversion to Jesus as the Son of God (Peace 1999:123–25). Each of these approaches explicitly posits a missional purpose for Mark. Evidently, spirituality and mission are dual concerns for Mark. A look at the patterns in Tables 15 and 16 below shows a consistent tie between the two. My most important finding was that Mark portrays a close connection between Jesus's withdrawals and his mission in words and deeds of compassion, welcome, forgiveness, suffering love, authority, and power.

---

34. In his important book *Conversion in the New Testament Paul and the Twelve*, Peace argues that St. Paul's encounter with Jesus on the Damascus road is the primary biblical illustration of conversion as an event, while Mark shows the disciples gradually and progressively responding to Jesus as Lord and Messiah. The latter illustrates conversion as a process, which Peace holds is the more effective and normative pattern both in Scripture and in the evangelistic experience of the contemporary church (1999:17–125; see also Wright 1999:30). Peace argues that in our instant society, we have focused on the former to the exclusion of the latter, which has been detrimental in terms of following-up converts. The lack of follow-up and spiritual formation in the Protestant church have been the unfortunate byproducts of this skewed emphasis. Peace holds that the natural focus on follow-up, which comes through the patient building of relationships, inherent in process evangelism, would go a long way to redress the problem in the church today. In this view of conversion, spiritual formation was inherent in Jesus's mission, and not just a preparation for it (1999:304–29).

Table 14: Jesus's Withdrawals from the Crowds in the Synoptics (Adapted from Throckmorton 1992)

Withdrawals of Jesus and Disciples	Matthew	Mark	Luke
Jesus's baptism (1992:14)	3:13–17	1:9–11	3:21–22
Jesus's temptation (1992:16)	4:1–11	1:11–13	4:1–13
Jesus's early morning prayer (1992:22)		1:35	4:42
Jesus's pattern of withdrawal (1992:38)		X	5:16
Choosing the Twelve (1992:72)		3:13–19	6:12–16
Retreat with disciples—Sermon on the Mount (1992:24–38)	5:1–7:29	X	
Taking disciples away for rest (1992:89)	14:13	6:30–32	9:10
Jesus's night in prayer (1992:91)	14:22–33	6:45–52	
Transfiguration (1992:101–103)	17:1–13	9:2–13	9:28–36
Last Supper (1992:183–186)	26:17–30	14:12–26	22:14–39
Gethsemane (1992:188–189)	26:36–46	14:32–42	22:39–46
Jesus's two synoptic commissions (1992:207–10)	28:16–20	X	24:36–39
X indicates the withdrawals omitted by Mark			

Three important withdrawals that I selected are omitted by Mark, indicated by an "X" in Table 14 above. The first is Luke's grammatical structure for the verb "withdraw" in verse 5:16, which indicates this was a regular pattern for Jesus. The second is Matthew's introduction to the Sermon on the Mount: "When Jesus saw the crowds, he went up the mountain; and after he sat down, his disciples came to him" (Matt 5:1). Mark and Luke include material from the Sermon, but neither includes an introductory description of Jesus's retreat to a mountain. The third withdrawal, which I will treat separately at the end of this chapter, occurs when the disciples withdrew from the crowds and Jesus commissioned them. Except for these cases, Mark includes all the other retreats I selected. My approach was to examine Mark's portrayal of each occasion and, where needed, to fill in the picture by comparing how Matthew and/or Luke portray the event.

Jesus's Retreats from the Crowds in Solitude or Community

In this section, I summarize my findings regarding how space and time were demarcated in Jesus's retreats, which particular inner disciplines were practiced, what experiences of grace were observed, and which ministries in word and deed Jesus engaged in after his retreats. Finally, I describe my observations regarding centrifugal and centripetal mission.

Table 15: Mark's Gospel, Part A: Jesus's Rhythms of Spirituality and Mission

Event	Time and Space/Place	Inner Discipline Practiced/ Taught	Grace: Divine Initiative/ Power	Outward Mission Practiced
Jesus's baptism (1:9–11) In community	*Time*: Perhaps 2–5 days to travel from Nazareth to Jordan *Place*: Jordan River	Baptism Silence: hearing the voice of God's love Solitude	John sent by God to prepare the way Spirit descends on Jesus like a dove A voice addresses Jesus, "You are my beloved Son"	
Jesus's temptation (1:11–13) In solitude	*Time*: 40 days *Place*: Wilderness	Obedience Solitude Silence Fasting	The Spirit sends Jesus into the desert Angels visit Jesus to minister to him	Begins ministry (1:14–34) *Word*: Proclaims gospel of God,→ calls disciples→ *Word*: Teaches in the Capernaum synagogue→ *Deed*: Heals demon-possessed, Peter's mother-in-law, and other sick brought to Jesus←

Jesus's early morning prayer (1:35) In solitude	*Time*: Early in the morning while it was still dark *Place*: A lonely place	Prayer Solitude		(1:36—3:6) *Word*: Preaches elsewhere→ *Deed*: Exorcisms in synagogue→ *Deed*: Heals the leper, paralytic, withered arm←, Opposition←
Choosing the Twelve (3:13–19) In community	*Time*: Unstated *Place*: Up in the hill country	Commissioning Sending Community	Jesus initiates	(3:2—5:17) *Word*: Teaches← *Deed*: Calms storm and demoniac←
Taking disciples away for quiet rest—interrupted (6:30–33) In community	*Time*: After disciples' mission and John's death *Place*: Boat on the way to a lonely place	Community Quiet rest Silence	Jesus initiates	(6:33–44) *Deed*: Feeds the 5,000←

→*Indicates centrifugal mission*   ←*Indicates centripetal mission*

Table 16: Mark's Gospel, Part B: Jesus's Rhythms of Spirituality and Mission

Event	Time and Space/Place	Inner Discipline Practiced/ Taught	Grace: Divine Initiative/ Power	Outward Mission Practiced
Jesus's night in prayer (6:45–52) In solitude	*Time*: After feeding 5,000 and sending them and disciples away—from day's end until between 3 and 6 a.m. *Place*: On the hillside near the Sea of Galilee	Prayer Solitude Silence Intercession	Jesus walks on the water approaching the disciples in the boat The wind immediately ceases when Jesus gets in the boat	(6:53–56) *Deed*: Heals those who touch him ←
Transfiguration (9:2–13) In community	*Time*: 6 days after Jesus predicted his death *Place*: A high mountain	Silence Listening to God's voice Community Seeing Jesus without distraction	Jesus initiates Jesus's clothes become dazzling white/ Moses and Elijah appear God speaks, "This is my Son, my Beloved; listen to him"	(9:14–50) *Deed*: Heals demon possessed boy ← *Word*: Teaches his disciples about prayer, true greatness, humility, and their mission →
Last Supper (14:12–26) In community	*Time*: Evening *Place*: A house	The Lord's supper Singing hymns— Psalms Praying Psalms Community	Jesus initiates Miraculous leading to the house	(14:53—16:8) *Deed*: Jesus's suffering—his trial and death on the cross; and vindication—his resurrection
Gethsemane (14:32–42) in solitude and in community	*Time*: More than one hour *Place*: Mount of Olives	Prayer Watching Solitude Community	Jesus initiates	

→ *Indicates centrifugal mission*   ← *Indicates centripetal mission*

Space and Time Demarcated

Jesus frequented solitary places—a pattern that later appeared in *eremitic* monasticism.[35] He sought solitude on his way to the Jordan, in the wilderness, on a mountain, on a hill next to the sea, and in a garden near Jerusalem.[36] Luke's reference to the Garden of Gethsemane as "the place" (*ho topos*) where Jesus prayed (Luke 22:40) may indicate this as one of his regular places of retreat.[37] He took his disciples to places such as these for communal spiritual practices, which anticipated the *cenobitic* monastic tradition in which monks or nuns lived in community. On at least one occasion, the crowds found Jesus as he and his disciples had crossed the lake to a deserted place for extended rest and retreat. His need for solitude was not an impenetrable boundary through which people could not reach him. On this occasion, Jesus ministered to them with compassion, for they were "sheep without a shepherd" (Mark 6:30–34). Immediately after feeding the crowd and sending the disciples away, he sought his Father in prayer on a mountain for a good part of the night.[38] Jesus came to these lonely places early in the morning (Mark 1:35) and late at night (Mark 6:45–52). Needing unhurried reflection and prayer for discernment in selecting those who would lead his movement after he was gone, Jesus spent an entire night in prayer in the setting of a mountain (Luke 6:12–16). He spent an hour in the agony of watching against the encroaching powers of evil, accompanied by three of his disciples, who could not stay awake (Mark 14:32–42). Taking the twelve away to the upper room for the Passover (Mark 14:12–26) and to rural areas for instruction and prayer[39] constituted a counter-temple movement that symbolized to all who noticed that Jesus was recon-

---

35. The eremitic tradition of spirituality emphasizes solitude in a deserted place—*eremon topos* (Mark 6:32), made famous by St. Antony. The cenobitic tradition refers to monks who live in community.

36. In the order I mention these places, see Mark 1:1–13; 9:2–13; 6:45–52; 14:32–42, and parallels (see Table 14).

37. New Testament scholar David M. Stanley suggests this in *Jesus in Gethsemane* (1980:214).

38. The duration was likely for a minimum of about six hours. This computation is based on Mark's comment that Jesus was already in solitary prayer on the mountain by nightfall (6:47) and did not approach the boat until early morning (6:48).

39. E.g., Matt 5–7 and Luke 6:12–16.

stituting a new Israel and a new temple in a new place—i.e., himself (Wright 1996:362).

According to the synoptic writers, the different durations of time that Jesus set aside for communion with his Father were an hour, about six hours, all night (nine to thirteen hours), and fifty or so days. The places he went included a river, a desert, a lonely place, a hillside, a mountain, a house, and a garden.

Inner Disciplines Practiced

My examination of the synoptic writers shows that Jesus and his disciples practiced a number of inner disciplines during these withdrawals (see Table 17 below). They included baptism, community, silence—listening to the "voice of the one who calls us the beloved,"[40] solitude, and prayer. To Mark's brief description of Jesus's journey to the Jordan and the wilderness,[41] Matthew and Luke add fasting,[42] authoritative prayer over evil, quoting Scripture from memory in order to resist the devil,[43] meditation, and discernment or spiritual direction.[44] The synoptic writers also show Jesus's obedience to the Spirit's leading[45] in opposition to the devil and the crowds, prayer for workers in the harvest,[46] prayer

---

40. Nouwen derived his definition of a spiritual discipline, applied here to silence, partially from the experience of Jesus hearing the voice of the Father calling him "beloved son" at his baptism (1993a).

41. Mark's use of the adverb *euthyos* (immediately) just after Jesus's baptism and before his temptations indicates that the two incidents were parts of a single journey (Mark 1:12).

42. See Matt 4:2 and Luke 4:2.

43. See Matt 4:3, 7 and Luke 4:3, 4. The "prayer of authority" is Richard J. Foster's term for prayer against the demonic (1992:229–42). Scripture memorization and meditation are implicit in Jesus's ready responses to the devil's temptation and his immediate recall of Deut 8:3b and 6:16. But then, the devil also knew Scripture, as indicated by his deceptive use of Ps 91:11–12 (Matt 4:6; Luke 4:10–11).

44. Somehow, Jesus was able to discern the activity of the devil in these wilderness temptations. Implicit in Matthew's and Luke's portrayals of these was Jesus's discernment of their source as coming from the devil rather than from God the Father or himself. Discerning the source of an experience is a primary function of spiritual direction, which Jesus does here for himself and repeatedly for his disciples and others throughout the Gospels.

45. "Saying yes, saying no" is a spiritual practice classified by Dorthy Bass (2003:see Table 3).

46. See Matt 9:38; Luke 10:2. Neither text is one of the ten withdrawals I selected;

Table 17: Summary of Jesus's Practices of Spirituality and Mission in the Synoptics

Time and Space/ Place	Inner Disciplines Practiced	Grace: Divine Initiative/Power/ Love	Outward Mission Practiced
Time: 40 days Early in the morning (twice) 1 hour All night (twice)	Baptism Community Silence (listening to God's voice of love) Solitude Prayer Fasting (Matt, Luke) Prayer of authority over evil (with Scripture memorization) Meditation Discernment Spiritual direction Obedience Prayer for workers in the harvest (Matt, Luke) Prayer in selecting apostles (Luke)	*Journey to the Jordan and wilderness:* Father's voice of love heard at Jesus's baptism Spirit seen descending as a dove on Jesus Spirit leads Jesus to the wilderness Angels attend to Jesus *Retreat with Disciples:* Jesus's initiates each of the disciples' retreats *Night in Prayer:* Jesus walks on water toward disciples Peter walks on water toward Jesus Immediately wind ceases and boat arrives on the other side when Jesus comes	*Deed:* Has compassion on the poor, powerless, sick, marginalized, and Gentiles Welcomes sinners and eats with them Forgives those who persecute him Heals Miraculously feeds multitudes Willing for the crowds to interrupt his retreat temporarily Prays for his executioners' forgiveness Dies for the world's sin and rises again

Jesus's Rhythms of Spirituality and Mission 93

Time and Space/ Place	Inner Disciplines Practiced	Grace: Divine Initiative/Power/ Love	Outward Mission Practiced
Space/Place: Jordan River Wilderness Lonely place Mountain (five episodes) Hills Upper room Mount of Olives	Commissioning and sending leaders Quiet rest/sleep (Mark, Luke) Recollected prayer- Thanksgiving/ praise Lord's Supper Singing/praying Psalms Watching Prayer of surrender Sacrifice Prayer of abandon Prayer of blessing Prayer of lament Lord's Prayer Prayer of forsaken Study of Scriptures (Luke)	*Transfiguration*: Jesus's face and clothes turn dazzling white Elijah and Moses appear Father's voice of love *Dark Night*: Angel appears to Jesus Jesus heals soldier Earthquake and darkness *Commissionings*: Jesus appears suddenly to disciples in a room Jesus tells the eleven to meet him on a mountain in Galilee	*Word*: Proclaims the kingdom Teaches with authority Heals the sick and demonized with a word He called people to follow him Selects leaders to be itinerants with him Pronounces absolution Responds to conflict and opposition Promises a place in paradise to the thief on the cross Gives two worldwide commissions

to discern God's selection of leaders (Luke 6:12), commissioning and sending of leaders, quiet rest and sleep,[47] recollected prayer,[48] and the Lord's Prayer (Matt 6:8–15).[49] During Holy Week, we see Jesus engaged in the practices of thanksgiving, praise, worship, the Lord's Supper,

---

yet, in both texts Jesus met with followers (the Twelve in Matt 10:1 and seventy in Luke 10:1) away from the crowds to give instructions for a short-term mission, which included the command to pray that the Lord would raise up laborers.

47. Jesus lauds rest in Mark 6:31 and fails to censure sleep or drowsiness in Luke 9:32, as he does in Gethsemane.

48. They saw "Jesus only" without distractions (Mark 9:8b)—a key characteristic of centering prayer.

49. Christian spiritual direction helps others practice disciplines that Jesus modeled and taught.

singing and praying the Psalms, keeping watch, the prayer of surrender, the discipline of sacrifice, the prayer of abandon, the prayer of blessing, and the prayer of lament. And after the first Easter, the risen Jesus opened the disciples' minds to Scripture—the discipline of study, and he confronted their awareness of fear and doubt that was occasioned by his sudden and miraculous appearance at their Jerusalem gathering (Luke 24:33–49).[50] These disciplines—half of which were forms of prayer—were practiced by Jesus sometimes in solitude and other times in community with his disciples. Jesus did not let the press of the crowds cut him off from these necessary inner rhythms to which he felt God calling him, nor did he allow Jewish leaders' criticisms, expectations, or notions of kosher spirituality deter him from practicing these in unconventional ways in terms of space and time. In selecting the Twelve Jesus implicitly claimed that his community, not the religious leaders and institutions of his day, was the true Israel (Wright 1996:300). As Nouwen points out, in Luke's version of the call of the Twelve (6:12–17) Jesus modeled a new three-fold configuration of spiritual practice for the true Israel.[51] He communed with God in solitude on the mountain, he had community with the Twelve apostles he selected, and then together they did ministry. Communion, community, and ministry constitute the normative "disciplines of the Beloved" (Nouwen 1993b) under which all

---

50. Becoming aware of God's presence and its affects upon our emotions is called the discipline of *examen* in the Ignatian tradition.

51. Wright and others see Jesus's calling of the Twelve as an implicit reconstitution of Israel. "Israel had not had twelve visible tribes since the Assyrian invasion in 734 BC, and for Jesus to give twelve followers a place of prominence . . . indicates pretty clearly that he was thinking in terms of the eschatological restoration of Israel" (1996:300). Wright also suggests that Jesus's inner core of confidants—Peter, James, and John—constituted a "Davidic symbol echoing the three who were David's closest body guards," and that Jesus was implicitly functioning like David as Israel's wandering and already anointed king who was waiting to be enthroned (1996: 300). Ched Myers et al. also see the selection of the Twelve as a clear attempt to renew Israel. But for them, the calling of the Twelve does not imply a renewal of Israel's monarchy, but rather harks back to the time when Israel was a confederacy of twelve self-governing tribes before they had been centralized under the monarchy in conformity with surrounding cultures rather than YHWH's will. Myers sees this as an egalitarian period of Israel's history without the abuses of state power typical of the monarchy, which Israel's prophets had repeatedly decried (1997:32–33). Whether Jesus is harkening back to the period of the monarchy or confederacy, both Wright and Myers believe that Jesus's selection of the Twelve must have been seen as a critique of Israel's leaders and her disobedience, as well as an attempt to renew her life.

other disciplines can be subsumed. For example, meditation is a form of communion in solitude.

Grace Observed

What incidents of divine initiative, power, or acceptance were associated with Jesus's withdrawal according to the synoptic writers? God prepared the way for the inauguration of Jesus's ministry by sending the prophet John the Baptist. At Jesus's baptism in the Jordan River, the Father's declaration of love for his son was heard and the Spirit was seen descending upon Jesus in the form of a dove (Mark 1:9–11). Jesus, full of the Holy Spirit, was led by the Spirit into the wilderness to be tempted by the devil, after which angels from heaven attended his physical needs. Jesus initiated each of the retreats to which the disciples were invited (Mark 1:11–13). On the night Jesus sent his disciples across the Sea of Galilee, Jesus walked on the water towards them, Peter walked on the water towards Jesus, and the wind immediately ceased when Jesus got into the boat (Mark 6:45–52). On the Mount of Transfiguration Jesus's clothes and face became dazzling white, and Elijah and Moses appeared. The voice of the Father was again heard, calling Jesus his "Beloved Son" and commanding the disciples to listen to him (Mark 9:2–13). Jesus's prayer in Gethsemane was accompanied by the appearance of an angel.[52] Jesus's prayers of lament and abandonment on the cross were accompanied by an earthquake and three hours of pitch black darkness. In his resurrected state, Jesus appeared suddenly to his followers in a house in Jerusalem, where he commissioned them to bear witness of him (Luke 24:45–49), and he appeared to the eleven on a mountain, where he gave the commission to make disciples of all nations (Matt 28:16–20). Divine initiative, power, or acceptance was associated with each occasion of Jesus's withdrawals and/or his subsequent mission.

Outward Mission in Deed and Word

Closely associated with Mark's portrayals of Jesus's withdrawals for communion with God, shown in Tables 15 and 16 above, are descriptions of Jesus engaging in mission—in deed and word—and doing so with compassion, welcome, forgiveness, suffering love, authority, and

---

52. The angelic visitation occurs only in Luke's version (22:43).

power. Jesus's inclusive mission radically departed from that of first century Judaism, which had excluded sinners, Gentiles, the poor, the marginalized, and the powerless. After his lengthy journey to be baptized and to spend forty days in solitude,[53] Jesus returned to Galilee to commence his public ministry (Mark 1:14–34). There, he taught with authority, proclaiming the good news of the kingdom and healing the sick and demonized.[54] People were amazed at the authority with which he taught and the power by which he healed. He invited people to come and follow him. He discarded patterns typical of rabbis of his day by utilizing itinerant apprenticeships instead of residential schools. In the Synoptics, Jesus, not his followers, initiated these apprenticeships, departing from the tradition of rabbinic schools in which students initiated the relationship with a rabbi under whom they wished to study.

Upon being discovered in solitary early morning prayer (Mark 1:35–38), Jesus told his disciples of his intention (presumably received in prayer) to extend his ministry of teaching and healing beyond Capernaum to the surrounding towns. And so he did, preaching and performing exorcisms in synagogues throughout Galilee (1:39). After Jesus's selection of the Twelve (Mark 3:13–19) came conflict and opposition from Jesus's own family and from the religious leaders. Further teaching and demonstration of kingdom power (Mark 3:20—6:6) prepared Jesus's followers to be sent out on mission themselves (Mark 6:7–13). Jesus's subsequent interrupted retreat was followed by healing, teaching, and the miraculous feeding of five thousand. He practiced

---

53. Myers et al. suggest that Jesus's trek in the wilderness might be like a Native American's vision quest, which is "at once an outward adventure beyond the margins of society; an inward passage of purification and self-encounter; and a journey 'in the spirit' to discover the identity and destiny of one's people. Might Jesus be somehow interiorizing and reliving the experience of Israel? 'For forty days' (1:13) is clearly meant to invoke Israel's forty years of 'testing' in the wilderness" (1997:8).

54. As Peace argues, though Jesus's ministry is different from the rabbinic teaching, Mark portrays Jesus as a teacher (1999:171). Jesus is most commonly addressed as *didaskale* (teacher), and the term *didache* (teaching) often refers to Jesus's public ministry (1999:166 n. 22). Peace observes that teacher is the first role by which Mark introduces Jesus and the first role by which the disciples relate to him. Mark introduces a total of six titles for Jesus, each of which constitutes a new stage in the gradual conversion of the disciples to Jesus: Teacher (1:16—4:34), Prophet (4:35—6:30), Messiah (6:31—8:30), Son of Man (8:31—10:45), Son of David (10:46—13:37), and Son of God (14:1—15:39). Peace thinks these titles provide a six-stage model for "process evangelism," which connects well to the contemporary cultural scene (1999:319–29).

suffering love in welcoming people at inopportune times. Immediately following the miraculous feeding Jesus spent another night in solitary prayer and community with his disciples in a storm, which culminated in the ministry of healing on the other side of the Sea of Galilee. Jesus's communion with his Father released divine energy in his mission (Mark 6:45–56).

After experiencing glory on the Mount of Transfiguration Jesus faced the power of the demonic and the prospect of his own death. He healed a demonized boy and resolutely set his face toward the culmination of his earthly mission (Mark 9:2–50). In celebrating the Passover with his disciples in the upper room and in withdrawing to the Garden of Gethsemane to keep watch against the encroaching evil, Jesus was being prepared to pour out his life on the cross the next day. Prayer and mission were inseparably linked with Jesus on the cross. Jesus's God-forsaken cry—a lament from Psalm 22[55]—is included by Mark and Matthew only.[56] Only Luke includes two other prayers from the cross. The first is, "Father, forgive them; for they do not know what they are doing" (Luke 23:34). Between this and the second prayer, only Luke includes Jesus's conversation with the repentant thief. As Jesus hung on the cross suffering for the world's sin in the face of ridicule from the soldiers, the crowd, and religious authorities, his redeeming love also focused one of the criminals crucified beside him (23:40–43). Jesus reached out with words of hope and the promise of paradise to this broken, repentant, dying man. Jesus's last words cried out from the cross were also prayer; "Father, into your hands I commend my spirit" (23:46). His obedience to his Father, even unto death, inspired the martyrdom of early Christians facing persecution (Bockmuehl 1992:64).[57] Jesus's prayer preceding his mission to the repentant thief and prayer for his enemies accompanied his martyrdom and sacrifice for their sin. His obedience to his Father took him to the cross. There he defeated evil in all its forms, forgiving sin and liberating the repentant from the oppression of the spiritual, religious, and structural powers of evil.

---

55. "Prayer of forsaken" is Richard Foster's term for the prayer of God's absence (1992:17–26).

56. Cf. Mark 15:34 and Matt 27:46.

57. To imitate Christ, early Christians anticipated following him in his martyrdom.

Centrifugal-Centripetal Mission

Centrifugal mission preceded centripetal mission in Jesus's ministry. But when mission is accompanied by compassion, healing, transformation, and authority, people, often in crowds, are drawn to the missionary—just as they were to Jesus—because of the signs of the kingdom that accompany her or him. As we have already mentioned, this movement towards the missionary is centripetal mission. But centripetal mission is dangerous because of the inevitable animosity, jealousy, threat to political power, and opposition it invites from those with religious influence, as well as for the unpredictability of the crowds who come. Thus, centripetal mission may necessitate the missionary becoming subversive, as Jesus often was. But an equal danger lies in its potential to consume the missionary with busyness, exhaustion, and prayerlessness unless adequate inner rhythms are created, protected, and honored. Jesus felt the need for periodic escape from the crowds and their needs, which pressed in upon him. If this was true for Jesus, must not it be for his disciples?

Table 17 above summarizes the synoptic authors' portrayal of Jesus's practices of spirituality and mission in terms of space and time (column 1), the disciplines Jesus practiced (column 2), the manifestations of grace associated with Jesus's retreats (column 3), and his missional works that followed these episodes (column 4). At a glance, we see the inseparable tie between Jesus's retreats for communion with his Father, grace, and his subsequent healing and transforming mission.

Jesus's Teaching on Spirituality and Mission

Having studied the spiritual disciplines that Jesus practiced when he retreated from the crowds and how these related to his mission, I now examine what he taught about the relationship between spirituality and mission in Matthew 5–7, John 15, and Matthew 28:16–20. My findings from these teaching blocks, given in retreat settings, are displayed in Tables 18, 19, and 20 below.

The Sermon on the Mount (Matt 5–7)

My research of Jesus's teachings in Matthew 5–7 yields findings in six areas:

1. *Metaphors for Spirituality and Mission.* Jesus draws upon Old Testament images of Israel as a tree (7:15–20) that YHWH had planted and as light[58] and salt, which he called her to be for the world (5:13–16). Each of these images signify what Israel was to be—a good tree, a shining light, and flavorful salt—as well as what she was to do for the sake of the nations—produce good fruit, dispel darkness, and preserve the flavor of YHWH's righteousness (lit. justice). These images suggest that what Israel was and did would naturally flow from the heart and character of her people—but that was the problem, especially among her spiritual leaders. The righteousness of the scribes and Pharisees was inadequate for the kingdom, said Jesus (Matt 5:20).[59]

2. *Grace and Virtue—Imitation and Participation.* Jesus spurned these leaders' religious practices and notions of virtue in both inward and outward realms. In the Beatitudes he spoke of humility, mourning, mercy, purity—heart attitudes, which attend divine blessing (5:3–11). He spoke against external acts like divorce, adultery, murder, and taking oaths (5:27–42), and also against lust, anger (5:21–30), retaliation, hatred of enemies (5:38–48), finding security in money (6:19–21), divided loyalty, worry about the necessities of clothing, food, and the length of one's life (6:24–34), and being judgmental (7:1–5). He asked his followers not to merely endure persecution, but to welcome it with rejoicing (5:11). The Sermon was a radical critique of Israel's spiritual leaders and a call for his disciples to imitate their heavenly Father rather than them (5:48).

> The scribes and the Pharisees do indeed teach a way of being faithful to God, a way of behaving in accordance with God's covenant. But God's own sovereign rule ... is even now breaking in; and those who want to belong to the new world he is opening up must discover a way of covenant behaviour that goes far, far beyond anything the scribes and Pharisees ever dreamed of. (Wright 2004a:41)

---

58. See Old Testament portrayals of Israel as a tree (Isa 6:13; 65:22) and a light (Isa 42:6; 49:6).

59. Wright, while admitting that there were many humble and pious scribes and Pharisees who were exceptions to Jesus critique, sees the Pharisees as comprising a "hard-line pressure group" who, in their rigorous attempts to follow their interpretation of the Torah, were harsh in their judgment of others (2004a:69).

Indeed, Jesus was describing the life of the Father in human existence. But imitation of the Father was only possible by participation in his life. George E. Ladd thinks kingdom righteousness "goes behind the act, to the heart, and deals with what a man is in himself before God.... What you *are* is more important than what you *do*.... It is obvious that such a heart righteousness can itself be only the gift of God. God must give what He demands" (1959:83).

3. *Spiritual Practices.* Jesus's teaching gave his disciples means by which they could participate in and imitate the Father's life: spiritual practices, especially prayer—"the single most important expression of both participation in Christ and imitation of Christ" (Bockbuehl 1992:57). Practices mentioned include praying with love for one's enemies (5:44), solitary prayer in secret (6:5–6), the Lord's Prayer with its forgiving of debtors (6:9–15), secret fasting (6:16–18), and petitionary prayer (7:7–11). Such hidden disciplines provide ways of seeking first the kingdom of God by nourishing secret communion with God, which bears fruit in kingdom righteousness, which blesses neighbor and enemy alike (6:33). Absent is any direct mention of fellowship or community.

4. *Necessity of Solitude.* In all of Scripture only in the Sermon on the Mount do we find an explicit command to pray in solitude (Matt 6:6). The purpose of solitude, Jesus said, is so that prayer is not practiced for the notice or approval of others: "And whenever you pray, do not be like the hypocrites; for they love to stand and pray in the synagogues and at the street corners, so that they may be seen by others" (Matt 6:5). This is the great danger of communal spiritual practice. In my view, Jesus's call for solitude and secrecy forms the crux of his critique of Israel's spirituality. These free us from the power of human approval and from the shackles of prevailing spiritual practices that have become ends in themselves, actually keeping God and others at bay. Without solitude and secrecy, a faith community will inevitably conform to its own culture; its only reward is human, not divine. Biblical scholar Robert Doherty says,

> Seeking approval from others, letting some individual or some social scene become the norm for our actions, we wear certain masks and play certain games to hide the truth. Thus we become more and more *unreal* before self, before others and be-

fore the real God.... Perhaps the single most significant element in all spiritual experience ... is solitude, or "silence of the heart." (2003:3)

5. *The Triad of Prayer, Fasting, and Almsgiving in Early Christian Expansion.* According to theologian Joseph F. Wimmer, the only place in the Bible where fasting, prayer, and almsgiving appear together is in Matthew 6. The three are each mentioned extensively in the Old Testament, but never jointly in the same reference. However, the linkage of the three together came to be universally affirmed by the church fathers. These disciplines, the first two inward and the last outward, became a "golden thread" for the early church, explicitly linking spirituality and mission during the rapid spread of Christianity in the Roman Empire (1982:52–53). These were normative minimal practices of early believers for their participation in and imitation of Christ, based on his words, "So whenever you give alms ... pray ... fast" (Matt 6:2, 5, 16).

6. *The Priority of Spirituality in Mission.* "I never knew you. Go away from me" (Matt 7:23)—tragic words that Jesus will speak to some who did "deeds of power" in his name but without obediently and intimately knowing him. Jesus's intimacy with his followers, cultivated by spiritual practices, must undergird works of exorcism and power (7:21–22). The latter are necessary signs of the kingdom but not sufficient in themselves to produce intimacy with Jesus. The primary fruit in the new Israel is not power, but humble obedience to God flowing from intimate knowledge of Jesus.

The True Vine (John 15)

What did Jesus teach concerning spirituality and mission in John 15? I find at least five areas in which his use of vine imagery speaks to the question:

1. *Abiding in the Vine.* Theologian Sharyn E. Dowd says that spirituality in John's gospel can be summarized by the word abide (*meno*) and the metaphor of the vine. Jesus said, "Abide in me as I abide in you. Just as the branch cannot bear fruit by itself unless it abides in the vine, neither can you unless you abide in me" (15:4). There are two sides to abiding: Jesus in us and we in him. In this "life-giving union" Jesus remains with

Table 18: Summary of Jesus's Teaching on Spirituality and Mission(Adapted from Sermon on the Mount [Matt 5–7] and upper room discourse [John 15])

NT Reference	Metaphor/ Explicit Teaching	Inward Spiritual Function/Practice	Outward Mission Function/Practice
Matt 5–7	Salt (5:13) Light (5:14–16) Tree (7:15–20)	Salt is flavorful, has savor Light by nature shines brilliantly, is transparent and reflected Inner character and being must be that of a good tree: • *Virtues*: humility, suffering loss, spiritual hunger, mercy, purity (5:3–8) given by God as gifts, which should replace … • *Bad fruit*: lust and anger (5:21–30), retaliation and hatred (5:38–48), greed (6:19–21), divided loyalty, worry (6:24–34), and being judgmental (7:1–5)	Preserves and gives flavor Dispels darkness so others can see our good works and glorify God Good trees produce good fruit from inner character Bad trees produce bad fruit from inner character
	Explicit teaching	Jesus commands disciples to pray: • For enemies who persecute them (5:44) • In secrecy and solitude (6:5–6) • With few words (6:7) • The Lord's Prayer with the condition that they forgive those who wrong them (6:9–15) • In the form of asking, searching and knocking (7:7–11) Jesus commends fasting (6:16–18): • In secret without the notice or approval of others • With joy and happy appearance	Jesus blesses those who: • Make peace (5:9) • Extend mercy (5:7) Jesus commands his followers to: • Love their enemies (5:44) • Give alms secretly (6:2–4) • Not judge others (7:1–5)

NT Reference	Metaphor/ Explicit Teaching	Inward Spiritual Function/Practice	Outward Mission Function/Practice
John 15	Vine and branches	The branches (the disciples) remaining in the true Vine (Jesus)	Abiding produces grapes, crushed into wine
	Explicit teaching	• *Abiding* (15:7): communion, word, prayer, obedience, and joy in love • *Loving one another* (15:12): community • *Pruning*: suffering loss and fruit (15:2) • *Lord's Supper*: see synoptic parallels	*Bearing witness* (15:27): mission in word emphasized in spite of opposition

us and makes his home in us so that we may "live and breathe and relate to others out of . . . relationship to the Risen Christ" (1989:69).

2. *Participation and Imitation*. The metaphor of the vine emphasizes participation of the branches (followers of Jesus) in the life of the vine (Jesus)—the true Israel.[60] But in this passage "the image of participation naturally gives rise to that of imitation, which was a practice deeply ingrained in the Jewish understanding of the teacher-disciple relationship" (Bockmuehl 1992:57). Jesus equates imitation with fruit bearing when he says, "My Father is glorified by this, that you bear much fruit and become my disciples" (15:8). The disciples' obedience to Jesus and their abiding in him are to mimic his obedience to the Father and abiding in the Father's love (15:10). The disciples' love for one another is to be patterned after Jesus's love for them, even unto laying down their lives for each other (15:12–13). And the disciples' relationship with the world would be patterned after that of Jesus; just as the world hated him, it would hate them too (15:18–19). Such imitation is impossible without participation—"Apart from me you can do nothing" (15:5).

---

60. Ps 80:8–9 portrays Israel as a vineyard planted in Canaan during the conquest, but Isa 5:4–6b gives a picture of Israel as a vine gone wild. Colin Brown notes, "Whereas Israel was the vine or the vineyard in the OT, the vine is now narrowed down to Jesus himself" (1979:920).

3. *Spiritual Practices.* Charles R. Miller argues that in this passage Jesus explicitly commands his disciples to practice three normative disciplines: abiding (15:7), loving one another (15:12), and bearing witness (15:27)—what he calls the "upper room lifestyle" (2007:77–95)—which are similar to communion, community, and ministry (Nouwen 1993b). Abiding involves dwelling in Jesus's love (15:9), letting his word abide in us, praying, and obeying him (15:7, 10). Abiding can be done as a community, just as the disciples experienced in this setting and after he ascended. It can also be done in solitude, though John 15 does not explicitly say so. In any case, abiding results in joy (15:11) or ecstasy[61] and fruitfulness (15:16), even when being hated on account of Jesus (15:19–21). Paradoxically, from pruning and loss comes more fruit (15:2). From the crushing of grapes comes wine, and from Jesus's death comes life. The synoptic writers say that wine, the fruit of the vine, was part of this Passover meal—a detail John fails to mention. Only the synoptic writers have Jesus actually blessing the bread and wine, details with which John's readers were most certainly familiar.[62] The vine imagery of John 15 implicitly commends the practice the Lord's Supper.

4. *Instructions and Imagery for Mission.* John 15 emphasizes mission in word, bearing witness verbally to Jesus even as the Holy Spirit does (15:26–27). Only by the Spirit can the disciple effectively and joyously give testimony on behalf of Jesus in the face of difficulty and opposition. Fruitfulness in mission grows out of the disciple having been with Jesus (15:27), which provides first hand experience of the Lord to which the disciple can testify. Mission in deed is only implicit.

5. *The Priority of Spirituality in Mission.* Jesus clearly teaches that without abiding mission cannot be done. Without the Spirit's testimony to Jesus, a disciple's testimony to him is useless. In this text and in the Sermon on the Mount Jesus clearly teaches that any spirituality not expressed in outward mission through word and deed is not a normative spirituality. Nor is any mission that lacks firm roots in inward communion with

---

61. In discussing John 15, ecstasy is the term Nouwen (1986) and Doherty (2003) use instead of joy.

62. Wright says, "John does not describe the meal itself; presumably he supposes that his readers know the story of it well enough from other traditions and from their regular experience of the eucharist" (2004c:44). L. William Countryman makes essentially the same point (1987:7).

God true to the primitive patterns that Jesus taught. This is made clear in Table 18 above and Table 19 below.

The Risen Jesus's Commissions: Radical Flexibility

Having looked at Jesus's teaching about spirituality and mission on the night before his death, we conclude this chapter with his synoptic post-resurrection commissions. Mark's Gospel ends abruptly at the empty tomb (Mark 16:8) with no post-resurrection appearances to his disciples and no worldwide commission.[63] Matthew and Luke record commissions given by the risen Jesus to his disciples in secluded settings (Matt 28:16–20; Luke 24:36–39).

Matthew's version—the Great Commission—is given on a mountain. Unfortunately, this is missed in most references to it, which generally begin with verse 18, not verse 16.[64] By so doing, mission gets conceptually removed from its necessary moorings in spiritual practice. Starting in verse 16, we begin with: "Now the eleven disciples went to Galilee, to the mountain to which Jesus had directed them. When they saw him, they worshiped him; but some doubted. And Jesus came and said to them . . . go[65] therefore and make disciples" (Matt 28:16–19). I suggest we start any discussion of the commission with verse sixteen, as Karl Barth has done (1961:55–71). Yet, neither he nor most scholars

---

63. Though a shorter and a longer ending (16:9–20) eventually appeared in later manuscripts, each with a commission, neither was written by Mark. Wright thinks that the longer ending (Mark 16:9–20) reflects how Christians in the late second or early third century viewed Easter and how they saw the gospel spread (2001:226).

64. See for example, David J. Hesselgrave's article, which refers to Matthew 28:18–20 three times (2000:412, 413, 414), though once he makes reference to verses 16–20 (2000:413). See also David Bosch's article "The Biblical Foundation of Mission," in which he critiques William Carey, founder of the modern Protestant mission movement, for his inadequate biblical use of verses 18–20, but also himself fails to start with verse 16 in his very illuminating treatment of the Great Commission (1978:34, 43). Wright, however, has treated Matthew 28:16–20 as one unit in his commentary (2004b:204–10), while D. A. Carson has split verses 18–20 into its own unit, which he titles "The Great Commission" (1984:591–99).

65. Literally "as you go." Bosch explains that the verb "go" (*poreuthentes*) is "an aorist participle, [and] is an auxiliary simply reinforcing the action of the main verb. It does not command the disciples to go into all the world. It is simply taking it for granted that they will do this, and so they are told that, while going into the world, their principal responsibility will be that of 'making disciples'" (1978:43). See also Hesselgrave (2000:413).

Table 19: Contrasts in Jesus's Teaching on Spirituality and Mission: The Sermon on the Mount Compared with John 15

Sermon on the Mount (Matt 5–7)	The True Vine (John 15)
Normative triad of practices—the golden thread: • Prayer in solitude and secrecy • Fasting and secrecy • Almsgiving and secrecy *Other spiritual disciplines taught as normative:* • Rejoicing when persecuted for Jesus • Prayer of blessing, forgiveness of enemies • Seek reconciliation to enter into prayer • The Lord's Prayer • Worship (in the Lord's Prayer) • Petitionary prayer • Silence implied in story of foolish builder • Simplicity: serving one master and seeking first the kingdom • Obedience to teachings and word of Jesus *Solitude (explicit), Community (implicit):* • Solitude and secrecy explicitly taught • Community not mentioned, only implied	*Normative triad of practices—three priorities:* • Abiding • Loving believers • Bearing witness *Three practices explained, other disciplines:* • Abiding in Jesus's love through prayer and letting his word abide in the heart of the disciple • Community with believers: expressing costly love towards followers of Jesus • Bearing witness of Jesus to unbelievers • Obedience to Jesus's word • Celebrating Lord's Supper implied *Community (explicit), Solitude (implicit):* • Solitude not mentioned, only implied • Community explicitly emphasized

Sermon on the Mount (Matt 5–7)	The True Vine (John 15)
Imitating Father (explicit), Participation (implicit): • Inner virtues commended: humility, meekness, spiritual hunger, mercy, purity, peace-making, forgiving, joy in adversity • Inner sins warned against: lust, anger, greed, divided heart, worry, and judging *Mission in deed emphasized:* • Peace making • Extending mercy • Blessing persecutors and those who despitefully use us • Non-retaliation • Sacrifice: give to all who ask • Loving our enemies • Almsgiving • Suspending judgment *Suffering comes from mission or relationships:* • Facing persecution with rejoicing • Forgiving those who despitefully use us	*Imitation and participation (both explicit):* • Abiding in Jesus has fruit of ecstasy, fulness of joy • Pruning produces more fruit • Imitating Jesus's self-sacrificing love • Imitating his endurance under persecution *Mission in word emphasized:* • Verbal testimony to Jesus • Experiencing the world's hatred for and opposition to Jesus *Suffering comes from mission or may be inward only:* • Pruning for more fruit and full joy • Willingness to lay down one's life for other disciples • Facing world's hatred toward Jesus

make what seems to be an obvious observation—namely, that there are two commissions here, an inner and outer one. First, Jesus directed his disciples to the mountain—there to meet him, see him, worship him, and experience his unconditional love, especially in their doubt (or perhaps hesitation).[66] Second, in the context of their obedience to the inner

---

66. Hesitation rather than doubt appears in Wright's translation of Matt 28:16–20 (2004b:204), though as Wright points out in his commentary, the term can mean either (2004b:206).

commission, he gave them the outer commission to make disciples of all nations. Wright comes closest to this assertion in his commentary on Matthew:

> The scene begins on a mountain. No surprises there: a great deal in Matthew happens on a mountain. The temptations; the Sermon on the Mount; the transfiguration; the final discourse on the Mount of Olives; and now this parting scene. Moses and Elijah met the living God on a mountain, and they have appeared in this gospel talking with Jesus; now Jesus invites his disciples to meet him, so that they can be commissioned in turn. (2004b:205)

Keeping mission firmly linked to spirituality by starting our discussion with verse 16, not 18, will guard our mission theology from lapsing into Pelagianism (legalism).[67] This helps keep mission practice in the realm of the gospel rather than duty or law, as Leslie Newbigin has so forcefully argued (1989:18). But to accomplish this, spirituality itself must not become Pelagian. Precisely here, Matthew 28:16–18a, I believe furnishes some of the most pointed patterns in all of Scripture for keeping spiritual practices from devolving into a new legalism (see Table 20 below). Matthew's words can help us discern whether our spiritual discipline is about Jesus or us; his initiative or ours, his guidance or ours, his power or ours, his control or ours. Do we catch a fresh vision of Jesus and find ourselves released to new adoration of him, or is our practice the focus? Does our discipline become so rigid that if Jesus himself wanted to change it midstream, so that we could express his compassion to others, he could not? Mission spirituality must be radically flexible, never absolutized. Thus, we must always be ready to subvert any practice that supplants Jesus himself.

---

67. This term derives from a fierce fifth century debate between Augustine and Pelagius, a British lawyer, over the role of grace in the exercise of human will. Pelagius held that the will unaided by divine grace was capable of good—a view strongly opposed by Augustine. Alister McGrath summarizes the two positions: "For Pelagius, humanity merely needs to be shown what to do and can then be left to achieve it unaided; for Augustine, humanity needs to be shown what to do and then must be gently aided at every point" (1988a:43).

Table 20: Keeping Spiritual Practices from Becoming a New Legalism

Matthew 28:16, 17, 18a
"Now the eleven disciples went to Galilee, to the mountain to which Jesus had directed them. When they saw him, they worshiped him but some doubted. And Jesus came to them."

Observations of the Text	*Discernment Questions for Practicing Spiritual Disciplines*
Being a disciple involves going to a particular place (a mountain in Galilee)—at a particular time (now) to encounter Jesus—i.e., *practicing various spiritual disciplines or exercises*. These practices constitute the human action or human effort to create open space, as Nouwen puts it (*spirituality from below*). Not all who think of themselves as disciples or are viewed as such actually practice spiritual disciplines (note that eleven, not twelve, went to the mountain). Some practice them from below but not from above. *Jesus initiates a spiritual discipline* with his disciples, shapes it (place and time), guides them in its practice (*Jesus directed them*) and empowers them in it (*he came to them*). This is *spirituality from above*.	Where is the mountain (i.e., the place where we will practice the disciplines of intimacy) to which Jesus is directing us to encounter him (place)? When (time)? Has God initiated, shaped, guided, and empowered our practice of the discipline? Or have we? Do we describe and experience the spiritual discipline primarily from above and only secondarily from below? Over time, does the discipline result in a fresh vision of Jesus? Does it focus on and point to him or to the discipline, practice, or exercise itself? Over time, does it result in renewed worship of Jesus? Is it life giving, and does it spill into and shape everyday life?
Jesus is the focus of a discipline, not the discipline itself—*they saw him*. The practice of a discipline over time makes us aware of Jesus—who he is and what he says and does. The practice of a discipline over time *releases us anew to worship him* (*they worshiped him*). The practice of a discipline also *surfaces inner doubt and struggle*—we become more aware of the fallen part of our nature, which lurks beneath the surface (*some doubted* or *hesitated*).	Over time, does it result in a new awareness of our fallen and hesitating response to God?

Summary

Originating from the center of a historic faith tradition, Jesus's spirituality can redress the collapse of space/time with potent rhythms of spiritual practice for individuals and communities, overflowing into transforming healing mission. In this chapter, I have found that:

1. Jesus drew from Israel's daily, weekly, monthly, and annual spiritual practices, which had supplanted God, kept others at bay, and truncated her mission. He subverted these practices symbolically by practicing them in powerfully new ways and by teaching his disciples about them.

2. According to the Synoptic Gospels, Jesus's frequent retreats from the crowds in solitude or with his disciples constituted a departure from the religious practices of the day in terms of time and space. These retreats lasted an hour, part of a night (five to six hours), all night (nine to thirteen hours), and approximately fifty days, in places that included a desert, a lonely place, a hillside, a mountain, a room, and a garden—most of which were not customary places for prevailing spiritual practices.

3. Mark portrays Jesus's withdrawals from the crowds as being intimately associated with his empowered mission in deed and word. Grace attends every withdrawal and/or subsequent mission. Spirituality is inseparably tied to mission.

4. In the Sermon on the Mount Jesus teaches that virtue is a gift flowing from participation in and imitation of the Father. The virtues Jesus commended and the vices he condemned in the Sermon are keys to obeying the great commandment and provided the basis for the cardinal virtues and the seven (or eight) deadly sins and in the later development of spiritual theology.

5. Jesus commanded secret solitude—the crux of his critique of Jewish spirituality and the heart of every subversive spirituality. Solitude (abiding), community (loving one another), and ministry (bearing witness) were normative, as were fasting, prayer, and giving alms (the golden thread).

6. The Great Commission (Matt 28:16–20) provided Jesus's disciples with a radical flexibility for keeping spiritual practices from supplanting him and his mission. Chapter 4 addresses how they did.

4

The Early Church's Rhythms of Spirituality and Mission

> Christ commands his followers to withdraw . . . for prayer. The apostles and, after them, the holy Fathers did just that.
>
> —Gabriel Bunge (2002:53)
>
> The enthusiasm to evangelize which marked the early Christians is one of the most remarkable things in the history of religions.
>
> —Michael Green (1970:286)

HAVING EXAMINED JESUS'S RHYTHMS OF SPIRITUALITY AND MISSION IN the last chapter, this chapter is devoted to the rhythms of the spirituality and mission that emerged among early Christians after Jesus was gone. I look closely at two groups—first, the original apostles, and second, the apostolic fathers, who wrote the earliest non-canonical Christian texts from about 70 to 150. I also briefly consider Origen, Antony, and St. Benedict, who lived during the late second to the mid–sixth centuries.

The period from the Day of Pentecost in 30 AD through the first half of the second century was critical for the fledgling movement, as it grew from a small Jewish sect into a widespread Gentile-Jew fellowship, which penetrated Greek, Syriac, Latin, and other cultures. The movement, which could have easily failed, did not, but its mission work is largely hidden from us except for the Book of Acts. We have no idea who planted the churches in the three cities that became the main centers of Christian influence after 70 AD: Antioch, Rome, and Alexandria.[1] From 90 to 120 we

---

1. Paul E. Pierson calls these missionaries Christianity's "non-name offense" (1998:73). Mark Noll identifies the fall of Jerusalem in 70 AD as the first key turning point in Christian history (2000:23–46).

have only nine or ten texts—known as the Apostolic Fathers—and we can only infer from them what kind of spirituality and mission occurred in those years. Do these texts disclose any of the rhythms of spirituality and mission that Jesus modeled and taught? This can be difficult to answer, as the new faith responded with great flexibility, adapting indigenously to the new cultural contexts into which it spread.[2] However, there are hints of generalized patterns, as we shall see.

But first, we will consider Acts, the first mission history text (Pierson 1998:60)—by finishing the examination of my second research question concerning how space and time with God relate to mission in the New Testament. The remainder of the chapter will address part of my third research question about how space and time with God relate to mission in selected spiritual classics from first and second millennia—in this case, the Apostolic Fathers and Origen's works on prayer and martyrdom. First, we see how these spiritual and missional practices were infused by what Stanley P. Saunders calls an "eschatological imagination," which remolded perceptions of space and time (2002:159).

Eschatology and Early Christian Spirituality

Though Jesus brought God's reign to a climax in his death and resurrection, his disciples only faintly began to grasp its nature and significance. Thus, in his post resurrection appearances he continued to teach them about the kingdom (Acts 1:3). Just prior to Jesus's ascension, they asked him if he was now going to restore the kingdom to Israel, to which he replied, "It is not for you to know the times" (Acts 1:7). Instead, they were to receive power from the Holy Spirit to be his witnesses in all places and times to the end of the age (Acts 1:8; Matt 28:18–20). The kingdom that had finally fully come in Jesus was to be spread until all creation was fully renewed at his appearing (Rom 8:21), when all confess Jesus as Lord (Phil 2:10–11). The eschatological kingdom was both now and not yet. John D. Zizoulas and many others note that Christianity inherited from Judaism the eschatological expectation of God's coming rule, which was reworked by Jesus and the apostles around himself

---

2. Thus, it is customary to speak of missions (Walls 1996:3–42; 2002:13) and spiritualities (Reilly 1978:43–45) in the plural to describe the new faith's adaptability to many cultural settings and forms.

(1982:23–26),[3] and that this expectation became a central feature in early Christian spirituality and mission. Living in the last days inaugurated by Jesus, Christians loved the prospect of his immanent appearing, which they expected from his ascension onward. This fueled their contagious witness to the point of death itself (Zizoulas 1982:25). In case studies of Matthew, Galatians, and Ephesians, Saunders concludes that "the rhetoric of eschatology was formative of early Christian spirituality." He believes that "through such discourse the New Testament writers reshaped the community's perception of time and space, and enabled their audiences to 'learn Christ'" (2002:156). Here Saunders is quoting Ephesians 4:20, which contrasts the Ephesians' former identities in Gentile paganism with the formation of their new identities "in Christ" (Eph 4:22–24)—part of the new creation in which space and time are redefined relationally (recall Torrance in chapter 2). "In Christ" constitutes the new relation to God in which time (*kairos*)[4] is experienced in its fullness through God's graced plan and all things in heaven and earth are brought together spatially—an eschatological reality (Eph 1:10). Being "in Christ" is conveyed in love and in bodily life. Spirituality affirms creation and relationships (Zizioulas 1982:29, 36–37).

N. T. Wright holds that through baptism and the Lord's Supper believers mysteriously participate here and now in the past events of Jesus's death and resurrection and in the future events of the *eschaton*. In baptism, believers experience the final judgment that "comes forward in time" to Good Friday and Easter Sunday. The final completed renewal of all creation has already begun in Jesus's resurrection from the dead. Likewise, the Lord's Supper is infused with the past and future events of Good Friday and the great banquet at the Parousia (Wright 2007).

3. Wright argues that early Christians interpreted the resurrection eschatologically because they were Second Temple Jews with a worldview that was eschatological in outlook—which, except for Sadducees, anticipated a general resurrection of the dead on the Day of the Lord. Early Christians applied this to Jesus, with his resurrection serving as the new center (2003:27). Wright claims that New Testament scholars employ at least ten meanings of the term (2003:26). He views eschatology as "the climax of Israel's history, involving events for which end-of-the-world language is the only set of metaphors adequate to express the significance of what will happen, but resulting in a new and quite different phase *within* space-time history" (1996:208).

4. Commenting on Eph 1:10, Francis Foulkes writes that "the word used for *time* is not *chronos*, which connotes the passage of time in days and months and years, but *kairos*, which speaks of particular times, the decisive times of fulfillment in the purposes of God" (1989:61).

In both practices eschatological events are made present to believers—
even if only partially. Saunders writes,

> In short, eschatology provided the early Christians with the
> means to reorient notions of both time and "space," that is, the
> ways they might relate to God, to one another, and to the rest of
> creation.... God's actions are not limited by our cultural con-
> structions of time. For the New Testament writers, the qualities
> associated with "the last days" lie not only in the future but also
> in the past and especially in the present, wherever and whenev-
> er God pours out the Spirit and restores a broken creation. "The
> last days" are a "kind of time" characterized more by content,
> experience, and relationships than by location or an abstract
> line. (2002:159)

The Apostles' Practice of Spirituality and Mission in Acts

So the apostles' spiritual and missional practices were inspired with an eschatological worldview. But to what extent did Jesus's rhythms of spirituality and mission and his teaching on these continue among the original apostles after the ascension? The best text, of course, to help get at this question is the Book of Acts.[5] Acts contains virtually no explicit teaching on prayer or spiritual practice, but it is filled with narrative descriptions of them. A cursory reading of Acts shows the primitive church praying repeatedly and often. The content of some of these prayers are recorded.[6] Except for my brief look at one prayer (Acts 4:24–30), I will study only selected withdrawals for prayer and worship. Also, since most scholars agree that Luke wrote both Acts and Luke, each comprising half of a complete work (Acts 1:1–2),[7] it makes sense to compare the two with respect to prayer, a subject that Luke mentions more frequently than any other New Testament author according to

---

5. For a history of various views of Acts's historicity since the Tubinger school's radical denial of its historicity under the influence of F. C. Bauer and his son-in-law, Zeller, see Longenecker (1981:225–29). For a more recent overview of the scholarly discussion of Act's historicity, see Witherington (2004:1–85). On the view that Luke whitewashed the church in Acts, see Wright (1992:452).

6. See 1:24–25; 4:24–30; 7:59; 8:29; 9:4–5, 10–16; 10:13–15.

7. On the unity of Luke-Acts, see Longenecker (1981:231–32 238–39).

biblical scholar Leonard Doohan (1987:120) and others.[8] Luke gives us a baseline of prayer, which Appendices D and E help us see. Do the rhythms of prayer in Acts look anything like those of Jesus in Luke? Doohan thinks so.

Rhythms of Prayer and Mission: Luke and Acts Compared

In *Luke: The Perennial Spirituality*, Doohan argues that the structure of Acts recapitulates that of Luke, and that the progression of the church's life follows that of Jesus—a widely held view among scholars (1985:50–55).[9] Though I did not include my findings for Luke in chapter 3, my research shows that he mirrors Mark in portraying Jesus's mission as inseparably bound to his retreats.[10] In Doohan's research of Luke-Acts, he has found and classified three types of prayer: personal, community, and ritual or set prayer.[11] Set prayer can be done in community or solitude. Doohan cites over twenty cases of prayer in Luke and nearly that in Acts (1985:104–5, 120–22).

I examined fourteen passages in Acts in which the church and her leaders were gathered away from the crowds for prayer.[12] I should note that most of the withdrawals were not intentional retreats to lonely places like those of Jesus, but rather, these occurred in homes, prisons, or during long journeys in the course of the church's life and mission (see Tables 21 and 22 below). In the passages I selected, prayer or worship was practiced corporately eleven times and in solitude on three occasions. Though I did not do so, I might have

---

8. David Crump (1999), Barbara E. Reid (1994:40, 50), and Bonnie Thurston (1993:55–56) have also noted Luke's emphasis on prayer.

9. See Longenecker on the recapitulation view of Luke-Acts (1981:232–35). On parallels between the narrative structure of the closing chapters of Acts and those of Luke, see Wright (1992:375).

10. See Appendices D and E. Shin Asami (2004) has detected a major shift in Jesus's ministry right after each of his retreats in Luke's Gospel. For a similar view, see Charles H. Talbert (1982:237–49).

11. Some in liturgical and free church traditions pit liturgical and spontaneous prayer against each other, which I think mistakenly absolutizes one at the expense of the other. For affirmation of both forms of prayer, see Moule (1961:7 ff), John Koenig (1992:137–41), and Frank C. Senn (1983:95–110).

12. Since Acts contains virtually no episodes of leaders seeking God in lonely places as in Luke, I tried to select incidents in which some kind of withdrawal (by choice or forced) from normal affairs took place.

included several lengthy periods of isolation from normal ministry when prayer doubtless occurred in solitude or community, though not explicitly mentioned. These include Paul's two year imprisonment under Felix, his three months in Malta, and his two year house arrest in Rome (Acts 24 and 28). I will begin with corporate prayer.

Table 21: Acts, Part A

Event	Time and Space/Place	Inner Discipline Practiced/ Taught	Grace: Divine Initiative/ Power	Outward Mission Practiced
Waiting for the Spirit/ Pentecost (1:6—2:4) In community	*Time*: Constantly (for ten days) *Place*: Upstairs room in the house where they were lodging	Constant prayer together with the eleven and a wider group of disciples Community Leadership selection and commissioning Extended waiting on God for the Spirit's work	Initiated by Jesus in his command to wait for the Spirit and his promise that they would bear witness (Acts 1:4–5, 8), wind rushed in, tongues of fire Disciples filled by Spirit, tongues descend on them	(2:5–41) *Word*: Hearing the noise, crowd gathers, sixteen language groups hear the disciples in their own tongue ← *Word*: Peter proclaims the gospel in story, 3,000 baptized
Gathering of first Christians in Jerusalem (2:42–47) In community	*Time*: Daily *Place*: Temple, private homes	Prayer Praise/worship Apostles' teaching small groups Fellowship Breaking bread Sharing possessions Hospitality	Sense of awe Marvels and signs through the apostles Joy	(2:47) *Word & Deed*: Daily conversions ←

Peter and John attending the temple's hour of prayer (3:1–10) In community	*Time*: 1 hour at 3 o'clock in the afternoon *Place*: Temple in Jerusalem	Community Worship Praise Set prayer	Miraculous healing	(3:6—4:23) *Deed*: Healing lame man at the Beautiful Gate← *Word*: Peter speaks to those who come running←
Corporate prayer after release (4:24–32) In community	*Time*: After they were released by authorities and warned not to speak in Jesus's name *Place*: Building where their friends were	Testimony: told what God did Corporate prayer in raised voice Praise and worship of Creator Submitted threat to God asking for boldness in Jesus's name	Earthquake shakes building	(4:33) *Word*: Apostles bear witness with great power to Jesus's resurrection→ *Deed*: Believers held in high esteem because of care for needs
Appointing of deacons (ch. 6) In community	*Time*: Disciples' growing conflict over widow care *Place*: Jerusalem	Prayer Ministry of word Service: waiting tables		*Deed*: Martyrdom of Stephen← *Word*: Expansion of the church

→*Indicates centrifugal mission*   ←*Indicates centripetal mission*

Corporate Spiritual Practice in Acts: Daily, Weekly, and Occasional or Annual Rhythms

A casual reading of Acts shows clearly that the apostles and those they influenced practiced corporate spiritual disciplines far more than solitary ones. While Jesus prayed in solitude somewhat more than in community (four of my selected Lukan retreats were solitary, while three were communal),[13] the early church prayed predominantly in commu-

---

13. Two other retreats in Luke had both solitary and communal aspects (see Appendices D and E).

nity, though not exclusively so. Of the selected texts in Acts, eleven contain explicit references to corporate prayer and three to solitary prayer.[14] I argue here that in Acts the rhythms of withdrawal for prayer followed by immediate mission recapitulates similar patterns in Luke, but with notable contrasts.[15]

1. *Occasional/Annual Rhythms.* Before Jesus began his ministry he spent forty days in solitude.[16] Before the church's ministry commenced at Pentecost, the disciples gathered for ten days of continual prayer in an upstairs room (1:13-14), where they awaited the Spirit's outpouring, which Jesus had promised (1:8).[17] The Spirit's descent and baptizing of them with tongues of fire (2:1-4) echoed the Spirit's descent upon Jesus at his baptism.[18] After forty days of hesitating worship of the risen Christ followed by his ascension, and ten days of corporate prayer culminating in the baptism of the Spirit, Peter preached powerfully, with three thousand being baptized (2:14-42). Following his trek to be baptized and spending forty days in solitude, Jesus preached and healed with authority and power.[19] Acts does not seem to portray widespread annual practices of extended corporate prayer, though there are hints of such in connection with the annual Jewish festivals. Paul spent days with the Philippians for the Feast of Unleavened Bread, and likely the Passover (20:6),[20] which I. Howard Marshall thinks was a Christian Passover or the beginnings of an Easter celebration (1980:325), a view not shared by Richard N. Longenecker.[21] Whatever

---

14. The eleven episodes of corporate prayer are displayed in Table 21 above and Table 22 below. The three episodes of solitary prayer are displayed as the first three episodes in Table 22: Philip's sojourn; Saul's Damascus Road encounter of the risen Christ; and the visions given to Cornelius and Peter during their separate observances of an hour of prayer.

15. See Table 21 above and Table 22 below.

16. See Luke 4:1-13.

17. See Luke 24:49.

18. See Luke 3:21-22.

19. See Luke 4:14-41.

20. See Longenecker (1981:507). For the origins of Easter, see Bradshaw (1999:81-97).

21. For commentary on Paul's celebration of the Feast of Unleavened Bread in Phillipi (Acts 20:3, 5-6) and his aim to get to Jerusalem by Pentecost (20:16), see Longenecker (1981:506-7, 510).

the case, after leaving Philippi, Paul was in a hurry to reach Jerusalem by Pentecost (20:16). These occasions may have been precursors to celebrations of Easter and Pentecost. By the second century, both had become occasions in the church's annual calendar at which believers practiced extended prayer and welcomed new converts in baptism—a clear linkage between corporate prayer and mission.[22]

2. *Daily Rhythms.* In Acts, the church gathered daily for corporate prayer and worship in homes of various sizes, accommodating groups ranging from a few to 120 (Acts 1:15),[23] and in the temple and synagogues. Also, they devoted themselves to apostolic teaching, shared meals together (the initial setting for the Lord's Supper),[24] and held property in common. These daily practices nourished the initial expansion of the church as evidenced by signs, wonders, daily conversions, and a sense of awe (2:42–47). This echoes how Jesus's daily prayers in solitary places sustained the initial expansion of his ministry.[25] As seen in chapter 3, Jesus prayed at set hours of daily prayer—the Shema and the Eighteen Benedictions. Phyllis Tickle says that as the Diaspora spread to cities of the Roman Empire, Jewish prayer came to revolve around the customary ringing of bells—roughly at six, nine, noon, three, and dusk (2001:viii).[26] The church followed suit, as seen in Peter's and John's temple visit for afternoon prayer (3:1) and in Peter's rooftop prayer at noon (10:9).

---

22. By this time, according to R. E. Nixon, Pentecost became a Christian feast, second only to Easter in importance, and it was called Whitsunday, as it became a regular occasion for baptisms of new converts who dressed in white (1978:763). On Passover-Easter as a time of baptism, see Chilton (2002:94).

23. Based on archaeological finds, John Koenig guesses the typical house held 20–30 (1992:130).

24. Robert and Julie Banks summarize William Barclay's five movements or shifts that have occurred in the celebration of the Lord's Supper over time: "from home to church building, from real to symbolic meal, from simplicity to elaboration, from experience to dogma, from concrete to abstract [and] from layperson to priest . . ." (1986:60). These, they argue, have greatly impoverished the Lord's Supper.

25. See Luke 4:42 for Jesus's episode of solitary prayer and 4:43–5:14 for his subsequent mission. See 5:16 for his continuous pattern of solitary prayer and 5:17–39 for his subsequent mission.

26. Bells rang at about six or at dawn (prime, the first hour) to open the business day, nine (terce, the third hour), noon (sext, the sixth hour) for lunch break, three (none, the ninth hour), and then at six (vespers, the evening hour) to close markets (Tickle 2001:viii).

Acts 4 illustrates how daily corporate prayer sustained the church in her early mission. Theologian John Koenig says that "Acts 4:24–30 is the longest prayer of the church on earth recorded in the New Testament, so we shall do well to give it close attention" (1992:140). When John and Peter were released from prison, believers "raised their voices together to God" (4: 24) upon hearing of the authorities' ban against speaking publically in the name of Jesus (4:18). Their Trinitarian prayer included abounding praise of God's person, his creative power, and his sovereign rule to which Israel and all nations are subject and which now is fully realized in Jesus (4:24–29). Koenig thinks "overflowing praise" was normative for all spontaneous and liturgical forms of prayer in the infant church. And so was, Koenig suggests, their petition that God grant them "all boldness" in speaking the word and give them signs, wonders, and healing through Jesus's name (1992:140). After praying, an earthquake shook their gathering place; they were filled with the Spirit and began to speak boldly of Jesus (4:31). The apostles powerfully preached the resurrection (4:33). The ongoing corporate worship, fasting, and prayer of believers in Antioch allowed them to hear the voice of the Spirit saying, "Set apart for me Barnabas and Saul [Paul] for the work to which I have called them" (13:2–3). Through the laying on of hands they commissioned Paul and Barnabas for their first missionary journey to plant churches and later select church leaders on their return to Antioch (14:21–28). These corporate practices were ongoing, and appear to have been daily and weekly. This Spirit-directed leadership selection process echoes Jesus's extended solitary prayer by which he gained discernment for his crucial selection of the Twelve. Once he selected his apostles, he immediately took them with him in ministry and then he sent them out on their own to preach and heal.[27]

3. *Weekly Prayer Rhythms.* The weekly Sabbath worship in the temple and in synagogues influenced corporate worship in the early church. Believers adopted a weekly pattern of meeting in homes or larger private venues primarily on the first or seventh days of the week, though they met together on other days for fellowship and prayer (2:46–47), as mentioned already. The features common to weekly synagogue and Christian worship, according to Everett F. Harrison, included "prayer, confession of faith, reading of Scripture, an exposition or homily, and

27. See Luke 6:12–19; 9:1–10.

the blessing of the congregation at the close. The word *synagogue* could even be used to refer to a Christian gathering (see Jas 2:2)" (1985:132). Jewish synagogues, as well as places devoted to Jewish prayer in urban centers where no synagogue existed, provided the apostles important venues for weekly corporate prayer and for evangelizing Jews and "God-fearers."[28] For the apostles, prayer and mission were linked at these places on Sabbath. Prayer was not only a preparation for mission, it was a part of the mission itself, just as it was for Jesus in Luke, where he engaged in healing and teaching on six different Sabbath occasions.[29] People were either amazed by his authority and power, on one hand; or so enraged by his subversion of their traditional spiritual and economic practices, on the other, that they began plotting to harm him. Five passages in Acts portray the apostles engaged in teaching on the Sabbath with the same two reactions.[30] Jesus's explosive redefinition of the Sabbath around communion with himself and compassion, not code or custom, was reflected in the apostles' weekly rhythms in Acts.

Solitary Spiritual Practice in Acts

Acts contains several explicit cases of solitary spiritual practice.[31] In them we see individuals practicing prayer or some important aspect of it—often in concert with worship, fasting, and other disciplines. Likewise, these cases are accompanied by manifestations of divine power, such as dreams or healing. The Ethiopian eunuch's conversion and baptism was a direct result of Philip's attentiveness to God's voice, his willingness to obey, and his immersion in the Scriptures, each of which is characteristic of authentic prayer (8:26–39). Saul's three days

---

28. The Gangites River, a mile and one half from Philippi, may have been the Jewish place of prayer where Lydia, a God-fearer, met Paul one Sabbath (Acts 16:11–15; see Longenecker 1981:460). God-fearers were Gentiles drawn to monotheistic worship who had not yet become Jews (see Arthur F. Glasser 1989:145, 253, 255).

29. See 4:16–30; 4:31–36; 6:1–5; 6:6–11; 13:10–17; 14:1ff.

30. See 13:14–41; 14:44–52; 16:13–15; 17:1–9; and 18:1–6.

31. Acts also has cases of implicit solitary prayer: Paul's two-year captivity under Felix (24:24–27); a fourteen-day voyage from Crete to Malta (27:9–44); a three-month stay in Malta (28:1–15); and his two-year house arrest in Rome (28:16–31). In these, Paul undoubtedly practiced prayer and worship, though this is not explicitly mentioned in the text. These incidents occurred on his final trip to Rome, which Wright thinks echoes Jesus's final journey to Jerusalem (1992:375). Paul, like Jesus, engaged in missionary activity during his last journey towards impending danger and death.

Table 22: Acts, Part B

Event	Time and Space/Place	Inner Discipline Practiced/Taught	Grace: Divine Initiative/Power	Outward Mission Practiced
Philip's sojourn (ch. 8) In solitude	Place: Samaria/Jordan River	Listening prayer Scripture	Angel of the Lord and Spirit speak	(8:26–40) Word: Conversion of Ethiopian→
Saul's conversion (9:1–19) In solitude	Time: 3 days Place: Road to Damascus/Judas's home in Damascus	Prayer/obedience Worship/fasting Solitude Community	Vision/voice of Jesus Blindness/healing Filled with Spirit	(9:19–29) Word: Mission in Damascus and Jerusalem→
Cornelius/Peter's hour of prayer (10:1–23) In solitude	Time: 3 p.m. and noon Place: Rooftop of house	Set hours of prayer Spontaneous prayer/hospitality Worship	Visions; supernatural timing and message	(10:24–48) Deed: Hospitality← Word: To Joppa→ Word & Deed: Gentile mission→
Church's prayer for Peter (12:1–19) In community	Time: Late at night Place: John Mark's mother's home	Fervent prayer in community Watching/praise	Angel appears to Peter in prison and frees him	(12:24) Word: Continued to grow→
Antioch church praying (13:1–3) In community	Time: Before first missionary journey Place: Church	Fasting/worship Prayer/community Commissioning Laying on of hands	"Separate me Paul and Barnabas," says the Spirit	(13:4–5) Word: Barnabas and Paul begin first missionary journey in Cypress→
Apostles' selection of elders (14:21–28) In community	Time: While returning to Antioch Place: Lystra, Iconium, Antioch	Prayer/fasting Taught sacrifice/suffering Leadership selection Testimony/story	Grace for the missionary task (Acts 14:26)	(14:25) Word: Message given at Perga→

Jerusalem conference (ch. 15) In community	Time: Conflict over circumcision after first missionary journey Place: Jerusalem	Worship (implied) Prayer (implied) Community debate Testimony/story	Unanimity	(15:35) Word: Paul and Barnabas teach and preach in Antioch→
Paul and Lydia praying/Paul and Silas praying in prison (16:6–34) In community	Time: Sabbath, midnight Place: Riverside, prison	Prayer/worship Baptism/hospitality Singing praise Sacrifice/suffering	Earthquake Miraculous release	(16:11–34) Word: Conversion of Lydia and household→ Deed: Exorcism Word & Deed: Conversion of jailor←
Corinth vision (18:9–10) In solitude	Time: Night Place: House of Titus Justus	Solitude/sleep Worship Community Hospitality	Vision-guidance/ divine affirmation	(18:11) Word: Teach word for 18 months in Corinth

→Indicates centrifugal mission ←Indicates centripetal mission

of solitude in Damascus after being blinded by a vision of the risen Lord preceded his healing and subsequent mission there (9:9–22). The hours of prayer kept by Cornelius and Peter prepared Peter to obey an unnerving vision that reversed the course of the infant church so she could welcome Gentiles in her life and mission (10:2–3, 9). In these episodes, as in Luke: no spirituality, no mission.

Peter's and Paul's Solitude: Subverting a Granite Impediment

The solitary prayers of Peter and Cornelius—accompanied by visions through which God guided them to each other—started a difficult transition towards inclusion of Gentiles in the church's life. Likewise, Paul's three days of solitude in Damascus (9:1–19), following his sudden encounter with Jesus on the Damascus road and his years in the Arabian desert (Gal 1:17),[32] proved critical to the church's radical redefinition of her mission. Wright describes this desert sojourn:

> Paul was stopped in his tracks, just as Elijah had been. Elijah, dejected and depressed, went off to Mount Sinai to meet his God afresh, to learn about the still small voice as well as the earthquake, wind and fire. Saul of Tarsus went off, probably to Sinai (he says "Arabia," which is where Sinai was) most likely for a similar private wrestling with the God he worshiped. (2002:9)

We can only surmise what occurred in Arabia, but certainly Paul had unhurried time to meditate on the Scriptures and rethink Israel's role in God's purposes in view of his encounter with the crucified and risen Jesus (Glasser 2003:289). Shockingly, as Paul had heard from Ananias in Damascus, the Gentiles were objects of divine love and could be counted within God's covenant people, and he, Paul, was being sent to them, not just to the Jews (Acts 9:15). John V. York says the idea of Gentile inclusion was "so odious to the Jewish audience" (2001:87) that they began shouting for Paul's death the minute he mentioned his divine call to the Gentiles (Acts 22:22).

So persistent was Jewish exclusion of Gentiles among the early Jewish followers of Jesus, that, without supernatural intervention given to Peter and Paul during their times of solitude and their subsequent mission activity, Christianity might have remained permanently trapped within Israel's truncated mission and the church might never have become a worldwide faith in its own right. God had to blast away at this granite impediment by calling Peter and Paul into solitude, where he spoke forcefully and acted visibly. Both men obeyed God even though it seemed counterintuitive and violated the most basic assumptions of first century Judaism.

Space/Time, Grace, Spiritual Practice, and Mission: Echoes and Contrasts in Luke and Acts[33]

The church's withdrawals for prayer in Acts both echo and modify Jesus's patterns in Luke:

---

32. Arthur Glasser thinks Paul stayed in Arabia several years (2003:289).
33. See Tables 21–23 and Appendices D and E.

1. *Space and Time.* Like Jesus, the church in Acts created time and space for God. They prayed and worshiped daily, for one hour, three days, ten days, late at night, on Sabbaths, and at midnight. Their prayer and worship occurred in a big upstairs room of a house, in private homes, in the temple, in synagogues, at the Jordan River, on a rooftop, at congregations' regular gathering places, on ships, and in prisons. In contrast, Jesus prayed more frequently in lonely desert places.

2. *Grace.* Both were accompanied by incidents of divine initiative and power: hearing God's voice, angel visitations, healing, and physical manifestations of God's Spirit or glory. Grace seeks Gentiles in Acts 15, but grace seeks wayward Israel—a lost sheep and a lost son—in Luke 15.

3. *Spiritual Practice.* In Luke, solitude and prayer enabled Jesus to hear his Father's voice as he redefined Israel's spirituality and mission. Solitude prepared Peter and Paul to hear God's welcoming heart for Gentiles and to redefine the church's mission. Jesus and the church share many practices: communion—prayer, fasting, worship, thanksgiving, pilgrimage, solitude, Scripture meditation/memory; community—fellowship, teaching; ministry—proclamation, healing, discernment, selecting leaders, hospitality, suffering love. Jesus's dying prayer for his executioners' forgiveness (Luke 23:34) is echoed in Stephen's martyrdom (Acts 7:60). In contrast, Acts has less solitary prayer and more communal prayer. Jesus's solitary prayer fueled the earlier stages of his movement while communal prayer fueled the church's early mission in Acts. Praying in community becomes more frequent as Luke unfolds while praying in solitude becomes more frequent as Acts unfolds.

4. *Mission Practice.* In Acts, every withdrawal for prayer is followed by mission in word and deed, just as in Luke. For both books, prayer preceded empowered mission to which significant opposition emerged, resulting in martyrdom. And in both, withdrawal for prayer preceded major transitions in ministry. Mission was both centrifugal and centripetal in both. In contrast, prayer in extended solitude preceded the beginning of Jesus's ministry in Luke while extended prayer in community preceded the beginning of the church's ministry in Acts. Jesus's first public ministry was centrifugal while the church's mission on the day of Pentecost was centripetal. Jesus's prayer in solitude preceded his

selection of the Twelve while communal prayer preceded leadership selection of Paul and Barnabas for the first missionary journey.

Table 23: Rhythms of Prayer and Mission: Parallels and Contrasts Between Luke and Acts

Luke	Acts
Extended prayer/worship in *solitude* preceding the beginning of Jesus's ministry in Galilee. John baptizes Jesus, and the Spirit falls on him and leads him to the desert. *Time*: 40+ day pilgrimage of prayer, Scripture, worship, fasting, and spiritual conflict with the devil *Place*: Jordan River/wilderness (3:21-22; 4:1-13) *Mission*: Jesus preaches good news to the poor, imprisoned, blind, and disenfranchised (4:14-41)	*Extended prayer/worship* in *community* preceding the beginning of church's ministry in Jerusalem. The Spirit baptizes the disciples as tongues of fire fall on them. *Time*: 10 days waiting in constant corporate prayer *Place*: Upper room where they were staying (Acts 1:12—2:4) *Mission*: Peter preaches Jesus's resurrection, repentance, and forgiveness; 5,000 were baptized (Acts 2:5-41)
Daily prayer/worship in *solitude* sustains Jesus in the initial expansion of his mission. *Times*: Early in the morning, regular (daily) *Places*: Lonely places (4:42; 5:16) *Mission*: Jesus's teaching, healing, compassion, and welcome to everyone draws crowds and followers as well as opposition *Transition*: His mission expands to new towns in Judea as opposition intensifies (4:43—5:15, 17-39)	*Daily prayer/worship* in *community* sustains the initial expansion of church in her mission. *Times*: Spontaneous, daily at set hours *Places*: Homes, the temple (Acts 2:42-47; 3:1-10; 4:24-32) *Mission*: Daily conversion, healing, and bold proclamation draw high esteem and persecution *Transition*: Church expands from Judea as persecution increases (first martyrdom) (Acts 2:47; 3:6—4:23; 6:7)
Extended prayer in *solitude* preceding Jesus's crucial leadership selection of the Twelve, training them and sending them on their first mission of preaching and healing. *Time*: All night in prayer waiting for discernment *Place*: On a mountain (6:12-16; 8:1—9:10)	*Ongoing prayer/worship* in *community* preceding the leadership selection of Paul and Silas for their first missionary journey and their later selection of elders. *Times*: Ongoing and regular, daily and weekly *Place*: Antioch (Acts 13:1-3)

Luke	Acts
Extended prayer in *community* practiced by Jesus and his disciples at the Transfiguration / Last Supper, leading to his *redeeming death*. *Places*: On a mountain / In the upper room *Times*: Unknown length, with Moses and Elijah appearing (9:28–36) / 5–6 hours (22:14–39) *Mission*: Corporate prayer at the Transfiguration and the Passover meal prepares Jesus for his journey to Jerusalem and his saving death*Transitions*: Jesus sets his face toward Jerusalem to die at the hands of the religious and political leaders. His mission flourishes after his death and resurrection. (9:22–24:51)	*Extended prayer* in *solitude* practiced by Paul / Peter leading to a *redirected mission* for the church. *Places*: In a house and at Sinai in Arabia (where Moses and Elijah had met God) / On a rooftop *Times*: 3 days and 2 years (Acts 9:1–19) / Beginning at noon, spontaneous (10:1–23; Gal 1:17) *Mission*: Paul and Peter begin the Gentile mission and persuade leaders in Jerusalem to transform the church's mission to include Gentiles, not just Jews*Transitions*: Solitude launches Paul's ministry and formes him spiritually and theologically in Arabia. Solitude helps Peter welcome Gentiles and prevail at the Jerusalem council. Gentile mission expands amidst persecution. (Acts 9:20—16:40)

The Apostolic Fathers

What little we know about the church's growth right after the New Testament[34] (especially from 90 to 120) depends heavily on a collection of writings that, by the late seventeenth century, became known as the Apostolic Fathers. While Acts is primarily narrative, the Apostolic Fathers are mostly instructional. The term grew out of the common belief that these writings were authored by leaders who either knew the original apostles or sat under their teaching.[35] The Apostolic Fathers

---

34. In Wright's historical reconstruction of the early church, he identifies ten fixed historical points from 30 to 150 AD accepted by most historians: 30—the crucifixion of Jesus; 49—Christians expelled from Rome by Claudius; 49–51—Paul resides in Corinth, then Ephesus; 62—James's martyrdom in Jerusalem; 64—persecution by Nero in Rome after the fire; 70—Jerusalem's fall; c. 90—Jesus's family members investigated by Domitian; c. 110–114—persecutions by Pliny in Bithynia; c. 110–117—Ignatius's letters and martyrdom; and c. 155—Polycarp's martyrdom. Wright faults scholars for widespread generalizations about the early church that ignore or distort these fixed points (1992:341–58).

35. According to Jefford, Harder, and Amezaga, the origin of the term traces back to J. B. Cotelier, a seventeenth century patristics authority (1996:1). Jefford et al. covers the

thus had great influence among later patristic church leaders (see Table 24 below).³⁶ Simon Tugwell, an authority on Christian spirituality, describes the Apostolic Fathers:

> They reflect a variety of very different situations in different Christian [sic] communities. Clement, writing from Rome in about 95, addresses himself to the church in Corinth, which was torn by schism; the Didache and the letter ascribed (falsely) to Barnabas may come from Palestine or Syria or from Egypt, and the major problem they deal with is posed by the temptation to adopt Jewish practices. Ignatius flashes across the scene on his way to be martyred in Rome early in the second century. Hermas was called to intervene in a crisis in the Roman church, probably towards the middle of the second century, precipitated by the relentless perfectionism of some teachers in the church who disallowed the possibility of any further repentance for Christians [sic] who had fallen into sin (1984:2).

Tugwell's description here omits writings usually included in this collection: *2 Clement* (*2 Clem.*), the *Letter of Polycarp to the Philippians* (*Pol. Phil.*), the *Martyrdom of Polycarp* (*Mart. Pol.*), the *Epistle to Diognetus* (*Diogn.*), and sometimes the *Fragments of Papias* (*Pap. Frag.*).³⁷

As Tugwell observes, the period in which the Apostolic Fathers were written was a time in which the church had no universally recognized canon. Her institutional structures, though more developed than in Acts, were still rudimentary. Although local deacons, elders, and bishops were accorded increasing authority, itinerant teachers with no organizational status were still prevalent. Though the church was distinguishing herself from Judaism and gnosticism and responding to the new challenges of philosophies, religions, and governments in the locals where she had spread, many elements of orthodox theology were not yet fully defined. Tugwell thinks heretical versions of Christianity may have outnumbered what we consider orthodox groups during this period (1984:2). In his introduction to *The Apostolic Fathers*,³⁸ Michael

---

Apostolic Fathers' sources, forms, dates, settings, occasions, authors, traits, and uses of Scripture in *The Apostolic Fathers* (1996).

36. The patristic period of church history is generally considered to span from the second to the fifth centuries.

37. Jefford et al. (1996) excludes the *Fragments of Papias*, whereas Holmes (1999) includes them.

38. The best revised edition of the classic translation of the Apostolic Fathers by J.

Table 24: Church Fathers Who Read the Apostolic Fathers (Adapted from Jefford et al. 1996:4–5)

Writings	Irenaeus	Clement of Alexandria	Tertullian	Hippolytus	Origen	Eusebius	Athanasius	Jerome
1 Clement Early canonical status	✓	✓	✓		✓	✓		✓
Didache Teaching of the Twelve		✓				✓	✓	✓
Letter of Barnabas		✓	✓		✓	✓		✓
Letters of Ignatius	✓				✓	✓	✓	
Letter of Polycarp to Philippians	✓		✓			✓		
Martyrdom of Polycarp			✓		✓	✓		
Shepherd of Hermas early canonical status	✓	✓	✓		✓	✓	✓	✓
2 Clement to Corinthians, early canonical status								
Letter to Diognetus		✓						

W. Holmes argues that from this diversity grew a clearer idea of the limits of the faith (1999:81).

The primary research question for my study of the texts (shown in Table 24 above) is, how does space and time for God relate to mission in the Apostolic Fathers? This question subsumes several others. What spiritual practices did the apostolic fathers portray? How did they demarcate time and space for these? What mission practices did they portray? After reading the Apostolic Fathers in light of these questions, I was struck by their frequent mention of both spiritual and mission practices. However, the spiritual practices mentioned are chiefly communal rather than solitary—a pattern we have observed in the first part of Acts. A major factor for this seems to be the apostolic fathers' oft-repeated concern that the church maintain her unity in the face of threats.[39] Although solitary practices appear rarely compared with the mention of communal ones, the apostolic fathers do teach solitary spiritual practice, which is key for my main argument.

A Case for Solitary Spiritual Practice in the Apostolic Fathers

In this section, I cite six evidences for solitary practice in the Apostolic Fathers—one narrative, four didactic, and one apocalyptic (*Shepherd of Hermas*). I begin with the narrative.

1. *Narrative Evidence.* In at least one case, a withdrawal for solitary as well as communal prayer is described in the only narrative work among these writings, the *Martyrdom of Polycarp*. Polycarp, the bishop of Smyrna (70–c. 155), had been seen by Irenaeus in his youth.[40] Wright considers Polycarp's martyrdom one of the ten fixed historical points of late antiquity (1992:346–348)[41] and most historians view

---

P. Lightfoot and J. R. Harmer is that of Michael W. Holmes (1999), which I use here. Of this edition, Jefford writes, "the text undoubtedly should be recognized as a superior collection of materials when placed in comparison with the commonly used edition of the apostolic fathers that was published by Kirsopp Lake" (1995 83).

39. For example, see Ignatius's instructions to the Ephesians on singing hymns to Christ in unanimity (1999:4.1–2), his instructions on unity to the Magesians (1999:7.1–2), and also Clement of Rome's teaching (*1 Clem.* 46.1—47.7).

40. In *Against the Heresies* (1956:3.3), Irenaeus portrayed Polycarp as a true pastor and teacher of the apostolic tradition because he had been taught by the apostles and had talked to other eyewitnesses of Jesus.

41. Wright thinks these fixed points are woefully unaccounted for when most historians try to fill in the huge gaps of early church history (1992:341, 345; see also

the *Martyrdom of Polycarp* positively. The work was probably written by believers in Smyrna who had seen Polycarp's death and wanted to preserve his memory and legacy (Jefford et al. 1996:86–88). Polycarp's solitary prayers feature prominently in this work, as does his hospitality to those who arrested him not long after he had gone reluctantly into hiding.

> So he withdrew to a farm not far distant from the city [Smyrna], and there he stayed with a few companions, doing nothing else night and day except praying for everyone and for the churches throughout the world, for this was his constant habit. And while he was praying he fell into a trance three days before his arrest, and he saw his pillow being consumed by fire. And he turned and said to those who were with him: "It is necessary that I be burned alive..." [As the search party neared his cottage] though he still could have escaped from there to another place, he refused, saying, "May God's will be done." So when he heard that they had arrived, he went and talked with them, while those who were present marveled in his age and his composure. ... [He] ordered that a table be set for them to eat and drink as much as they wished at that hour, and he asked them to grant him an hour so that he might pray undisturbed. When they consented, he stood and prayed, so full of the grace of God that for two hours he was unable to stop speaking; those who heard him were amazed, and many regretted that they had come after such a godly old man. (*Mart. Pol.* 1999:5.1–2; 7.1–3)[42]

In this passage Polycarp and his companions practice extended communal prayer, which lasted a number of days—as was "his constant habit" (*Mart. Pol.* 1999:5.1). Polycarp's intercession was interrupted by a vision, typical of mystical encounters that sometimes attend sustained prayer. The vision, which predicted his own martyrdom, was a form of solitary prayer because Polycarp, and not his companions, fell into a visionary trance.[43] He also practiced solitary prayer after his arrest and

---

n. 34 above). There are hagiographic details that present the bishop quite favorably, which raises questions about its reliability. But the dominant view is that "compared to many of the later accounts of martyrdom the story is told with a good deal of restraint, and may be judged to provide a generally reliable account of Polycarp's martyrdom" (Holmes 1999:224–25).

42. Here and elsewhere 1999 indicates Holmes's edition of the Apostolic Fathers.

43. This solitary form of hearing God is to be distinguished from the voice he heard in the stadium, which was communal because it was heard by others (*Mart. Pol.*

betrayal by a Christian slave. "So full of the grace of God" was Polycarp that he prayed alone for two hours, interceding for all the churches and people he knew (1999:7.3).[44] As with Jesus the night before his death, Polycarp's extended prayers prepared him for his coming trial, death, and witness.

Upon entering the stadium, where he would be martyred, he heard a voice from heaven saying, "Be strong, Polycarp, and act like a man" (*Mart. Pol.* 1999:9.1), which surely inspired his response to the magistrate, who commanded him to revile Christ and swear an oath to Caesar. Polycarp replied:

> "For eighty-six years I have been his servant, and he has done me no wrong. How can I blaspheme my King who saved me"?
> .... As he spoke these and many other words, he was inspired with courage and joy, and his face was filled with grace, so that not only did he not collapse in fright at the things which were said to him, but on the contrary the proconsul was astonished. (1999:9.3; 12.1)

Polycarp's life ended in prayer and worship. "I bless you because you have considered me worthy of this day and hour, that I might receive a place among the number of the martyrs in the cup of your Christ," he prayed. His final words were, "I praise you, I bless you, I glorify you, through the eternal and heavenly High Priest, Jesus Christ, your beloved Son, through whom to you with him and the Holy Spirit be glory both now and for the ages to come. Amen" (*Mart. Pol.* 1999:14.2).

2. *The Didiche.* The next piece of evidence for solitary prayer is found in the *Didache* (teaching), which contains some of the earliest non-canonical instructions for baptismal candidates and church leaders. It was compiled gradually between 70 and 150 in either Syria, Palestine, Egypt, or Asia Minor.[45] The *Didache* implicitly teaches solitary prayer in its inclusion of the golden thread of prayer, fasting, and almsgiving: "'Bless those who curse you,' and 'pray for your enemies,' and 'fast for those who persecute you.' . . . 'Give to everyone who asks you, and do not

---

1999:9.1).

44. Although some of his captors heard Polycarp's prayer, I consider this to be solitary prayer, since he wanted to pray undisturbed and his captors obviously did not pray with him.

45. See the overviews of the *Didache* by Jefford et al. (1996:32–52) and Holmes (1999:246–48).

demand it back'" (*Did.* 1999:1:3, 5). Here spiritual and mission practices merge. Even inward prayer and fasting move outward towards enemies and persecutors—part of a mission spirituality for believers wanting to be faithful witnesses to Jesus in the face of persecution and possible martyrdom. But were fasting and prayer to be practiced in solitude as well as with believers? Yes! The *Didache* instructs believers to fast on Wednesdays and Fridays, not as "the hypocrites"—referring to Jews who fasted on Mondays and Thursdays (*Did.* 1999:8.1). To fast twice a week could not have been done exclusively with others and thus involved some solitude. Immediately after this instruction we find Matthew's version of the Lord's Prayer (1999:8.2) followed by the command, "Pray like this three times a day" (1999:8.3).[46] To follow this practice required solitary prayer some of the time, even while in "the daily presence of the saints" (1999:4.2).

3. *Dependence on Matthew*. Another piece of evidence for solitary prayer in the Apostolic Fathers is their strong dependence on Matthew's Gospel (and his sources). Michael Holmes's index of biblical references shows that Matthew's material appears in the Apostolic Fathers sixty times—more than twice the total of the next most frequently quoted New Testament book, Luke, which is cited thirty times (1999:604).[47] The apostolic fathers were very familiar with the only biblical passage in which Jesus explicitly commands solitude: the Sermon on the Mount. According to Jefford et al., the *Didache* alone contains thirty references to Matthew, ten of which refer to Matthew 5–7, with four allusions to Matthew 6:1–18[48]—the specific section in which Jesus commanded solitary prayer and fasting. The author(s) of the *Didache* clearly knew Jesus's command, "But whenever you pray, go into your room and shut the door and pray to your Father who is in secret" (Matt 6:6). Readers

---

46. Reflecting a consensus, E. Glenn Hinson holds that this occurred at nine, noon, and three (1996:81).

47. Following Luke, there are twenty-five references to 1 Corinthians, twenty-one to Acts, seventeen each to John and Mark. Philemon, 2 Peter, 2 and 3 John do not appear in the Apostolic Fathers (Holmes 1999:604–5).

48. The four allusions to Matt 6:1–18, according to Jefford et al., are: (1) *Did.* 8.1, which refers to fasting and hypocrites in Matt 6:16–18, 20; (2) *Did.* 8.2a, which refers to praying and hypocrites in Matt 6:5; (3) *Did.* 8:2b, which refers to the Lord's Prayer in Matt 6:9–13; and (4) *Did.* 15.4, which refers to fasting, prayer, and almsgiving in Matt 6:1–18 (1996:48).

were expected to recall and obey these words in the instruction, "As for your prayers ... do them all just as you find in the gospel of our Lord" (*Did.* 1999:15.4).

4. *Letter of 1 Clement.* Some of the earliest evidence for solitary prayer outside the New Testament is found in *1 Clement*, which is devoted to the issue of church unity. In about 95–97, leaders in the church at Rome led by Clement[49] wrote a letter to the Corinthian church about a rebellion there that had succeeded in deposing her leaders (Holmes 1999:22–23). "Let us therefore root this out quickly, and let us fall down before the Master and pray to him with tears, that he may be merciful and be reconciled to us" (*1 Clem.* 48.1). "Love knows nothing of schisms ... love does everything in harmony.... without love nothing is pleasing to God. In love the Master received us" (*1 Clem.* 49.5–6). Then Clement urges each one involved "to confess his transgressions rather than to harden his heart" (*1 Clem.* 51.3). He cites the dire consequences of Israel hardening her heart in rebellion and reminds them that Moses went to the mountain to humbly fast for forty days and nights (*1 Clem.* 53.2). This served as a warning to the troublemakers. But it could also have suggested to the presbyters that they, like Moses, were called to fast and humbly intercede in extended solitude to divert judgment. "What mighty love! ... [Moses] asks forgiveness for the multitude, or demands that he himself also be wiped out with them" (*1 Clem.* 53.5).

5. *Letters of Ignatius.* Early evidence for solitary prayer is also found in the letters of Ignatius, bishop of Antioch, written in chains to various churches on his way to martyrdom in Rome (110–17)—another of Wright's fixed historical points of history in late antiquity (cf. n. 34). Writing to the Trallians (*Trall.*), Ignatius claims that his chains, which presumably confined him to long periods of solitude, actually called the Trallians to unity and corporate prayer. "My chains, which I carry around for the sake of Jesus Christ while praying that I might reach God [martyrdom], exhort you: persevere in your unanimity and in prayer with one another" (Ign. *Trall.* 1999:12.2). To the Ephesians (*Eph*), he wrote more explicitly. "For if the prayer of one or two has such power,

---

49. Later tradition says that Clement was bishop of Rome, which is unlikely. By the end of the first century, the office of one bishop had not yet replaced the plurality of leaders in Rome (Holmes 1999:23).

how much more that of the bishop together with the whole church!" (Ign. *Eph* 1999:5.2). Here Ignatius argues that because solitary prayer is effective (as is praying with another), prayer with the bishop and the entire church is even more so.[50] For Ignatius, the power of corporate prayer trumps that of solitary prayer, but in commending the former, he is also advocating the latter.

6. *Shepherd of Hermas*. Strong evidence for solitary prayer abounds in the *Shepherd of Hermas*, written in two phases and circulated separately by an unknown author in Rome (Holmes 1999:330). Its hopeful message countered a perfectionist school that taught that repentance for post-baptismal sin was impossible—a view that seriously threatened the church in Rome by the mid second century. The first phase—chapters 1–24—consists of four visions (*Vis.*) given to Hermas while he prayed in solitude,[51] written in the late first century[52] in the style of Jewish apocalyptic writings.[53]

The second phase (chapters 25–114) was written sometime in the middle of the second century. The fifth vision begins the second section, introducing the angel of repentance, who gives Hermas twelve mandates (*Man.*) and ten similitudes (*Sim.*) that offer repentance after baptism. These are given to Hermas after he had prayed and sat down on his bed, presumably in solitude (*Herm. Vis.* 1999:5.1). The revelations, shown in Table 25 below, call Hermas to repent of deficient parenting, deficient fasting, and a deficient heart. Similitude 9 warns of deficient solitude after describing its joys. In a time of solitude with the Spirit, Hermas experiences joy, graciousness, play, silence, sleep, unceasing prayer, and sustained meditation on the word (*Herm. Sim.* 1999:9.10.5–9.11.9). The

50. Ignatius's letters urging unity with the bishop argue for an early appearance of an episcopal form of governance in some cities—with leadership consisting of one bishop, the presbytery (elders), and deacons. Other cities such as Rome only had elders and deacons during the time of Clement (see n. 49 above).

51. See *Herm. Vis.* (1999:2.1.1–2; 2.2.1; 3.1.2–5; 4.1.3–7; 5.1–7)—i.e., parts of Visions 2, 3, 4, and 5.

52. The early dating for the first section comes from the mention of Clement (8.3)—maybe Clement of Rome—and a less developed church structure than described in the second section (Jefford et al. 1996:139–41).

53. Holmes gives the typical features of an apocalypse: "(1) a revelation from God, (2) usually in the form of a vision or dream, (3) often given through a mediator, (4) who provides an interpretation of the vision, (5) whose contents usually concern future events, especially the end times" (1999:329–30).

Table 25: Solitary Prayer and Mission in the Shepherd of Hermas

Shepherd's Message to Hermas:
Hope—repentance for post-baptismal sin is possible! Counters second century perfectionism group in Rome, which denied this.

Section 1, Chapters 1–24

- Date: probably late first century
- Style: four visions like Jewish apocalyptic writings (Holmes 1999:139–141)

Four visions, all given to Hermas while praying in various solitary places	Repent of deficient parenting	*Vision 1*: A woman appears, claiming God is angry with Hermas for failing to confront his children's spiritual rebellion. He is to instruct them in hope of their repentance and inclusion "with the saints in the books of life" (*Herm. Vis.* 1999:1.3.1–2). How was he to do this? "For just as the blacksmith by hammering at his work completes the task he wants to do, *so also does the daily righteous word conquer all evil*" (*Herm. Vis.* 1999:1.3.2).
		The woman—an allegory for the church (Jeffords et al. 1996:154)—reflects the priority of mission to children and family as the center for spiritual formation in Rome in the late first century. For parents to daily teach children the word, they themselves would need to absorb it in church and in solitary meditation.

Section 2, Chapters 25–114

- Date: 100–150
- Style: mandates like Jewish Hellenistic homilies, similitudes like allegorical similes of *1 Enoch* (Holmes 1999:330)

One vision, twelve mandates, Ten parables-similitudes, all given to Hermas after prayer, probably in solitude	Repent of deficient fast	*Vision 5*: Angel tells Hermas to journal revelations so he can tell others.
		Similitude 5: Parable given to Hermas during extended solitude on a mountain while he was fasting and giving thanks to God. But his fast is deficient. Hermas learns that *a perfect and acceptable fast involves cleansing from all evil at the heart level* (*Herm. Sim.* 1999:5.1.5) and calculating the cost of the food from which one is fasting (only bread and water were allowed) and *giving it to orphans, widows, and the needy* (1999:5.3.7–9). The Shepherd teaches Hermas that solitude and fasting without compassionate care for others are insufficient. Here again we see the *golden thread of fasting, prayer, and almsgiving* woven together as they were in Matthew 6:1–18 and *Didache* (1999:1.3, 5).

	Repent of deficient heart	*Mandate 9:* "*Turn to the Lord with all your heart* and ask of him unhesitatingly, and you will know his extraordinary compassion because he will never abandon you, but will fulfill your soul's request" (*Herm. Man.* 1999:9.2). Compassionate acts flow from experiencing God's cleansing and love in prayer. God's extraordinary compassion for all is reflected in the Shepherd's commands regarding widows, orphans, and those in need (*Herm. Man.* 1999:8; *Herm. Sim.* 1999:2.8; 5.3.5). It is also seen elsewhere, such as helping God's servants in distress, hospitality, peacemaking, "respecting the elderly," encouraging the "sick at heart," restoring those who have repented, forgiving debts (*Herm. Man.* 1999:8.10) and rescuing everyone in distress, especially the suicidal (1999:10.4.2–3). In short, fruitful and faithful believers are "*always having compassion for every person, and from their labors they supplied every person's needs without reproach and without hesitation*" (1999:9.24.2). With compassion like this, even though only partially practiced by a part of the church, it is no wonder the early church grew.

solitude lasted from late afternoon or early evening until 8 o'clock the next morning, when the Shepherd returned (1999:9.11.7). When asked what he had eaten for dinner, Hermas told the Shepherd, "I dined on the words of the Lord the whole night" (1999:9.11.8). Later in Similitude 9, the Shepherd warns Hermas of a kind of barren solitude typical of some who absented themselves from contact with believers. Inasmuch as "they do not associate with God's servants but remain alone, they destroy their own souls" (1999:9.26.3). Such a solitude actually denies the Lord.

Time and Space for God Related to Mission in the Apostolic Fathers

The case for Christian solitary practice in the gaps of church history between 80 and 160 is crucial if later Christian spiritualities did more than just import Platonist solitary contemplation.[54] Yes, Christians did rightfully draw from Greek contemplative practices, but a dis-

---

54. Tugwell suggests that Ignatius's comments in his *Letter to the Ephesians* concerning silence and unity hints at a kind of mystical teaching typical of later spiritual writers that were influenced by neoplatonism—a loose term referring more or less to the renewal and influence of Plato's ideas beyond his own age (1986:3–4).

tinctly Judeo-Christian tradition of solitary meditation and prayer can be traced, as I have shown, from Jesus through the apostles to the apostolic fathers. So how did space and time devoted to these solitary practices and corporate ones relate to mission in deed and word in the Apostolic Fathers?

DAILY PRACTICES

The daily spiritual practices taught by the apostolic fathers were intricately bound to the mission activities they commended. We have seen how prayer, fasting, and almsgiving were closely interwoven in the *Didache* and *Shepherd of Hermas* (see Table 25 above). The three appear in the same verse of *2 Clement*,[55] the earliest surviving non-canonical sermon whose author and location remain unknown (Holmes 1999:102). *1 Clement*, the *Letter of Barnabas*, and the *Letter of Polycarp to the Philippians* also mention these three practices, but not in the same verse (see Table 26 below). Praying and alleviating the physical needs of the poor (almsgiving) were to be practiced daily, while fasting was to be semi-weekly (cf. below). The apostolic fathers command inner and outer practices.

1. *Inner Practices.* Daily prayer was to be frequent (Ign. *Eph* 1999:13.1), unceasing (Ign. *Pol.* 1999:1.3; Ign. *Eph* 1999:10.1), accompanied by intercession (Ign. *Pol.* 1999:1.3), thanksgiving (Ign. *Eph* 1999:13.1), and Scripture meditation and confession (*1 Clem.* 2.1–3). Praying the Lord's Prayer three times daily was likely widespread among Christians in this era, like daily fellowship (*Did.* 8.1, 4.2; *Barn.* 19.10).[56]

2. *Outer Practices.* Believers were to be ready at anytime to care for the tangible needs of others—"always having compassion for every person" (*Herm. Sim.* 1999:9.24.2)—while those ignoring orphans and widows were censured (*Barn.* 1999.20.2). Though the apostolic fathers emphasized daily acts of social compassion more than verbal witness, evangelism was still stressed as a daily part of the "way of light" described in the *Letter of Barnabas* (*Barn.* 19.10). This work, probably written in

---

55. *2 Clement* says, "Fasting is better than prayer, while charitable giving is better than both" (16.4).
56. For the liturgical origins of the daily offices of prayer, see Bradshaw (1992: 185–92).

Alexandria between 70 and 135,[57] instructs, "remember the day of judgment night and day, and you shall seek out on a daily basis the presence of the saints ... laboring in word and going out to encourage, and endeavoring to save a soul by the word" (*Barn.* 19.10). Ignatius writes, "I urge you, by the grace with which you are clothed ... to exhort all people, that they may be saved.... Devote yourself to unceasing prayers ..." (Ign. *Pol.* 1999:1.2–3). Notice Ignatius's emphasis on grace here. To the Ephesians he wrote, "Pray continually for the rest of mankind as well, that they may find God, for there is in them hope for repentance. Therefore allow them to be instructed by you, at least by your deeds" (Ign. *Eph* 1999:10.1). Daily compassion is mentioned by all nine apostolic fathers, whereas only four mention proclamation—five if we include martyrdom (see Table 26, right column).

To summarize, the daily inner disciplines commended by the apostolic fathers included prayer, confession, thanksgiving, praise, meditation on the word, intercession, fellowship with other believers, and teaching the word at home. The daily outer disciplines included acts of compassion to all in need, evangelism, and suffering joyously for the sake of Christ. And these were by grace.

Weekly Practices

The Eucharist was to be practiced every week, preceded by confession of sins (*Did.* 1999:14.1). These gatherings still occurred in homes during this era, but already the Eucharist had become separated from the breaking of bread and love feasts observed daily by Christians in the book of Acts (2:46). Weekly disciplines included fasting, practiced on Wednesdays and Fridays (*Did.* 1999:8.1)—which, we have seen, was part of the golden thread of fasting, prayer, and almsgiving. When the apostolic fathers wrote, evidently Christianity was still predominantly a way of life, rather than an institution centered in weekly gatherings in church buildings, which was characteristic of the third and fourth centuries.[58]

---

57. "Writing at a time when the level of antagonism between church and synagogue sill ran high, the anonymous author of *Letter of Barnabas* ... seeks to show by means of an allegorical interpretation of Scripture that Christians are the true and intended heirs of God's covenant" (Holmes 1999:270).

58. This may explain the scarcity of references to weekly practices in the Apostolic Fathers. But we must beware of sweeping generalities. Based on new Jewish and early

Extended and Occasional Practices

The Apostolic Fathers also mention disciplines practiced occasionally and over extended periods of time. I have mentioned Clement's allusion to Moses's forty days of solitude, fasting, and interceding (1 Clem. 43.5; 53.2), and how extended times with God related to mission in the *Shepherd of Hermas* and *Martyrdom of Polycarp*. The latter depicts Polycarp's bold witness and love for his persecutors, which emanated from hearing God's voice and receiving a vision during an extended time (a number of days) of continuous prayer and intercession (*Mart. Pol.* 1999:5.1—15.2). Hermas spent fifteen days fasting in extended solitude with the Lord before he receives the third vision (*Herm. Vis.* 1999:3). The extended meditation described in Similitude 9 lasted an entire night (*Herm. Sim.* 1999:9.11.1–9) and preceded an exposition of the gospel that must have been typical of the Roman church in the mid scond century (1999:9.12.1–8).

Silence, a discipline not yet mentioned, was most likely practiced daily, weekly, and certainly in extended times. Ignatius of Antioch tells the Ephesians that the mysteries of the Incarnation, virgin birth, and Christ's death done in God's silence are to be proclaimed loudly (Ign. *Eph* 1999:19:1). Hearing the silence of Jesus is connected to the true possession of his word and any subsequent proclamation of it (1999:15.2). Furthermore, "it is better to be silent and be real, than to talk and not be real." The things Jesus did in silence "are worthy of the Father" (1999:15.1). Thus, Ignatius commends the discipline of silence in our meditation upon God and he connects this silence with outward ministry in deed and word. I should note that based on this letter some have suggested the *Letters of Ignatius* exhibit traces of Hellenistic Gnosticism—a view that has been undermined by recent scholarship.[59]

The apostolic fathers commended many of the daily, weekly, and extended inner rhythms of spiritual life, especially corporate ones, and mission practices in both deed and word that were practiced by Jesus

---

Christian studies, Bradshaw argues for a more variegated development of Christian worship than had been thought (1992:185–205; 1999:24–42).

59. "The character of Ignatius's debt to Hellenistic culture is much debated. Gnostic affinities have been alleged on the basis of mythological elements in such passages as Ign. *Eph* 19 or the themes of 'oneness' and 'silence.' But recent investigations have indicated that these elements are also found in the wider popular culture" (Holmes 1999:133).

Table 26: Space, Time, Spirituality, and Mission in the Apostolic Fathers

Text	Spiritual Practices	Space/Time Demarcated	Mission Practices
1 Clement	Memorize/meditate on the word Contemplate the cross (2.1; 7.4) Prayer of confession (2.3) Confession (51.3) Praise/thanks (35.12; 38.4) Moses's intercessory fast (53.1–5)	Mountain/40 days	*Deed*: Mourn for neighbors' sins, considering them as one's own (2.6) Hospitality (1.2; 10.7; 11.1) Giving to poor (38.2)
Didache	Lord's Prayer (8.2–3) Pray for enemies (1.3) Fast (1.3; 7.4; 8.1) Communal property (4.8) Fellowship (4.2; 16.2) Eucharist (9.1–10.7; 14.1) Confession (4.14; 14.1) Hospitality (11.3; 12.2)	3 times daily at 9 am, noon, and 3 pm 2 times weekly on Wed. and Fri., and 1 or 2 days before baptism Daily, frequently On the Lord's own day On the Lord's own day 1–2 days for prophets	*Deed*: Almsgiving (1.5) Mercy on the poor (5.2) Baptism (7.1–4) Give if prophet asks money for others, not himself
Letter of Barnabas	Fasting (4.7; 14.2) Baptism (11.1–11) Extended time—Moses (4.7) Prayer/confession (19.12) Fellowship (19.10)	On mountain/40 days Daily	*Deed & Word*: Share all with neighbor (19.8), orphans, widows (20.2) Evangelism (19.10)
Letters of Ignatius -*Eph.* -*Magn.* -*Phld.* -*Rom.* -*Smyrn.* -*Trall.* -*Pol.*	Solitary/communal prayer (*Eph.* 5.2) Intercession for unbelievers (*Eph.* 10.1) Silence (*Eph.* 19.1; 15.1–3) Communal prayer (*Magn.* 7.1–2; *Trall* 12.2) Eucharist (*Eph.* 20.2; *Phld.* 4) Prayer (1.3)	 Continually More frequently Unceasing	*Deed & Word*: Martyrdom (*Trall.* 4.2; 12.2; *Rom* 6.3) Care for prisoners, hungry, orphans, and widows (*Smyrn.* 6.2) Word and deed (*Pol.* 1.2)
Letter of Polycarp to the Philippians	Prayer, fasting (7:2) Intercession (12:3)		*Deed*: Sick, poor, widows, orphan (6.1)

Martyrdom of Polycarp	Extended communal and solitary prayer (5.1–2; 7.3) Obedience unto death (9.1–11.3) Worship, prayer (14.1–3)	Number of days/At farm cottage/ 2 hours	Deed & Word: Hospitality to enemies (7.2) Testimony of Jesus, martyrdom
Shepherd of Hermas	Fasting, extended solitude Confession, repentance Prayer, thanks throughout	15 days before 3rd vision Days and all night Daily	Deed & Word: Social justice Teaching children in the word
2 Clement	Praise from the heart (9:10) Prayer, fasting (16.4)		Deed: Almsgiving (16.4)

and the apostles. They accorded acts of compassion and justice greater attention and priority than proclamation of the gospel, though the latter is mentioned by five apostolic fathers.

Grace, Spiritual Practice, and Mission in the Apostolic Fathers

My study of the Apostolic Fathers has found them in unanimous agreement with the New Testament idea of initiating and transforming grace. As in the Synoptics and Acts, God took initiative in speaking and sending divine guidance, power, visions, angels, and miracles in relation to spiritual practice and mission. We see this in *Martyrdom of Polycarp* and *Hermas*. The Apostolic Fathers teach the need of empowering grace for prayer, obedience, encouragement, wisdom, protection, and evangelism. Ignatius wrote, "I urge you, by the grace with which you are clothed, to press on in your race and to exhort all people, that they may be saved" (Ign. *Pol.* 1999:1.2–3). Polycarp is said to have "stood and prayed, so full of the grace of God that for two hours he was unable to stop speaking" (*Mart. Pol.* 1999:7.1–2). Clement of Rome prayed:

> We ask you, Master, to be "our Helper and Protector." Save those among us who are in distress; have mercy on the humble; raise up the fallen; show yourself to those in need; heal the godless; turn back those of your people who wander; feed the hungry; release our prisoners; raise up the weak; comfort the discouraged. "Let all the nations know that you are the only God," that Jesus Christ is your servant, and that "we are your people and the sheep of your pasture." (*1 Clem.* 59.4)

However, the apostolic fathers do drift away from another aspect of grace in the New Testament: Paul's declaration that nothing can separate believers from God's redeeming love (Rom 8:37–38)[60] and John's assurance that divine love and eternal life unambiguously belong to believers (1 John 4:16–18; 5:11–13). They depart from accepting grace and do not teach full assurance of salvation and forgiveness in the way Paul and John did. Rather, such certainty is suspended until after believers have attained various virtues or endured suffering or persecution.[61] At least two apostolic fathers taught that their martyrdom would attain the resurrection of their bodies.[62] Despite a few references that imply full assurance of salvation in the present, most deny the possibility.[63] This drift is especially evident in the *Shepherd of Hermas*. Though the Shepherd's long similitude of the willows offers hope of repentance for post-baptismal sin, it teaches merit and penance as evidence of true repentance and as a safeguard for moral virtue (*Herm. Sim.* 1999:8:1–11). "Perhaps the one theme most widely associated with the Shepherd is that of penance" (Jefford 1996:144). The Shepherd's views gained wide credence by the second century as Clement of Alexandria, Iranaeus, and Origin—in his early writings—accorded it scriptural status (Holmes 1999:329). By the year 207, after initially embracing Hermas, Tertullian described him as the "shepherd of harlots" because of his relative laxity compared to the Montanists with whom he had affiliated (Holmes 1999:329). Historian James Bradley notes that Tertullian established the theological foundation for Western medieval piety, in which penance was pivotal. Bradley

---

60. Holmes thinks that a great distance developed between the theological framework undergirding the piety of the mid second century Roman church at the time of Hermas and that of the Roman church in Paul's day, and that the situation in Rome at the time of Clement lay somewhere in between the two (1999:329). Clement seems closer to Paul than Hermas, based on *1 Clement* 32:4, quoted in n. 63 below.

61. One example of suspended certainty is, "So do you think that the sins of those who repent are forgiven immediately? Certainly not! But the one who repents must torment his own soul and be extremely humble in everything he does and be afflicted with a variety of afflictions; and if he endures the afflictions that come upon him, then assuredly the one who created all things and endowed them with power will be moved with compassion and will give some healing" (*Herm. Sim.* 1999:7.4).

62. See Ignatius (*Rom* 1999:2.2, 4.3) and Polycarp (*Mart. Pol.* 1999:14.2).

63. See *1 Clement* 32:4, which says we "are not justified through ourselves or through our wisdom or understanding or piety or works which we have done in holiness of heart, but through faith, by which the almighty God has justified all who have existed from the beginning."

thinks Tertullian went terribly wrong, but we should understand him in light of the persecution threatening the church of his day. Whenever the church suffers for the faith, she generally becomes more rigid and legalistic for intelligible reasons (Bradley 1997:tape 2). If fellow believers renounced Christ, sacrificed to Caesar, had sacred writings destroyed, and betrayed fellow believers who were then imprisoned or killed, how should the faithful relate to the unfaithful who are now penitent? For the church to survive, fellowship often was denied to these. Debate ensued as to how, when, or if these unfaithful could be allowed back into the fellowship. As persecution forced the church to meet in secret, a lengthy period of preparation for baptism emerged, in part, to screen out those who might prove to be unfaithful. In this context, penance became an important means of demonstrating fidelity and genuineness of one's repentance and faith (Bradley 1997:tape 2).

The shift away from accepting grace, seen in the apostolic fathers and even more in Tertullian, became a fixture in the Latin wing of the church.[64] This split between accepting and transforming grace has plagued the Western church ever since. She has tended to embrace one side of the divide at the expense of the other rather than holding both in necessary tension.

A Word about Origen, Antony, and Benedict

> The grace of God, immense and beyond measure, showered by Him on men through Jesus Christ, the minister to us of this superabundant grace, and through the co-operation of the Spirit, makes possible through His will things which are to our rational and mortal nature impossible.... Yet this impossibility becomes possible through the overflowing grace of God. (Origen 1954a:1)

These are Origen's first words in his classic text *Prayer*,[65] which reflects his belief that transforming grace is key to spiritual practices—much

---

64. The Latin system of jurisprudence may have been a key factor in moving the church towards this system in which penance and merit played such a key role. Wright asserts that by the sixteenth century the Protestant reformers read back into Paul's idea of the righteousness of God the practices of the Latin law court, while Paul was drawing from the legal traditions of the Hebrew law court (1997a:100–110).

65. I am using John O'Meara's translation of *Prayer* and *Exhortation to Martyrdom* (1954), which I prefer to Alistair Stewart-Sykes's newer translation (2004). References

like the apostolic fathers before him. But he, like most of them, did not teach accepting grace. Rather, he tied assurance to penance and merit, as can be seen in his *Exhortation to Martyrdom* (1954b:2). Origen (c. 185–253) was born possibly in Alexandria. When he was about seventeen his father was martyred in the persecution of Severus, which left Origen for a lifetime craving martyrdom himself.[66] He called it "the chalice of salvation" and made assurance conditional upon suffering for the gospel (Origen 1954b:25, 29, 38–41). But martyrdom—the ultimate act of imitating Christ and bearing witness to him—happens only as God "multiplies his graces towards those who through their contempt of this earthen vessel show with all their might that they love him with their *whole soul*" (1945b:2).[67] For Origen, mission, especially martyrdom, is impossible without grace accessed through prayer. Origen seeks to imitate not only Jesus's death, but also his prayer (1954a:13.1). He cites Jesus's prayers in solitude (Mark 1:35; Luke 6:12) and in community (Luke 11:1; John 11:41–42; 17:1). Jesus's extended night of solitary prayer (Luke 6:12) is mentioned. Prayer, fasting, and alms are good together (1954a:11.1). He discusses prayer in terms of time and space. Prayer should be practiced unceasingly but also at special times: "not less than three times each day" (1954a:12.2). Likewise, prayer can happen anywhere (1954a:31.4), but also in special places like a room in one's own house (1954a:31.4)[68] or where the congregation gathers for communal prayer (1954a:31.5). In prayer and "recollection of God" (1954a:8.2) "one must forget everything outside the soul" and learn to deal with distractions (1954a:9.1). He covers the four forms of prayer found in 1 Timothy 2:1—supplication, prayer, intercession, and thanksgiving (1954a:14.2–6). He discusses the Lord's Prayer (1954a:18.2–30.3). Both texts are saturated with Scripture—each paragraph strewn with biblical quotes—evidence of amazing recall. While I often differ with Origen's

to both these texts use section and subsection rather than page number; thus, Origen (1954a:1) refers to section 1, not page 1, of his *Prayer*.

66. Again, I am following O'Meara's biographical sketch in his introduction to Origen's *Prayer* (1954:3).

67. Origen's attitude here in section 2 of *Exhortation to Martyrdom* reflects the neoplatonic devaluation of the body and the separation of the senses from the intelligible. On Plato's and Origen's idea of the separation of these, see Torrance (1969:15).

68. Origen suggests that, if there is room, one create a sanctuary for prayer in some part of the home—evidence for oratories or small private chapels at the time (see O'Meara 1954:227, n. 673).

adoption of Plato's ideas, he still exhibits a deep and biblically shaped spirituality. Though scholars rightly point out that Origen was part of the Alexandrian neoplatonic tradition,[69] overemphasizing Origen's debt to Plato conceals Origen's debt to the tradition of Jesus's spirituality, which came to him by way of the apostles and apostolic fathers.[70] Jesus's spiritual practices deeply shaped Origen. We cannot reduce him solely to a practitioner of Greek contemplation devoid of patterns of spiritual practice seen in the Gospels and Acts. His enormous influence on the history of spirituality derives partially from a biblical core. Patristic scholar Robert L. Wilken (2003) is impressed by the central role the Bible plays in shaping the original and coherent thought among early Christians, which was not divorced from the practice of virtues—most importantly, love. He thinks Adolf Harnack's popular notion of the Hellenization of Christianity has outlived its usefulness, and argues instead that Christianity imported elements of Greek thought that could be used in the service of the gospel, but in a way that does not erase the knowledge and practice of a biblical tradition—precisely my conclusion on Origen. Origen was brilliant in his study and teaching of philosophy, communicating the gospel in terms of Greek philosophy and literature. In his *Church History,* Eusebius cites Porphyr, who described his opponent Origen as follows:

> His way of life was Christian and against the law, but ... he played the Greek, putting a Greek spin on foreign fables [the gospel]. ... He also used the books of Chaeremon the Stoic and Cornutus, where he learned the allegorical [method of] interpretation ... and applied it to the Jewish Scriptures. (Maier 1999:6.19)[71]

Here we glimpse Origen's adoption of Greek thought forms, which he utilizes in communicating the gospel. His mission was indigenous, but

---

69. Rowan Williams mentions the debate over whether Origen, the disciple of Plato, or Origen, the disciple of Jesus, prevails in his heart and writings (1980:37). See also Anthony Merideth (1986:118).

70. Origen argues for praying at least three times each day, in part on the basis of Peter's rooftop prayer at noon (1954a:12.2). According to Jeffords et al., Origen read five of the apostolic fathers (1996:5). See Table 24 above.

71. Here I use a very accessible translation of Eusebius's *Church History* by Paul L. Maier (1999). Citations refer to books and sections, not pages. Hence, (Maier 1999:6.19) refers to book 6, section 19 of Eusebius's *Church History.*

subverted both Greek ideas and Roman authority.[72] Following the death of Origen's father, who had immersed his son in the study of Scripture and philosophy, Origen began teaching in the Alexandrian catechetical school at a time of acute persecution (1999:6.2). Years of teaching and modeling a life of prayer, discipline, study, and meditation on Scripture "inspired a large number of students . . . [and] won over some unbelieving pagans, scholars, and philosophers" who were later martyred (1999:6.3).

Origen's Influence on St. Antony and the Eremitic Tradition

Fred Noris writes that "the positive contributions of this ascetic, exegete, mystic, mission theologian and spiritual director, with all its deficiencies,[73] towers over that of nearly all others" (2000:1022). John A. McGuckin says, "Origen has been called the 'father of Christian mysticism'. . . . His writings were highly influential in the century following him, when the movement of ascetics that soon came to be called 'monasticism' began" (2001:56–57). Origen read the Song of Solomon as an allegory of God's love—echoed in later monastic writing (2001:56). And he developed the concept of a ladder of progressive purity[74]—the window through which we see God (Matt 5:8)—a key feature of the desert fathers and mothers, monasticism, and the spiritual theology they formed.[75] Almost forty years after the Edict of Toleration in 313, the story of Antony (c. 251–356) stirred the imagination of believers and unbelievers alike, notes patristic scholar Robert C. Gregg (1980:5). Seeking God, Antony

72. Henry Chadwick notes Origen's antipathy for paganism, yet his mastery of its culture (1990:52).

73. Origen indicated belief in the pre-existence of the soul, the subordination of the Son to the Father, and a universalism in which even Satan would be saved—views that were later rejected at the Council of Constantinople in 543. Yet, Origen himself was never condemned as a heretic (O'Meara 1954:6).

74. See Meisel and Del Mastro on Origen and the origins of asceticism (1975:13).

75. According to Princeton theologian Diogenes Allen, the branches of spiritual theology are: (1) ascetic theology—the purgation of the seven deadly sins and the development of the cardinal virtues, which remove barriers to love of God, others, and self in the active life; and (2) mystical theology, which focuses on the vision of God in the contemplative life through (a) illumination indirectly by discursive meditation on images in Scripture, nature, and human nature and (b) union with God by direct meditation without images (1994:7–20; see Appendix F). Origen was the first to use Martha as a metaphor for the active life and Mary as a metaphor for the contemplative life (Merideth 1986:117).

fled to the Egyptian desert from a society in which Christianity would emerge into a new epoch with the resources and power of Rome now with her. Antony's journey—requiring sole dependence on God in a fight against evil—was a quiet protest against empire and church in the tradition of Jesus's and John the Baptist's desert sojourns. His years of solitary practice became seen as a new form of martyrdom. The wildly popular *Life of St. Antony* (1980), written by Athanasius (c. 295–373), was used in the battle with Arius over the deity of Christ mentioned in chapter 2. William A. Clebsch notes the contribution of Origen's allegorical method—finding the spiritual meaning behind the literal sense of Old Testament texts, which found Christ everywhere and especially in the Psalms. This method supplied Athanasius an argument against Arius and a means to find the pre-existent Christ in the Psalms, which Antony and other monks sang perpetually in the Egyptian desert (1980:viii–xi). Praying or singing the psalms daily in sequence each month is a legacy from Antony and his monks that became a normative spiritual practice for Christian believers over the centuries (Peterson 1992:100–105).

Granted the hagiographic nature (exaggerated portrayal of a hero) of *The Life of St. Antony*, we can still detect something of Antony's discernment, healing, and power over evil, which emanated from his many years of solitary spiritual practice. Those we call the desert fathers and mothers also flocked to the desert by the thousands. Nouwen notes that some found a "furnace of transformation" in the disciplines of solitude, silence, and prayer, which shaped them deeply into the image of Christ—the positive side of the movement emphasized by Nouwen (1981:13–18). Others met spiritual, moral, and physical ruin through extreme and bizarre practices—the negative side of the movement chronicled by those like Willard (1988:139–144). Over time, these mothers and fathers began to find each other out of necessity for guidance and mutual support in their difficult venture. They formed quasi-communities of hermits, or anchorites, who lived in semi-seclusion, often gathering weekly for the Eucharist, spiritual direction, fellowship, and prayer.

Origen's Influence on St. Benedict and the Cenobitic Tradition

Origen's influence upon Benedict of Nursia (c. 480–547) can be traced through Gregory of Nyssa (c. 335–95), Evagrius Ponticus (345–99), and Evagrius's disciple John Cassian (c. 360–435). This is unquestioned though the particulars are widely debated.[76] Cassian provided an important link to St. Benedict, the founder of the Benedictine order and a key figure in the origins of Western monasticism, as explained by Mary Margaret Funk.[77]

> The *Rule of St. Benedict* (*RB*),[78] written one hundred years after the time of the desert fathers and mothers, was an extension of the same spirit. Benedict, in his short rule, refers seventy-eight times to Cassian's *Conferences* (*Conf.*) and sixty-eight times and to the *Institutes* (*Inst.*).[79] (2002:10)

Commenting on the *Rule of St. Benedict* is not within the scope of this study, except to say two things. First, Benedict's *Rule* represented a moderation of the disciplines practiced in the desert.[80] Second, it created close-knit spiritual communities of spiritual practice, virtue, and compassion at a time when the Roman Empire was crumbling under impact of barbarian invasions from without and the demise of its institutions from within.

---

76. For a discussion of Origen's influence on Gregory of Nyssa, Evagrius Ponticus, John Cassian, St. Benedict, and others, see Bamberger's introduction to his translation of Evagrius's *Praktikos* and *Chapters on Prayer* (1981). In the preface to this work, Jean Leclercq sums up the scholarly consensus: "Historians have sufficiently demonstrated that Evagrius depends on Origen and Gregory of Nyssa so that there is no need to insist upon it here" (1981:xi).

77. See Funk's *Thoughts Matter* (2002), a readable commentary on Cassian's two works, which provides a contemporary rendition of his counsel to monks as they progressed more deeply in God through three renunciations: (1) of one's past way of life; (2) of deadly and distracting thoughts—the genesis of the seven or eight deadly sins; and (3) of distorted images of God (see *Conf.* 3).

78. For an accessible translation of the *Rule of St. Benedict*, see Benedict (1975).

79. For readable translations in contemporary English of these two influential works by John Cassian, see his *Conferences* (1985), which includes nine of his twenty-four conferences, and his *Institutes* (2000), which are unabridged.

80. On this point, see Jean Leclercq (1985:117–18), within his discussion of the beginnings of the Benedictine monasticism in its uniquely urban centers (1985:116–19).

Summary

In this chapter, I examined the early church's rhythms of spirituality and mission; what was practiced in Acts and what was taught by the apostolic fathers. I also looked at what Origen taught about prayer and mission in his *Prayer* (1954a) and *Exhortation to Martyrdom* (1954b). I have found that:

1. What Jesus practiced during his withdrawals from the crowds in Luke, the church practiced in Acts, but with some contrasts—most notably that the church withdrew primarily in community and less so in solitude. These withdrawals lasted for ten days, three days, or one hour, and occurred late at night, daily, weekly, or at midnight. They occurred in places including private homes, an upstairs room of a house where they stayed, the temple, synagogues, prisons, and ships, as well as congregations' regular gathering places, a rooftop, and the Jordan River. Jesus, by contrast, prayed more frequently in lonely desert places and less in community than did the church in Acts.

2. The apostles' withdrawals for prayer were closely tied to subsequent mission practices, just as with Jesus's rhythms in Luke. Connected with each of the fourteen withdrawals studied in Acts, mission happened usually by proclamation. As with Jesus, grace attended each withdrawal and subsequent mission.

3. During the initial phase of the church's mission in Acts, corporate prayer preceded and sustained her mission more than solitary prayer, whereas Jesus's early mission was sustained by solitary prayer. But it was not long before solitary prayer became a crucial factor in God dynamiting the granite impediment of the Jewish exclusion of Gentiles from the church's mission. Divine intervention came to Peter and Paul in their solitude and meditation to change the course of the church's mission.

4. Jesus's prayer for the forgiveness of his executioners in Luke is recapitulated in the dying prayer of Stephen for those who were stoning him. Such suffering love and forgiveness of persecutors are earmarks of authentic mission spirituality. For early Christians, to imitate Christ meant to imitate him in his death. Like Origen and Ignatius of Antioch, they expected to be martyred.

5. Though communal spiritual practices predominate in the Apostolic Fathers, good evidence for solitary spiritual practice was also found. Both kinds of practice, commended explicitly or implicitly, are associated with outward mission, usually in deed. This is not seen primarily in retreat episodes, which require narrative texts, but by the close proximity to each other of references to spiritual and mission practices in didactic texts or letters. Prevenient and transforming grace are present but, sadly, accepting grace disappears—replaced by merit and penance.

6. Origin drew from, but subverted Greco-Roman culture and authority in his indigenous proclamation of the gospel and in his spirituality. His spirituality and his mission were expressed in neoplatonic ideas and practices, but a tradition of New Testament spirituality also found its way through the apostolic fathers to his own practice of spirituality. He echoes their focus on transforming grace in relation to mission and prayer. He held that both the golden thread—fasting, prayer, and almsgiving—and the three disciplines of communion, community, and ministry were normative and to be pursued relentlessly. He helped shape the eremitic and cenobitic monastic traditions, which played key roles in the medieval church and in the spiritualities and missions that emerged later in the modern age. To that story I now turn.

5

Rhythms of Spirituality and Mission in the Modern Age

> Throw out all hindrances to grace if you really want to be filled with grace. How can you do that? Be alone in secret ... pour out devout prayer to God. ... Not even the gift of preaching, the gift of miracles, the gift of reasoning, no matter how highly developed, has real value without grace.
>
> —Thomas à Kempis (1982:234, 241)

HAVING EXAMINED THE COLLAPSE OF SPACE AND TIME IN NORTH America since 1950 (chapter 2) and sampled the spirituality and mission of Jesus and the early church (chapters 3 and 4), I now turn to the modern era—from about 1450 to the mid twentieth century.[1] The texts I select were written during a period spanning four hundred years, which saw the gradual separation of time from space resulting in radical shifts described in chapter 2. I find correlations in these texts similar to those seen in pre-modern texts.

After sketching a backdrop for late medieval spirituality, this chapter analyzes the rhythms of spirituality and mission in three movements that contributed to modern missions. First, the *Devotio Moderna*, a late medieval movement, was founded by Geert Groote (1340–1384) near the close of the pre-modern age. It produced *The Imitation of Christ* by Thomas à Kempis, the most translated book beside the Bible (1982:cover). After the printing press and Protestant Reformation ended the movement, its influence lived on in Catholic and Protestant spiritualities. Second, the Society of Jesus, begun by Ignatius of Loyola

---

1. Here I follow Charles Jencks, who dates the modern age from 1450 to 1960 (1996:56).

(1491–1556), became an impetus for modern Catholic missions. Third, the First Great Awakening in eigtheentgh century America produced Jonathan Edwards and David Brainerd, whose diary inspired nineteenth century Protestant missions—a period I will touch on briefly.

In this chapter, I finish addressing my third research question concerning how space and time with God relate to mission in selected second millennium classics. The secondary questions are: How are time and space for God demarcated? What spiritual disciplines are practiced? Is grace associated with these? Is mission practiced in word or deed, centrifugally or centripetally?

A Backdrop for Late Medieval Spirituality

After the emergence of the desert fathers and mothers and the monastic movement they inspired, the church experienced major ebbs[2] and flows in her mission from about 500 to 1000. During these years, according to Stephen Neil, the gospel spread among barbarian peoples in large part through monasticism, martyrdom, and royal favor (1986:57). Monasticism—founded on vows of poverty, celibacy, and obedience—could devote undivided attention to prayer, virtue, learning, manual labor, agricultural reform, and preserving sacred texts. Though most monastic groups in this era did not begin as missionary communities, except for Celtic ones, they became missional as people flocked to them for help. Until the fifteenth century, most missionaries came from monasticism (Pierson 1998:78). Yet, at the beginning of the tenth century, Western Europe was only nominally Christian. "The Roman Empire has collapsed; the Viking Invasions are over; Europe is in chaos; feudalism is the order of the day politically; the papacy was at its lowest point" (1998:90). From the tenth to the fourteenth centuries several key political, social, and religious conditions formed the backdrop for the development of late medieval spiritualities and missions that emerged in Western Europe.

---

2. Two of the church's greatest defeats prior to modern times were the Muslim conquests during the seventh and eighth centuries in lands where she had been the strongest and the Viking invasions during the eighth and ninth centuries (Pierson 1998:86–89).

The Recurring Need for Reform

At the beginning of the tenth century, monastic orders themselves needed reform. In 910 the monastery at Cluny began the first great renewal in the practice of Benedict's Rule during this period. Over the next two hundred years of growing influence, organizational complexity, and wealth, this movement became lax and corrupt. In 1098 a group of reform-minded members gave birth to the Cisterian order (today's Trappists), which adopted a more rigorous practice of Benedict's Rule involving six hours of daily prayer (Pierson 1993:90–91). An even stricter community called the Carthusians was founded in 1084. Rather than embracing Benedict's Rule, they devoted themselves to seeking the solitude, silence, and prayer that Jesus practiced in the desert.[3]

Centralization, Abuse of Power, and Rationalization

From the tenth to the fourteenth centuries, Europe needed greater cohesiveness, connection, and organization. These fostered the solidification of nation states and religious institutions, and contributed to the growth of new monastic orders and the decline of older ones. As James F. McCue observes, "It is from about 1050 that we see a broad movement towards centralization and rationalization in both Latin Europe and the Latin Church" (1987:427). As they centralized, both state and church amassed increasing wealth and power. Since Constantine, the co-mingling of religious and political power had enticed the church to use violence and war to further her agenda, which in this era was seen in the tragic Crusades and Inquisitions of the Roman Catholic Church. The break between Eastern Orthodox and Western Catholic traditions in 1054 was further widened by the Latin Church's intransigence on the issue of papal supremacy, by the increasing rationalism of her medieval scholasticism, which separated theology from prayer,[4] and by

---

3. See Susan Muto (2000:35–36). A. S. Toon says that its rigorous eremitic elements prevented its rapid growth, but insulated it from the decline of monastic orders in the late medieval period (1978:196–97).

4. On the divide between Eastern and Western traditions, see Meyendorff (1997:439–53). For the separation of theology from prayer, see Philip Sheldrake (1992:4) and Diogenes Allen (1997:19).

the Fourth Crusade, which captured and ransacked Constantinople in 1204, making this Great Schism permanent.[5]

Urban Growth, Wealth, the Vita Apostolica, and the Mendicants

By the thirteenth and fourteenth centuries, "Europe was moving from a feudal, rural, agricultural society to one of trade, cities, and middle class" (Pierson 1998:97). This shift contributed to the decline of older monastic houses, which were located primarily in rural areas and not well suited to the new situation, and which had become wealthy, corrupt, and lax (1998:97-98). The thirteenth century saw the emergence of mendicant orders (*mendicare*, "to beg"), which renounced the opulence and power of the church and of lax monasteries. The mendicants grew rapidly, especially the Franciscans founded in 1210 and the Dominicans founded in 1216, also called Friars (*frère*, "brothers").[6] Philip Sheldrake writes,

> The emergence of the mendicant orders in the thirteenth century, represented both an evangelical and a social reaction to the wealth and power of society and of a Church that all too frequently aped the "values of the world".... Francis's vision ... is symptomatic of a wider spiritual movement in the late eleventh and twelfth centuries, known as the *vita apostolica*. (1992:58)

Typical of the *vita apostolica* was imitation of Jesus's itinerant preaching, service, simplicity, and poverty by women and laity in groups outside monasticism, like the Beguines and their male counterparts, the Begheads. Furthermore, new monastic orders developed branches called tertiaries for those who could not or did not want live by the entirety of their rule (Sheldrake 1992:117). Devotional spirituality of laity grew in this period. Pilgrimage to holy places with relics, shrines, or burial sites of saints became popular among the populace. "The rosary, meditations on the Passion and Books of Hours were effectively lay imitations of monastic rhythms" (1992:72).

Ewert Cousins sees two foci of medieval spirituality—the humanity and passion of Christ. These were evident in the spiritual writings of Anselm, a Benedictine; Bernard, a Cisterian; Francis of Assisi; and his

5. See Barbara L. Faulkner (1978:322-25) and C. T. McIntire (1978:479).
6. See T. L Underwood (1978:649).

biographer, Bonaventure, whose classic *Tree of Life* was incorporated into the widely influential *Vita Christi* (*Life of Christ*) by Carthusian Ludolph of Saxony (1987:377-82). By the early fifteenth century, monastic orders, including mendicants, were in grave decline, straying from their core values (Pierson 1998:102). Yet, as John Van Engen notes, from the Cistercians and Franciscans the *Devotio Moderna* and other medieval renewal groups inherited a centeredness in the person of Jesus to which they added their own emphasis on imitation and the virtues (1988:25).

Geert Groote and the Devotio Moderna: In Imitation of Christ

First appearing in the Netherlands in the latter part of the fourteenth century, the *Devotio Moderna* (lit. "Modern Devotion," also called New Devotion) attracted clergy, laity, women, and youth as it spread to Belgium and throughout Germany. The movement had three parts: (1) the Sisters of the Common Life for lay women; second, the Brethren of the Common Life for laymen and some priests; and finally, the Augustinian Canons Regular at Windesheim, a monastic community.[7] Rather than taking vows of poverty and begging for alms as did the medieval mendicant orders, members of the *Devotio Moderna* lived communally and earned income for their households by selling sacred texts they copied and by producing goods for the textile industry. Medieval scholar Heiko A. Obermann describes the dominant purpose of the movement as "the search for a new meditation technique for the working classes, directed toward the reformation of the soul . . . as the basis for the renewal of the communal life whether within or outside the monastic walls" (1988:2).

In his introduction to representative texts of the movement,[8] John Van Engen, Director of the University of Notre Dame's Medieval Institute, links the *Devotio Moderna* to the views of Luther and Calvin

---

7. See Kenneth Strand (1984:84, 97). Augustinian Canons Regular are distinguished from the Augustinian Hermits, which was a mendicant order to which Martin Luther belonged (see P. Toon 1978:88).

8. John Van Engen omits the *Imitation of Christ* because the widespread attention to this work tended to exclude attention to other texts of the *Devotio Moderna*. Until Van Engen's collection and translation, no collection of representative texts in English had been published (1988:back cover).

on sanctification. But on justification, he and most scholars now see little continuity.⁹

> Any close reading of these works, with all their emphasis on the will and disciplined training in the virtues together with merit and reward, could only bring horror to some Reformer with a radically Pauline and Augustinian theology of grace.... [Luther's] doctrine of justification by faith alone appears to have "short-circuited" the whole system in the most fundamental way thinkable: He declared himself "sinner" and "saved" at the same time. (J. Van Engen 1988:60)

But, as Van Engen notes, Luther expected Protestants to practice the *Devotio Moderna*'s devotional methods and its imitation of Christ's virtues in their sanctification (1988:60–61). From 1497 to 1498 Luther had attended a school for youth in Magdeburg, where he had been taught by Brethren of the Common Life.¹⁰ He had also read the movement's key text: *Spiritual Ascents* (1988:56). Regarding Calvin, Van Engen thinks Calvin's *Institutes* employ Modern Devotion language in describing future glory, contempt for the world, virtue, spiritual exercise, and progress, but "as the work of the Holy Spirit and as an act of gratitude rather than of a disciplined will" (1988:60–61). Most scholars now think the Modern Devotion's greatest continuity is with the Catholic Reformation, frequently noting parallels with Ignatius of Loyola.¹¹ Van Engen observes that "what the Modern Devout represented better than most others was a religious outlook that nearly all spiritual thinkers in the fifteenth century discovered for themselves or took for granted." Furthermore, "both Protestants and Catholics could read the literature generated by the Modern Devotion and, each in their own way, find it altogether appropriate and edifying" (1988:60–61).

---

9. Arguing for a strong continuity between the New Devotion and the Reformation were Hyma (1924), Landeen (1951, 1964, 1984), and others. Kenneth Davis sees closer ties with the Anabaptist wing of the Reformation. Both movements were "ascetic, conductual, lay-oriented, primitivistic, and perfectionistic" (1974:251).

10. See Landeen (1984:81). Before Landeen's groundbreaking work, most scholars felt that Luther had stayed in a dormitory run by the Brethren, but had gone to school elsewhere (Strand 1984:97). Additionally, Ignatius read Imitation of Christ while at Manresa (Sheldrake 2007:124).

11. Ignatius of Loyola drew most heavily from Ludolph of Saxony's *Life of Christ* (Ganss et al. 1991:19–26), a work also influential in the New Devotion.

Founder Geert Groote[12]

Geert Groote (1340–1384) was born to a wealthy family in the town of Deventer in the diocese of Ultrect (Jacob 1952:44). His father was the town treasurer before he and Groote's mother died from the plague when Groote was ten. Deventer's record keeping changed from Latin to Middle Dutch in 1359. As Van Engen notes, had Groote followed his father's vocation, he would have kept records in the vernacular language (1988:16). Instead, as leader of the New Devotion he translated spiritual texts into Middle Dutch so laity could access them for meditation in their heart language. This was an indigenous feature of the *Devotio Moderna*, reflecting shifts in the wider culture.

At age fifteen Groote began studying canon law and other subjects at the University of Paris, earning a master's degree by eighteen. Wealthy, successful, and brilliant, he lived apart from God until he had a dramatic change at the age of thirty-four.[13] After his conversion in 1374, Groote quit his well-paying cleric positions, called livings or benefices, in which he had practiced canon and other law. He began living a disciplined, penitential life, giving his parents' farm to a Carthusian house and traveling to Paris to shop for books "presumably to aid in his new study of the religious life" (J. Van Engen 1988:36–37). Under the influence of mystic Jan Ruusbroec (1293–1381), he took lengthy pilgrimages and retreats to a Carthusian monastery. Groote, however, felt led to nurture his spiritual life away from the cloister, under civil rather than religious authority and in cities not rural settings (1988:37; Jacob 1952:46–47). Groote opened his Deventer home to a group of poor women—eventually the first house of the Sisters of the Common Life (Hyma 1924:vii).[14]

In 1379, after five eremitic or solitary years, Groote began preaching as an itinerant deacon. He called for repentance from vice among the clergy and from indolence and greed within monastic orders (Jacob 1952:43–44, 48). His preaching mission attracted converts (Hyma

---

12. All scholars agree Groote is the founder. I have drawn primarily on J. Van Engen (1988:36–40) and an older, but excellent paper concerning Groote by Oxford historian E. F. Jacob (1952:40–57).

13. Accounts of his conversion differ. Jacob contends Groote's past was not profligate (1952:46–67).

14. The home had room for eight women in the front and eight in the back (J. Van Engen 1988:16).

1924:14), whom he encouraged to form voluntary groups in private houses. "Each community demanded, above all, a genuine commitment to the spiritual life" (J. Van Engen 1988:39). But in 1383 his preaching was banned and he had to flee for safety amidst the outrage created by his 1383 sermon to the clerics of the diocese of Utrecht. He had decried as mortal sin both the common clergy practice of concubinage and knowing participation in masses led by such priests (1988:38-39). Meanwhile, men had been forming voluntary clusters in Deventer and Zwolle dwellings even as the women had in Groote's home (1988:38-39). In the year after the ban Groote focused on his disciples, one of whom became his successor: Florentius Raderwijns. At Raderwijns's urging, Groote finally consented to his disciples' wish to pool their possessions and live in common, a move that was sure to be opposed by the mendicant orders as an invasion of their turf. Groote wrote a constitution with voluntary resolutions, rather than the fixed vows typical of the orders, for the men's and women's houses (Hyma 1924:43-45; Jacob 1952:52-53). In 1384 Groote died from the plague (J. Van Engen 1988:38).

Development of the Movement

After Geert Groote's death, the New Devotion grew for the next 130 years, until the printing press and the Reformation finally ended the movement by the late sixteenth century. The movement developed along two distinct branches.

1. *Growth of the Brothers and Sisters of the Common Life.* Under Raderwijns (1350-1400), the Brethren of the Common Life grew to six houses in Deventer, Zwolle, Amersterdam, and elsewhere. During this period, the movement's other great leader was Gerard Zerbolt of Zutphen (d. 1398), author of *Spiritual Ascents*. By 1420, there were eleven houses for the brothers. The most important leader in the second generation of the New Devotion was Dirk Herxen (1381-1457), who began convening all the Dutch houses annually in 1431. The number of brother houses grew to twenty in 1460, thirty-nine in 1500, and forty-one in 1517 (J. Van Engen 1988:20, 43, 52). The sisters grew more rapidly. Estimates for the number of Dutch sister houses in 1460 range from thirty-four to 106, while the number in Germany was 60 (1988:18). Typically these

> were larger medieval houses of a kind still to be seen in northern European cities. They had an inner courtyard allowing privacy in work and other business, different wings and floors applied to various purposes, and fairly severe front on the street with a single door or gate.... If the number of devout required and their income permitted, buildings might be added or annexed, beginning often with a chapel and/or work rooms (i.e., a library and copy area for the brothers, a sewing area for the sisters). Larger houses might add a separate kitchen, refectory, or dormitory. All remained houses in a city, often near the parish church ... once a day or once a week ... they walked out in single file and in silence to hear mass.... For all of them, family, friends, the world and its amusements, even (as some stories make clear) old lovers, were only one door away, with nothing to block them—no walls and no vows—except their own resolve and the internal pressures exercised by their community. (J. Van Engen 1988:22)

The mission of the Brethren and Sisters of the Common Life had five key features: (1) use of the vernacular, (2) schools or dormitories for youth,[15] (3) social ministry—income above house expenses was given to the poor, (4) business activity in towns, and (5) evangelism through weekly collations—meetings open to all the community to hear the brothers teach Scripture, which drew opposition from religious leaders.[16]

2. *The Windersheim Congregation of Canons Regular*. Constituted under religious, not civil authority (Oberman 1988:2), this branch grew the fastest. Under canon law for religious orders, the Windersheim Congregation escaped mendicant opposition to "middle way" gatherings, which lacked legal protection (J. Van Engen 1988:20). Eventually many, like Thomas à Kempis, found it easier to join the Windersheim Congregation in order to gain a more stable and ordered spiritual life.

---

15. Hyma estimates the number of boys taught in schools or dormitories run by the Brothers to be point to be 1,200 in Zwolle and a large number in Deventer (1924:123). R. R. Post's massive *The Modern Devotion* criticizes Hyma and others for evaluating the New Devotion's contributions too highly—especially its educational efforts (1967:419, 558, 457, 568–76, 613–18, 628–30). For a book review that presents a more positive assessment than Post's and a needed corrective, which is now echoed in J. Van Engen and other scholars, see Kenneth Strand (1969:65–76).

16. Collations threatened the teaching monopoly of the Dominicans and the priests (J. Van Engen 1988:52).

Also, many congregations started out as brother or sister houses before becoming a Windersheim house or a house in another order (1988:8–9, 20).[17] The more legally acceptable branch grew from the initial congregation at Windersheim (1387) into a union of four houses by 1395, and then to thirty under John Vox de Heusden (1391–1424). Eventually, there were a total of ninety-seven houses throughout Holland and Germany; eighty-four houses for men and thirteen for women (1988:20–21).

Their Rhythms of Spirituality and Mission

In this section, I survey the New Devout's daily, weekly, monthly, and annual or occasional rhythms of spiritual practice and look at how these relate to mission. First, two notes about their practices:

1. *Flexibility*. In a sermon for laity, Groote argued that practices were to be radically flexible means towards the goal of "righteousness, peace and joy in the Holy Spirit" (Gal 5:22–23).

> In seeking these three, a man should let every external religious exercise go. For all external exercises, whether fasting, scourging, keeping vigil, much psalm-singing, many Our Father's, manual labor ... have only so much good and profit as they bring righteousness, peace, and joy in the Holy Spirit. Men should do such works only in order to acquire those three and measure accordingly whether to do more or less. Any exercise that gets in the way of righteousness, peace, and joy in the Holy Spirit, or any one of the three, is harmful, burdensome, and improper for a man. It comes rather as man's enemy, the devil, and from man's own perverse conceit and self-absorption. (Groote 1998a:92)

Groote and other members of the movement wrote resolutions and intentions (not vows) of the disciplines they wished to practice—like a rule or rhythm of life.[18] These reflected a diversity of need and were

---

17. Recent scholarship has emphasized the differences between the Windersheim Congregation and the other two branches of the New Devotion. Though most Windersheim houses were located in rural areas withdrawn from the world, and though they adopted a more ordered life prescribed by non-voluntary vows, still they preserved the spirit of the *Devotio Moderna* in most respects (J. Van Engen 1988:21).

18. For practical discussions on developing a rule of life—a written statement of the particular cluster of spiritual disciplines that are life-giving at a particular time and place in one's life—see Marjorie Thompson (1995:137–46), Chan (1998:190–98), and Peterson (1992:97–115).

flexibly practiced. If inner transformation did not result they were discarded—an approach which deeply subverted the fixity of monastic vows of the day.

2. *Shifts in Several Stages of the Movement*. As the movement developed, houses began to write "customaries," the equivalent of a written rule of life for an individual house. The best example of these is *The Customary for Brothers*, probably written by Dirk Herxen, rector of the brother house in Zwolle, which was the largest house in Holland (1988:155–75). Customaries reflected a distinct formalization of the movement, which developed in its second generation when Herxen emerged as its leader and convened annual meetings of all the Dutch houses. Philip Sheldrake calls this the maintenance-stability stage of a movement, which in his scheme represents the second of three stages typical of all spiritual movements (see Table 27 below). In this stage, less flexibility and more structure emerge as the movement grows. Though more standardization can be detected in the second stage of the New Devotion, its customaries still reflected the unique character and needs of the local community in each house—far more flexible than most orders of the day (J. Van Engen 1988:48).

Daily Practices

I will now look at the daily practices in the first two stages of the movement (see Table 28 below). The emergence stage (1374–1390) is comprised of Groote's conversion, his five eremitic years, his four years of itinerant preaching, his final year of leadership selection, and the six years under his successor, Radewijns. The maintenance-stability stage lasted over one hundred years (1390–1500). The daily practices detected during his conversion and eremitic years can be divided into three groupings: communion, community, and ministry.

1. *Communion*. Shortly after his conversion, Groote wrote his *Resolutions and Intentions* (J. Van Engen 1988:39), which give the best picture of his eremitic years. It begins with these words: "I intend to order my life to the glory, honor, and service of God and the salvation of my soul; to put no temporal good of body, position, fortune, or learning ahead of my soul's salvation; and to pursue the imitation of God" (Groote 1988b:65). This is a remarkable prayer of relinquishment, a key to being

Table 27: Sheldrake's Three Stages of a Spiritual Tradition[19] (Adapted from Sheldrake 1992:75–79)

Stage 1: Emergence	Origins
Historian's tasks: Identify early principles from • the stories of the initiators • the internal context of the tradition • the external context of the surrounding society Identify resulting praxis in terms of space/time with God Identify missional activity	• Founding group or individual responds to the needs of a new cultural milieu in light of the gospel • Greatest flexibility, as structures are not yet set • Strong sense of fluidity and purpose
	Expansion
	• Begins when new spirituality is seen as answering the felt needs of society • New people join original group or affiliate in some way with the new spirituality • Founding core group brings together resources to translate vision into coherent patterns • New groups beyond the birth place want to share in the vision

---

19. Sheldrake's scheme has three stages: (1) emergence, (2) maintenance-stability, and (3) senility-breakdown (1992:75–79). In the latter, a movement will breakdown if it is not flexible enough to respond to new cultural conditions by developing a new synthesis between its founding principles and the new situation. By 1450, the use of moveable type had been spreading gradually, replacing the use of parchment and the painstaking manual work of copyists (Latourette 1975:606). Thus, in its maintenance-stability stage, when the New Devotion was in its prime, spreading rapidly in Germany, the introduction of printing contained the seeds of the movement's demise. When the Reformation engulfed Holland and Germany during the final stage of the *Devotio Moderna*, the Reformers removed singleness as a condition for devotion to Christ, and they destroyed penance and merit as a motivation and foundation for holiness. Unable to form a new synthesis with the new economic, social, and theological realities, the movement died out by the end of the sixteenth century.

Stage 2: Maintenance-Stability *Historian's tasks:* Note if first principles change Note changes in players, internal and external contexts Note standardization of spiritual and missional practice	• Flexibility is replaced by more detailed formulation and structure (such as the creation of a rule) • Tradition has its own momentum; change is harder • Certain options are now chosen and rejected, which should not be read back into the emergent stage • Tradition has become respectable and socialized • Protectiveness develops among those who benefit from the movement against anything that threatens the movement
Stage 3: Senility or Breakdown *Historian's tasks:* Note if rigidity is lethal Look for any new synthesis between tradition and culture Identify new forms of first principles that are expressed in the new synthesis	• Rigidity becomes intensified • Disconnection between values of the tradition and the needs of contemporary society threaten the tradition • Original vision does not seem to work presently • Structures are more important than their meaning • Rules do not meet needs in new context and are bypassed *Two options:* • Flexibility: new synthesis between tradition and culture • Death

an unreserved follower of Jesus. His *Resolutions* also included simplicity, Scripture reading, spiritual reading, singing psalms, secrecy, sacrifice (celibacy and relinquishing ownership), and the golden thread of unceasing prayer, fasting, and almsgiving (1988b:65–71).

2. *Community.* Groote devoted a whole section of his *Resolutions* to the Eucharist and corporate worship. He probably celebrated these daily, since the church in Deventer was close to his home (1988b:71–73).

3. *Ministry.* Groote rejected academic pursuits because they "would draw you away from the salvation of your neighbor ... [and] also away from prayer, purity of mind and contemplation" (1988b:69). Early in his spiritual journey, inward prayer and contemplation were explicitly linked to outward mission. Peacemaking and suffering love were also among his resolutions (1988b:69–70). As for almsgiving, "It is evil to forsake, even for contemplation, any godly usefulness to your neighbor and especially the justice another cannot do" (1988b:70). "Allot yourself therefore a frugal portion of clothing and food, more to the poor and the deserving and more still for the salvation of souls. Never give anything to someone not in need . . ." (1988b:75). In his resolutions, mission included both deed and word, with word apparently having greater priority.

During Groote's four years of public ministry (1379–1383), new practices emerged.[20] The emphasis shifted from compassionate justice and hospitality to proclamation. Groote's itinerant preaching in Middle Dutch (the common language) was an indigenous form of centrifugal mission. But he was also subversive in calling for complete repentance from all that impedes full imitation of Christ, and he challenged the patterns and powers of church and culture that stood in the way. The second new feature was voluntary formation of small, highly committed groups of followers in the wake of Groote's preaching, and his selection of twelve leaders and a successor after he was banned from preaching. A third innovation during this period was the conversion of New Devout houses into economic units for communal living and working—a new

---

20. Not surprisingly, as Groote began to live out his intentions and resolutions, some new daily practices emerged throughout his apostolate, which were not mentioned in his *Resolutions*. These appear in his sayings, letters, sermons, and biographical material that have come down to us.

practice at the end of Groote's life, which drew suspicion. Though his *Resolutions* made little mention of love and unity among brothers and sisters, this was a major concern in "A Sermon Addressed for Laity" (1988a:92–97). Groote knew the small groups he established needed to learn to live with each other in peace and love—a need that would become further taxed by communal living. Finally, in his sayings written during this period Groote introduces the practice of praying the psalms before retiring at night, which would determine one's thoughts upon rising (1988c:77), and in a letter on suffering he emphasizes affectionate meditation on the cross and inward chewing and reflecting on the words of Scripture (1988d:85, 87).

In the second stage of the movement, living from a common pot bound members more closely together than previously and likely fostered greater structure. *A Customary for Brothers* sets forth a detailed daily schedule for corporate and solitary prayer,[21] spiritual reading (one hour), manual labor (six to eight hours), silence, and rest. Spiritual direction with a confessor and short, frequent, ejaculatory prayers were also prescribed. In spite of increased standardization, flexibility still persisted, as seen in the proviso that if need or obedience dictated the men could diverge from their set hour of private spiritual reading (Herxen 1988:156–59). All brothers and sisters kept journals along with their contemplative Bible reading, keeping notebooks "(*rapiaria*) of those passages they found most compelling" (J. Van Engen 1988:25–26).[22] Sisters of the Common Life practiced similar daily disciplines, as portrayed in texts about their exemplary lives.[23] Gese Broekelants (d. 1407) was "especially devoted to the passion of our dear Lord, so that at times she would burst out into many tears," and she confessed her faults to everyone (J. Van Engen 1988:123–24).[24] Key leader Salome Stricken

21. In the chapel they said matins (between 3 and 4 a.m.) and prime (6 a.m.). The rest of the hours they said privately (1988:157): terce (9 a.m.), sext (noon), none (3 p.m.), and vespers (6 p.m.)

22. These notebooks stood in the monastic tradition of medieval *florilegia*, which the New Devout made accessible outside the boundaries of monasteries (J Van Engen 1988:25–26).

23. For a survey of literature by women of the New Devout, see Scheepsma (1995:27–40).

24. The description of Broekelants comes from "Some Edifying Points from the Lives of the Older Sisters," written by an unknown sister who described sixty-seven women who lived in the first phase of the movement. J. Van Engen has selected eleven

(1369–1449) emphasized submission, hymn singing, and the practice of *examen*.

> I wish your hearts to be occupied with nothing other than affectionate meditation on the Lord.... At all times and places, moreover, lift your hearts up frequently to our most loving Lord Jesus Christ in brief prayers . . . ; for instance in the psalm "Create in me a clean heart, O God" or the hymn "Come Holy Spirit".
> . . . Each hour you should also look into yourself to examine your progress or decline, carefully reflecting on what gladdens or saddens you, what you love, what you hope in. Each evening as you sit before your bed, carefully scrutinize how you spent the preceding day. (Stricken 1988:178–179)

Weekly Practices

Except for Mass and corporate worship, New Devotion texts lack references to weekly practices. One exception is "On the Life and Passion of Our Lord Jesus Christ, and Other Devotional Exercises" (Radewijns 1988:187–204). This falls into a genre of texts called exercises, which did for individuals what customaries did for houses. They provided prayers and guided emphatic meditation (affective imagination) on the life and death of Jesus and for the assimilation of his virtues. They were structured so that, over time, the same exercise could be repeated on Mondays, a different exercise repeated on Tuesdays, yet another on Wednesdays, and so forth. Emphatic meditation, prayer, and fasting were typical of Franciscans and other medieval orders. These were taken over by the New Devout, but their assimilation of virtue in imitation of Christ was distinctive to them (J. Van Engen 1988:50).

These inner corporate and solitary weekly practices were typical of all houses of the New Devotion and fueled the movement's primary evangelistic activity: the weekly collations held on Sunday afternoons open to all in the community. These replaced Groote's preaching missions as the primary means of recruitment after his death. The collations themselves were quite flexible, spontaneous, and personal in the way they were conducted. This mission practice was centripetal and was located at a fixed location, in contrast to Groote's four-year preaching

---

of these lives to translate (1988:46, 121–36). This text and others like it served to celebrate and teach the way of life to the next generation of the movement (1988:45).

campaign, which was highly mobile and centrifugal. Collations were opposed because they usurped Dominican teaching.

Monthly Practices

A Customary for Brothers contains the following instructions for the house in Zwolle: "As far as possible we arrange it so that in preparation for such feast days we withdraw a day or two from all major tasks and distractions that can conveniently be put off" (Herxen 1988:174). Herxen mentions seventeen feast days that the house celebrated each year, which means that, on average, every three weeks the brothers at Zwolle were able to enjoy a one or two-day retreat for extended personal communion with God away from their customary routines.[25] Given Herxen's widespread influence through the annual convention of Dutch houses he convened, these patterns likely spread well beyond Zwolle. These one- or two-day retreats allowed the New Devout to "find a convenient and unhurried time for meditating on God's love," in the words of Thomas à Kempis in the *Imitation of Christ*, which devotes a whole section to solitude and silence (1982:44–48).

For feast days in sister houses, Stricken advised a period of mutual confession between the sisters for one or two hours (Stricken 1988:185). Some authorities feared that the New Devout would use this practice, known as "fraternal correction," as a substitute for regular confession with a priest (J. Van Engen 1988:17). They also held colloquies, monthly gatherings of houses for members to share the concerns and needs of the community with one another and the rector (Herxen 1988:166).

Annual or Occasional Practices

There was little, if any, opportunity for members of the New Devotion to take annual retreats or pilgrimages away from their houses for a week, two weeks, or a month, as did the early followers of Ignatius of Loyola more than a century later. The New Devout did not take lengthy periods of solitude in spite of beloved examples like Antony, the desert fathers,

---

25. The feast days celebrated were: Easter, Ascension, Pentecost, Corpus Christi, the Visitation, Mary Magdalen, the Assumption, the Nativity of Mary, St. Michael's, All Saints, the Conception of Mary, Christmas, Epiphany, the Purification, the Enthronement of St. Peter, and the Annunciation (Herxen 1988:174).

and Groote in his eremitic years.[26] The movement's pattern of monthly one- or two-day retreats was undoubtedly key to the empowerment of its spirituality and mission. Yet, I suggest that the limited opportunity for the New Devout to move into more extended solitude, as their founder had initially done, kept them from patterns that may have deepened their transformation and furthered their impact.

Table 28: The New Devout's Emerging Spiritual and Mission Practices (Adapted from J. Van Engen 1988; Sheldrake 1992; Miller 2007; Jacob 1952; Hyma 1924)

Stage 1: Emergent (1374–90)	Stage 2: Maintenance (1390–1500)		Stage 3: Senility or Breakdown (1500–1600)
Groote's Resolutions	Groote's Apostolate	1st & 2nd Generations	Demise
Daily Practices	New Practices	New Practices	Factors Leading to Demise
Solitude: • Prayer of surrender • Simplicity • Fasting • Study Scripture • Study fathers and classics • Singing the Psalms • Slowing, interiority	Abiding: • Praying the Psalms • Affective meditation use of imagination • Meditation on cross • Celibacy	Commitment 1: • Praying the hours, vigils • Examen • Hymns • Journaling notebooks • Work: unceasing prayer • Ejaculatory prayer • Rest • Manual labor	External cultural shifts (from / to): • Copying / Printing press • Celibacy / Marriage • Penance / Assurance • Protestant Reformation in Dutch & German lands Internal shifts (from/to): • Founder's long retreats / Shorter 1- or 2-day retreats • Preaching / Collations • Centrifugal / Centripetal
Community: • Eucharist • Centering prayer • Silence	Loving one another: • Hospitality • Starting small groups • Selecting leaders • Living in common	Commitment 2: • Mutual confession • Submission	

26. See the section on vagrancy in *A Customary for Brothers*. "The source of all evil is useless wandering about. We propose therefore to make trips difficult." Trips more than a mile from the city required a brother to accompany him to help restrain the lure of contact with the world (Herxen 1988:174–75).

Ministry: • Almsgiving • Compassionate service • Peacemaking • Suffering, forgiving love	Bearing witness: • Preaching mission draws followers and opponents • Copying, "tent making" • Visiting sick	Commitment 3: • Schools for youth • Selling copies in vernacular • House profits to poor	
Weekly Practices: Eucharist Corporate worship	None new	Exercises, affective meditation on Christ Collations	None new
Monthly Practices: None	None new	One-or two-day retreats House sessions for "fraternal correction" Colloquies, house unity	None new
Annual/ Occasional Practices: None	Silent retreats Spiritual direction Pilgrimages	Colloquies, Dutch unity Dying well	No extended retreats or sabbaticals

Stage 1 Shifts	*Stage 2 Shifts*
Groote and followers move from / to: • Fixed vows / Flexible resolutions outside orders • Wealth / Simplicity & hospitality to poor women • Cognitive study of Scripture / Heart meditation • Daily solitude / Occasional long solitary periods • Isolation / Preaching & starting small groups • Latin / Vernacular heart language of laity	Movement from / to: • Individual / Communal living & working • Individual / Communal compassion for poor • Less / More structure through customaries • Preaching / Evangelistic collations • Existing schools / New training for youth • Isolation / Annual colloquies of Dutch houses

Though negative examples of mindless submission can be cited,[27] I offer a counter example, which became an annual practice for many houses. Each year, Herxen called to the house at Zwolle rectors of other congregations from whom they accepted outside counsel and to whom they submitted unresolved disputes. This form of voluntary submission to others, who carefully and gently listened to each person in the community, is exemplary (1988:165–66).

Finally, the New Devout and other medieval movements held to a practice of contemplating the final judgment and their own death. The New Devout practiced dying well, accompanying their own to death's door in a loving community of prayer. Broekelants (d. 1407) is a good example:

> As her death drew nearer . . . it seemed as if she had died. But when she came back to herself, she said warmly . . . "O good Jesus, where have you been so long?" And when death came over her, she seemed so joyful that it was as if she was laughing at it. That arose from her good conscience which she felt within her, for the Holy Spirit was bearing witness to her spirit that she was a child of God. (J. Van Engen 1988:125)

Grace

Not all of the New Devout exhibited the assurance of being God's child to the degree Broekelants did. In fact, the idea of assurance was neither explicit nor implicit in texts of the *Devotio Moderna*. The movement inherited the theological structure of medieval piety, based on merit and penance, which kept believers from the notion of God's accepting grace.[28] In a letter to one disciple, Groote argued that suffering increases virtue, reward, and merit (1988d:86). In another letter he wrote, "For he who stands firm to the end will be saved (Matt 24:13)—not he who begins, but he who finishes, not he who wavers but he who keeps the Word of God he has received; he will gain the reward" (1988e:78). In Gerard Zerbold's *Spiritual Ascents*, penance is the first ascent, which is

---

27. Salome Stricken instructs sisters not even to get a drink without permission. Quoting Groote, she commends mindless submission, even if ordered to set the house afire or to dismantle the roof (1988:179, 182).

28. For an excellent survey of the theological structure and origins of medieval piety, see Bradley's lecture (1997).

comprised of three steps: contrition, confession to a confessor, and satisfaction (1988:257-59). The texts of the Modern Devotion universally reflected this perspective. The idea of accepting grace and the assurance of salvation in the present was inconceivable to the New Devout, as it had been for believers since the *Shepherd of Hermas* in about 150.

But did the New Devotion emphasize empowering grace in conjunction with its spiritual practice and mission? My answer is a qualified yes. Though the New Devout placed high value on resolution based on their optimistic view of the role of the will, yet grace as God's enabling power is emphasized in their texts. For à Kempis, grace was "the teacher of discipline" and "the nurse of my devotional life" (1982:242). In *The Spiritual Ascents*, Gerard Zerbolt said that our heart desire for God should lead us to ascend to him through various exercises, which cannot be done by our virtue but only by "resting constantly on the aid of the Almighty" (1988:245). He concluded with three descents into various ministries of love to fellow believers and to those needing conversion. Citing Gregory and Bede, Zerbolt wrote of the role of grace in verbal witness of Christ (1988:312-14).[29]

Finally, grace originates with God, not us. God pours out his love in grace, which awakens in us a response of repentance, faith, and love. The Apostle John wrote, "We love, because he first loved us" (1 John 4:19). Thus, God's love for us—not our love for God—is the most important issue. "In this is love, not that we loved God" (1 John 4:13). This is hardly present in *Devotio Moderna* texts. The predominant emphases—on our resolution, our will, our devotion to Christ, and our imitation of him—eclipsed God's gracious initiative towards us. This dimension of grace—prevenient grace—seems to take a back seat to human resolve and devotion, with few exceptions.[30]

To summarize, the New Devout believed firmly in empowering grace. Without it even penance and merit were impossible. Empowering grace was strongly associated with both spirituality and mission (see

---

29. In *The Imitation of Christ*, à Kempis devotes six sections to various aspects of grace. It was a key to his battle against his fallen nature (1982:240). Without it, he could not live with power, develop virtue, do ministry, or practice spiritual disciplines (1982:234, 241-42). When discussing prayer in the context of manual labor, Salome Stricken attributed even our desire for God to his grace (1988:182).

30. For traces of prevenient grace in New Devout texts, see J. Van Engen (1988:122), Herxen (1988:214, 220), and Dieburg (1988:236).

Table 29 below for examples of New Devout views on grace). But accepting grace and full assurance appeared nowhere in their teaching. Their emphasis on human will eclipsed the idea of prevenient grace in which God takes the initiative prior to human response, though traces of this idea can be found, albeit rarely.

Table 29: New Devotion Quotes on Empowering Grace (Adapted from J. Van Engen 1988; Demaray 1982)

Source	Idea	Quote
Thomas à Kempis: *Imitation of Christ*	Grace and spirituality	"When grace is missing, even a little resistance stops me in a dead faint." (1982:240)
		"Without Your grace I can do nothing; with You I can do anything because Your grace strengthens me." (1982:241)
		"Though I experience temptation, vexation, and trouble I fear no evil, so long as Your grace stays with me. Grace alone and by itself is my strength; grace alone gives advice and help. Grace alone is stronger than all enemies." (1982:242)
		"Throw out all hindrances to grace if you really want to be filled with grace. How can you do that? Be alone in secret; love being alone; don't desire a lot of conversation with people; pour out devout prayer to God in order to keep your soul contrite and your conscience pure; look on the whole world as nothing compared with grace; prefer being with God over external stimuli . . ." (1982:234)
	Grace and mission	"Not even the gift of preaching, the gift of miracles . . . no matter how highly developed, has real value without grace. . . . Without grace, I am but a withered branch, a stump unable to bear fruit." (1982:241–42)

Salome Sticken: A Way of Life for Sisters	Grace and desire for God	"May it be common among you to pray devoutly and to lift your hearts up to the Lord God during your labor, because the Lord God is to be sought and found not only in churches, through the prayers poured out there, but in every place and as present to everyone, *at* least to everyone who by grace desires him." (1988:182)
Gerard Zerbolt: Spiritual Ascents	Grace and spirituality	"You must therefore dispose your heart to these ascents [various spiritual exercises], not trusting to make the climb on the strength of your own virtue but resting constantly upon the aid of the Almighty.... Because this ascent is truly not in the power of the one walking or ascending but in the gift of God, you are advised ... to request the aid and counsel of God, for unless you are accompanied in all things by divine grace you will have no energy of your own." (1988:245–46)
	Grace and mission	"Insofar as you accept the grace of the highest inbreathing, recall your neighbor from evil, proclaim to the erring one the eternal kingdom.... and by daily exercise ... strive to convert others to the author of all grace and ever to increase the joy of the heavenly homeland." (1988:313)

Conclusion on the Devotio Moderna's Rhythms of Spirituality and Mission

The mission of the New Devout is unimaginable without the space and time they created for God in solitude and community. Their houses planted in the heart of fourteenth and fifteenth century towns, their private rooms, the chapels in these houses, the parish churches, and cathedrals in their towns comprised the holy spaces where they practiced their rhythms of imitating Christ. Their schedules were filled with daily spiritual practices and at least weekly mission practices. Also important were the one- or two-day silent retreats away from the pressures of daily life preceding the feast days, which occurred every several weeks. Appendix G displays the findings to my primary research question and its subsidiaries. It shows a close connection between time and space created for God and mission "in deed and word. Though the movement did not last beyond the sixteenth century, it survived in other forms such as 'reform Catholicism' and Puritanism" (Oberman 1988:3). Van Engen sums up its main emphases:

> "Imitation" is probably a misleading term for their outlook. Their emphasis fell neither on imitation in a strict sense, as in works of mercy, nor on "mystic union," as in the teachings of many late medieval authors, but rather on an individual and affective identification with particular moments in Christ's life, chiefly his passion, the result or purpose of which was ideally fourfold: to "relive" with Christ his virtuous life and saving passion, to have him ever present before one's eyes, to manifest his presence to others, and to orchestrate, as it were, all one's mental and emotional faculties around devotion to him. (1988:25)

Interestingly, "affective identification with particular moments in Christ's life" (J. Van Engen 1988:25) was also a central earmark of Ignatius of Loyola's *Spiritual Exercises* (1991c). Given the debt of the New Devout and Ignatius to a common spiritual text—Ludolph of Saxony's *Life of Christ* (J. Van Engen 1988:25, Ganss et al. 1991:19–26)—such a common characteristic is not surprising. To the discussion of Ignatius and his four classic texts we now turn.

Ignatius of Loyola and the Early Jesuits

In *Spirituality for Mission*, Reilly noted that the largest male mission order in the Roman Catholic Church in the twentieth century was the Society of Jesus (1978:76). So what kind of spirituality fueled the early life and mission of the Jesuits, which might account for its spread and longevity? Its founder, Ignatius of Loyola, wrote his *Autobiography* (Ign. *Autobiog.* 1991a), *Spiritual Diary* (Ign. *Diary* 1999b), *The Spiritual Exercises* (Ign. *Sp. Ex.* 1991c), *Constitutions of the Society of Jesus* (Ign. *Const.* 1991d), and almost seven thousand letters.[31]

---

31. These texts and ten of Ignatius's letters have been published by Paulist Press in The Classics of Western Spirituality series (Ganss et al. 1991). This volume was edited by Father George E. Ganss, S.J., who is an editor in the Institute of Jesuit Sources. Collaborating in the translation with Ganss were R. Divarkar, SJ, Edward Malatesta, SJ,

The Spiritual Exercises functioned for the early Jesuits in much the same way as did the various spiritual exercises written for individual use in the Modern Devotion. Just as the *Customary for Brothers* at Zwolle came to have an important structuring role for the whole movement in Holland, so the *Constitutions of the Society of Jesus* did later for the Society. As I apply my research question to these texts, an obvious subsidiary question presents itself: Why did the Society become a lasting presence in its work of renewal and world mission for almost five hundred years, while the New Devotion ceased to exist within a couple of centuries of its birth and explosive growth?

To address these questions, I will survey the life and mission of Ignatius, but give less attention to the movement after his death than I did to the New Devotion after Groote's death.[32] And so, I focus primarily on Ignatius's texts. As with the New Devotion, I will identify the daily, weekly, monthly, and annual or occasional spiritual and mission practices of Ignatius and his early followers, how time and space were demarcated for these practices, and how grace related to them.

The Autobiography (1521–38)

Ignatius was born to noble parentage in Northwest Spain in 1491, a time of momentous political and religious change. Feudalism was still giving way to powerful centralized governments, which were now exploring new lands looking for treasure and territory (Ganss et al. 1991:10). The unity of the Roman Catholic Church was under assault by forces that would eventually result in the Protestant Reformation. Where the church remained intact, it stood in need of moral, spiritual, and structural reform (1991:11–12). At age fifteen, Ignatius went to live in the home of the treasurer to King Ferdinand and Queen Isabella to be trained in court life, where he became known for gambling and ro-

---

and Martin Palmer, SJ, all scholars in some aspect of Jesuit spirituality, mission, and history. I also use *Draw Me into Your Friendship* (1996) by scholar David Fleming, SJ. Given the broad scope of this study, a full review of recent literature by scholars of Ignatius and early Jesuit spirituality is impossible. But such a review would include the biography by Candido de Dalmases (1985), *The First Jesuits* by John O Malley, SJ (1993), and David Lonsdale's *Eyes to See, Ears to Hear* (2000).

32. The reason is that Ignatius (1491–1556) lived for thirty-five years after his conversion compared to only ten years for Groote, thus Ignatius had far greater *direct influence* upon the early stages of his movement than did Groote upon the New Devotion.

mantic affairs (1991:14–15). The beginning of his *Autobiography* states that until age twenty-six Ignatius was given to "vanities of the world ... warlike sport ... [and] foolish desire to win fame." In 1521 he was wounded in battle, and would have died except for a miraculous healing (*Autobiog.* 1991a:[1, 3]).[33]

Ignatius's conversion occurred while he was convalescing at Loyola from August 1521 to February 1522. Here he had long periods of solitude and silence, devoted to meditative reading and the start of his lifelong practice of making notes on his readings, a form of journaling. He read Ludolph of Saxony's *Life of Christ* and *The Golden Legend* by Jacobus de Voragine, which contained stories of the saints (Ganss et al. 1991:15, 19).[34] To pass time, he imagined himself in these stories even as he had been prone to do with medieval fiction. But he found that spiritual texts left him fulfilled, not "dry and dissatisfied" like fiction. This was his first experience of discernment of spirits (Ign. *Autobiog.* 1991a:[6–8]). During his recovery, he took long solitary periods with God in nature, especially gazing at the sky and stars. His family noticed the change in his soul. When he had recovered, despite their opposition, he set off on a pilgrimage to the Holy Land, to which he sensed God calling him. He practiced nightly vigils and wrote out a lengthy three-day confession near Barcelona, after which he donned the garb of a penitent. He began to give away most everything given to him, the practice of almsgiving coupled with simplicity.

Leaving Barcelona for Jerusalem, he took a short detour to Manresa, which instead became an eleven-month stay and would affect the rest of his life (*Autobiog.* 1991a:[10–11, 13, 17–18]). In Manresa he begged for alms daily and went to the church three times a day, "finding great comfort" praying the hours (Ign. *Autobiog.* 1991a:[12–20, 26]). He began to have visions and illuminations from both God and the devil—the

---

33. Ignatius of Loyola's works are not usually referenced by page number, but by sections or subsections—each usually about a paragraph or two in length. Thus, (*Autobiog.* 1991a:[1, 3]) refers not to pages 1 and 3, but to sections 1 and 3 of Ignatius's unfinished *Autobiography*, which covers his life from 1521 in Pamplona to 1538 in Rome in at the end of his first year there (Ganss et al. 1991:57).

34. *The Golden Legend* treated the saints in order of the feast days on which they were honored. Regarding the hagiographic nature of this work, Ganss et al. write, "It is replete with tales, many of them about miracles, which are retold without any sense of critical scholarship; and its etymologies are fanciful. Yet beneath this exuberant foliage it also contained substantial historical and religious truth" (1991:16).

latter revealing himself as a beautiful serpent, which Ignatius initially mistook as a divine revelation due to the consolation it produced. Soon he had "great changes in his soul.... Sometimes he felt so out of sorts that he found no relish in saying prayers nor in hearing Mass nor in any other devotion he might practice" (*Autobiog.* 1991a:[21]). Perplexed by this, he sought counsel from spiritual people, though usually this proved disappointing (*Autobiog.* 1991a:[37]). Seeking spiritual direction to sort out God's voice amidst various stirrings in the soul would become an important feature of Jesuit life. Ignatius learned that consolations do not necessarily come from God, nor do desolations mean that God is not at work. I have illustrated the need for discernment and spiritual direction in Table 30 below, which could serve as a discernment grid for spiritual directors and those in discipling and mentoring roles [35]

This eremitic phase of Ignatius's life marked him in several ways. First, he experienced God as his personal teacher. Second, he received numerous visions of Christ in human form—between twenty to forty, he says. Third, he conversed distinctly with each member of the Trinity with great emotion, often to the point of tears. Fourth, what Ignatius later viewed as his greatest solitary encounter with God occurred in a natural setting beside the Cardoner River, not far from Manresa (Ign. *Autobiog.* 1991a:[27–30]). Ganss et al. point out that through this encounter Ignatius discovered that he was "not to remain a solitary pilgrim imitating the saints in prayer and penance, but to labor with Christ for the salvation of others. He also saw, somewhat dimly, that he ought to seek companions for this enterprise" (1991:31). Fifth, he wrote these and subsequent illuminations and revelations in a copybook, which became the rough draft of *The Spiritual Exercises,* completed by the time he left Manresa in March of 1523 (1991:27). These notes informed the counsel he gave others, who sought his counsel.

After his pilgrimage to Jerusalem in 1523, Ignatius began a period of study (1524–35) at the Universities of Barcelona, Alcala, Salmanca, and finally Paris, where he would earn a master of arts degree, which

---

35. Ignatius has one set of rules for discernment to guide retreatants during their first week (*Sp. Ex.* 1991c:[313–27]) and a different set for the second week (*Sp. Ex.* 1991c:[328–36]). James Wakefield notes the division between scholars who see the *Exercises* primarily as a means of making vocational decisions and those who see them primarily as a school of prayer (2006:195 n. 10). Wakefield views his Protestant version of the *Exercises* primarily as a school for prayer.

Table 30: Ignatius Discovers the Need For Spiritual Discernment and Direction (Adapted from Ign. *Autobiog.* 1991a:[19–37])

Source	In Consolation	In Desolation
God and his holy angels	God works through joy and an awareness of his presence and grace. Spiritual practice is a delight. Consolation was a part of Ignatius's initial spiritual journey.	God's works through hidden-ness, without an awareness of his presence. Spiritual practice seems dry. Desolation becomes redemptive. As Ignatius grew it was essential to his future life and work.
Our new nature	Affirmation of virtue, truth; often delayed	Resistance to evil, error; inner alarm
Our fallen nature	Instant pleasure in evil or pride in virtue	Finally bitter aftermath of evil, deceit
Devil and his fallen angels	The enemy works deceptively as an angel of light. This consolation at first appears to be from God but is not.	The enemy brings desolation that is not redemptive but destructive.

would allow him to teach anywhere in the world. His schooling at the college of Saint Barbe in Paris provided him the theory and methods upon which to base the future educational work of the Society, according to Joseph A. Tetlow (1992:24). However, during Ignatius's years of study, revelations and visions became infrequent, while persecution and false accusations increased. In spite of these conflicts and the time constraints of academic study, he attracted a growing number of followers, giving them the *Spiritual Exercises* and training others to do the same. This activity outside the confines of any order or ecclesiastical body drew suspicion in an age of inquisitions in which heretics were burned. Ignatius was examined and pronounced doctrinally sound, but was subsequently jailed for forty-two days at Alcala and eleven days when he was at Slamanca. He refused repeated efforts of acquaintances to get him out, always responding, "He for whose love I got in here will get me out, if he is served thereby." While in prison, he continued to teach and give spiritual exercises (Ign. *Autobiog.* 1991a:[58–60]). At the University of Paris he also suffered persecution. There he surrounded himself with followers from whom he selected a handful of associates, who would become the founding members of the Society of Jesus (*Autobiog.* 1991a:[73–86]). The new spiritual disciplines that he practiced during his years of academic work were study, caring for souls by giving the *Spiritual Exercises*, costly suffering love, and selecting and training leaders.

Time, Space, Spirituality, and Mission in the Exercises

In 1534 Ignatius's six companions each withdrew from their normal activities at the University of Paris for one month in solitary retreat to take the *Exercises*.[36] Jesuits ever since have done the same as part of discerning God's call to the Society.[37] In my view, this is a key factor for the Society's longevity. Jesuit spirituality includes a withdrawal that approximates the length of Jesus's solitary pilgrimage to the desert, a pattern that never developed in the *Devotio Moderna*.

Yet the *Exercises* were flexibly designed for other time spans as well. Ignatius "gave his Exercises to many kinds of persons and in many different ways; for example, for two or three days, or one week, or three, or four weeks" (Ganss et al. 1991:51). Indeed, the Nineteenth Annotation states, "A person who is involved in public affairs or pressing occupations but educated or intelligent may take an hour and a half each day to perform the Exercises" (*Sp. Ex.* 1991c:[19]).[38] This is called a "retreat in everyday life" in David Fleming's contemporary reading of the *Exercises* (1996:19). This flexibility regarding time renders the daily-weekly-monthly-annual/occasional scheme I have used to ana-

---

36. One of the associates, Simon Rodrigues, withdrew for an hour and a half each day, doing the *Exercises* over a number of months due to academic responsibilities (Tetlow 1992:25).

37. According to Ganss et al., all novices are required to take the full thirty-day retreat (1991:51).

38. The *Exercises* begin with twenty introductory explanatory notes about their use and practice. These are called annotations and are set off with brackets as are all 370 sections of the *Exercises* in the editions I consulted. Since I am referring to sections and not pages in my citations of the *Exercises*, I use the customary brackets within parentheses, hence the citation of the nineteenth annotation appears as (*Sp. Ex.* 1991c:[19]).

lyze spiritual texts somewhat inadequate in this case.[39] Yet the *Exercises* do address issues of time and space with respect to spiritual practice. Regarding a place for a multi-day retreat, the Twentieth Annotation proposes a location away from one's normal environs.

> Ordinarily ... an exercitant will achieve more progress the more he or she withdraws from all friends and acquaintances, and from all earthly concerns; for example, by moving out of one's place of residence and taking a different house or room where one can live in the greatest possible solitude, and thus be free to attend Mass and Vespers daily without hindrances from acquaintances. (*Sp. Ex.* 1991c:[20])

This illustrates the genius of the *Exercises*: their portability. They were not confined to a monastery, retreat center, the life of an order, or any particular time in the church's calendar. Indeed, they could be done anytime, anywhere. Ignatius suggests a "house or room" away from one's normal living environment. Deep formation in Christ and his mission became accessible outside the confines of typical monastic life, which accounts for some of the opposition to Ignatius, not to speak of his non-clerical status during his student years. The genius of the *Exercises* is also seen in their adaptability. The Eighteenth Annotation states, "The Spiritual Exercises should be adapted to the disposition of the persons who desire to make them, that is to their age, education, and ability" (*Sp. Ex.* 1991c:[18]).

The *Exercises* sometimes prescribe temporal boundaries for spiritual and mission practices and sometimes they do not. Examination of conscience (*examen*) is to occur three times daily while taking the *Exercises*—upon rising, after lunch, and after dinner—and twice daily otherwise. The five meditative exercises done daily during a multi-day retreat are to be given one full hour each (Ign. *Sp. Ex.* 1991c:[12, 24–26]). Works of mercy (giving alms) are commended, as is fasting if not physically harmful, but with no fixed time frame (*Sp. Ex.* 1991c:[212–213, 337–345]). Thus, Ignatius includes the same "golden thread" of the historic spiritual practices commanded by Jesus and seen in the early church and Geert Groote: fasting, prayer, and almsgiving. Inner spirituality finds expression in compassionate acts. Confession

---

39. I was alerted to this by Simon Chan in his critique of this study in the dissertation phase (2007).

is to occur daily while taking the *Exercises* and weekly otherwise. In normal life, the Eucharist should be received every two weeks, or preferably weekly, but daily while taking the Exercises (*Sp. Ex.* 1991c:[18, 20]). For retreatants taking the *Exercises*, prayer and mission merge in two locations: "The Call of the Temporal King" (*Sp. Ex.* 1991c:[92-99]) and "Contemplation to Attain Love" (*Sp. Ex.* 1991c:[230-37]). Here retreatants meditate upon the mission of the risen Lord to which they are called.

Other notable features in the *Exercises* that relate to time include:

1. The usual duration of the *Spiritual Exercises*—thirty days broken into four weeks

2. Unhurried time for tending one's desires and using affective imagination in meditation

3. Unhurried time for "making an election"—discerning God's will on a major question

4. Rules for discernment

I will treat these in order. First, the schedule of a usual retreat for those taking the *Exercises* involves thirty days divided into four successive weeks, which are not necessarily seven days each.[40] After the "Introductory Explanations" and the "Principle and Foundation," "the First Week" addresses the retreatant's sin in light of the cross and attempts to bring genuine confession and sorrow for sin. "The Second Week" deals with meditative exercises from the life of Christ prior to Passion Week. "The Third Week" focuses on the passion of our Lord and the Fourth Week on his resurrection. "The Fourth Week" prepares the retreatant to return to the world as a participant in Christ's mission.

Second, two earmarks of the *Exercises* are the use of the imagination[41] and paying attention to inner desires of the heart. On this Ignatius says the following:

> When a contemplation or meditation is about something that can be gazed on, for example, a contemplation of Christ our Lord, who is visible, the composition consists of seeing in imag-

---

40. Wakefield talks of movements, not weeks, in his Protestant version of the *Exercises* (2006).

41. For a discussion of biblical uses of the imagination, see J. Wakefield (2006:23-24, 197 n. 4-6).

> ination the physical place where that which I want to contemplate is taking place....
>
> When a contemplation or mediation is about something abstract and invisible, as in the present case about the sins, the composition will be to see in imagination and to consider my soul as imprisoned....
>
> The second prelude is to ask for what I want and desire. What I ask for should be in accordance with the subject matter. For example, in a contemplation on the resurrection, I will ask for joy with Christ in joy; in a contemplation on the Passion, I will ask for pain, tears, and suffering with Christ suffering. (*Sp. Ex.* 1991c:[47–48])[42]

To be aware of the heart's desires takes unhurried time in solitude, as does the meditative use of imagination. So does the thoughtful, rigorous examination of conscience prescribed in the *Exercises*.[43]

Third, when they took the *Exercises*, Ignatius's friends sensed God's call to participate in the mission to which God had called Ignatius. Ignatius called this "making an election," which could best be done in an unhurried extended retreat. In this environment, retreatants waited upon God and listened for a three-fold confirmation, consisting of (1) divine attraction in the retreatant's will, (2) clarification through consolations and desolations, and (3) a period of mental calm in which two methods[44] are used to test the spirits (*Sp. Ex.* 1991c:[175–87]).

Fourth, if Ignatius is known for anything, it is for his way of discerning the movements in the soul of either consolation or desolation and whether these might have either good or evil spirits as their source, as mentioned above. He devotes twenty-two sections to this issue (*Sp. Ex.* 1991c:[313–36]). The design of the *Exercises* provides the retreatant and her or his director reflective time for unhurried discernment throughout the retreat.

---

42. Ignatius used Ludolf's method of affective meditation on the life of Christ (Ganss et al. 1991:22).

43. Each of these is important in recovery from drug and alcohol addiction, which is why recovering addicts have seen many parallels between the *Exercises* and the Twelve Steps.

44. These two methods contain ten steps for discerning God's will (Ign. *Sp. Ex.* 1991c:[178–88]).

Founding and Early Growth of the Society

Ignatius and his six companions, having finished their degrees in Paris and having taken the *Exercises* and a vow of chastity and poverty, gathered in Venice in 1537 to wait a year for an opportunity to go on pilgrimage to Jerusalem (Tetlow 1992:26; Ganss et al. 1991:108-9).

They were ordained to the priesthood on June 24, 1537 (Ganss et al. 1991:41). Not long afterward, Ignatius and two associates went to Vicenza, where they spent forty days in a house outside the city devoting themselves to prayer (*Autobiog.* 1991a:[93, 94]).[45] Afterwards, they went out to preach. "Their preaching caused a great stir in the city, and many persons were moved with devotion, and they received in greater abundance the material goods they needed." In Vicenza, supernatural visitations and visions returned to Ignatius like he had experienced in Manresa. In one case God gave Ignatius assurance that a dying companion, Bassano, would be healed. He was miraculously restored (*Autobiog.* 1991a:[95]). Grace, spirituality, and centrifugal mission were powerfully linked during their stay.

At the end of the year of waiting, when no ship had sailed to the Holy Land due to a conflict between the Venetians and Turks, Ignatius and his companions made their way to Rome to place their services at the pope's discretion. "One day, a few miles before reaching Rome, he was at prayer in a church and experienced such a change in his soul and saw so clearly that God the Father placed him with Christ his Son that he would not dare doubt it" (*Autobiog.* 1991a:[96]). This vision came as a direct answer to Ignatius's longtime prayer to be with Christ, and was recounted to Jesuits in the early days as evidence of God's calling upon the newfound order (Ganss et al. 1991:41-42). At the time of the vision, Ignatius wondered if it meant that real or figurative martyrdom awaited him in Rome (Tetlow 1992:26). But once in Rome, his companions organized the wealthy to help the poor.

> Particularly during the first winter, 1537-38, severe itself and coming after poor harvests, the Companions helped house, clothe, and feed hundreds of people (a significant percentage of the city's population). Before long, they had launched an or-

---

45. This does not appear to have been an occasion when anyone took the *Exercises*, though some of Ignatius's exercises may well have been used in prayer. The companions apparently waited upon God in corporate and solitary prayer.

phanage, a home for prostitutes trying to start over . . . a refuge for persecuted Jews, and a school. . . . The school, to the astonishment of the Romans, was free. These efforts for the marginated and poor emerged from the experience of the Spiritual Exercises. (1992:27)

In the spring of 1539 after discussion and prayer, according to the procedures for making an election in the *Exercises,* Ignatius and his ten companions came to the unanimous decision that they should seek to become an apostolic order (Ganss et al. 1991:44–45). On September 3, 1539, they submitted a written application to the pope. On September 27, 1540, approval came in a papal bull from Paul III. "Ignatius and his ten companions were now a new religious order of clerics regular in the Church, the Society of Jesus" (Ganss et al. 1991:44–45). After being unanimously elected as the Society's first superior general by his companions on April 6, 1541,[46] Ignatius led the Society through a period of explosive expansion until his death in 1556. During these years he wrote the *Constitutions* (1991d) and almost seven thousand letters with the help of his close associate and secretary Polanco (Ganss et al. 1991:46, 56).

Part IV of the *Constitutions* outlines Ignatius's philosophy of education and how colleges should be structured (1991d:[307–509]).[47] The haphazard attempts to educate prevalent in European cities and towns had produced hunger for a more systematic and comprehensive approach to education, such as the Paris method, which Ignatius employed. He saw the opportunity and responded to the felt need. By the time of his death, Ignatius and his fellow Jesuits had established 33 colleges, including institutions in Goa and Brazil, with another 6 having been approved. That number increased to 372 in 1675, and to 612 in 1710. Jesuits also led 15 universities and 176 seminaries by the time the order was suppressed in 1773. All the colleges were governed from Rome under the philosophy laid out in the *Constitutions* (Ganss et al. 1991:48–49, 280).

In addition to the educational work of the Jesuits, their initiatives in foreign mission were also impressive. Xavier spearheaded the Jesuit mission in Goa where he arrived in 1542. His mission carried him to

---

46. Ignatius was given his charge on April 19, 1522 (Ganss et al. 1991:46).

47. Ganss's edition of the *Constitutions* demarcates subsections by brackets, thus (1991d:[307]) refers to a subsection, not a page.

Southwest India, where in one month he baptized ten thousand. In 1546 another twelve Jesuits went to India. Xavier's mission career took him to Japan, where he introduced Christianity and the Catholic Church. By his death in 1552, he left Jesuits in mission enclaves throughout the Far East. Jesuits also went to Brazil to start a mission in 1549 (Ganss et al. 1991:47–48).

Time, Grace, Spirituality, and Mission in Ignatius's Diary

The *Diary* (Ignatius 1991b), which covers approximately thirteen months from February 2, 1544 to February 27, 1545, provides a clear picture of Ignatius's spirituality as he carried out his daily responsibilities as general superior.[48] It portrays him at the pinnacle of his spirituality, which flourished rather than waned under the under the heavy responsibilities of leading the Society.

> Most but not all of the mystical experiences recorded in the *Diary* occurred during Ignatius' prayer in the morning. This prayer, including the Mass on which it was centered, seemingly lasted one to three hours daily. For the rest of the day throughout these almost thirteen months he engaged in his ordinary apostolic activities. He was governing the Society, which now had members in Portugal, Spain, Germany, Italy and India. He had spiritual care of the women living in the House of St. Martha and was confessor to the household of Margaret of Austria, who in 1543 had given him help in his work for the catechumens from Judaism. (Ganss et al. 1991:231)

It appears that Ignatius devoted himself to lengthy periods of private prayer in preparation for leading the Mass. "In my customary prayer from the beginning to the end, there was a great and constantly growing help of grace, with devotion that was very clear, bright, and warm. It resulted in much satisfaction and contentment, both in the preparatory prayer and in the chapel." He describes what ensued in the chapel. "While vesting I experienced fresh motions which lasted to the end, together with greater ones and with many tears." All during Mass "there was much interior devotion and spiritual warmth, not without

---

48. Ignatius, not wanting his *Diary* read, probably destroyed it, with only fragments surviving—the forty days in which he concluded his election concerning poverty, February 2 to March 12, 1544; and March 13, 1544 to February 27, 1545, describing special mystical encounters in prayer (Ganss et al. 1991:55).

Table 31: Ignatius on Empowering Grace for Spirituality and Mission (From Ign. 1991a:[88–89], 1991b:[76, 134, 153], 1991c:[20, 46, 49], and 1991e:[332, 338]; emphasis added)

Autobiography		Grace and mission	"In this hospice he [Ignatius] began to speak with many who came to visit him of the things of God, *by whose grace much fruit was derived*. As soon as he arrived, he decided to teach Christian doctrine every day to children, but his brother strongly objected to this, saying that no one would come. He replied that one would be enough. But after he began to do it, many came continually to hear him, and even his brother.
			Besides Christian doctrine, he also preached on Sundays and feast with profit and help to the souls who came many miles to hear him. He also made an attempt to eliminate some abuses, and *with God's help* some were set right" (1991a:88–89). The abuses he set right were a ban on gambling and concubinage in which many priests were participating. Also, "He got an order to be given that the poor should be provided for officially and regularly, and that bells should be rung three times at the Angeles, that is morning, noon, and evening, so that the people might pray as in Rome." (1991a:89)
Diary		Grace and spiritual practice	"During the first prayer [at Mass] I had much devotion, and later even more with warmth and *the assistance of copious grace*." (1991b:[76])"In my customary prayer from the beginning to the end, *there was a great and constantly growing help of grace*, with devotion that was very clear, bright, and warm. It resulted in much satisfaction and contentment, both in the preparatory prayer and in the chapel." (1991b:[134])"During the grace at table I had a partial perception of the Father's being and also of the Being of the Holy Trinity, and a certain spiritual motion impelled me toward devotion and to tears. Throughout the whole day I had neither experienced nor seen anything like it, although I had sought it many times. The great visitations of this day did not terminate in any distinct or particular Person, but in general in the *Giver of graces*." (1991b:[153])

	Grace, solitude, and the prayer of preparation	"The more we keep ourselves alone and secluded... the more do we dispose ourselves to receive graces and gifts... (1991c:[20])The preparatory prayer for all contemplations and meditations in *The Spiritual Exercises* is "to ask God our Lord for the grace that all my intentions, actions, and operations may be ordered purely to the service and praise of his Divine Majesty." (1991c:[46, 49])
Spiritual Exercises		
Letters	Grace and protection, with help to obey God's will	Salutation and Closing of Letter to Teresa Rejadell [I:99–107][50] "*May the grace and love of Christ our Lord be always our* protection and help.... I close, praying that the most holy Trinity by its infinite and supreme goodness *may bestow upon all of us plentiful grace* to know its most holy will and perfectly to fulfill it." (1991e:332, 338)[51]

tears" (*Diary* 1991b:[134–36]).[49] Ganss et al. note that tears associated with humble love, reverent joy, and affectionate awe, as seen in this entry, were common features of his morning prayers, as were visions, insights, visitations, touches, and speech. These are characteristic of what is called infused contemplation or mysticism. Key to these experiences are prevenient grace, divine initiative, God's power, and passivity on the part of the mystic (1991:230–31). Ignatius's experience of grace during these times with God undoubtedly influenced his teaching on grace. Though he was still working under the medieval system of penance, merit, and satisfaction, without a theology of accepting grace (*Sp. Ex.* 1991c:[82–89]), Ignatius experienced and taught prevenient and empowering grace. Both undergirded his view of mission (*Autobiog.* 1991a:[88–89]), spiritual practice (*Diary* 1991b:[134, 153]), and solitude and prayer (*Sp. Ex.* 1991c:[20, 46, 49]).

Grace, Time, Spirituality, and Mission in the Constitutions

The Society of Jesus has been governed by its massive *Constitutions* ever since they were completed, and this longevity bears witness to

---

49. As with Ignatius's *Autobiography* and *Constitutions*, citations for his *Diary* refer to subsections, not pages, thus (1991b: [134–36]) refers to subsections 134–36.

their flexibility, wisdom, and stature among spiritual classics.[50] Just as transforming grace permeates Ignatius's writings examined thus far, so grace pervades the *Constitutions*, written by Ignatius to shape his Society's spirituality and mission. "The end of this Society is to devote itself with God's grace not only to the salvation and perfection of the members' own souls, but also with that same grace to labor strenuously in giving aid toward the salvation and perfection of the souls of their neighbors" (*Cons.* 1991d:[3]). Grace is key to "the observance of all the Constitutions and in our manner of proceeding in our Lord," and as the Society would grow, unity could only be preserved by "the help of the grace of God" (1991d:[547, 662]). Table 31 above samples Ignatius's comments on grace in his other works.

Time was demarcated for spirituality and mission in the *Constitutions*. In Table 32 below I have displayed my findings regarding how much time for spiritual and mission practices was required of scholastics—Society members who studied at Jesuit colleges—compared with the more flexible requirements for Society members who were not scholastics. Ignatius felt that Jesuit education, which was free to Jesuits and non-Jesuits alike (*Cons.* 1991d:[478]), should require and maintain certain minimal daily, weekly, and annual or occasional practices for all its students.

1. *Daily Practices*. Ignatius believed that students who had not yet taken the Society's vows of poverty, chastity, and obedience should still be required to practice these each day as long as they lived in Jesuit houses and attended Jesuit colleges (*Cons.* 1991d:[282, 284]). These externs along with Jesuit students should also conduct an examination of conscience two times daily and spend an hour a day in prayer. Daily attendance at Mass was also required (1991d:[342]).

---

50. Before the *Constitutions* were accepted in 1558 by the Society's first General Congregation two years after Ignatius's death, he had introduced an experimental text in 1552. This was known as Text A. From 1552 until 1555, Text A was explained to various Jesuit communities throughout Europe. Another copy, Text B—known as the "Autograph"—was retained by Ignatius on which he made minor corrections until his death. Text B was approved in 1558 and remains the Society's governing law to this day (Ganss et al. 1991:56–67).

Table 32: Spiritual and Mission Practices Taught in the Constitutions (Adapted from Ign. *Cons.* [1991d] and *Sp. Ex.* [1991c])

	Spiritual Practices	Mission Practices
	Principle for Scholastics: "In regard to spiritual matters … While they [the scholastics] are applying themselves to their studies, just as care must be taken that through fervor in study they do not grow cool in their love of true virtues and of religious life, so also during that time there will not be much place for mortifications and long prayers and meditations." (1991d:[340]; see also [362])	
Daily	*Solitude / Abiding:* Poverty (1991d:[287]) Chastity Obedience (submission) (1991d:[282, 284]) *Examen* 2 times daily (1991d:[342]) 1 hour of meditation—for recitation of the Hours of Our Lady and other prayer forms adapted to one's personality (1991d:[342]) *Community / Loving One Another:* Mass heard daily (1991d:[342])	Works of mercy: almsgiving (1991c:[337–345]) Jesuits offered education free to anyone who qualified (1991d:[478])
Weekly	Confession every 8 days (1991d:[342]) Communion every 8 days (1991c:[342])	

	Solitude / Abiding:	When on Retreat with the Exercises:
Annual or Occasional	Taking the Exercises (1991d:[408])Making an election (discerning a major life/ministry decision) (1991c:[169–89])	Contemplating the call of Christ my King in his mission in the world (1991c:[92–99])
	Fasting commended if not physically harmful but no fixed time frame given (1991c:[212–13]) *Community / Loving One Another:*	Contemplation to attain love (1991c:[230–37]) Preaching and giving sacred lectures (1991d:[402]) Practice in administering the sacraments of confession and communion (1991d:[406])
	2-year probationary living in a Jesuit house or college[51] (1991d:[283])	Learning to give the Exercises (1991d:[408])
Principle for All Other Members: "In what pertains to prayer, meditation, and study and also in regard to the bodily practices of fasts, vigils, and other austerities of penances, it does not seem expedient to give them any other rule than that which discreet charity dictates to them, provided that the confessor should always be informed and also, when a doubt about expediency arises, the superior." (1991d:[582])		
Flexibly determined with confessor	"On the other hand, they should be vigilant that these practices may not be relaxed to such an extent that the spirit grows cold and the human and lower passions grow warm." (1991d:[582])	"On the one hand, the members should keep themselves alert that the excessive use of these practices may not weaken the bodily energies and consume time to such an extent that these energies are insufficient for the spiritual help of one's neighbor according to our Institute." (1991d:[582])

---

51. The contemporary term for this period is "novitiate" (Ganss et al. 1991:455 n. 19).

2. *Weekly Practices.* Ignatius wanted scholastics to go to confession and take communion weekly (1991d:[342])—often by sixteenth century norms. He was a champion of frequent communion.[52]

3. *Annual or Occasional Practices.* Novitiates seeking membership in the Society lived in Jesuit houses for a two-year probationary period to discern whether they were being led to the Jesuit life (*Cons.* 1991d:[283]). Having experienced the *Spiritual Exercises* themselves, scholastics—and perhaps novitiates and externs—were expected to lead others through them (1991d:[408]). Scholastics were also encouraged to preach, give lectures, take confessions, and administer communion (1991d:[402, 406]). Missionaries would need to be able to do all these. With respect to all other members of the Society, Ignatius insisted on a radical flexibility. On one hand he was concerned that time taken in spiritual exercises would not be allowed to usurp time for mission, while on the other hand, he advocated that spiritual practice not become so relaxed that spiritual passion cools while the fallen nature is stirred (*Cons.* 1991d:[582]). Mission practices and spiritual practices in both solitary and communal forms were embedded in the *Constitutions*. Spirituality and mission were not to be mutually exclusive.

Conclusion on the Early Jesuit's Spirituality and Mission

Table 33 below displays these practices in the first two stages of early Jesuit expansion, using Sheldrake's model (see Table 27). The focus in this study has been Stage 1 and the early years of Stage 2. The period after 1560 is beyond the scope of this study except to briefly discuss some basic internal and external threats to the movement, which could contribute to its senility or breakdown.

1. *Lack of Contextualization.* Stephen Neill points out that during Xavier's initial three years in Goa he was able to learn little of its difficult Tamil language, into which interpreters roughly translated the Creed, the Ten Commandments, the Lord's Prayer, and other prayers.[53] Xavier had "a wonderful capacity to attract youth," whom he taught to memorize these Christian texts and to, in turn, teach them to the older

---

52. Ganss et al. 1991:459 n. 31.

53. Neill notes that the translation of these interpreters later proved to be quite deficient (1986:128).

Table 33: Early Jesuit's Emerging Practices of Spirituality and Mission (Adapted from Ganss et al. 1991; Sheldrake 1992; Catherall 1978; Miller 2007; Ivens 1986)

Stage 1: Emergent (1521–40)	Stage 2: Maintenance (1540–1650)		Stage 3: Possible Breakdown (1650–)
Conversion, Deepening	Schooling, New Society	Growth of Society	Renewal of Society
Daily Practices Solitude: • Sacraments: Mass • Silence • Long solitude in nature; by a river, under sky • Affective meditation • Spiritual reading • Taking notes, journaling discernment of spirits • Vigils • Simplicity, poverty • Praying the 7 hours • Recollected prayer • *Examen* of conscience	*New Practices* Abiding: • Fixed vows of poverty, chastity, obedience, submission • Study; theological and biblical • *Examen* 3 times daily: morning, lunch, after supper	*New Practices* Commitment 1: • Flexibly worked out with confessors •	*Cultural Factors Aiding Early Growth:* • From feudalism to central government, gave a centralized structure for society • Age of exploration helped cross-cultural mission • Hunger for more structured education • Need for renewal in Roman Catholic Church • Catholic Reformation
Community: • Mass • Singing Vespers, Compline • Begging alms, poverty • Submission to authority	Loving one another: • Selecting a community of leaders • Training others to give the *Exercises*	Commitment 2: • Developing the *Constitutions* for the Society	

Rhythms of Spirituality and Mission in the Modern Age   195

Ministry: • Almsgiving • Giving spiritual counsel • Compassion & justice	Bearing Witness: • Suffering, forgiving love • Giving the *Exercises* to individuals	Commitment 3: • Establishing free schools • Cross cultural mission	*Factors Threatening Demise in Stage 3* External threats: • Protestant Reformation. Close relation to colonial monarchies • Expelled from Portugal (1759), France (1764), Spain (1767) • Papal suppression of Jesuits (1773) Internal threats: • Rigidity replaced the flexibility of *Cons.* and *Sp. Ex.* • Lack of contextualization in early Jesuit mission
Weekly Practices: Communion, confession	None new	None new	
Annual/Occasional Practices: 6-month solitary retreat 2-year pilgrimage 3 days of confession 1-week fast	30-day retreats Spiritual direction Fasting when possible Making an election 40 days of prayer	Extended periods of solitude provided by apostolic travel Dying well (Ignatius, Xavier, and others)	
Stage 1 Shifts Ignatius and followers move from / to: • Conversion of soldier / Soldier for Christ • Daily exercises in monasteries / Portable 30-day *Sp. Ex.* done in solitude anytime anywhere • Eremitic life / Cenobitic life in an apostolic order		*Stage 2 Shifts* Movement from / to: • Fixed rule / Flexible rhythms worked out under principles in *Cons.* with a confessor • European / worldwide cross-cultural mission • Costly scholastic schools / Free Jesuit colleges	

members of the community (1986:128). Sunday services consisted of a corporate rehearsal of these texts and prayers by heart (1986:128–29), an approach that Reilly finds primitive at best (1978:81). Yet, in spite of its initial limitations, not least of which was the lack of contextualization, the mission to Goa has survived even to this day (Neill 1986:129).

Later Jesuit missionaries to the Far East became experts in language and culture, expressing well the indigenous impulse of the gospel by adopting the dress and customs of the cultures to which they went (Reilly 1978:83).[54] In their first hundred years, "Jesuits were to lay their bones in almost every country of the known world and on the shores of almost every sea" (Neill 1986:127). Reversing the early lack of contextualization by various Jesuits undoubtedly contributed to the mission expansion of the Society.

2. *Rigidity*. In spite of the flexibility and effectiveness of contextualized methods used by some Jesuit missionaries, a rigidity emerged within the Society as a whole that hindered the indigenous impulse. As Sheldrake writes:

> There seems to have been a move towards a greater rigidity, both with regard to life-style and specifically with regard to interpretation of *The Spiritual Exercises* and approaches to prayer, which departs substantially from what seems to have been Ignatius's original intention and insight. While the original *Constitutions* of Ignatius Loyola presuppose that Jesuit communities will look very different, depending on work and context, a recognisably Jesuit style soon emerged in practice which meant that people travelling from country to country, and even continent to continent, existed within a fairly uniform framework of life. (1992:77)

3. *Other Threats*. The Jesuits' rigidity and lack of contextualization to French custom in eighteenth-century France helped fuel hostility towards them from a host of influential French groups, for various reasons (including historical Jesuit ties to an increasingly unpopular monarchy), which resulted in the Society's expulsion from France in 1764. External

---

54. Reilly gives the examples of Robert de Nobili (1577–1656) and the Tamil scholar Constantine Josephus Beschi (1680–1746) in India, and Matteo Ricci (1552–1610), Ferdinand Verbiest (1623-16–88), and others who worked to incarnate "Christianity in oriental forms and to approach the learned classes of society" (1978:83).

threats of ideological, anticlerical, legal, political, and governmental opposition emerged in other countries as well, resulting in Jesuit expulsion from Portugal in 1759 and from Spain in 1767. Fierce opposition in these countries eventually led to papal suppression of the Society in 1773, which was not reversed until 1814.[55] The eventual lifting of papal suppression and national expulsions and a recovery of some of the flexibility envisioned in the *Exercises* and *Constitutions* has strengthened Jesuit influence in more recent times.

Appendix H displays a summary of the findings to my primary research questions applied to Ignatius and the early Jesuits. It shows that the time and space Ignatius and his early associates demarcated for God were closely connected to their mission in both deed and word, indicating how space and time were demarcated, what disciplines were practiced, how grace was associated, and what mission practices in deed and word appeared. The early Jesuit mission activity was both centrifugal and centripetal. Whereas the New Devout were predominantly centripetal in their mission, the Jesuits were more centrifugal. They were always on the move, initiating ministries of preaching and compassion, and doing so in many cross-cultural settings. The Jesuits were apostolic, seeing the whole world as their mission and living to bring glory to God in all things at all times. They expressed the indigenous principle more strongly as the movement expanded its worldwide mission. But they also expressed the pilgrim principle through the practice of the *Spiritual Exercises* and the spiritual formation efforts of its schools and colleges.

Jonathan Edwards and David Brainerd

I now turn my attention to two Protestant leaders in North America who were both involved in mission to the Native Americans: Jonathan Edwards (1703–1758) and David Brainerd (1718–1747). Both were products of New England Puritan influences, which exhibited traces of the New Devotion. Though the *Devotio Moderna* had not survived as a movement, it survived in other forms, including Puritanism (Oberman 1988:3). The primary text I examine is the spiritual classic *The Life and Diary of David Brainerd* (1949), first edited and published by Jonathan Edwards in 1749, two years after Brainerd's death, according to George

---

55. Cf. Gordon A. Catherall (1978:531).

M. Marsden (2003:xiv).[56] My approach is to apply my research questions to select representative entries from various parts of the *Life* from the two sources that make up the text: Brainerd's diary and journal.[57]

David Brainerd's Rhythms of Spirituality and Mission

Marsden says that the *Life* was Edward's "*Religious Affections* in the form of a spiritual biography," and that his desire was to promote true spiritual awakenings through both books (2003:331).[58] The *Life of Brainerd* did influence subsequent awakenings and missions for at least a hundred years. It presents Brainerd's inner life with his external mission functioning as the scaffold (2003:332).

Diary (1718–42): Birth, Conversion, and Study at Yale

David Brainerd was born April 20, 1718, in Haddam, Connecticut (Edwards 1949:53). In his preface, Edwards discusses Brainerd's self

---

56. I also consult excerpts from Edwards's *Personal Narrative* and *Religious Affections* (2001). I refer to George Marsden's biography on Edwards (2003) and Philip Howard Jr.'s biographical sketch in the Brainerd text (1949). With this study's broad scope, a survey of literature on Brainerd and his context is impossible as in similar studies by Bradley (1997) and Reilly (1978). Any literature review, however, should include Joseph Conforti (1995) and Christopher Mitchell (2003).

57. The *Life* is referred to variously as *The Life of David Brainerd*, *The Diary of David Brainerd*, or *The Life and Diary of David Brainerd*. His journal is a different document from his diary. The copyright for the Brainerd text is held by Moody Bible Institute (1949), for which Philip E. Howard arranged the text in the order in which it appears in the Baker fifteenth printing in 2005. Howard explains why he used Brainerd's *Journal* for the period of his most fruitful work with Native Americans at Crossweeksung—from June 1745 to June 1746—instead of his *Diary's* entries for this period. Brainerd's *Journal*, which he kept for the Society for the Promotion of Christian Knowledge, the Scottish sponsor of his mission, "is more extensive, not so subjective, and probably gives a more complete picture of the conditions of the Indians and the effect of the gospel among them" (Howard 2005:7). Howard is following Edwards, who used Brainerd's journal rather than the diary entries covering the mission at Crossweeksung for similar reasons (1949:52).

58. Edwards's goal was a model spiritual biography (Marsden 2003:332). "Although the substance of the volume is edited diaries, it is often difficult to distinguish between author and editor.... [But] we can tell that Edwards, while mostly following Brainerd's words, also took some broad liberties, as editors of the time typically did.... The Brainerd that Edwards wished remembered exemplified (closely paraphrasing the 'Eighth Sign' of *Religious Affections*) 'the lamb-like, dove-like spirit of Jesus Christ! How full of love, meekness, quietness, forgiveness, and mercy!'" (2003:331–32). I will thus quote Brainerd but cite Edwards.

admitted "melancholy and dejection of spirit" (1949:46–47), which "destroyed his eagerness for play." Yet, he experienced no awareness of sin except on two occasions, one after his mother's death when he was eight (1949:57). In the winter of 1738, at the age of twenty, he felt a deep conviction of sin in light of God's holiness—a sense that became an earmark of those converted through his ministry. He writes,

> It pleased God, on one Sabbath day morning, as I was walking out for some secret duties,[59] to give me on a sudden such a sense of my danger and the wrath of God that I stood amazed.... Thus I lived from day to day, being frequently in great distress. Sometimes there appeared mountains before me to obstruct my hopes of mercy; and the work of conversion appeared so great, that I thought I should never be the subject of it. (1949:59)

Brainerd discovered that his previous experiences of spiritual solace had been based solely on duty, his affection for God, or "some good resolutions." Nothing in them centered upon the glory of God (1949:60)—a central theme for Edwards[60] and later for Brainerd also. This inner revelation came to Brainerd during a day set aside for solitude, prayer, and fasting in February of 1739 (1949: 60)—a frequent pattern, often weekly, throughout his *Diary*. Five months later, a breakthrough came during a three-day period of solitude and silence, which Brainerd described thus:

> I was walking again in the same solitary place where I was brought to see myself lost and helpless, as before mentioned. Here, in a mournful, melancholy state, I was attempting to pray; but found no heart to engage in that or any other duty....

---

59. By "secret duties" Brainerd and Edwards mean solitary meditation and prayer.

60. Louis Dupre and James A. Wiseman point out that it was 1 Timothy 1:17 that finally gave Edwards a positive view of predestination by focusing his attention not on his own destination but on the glory of God. This text was important to Brainerd also. Even after Edwards's conversion, "still, he felt the longing for God's presence and for holiness had at first depended greatly on his own efforts and constant self-examination. Suffering, sickness, and disappointment as a tutor at Yale gradually purified his attitude and transformed it into one of attentive waiting. Then in 1737 came the first revelations, the vision of 'the glory of the Son of God as Mediator between God and man.' This was followed by revelations of the Holy Spirit, the source of divine glory and the sweet guest of the soul. Edward's experience of the *theologia gloriae* brings him into close proximity with the man from whom church and dogma divided him so profoundly—Ignatius of Loyola" (2001:384).

> I had been thus endeavoring to pray ... for near half an hour; then, as I was walking in a dark thick grove, unspeakable glory seemed to open to the view and apprehension of my soul. ... It was a new inward apprehension or view that I had of God, such as I never had before....
>
> I stood still, wondered, and admired! I knew that I never had seen before anything comparable to it for excellency and beauty; it was widely different from all the conceptions that ever I had of God, or things divine.... My soul rejoiced with joy unspeakable to see such a God, such a glorious Divine Being; and I was inwardly pleased and satisfied that He should be God over all for ever and ever. My soul was so captivated and delighted with the excellency, loveliness, greatness, and other perfections of God, that I was even swallowed up in Him ...
>
> At this time, the way of salvation opened to me with such infinite wisdom.... If I could have been saved by my own duties, or any other way that I had formerly contrived, my whole soul would now have refused it. I wondered that all the world did not see and comply with this way of salvation, entirely by the righteousness of Christ. (1949:69–70)

This joy lasted a week. Darkness returned occasionally, but after each episode "the Lord returned graciously" (Edwards 1949:70). Brainerd's conversion came just prior to beginning his divinity course at Yale College in September of 1739, just before the Great Awakening broke out in New England. The consolations continued with the start of his life at Yale in 1740. "I enjoyed considerable sweetness in religion all the winter following" (1949:71). During a noontime getaway for a time of meditation in fields some distance from Yale, Brainerd was flooded with an overflowing sense of God's glory and a love for all humankind (1949:72). He wanted more time with God, but the "ambition in my studies" had a deadening affect on his spiritual life (1949:74).

Brainerd's entries in the fall of 1740 reflect several regular spiritual practices including "duties of secret prayer (Edwards 1949:72), self-examination, and the Lord's Supper. "Secret duties"[61] seem to have included morning and evening devotions, the latter probably lasting about an hour (1949:75–74). In these Brainerd may have practiced self-examination much like Ignatius's pattern. On October 18 Brainerd wrote, "Both morning and evening I spent some time in self-exami-

---

61. See Edwards (1949:59, 73).

nation" (1949:72-73). The Lord's Supper was the primary practice for meditating upon Jesus's death. The sacrament filled Brainerd with love, "so that my soul and all the powers of it seemed, as it were, to melt into softness and sweetness.... This love and joy cast out fear" (1949:73).

Diary (1742–1745): Deepening and Preparation

In the winter of 1742 Brainerd was expelled from Yale College for a disparaging remark he made privately about a faculty member (he removed this section from his diary). Yale never allowed him reentrance or graduation, a decision Edwards felt excessively harsh (1949:381-82).[62] Brainerd went on to study privately for the ministry. In this dark time, other disciplines appear: intercession and communal prayer with friends, which encouraged him (1949:85). On April 19 he prayed and fasted for his future. "I felt the power of intercession for precious, immortal souls; for the advancement of the kingdom of my dear Lord ... a most sweet resignation and even consolation and joy in the thoughts of suffering hardships, distresses, and even death itself, in promotion of it" (1949:80). Here is a prayer of surrender and resignation to the will of God, no matter the cost. Brainerd was licensed to preach in July of 1742 (1949:92).

In November of 1742, he was appointed to work for the Scottish Society for the Propagation of Christian Knowledge (SPCK) as a missionary to the Native Americans at Kaunaumeek (Edwards 1949:104).[63] His time there was a period of preparation through inward affliction, sickness, and little success, leaving only a handful of believers after a

---

62. Marsden explains the college's refusal to reinstate Brainerd in light of the growing split between Old Light and New Light Presbyterians—the latter represented by Edwards and the founders of Princeton College, who wanted to preserve Calvinism from Arminian and deist influences that were making inroads at Yale and Harvard. "His expulsion from Yale became a test case that symbolized the whole controversy. Who had the power to educate and hence to control ordination? The spat between Yale's Rector Thomas Clap and Edwards grew out of Clap's fears that Whitefield and his cohorts would destroy the near-monopoly that Yale and Harvard had on the supply of clergy. Clap also saw to it that Connecticut banned ordinations of those, such as Brainerd, who had not graduated from Yale, Harvard, or a European university. In 1744, new Light Presbyterians ordained Brainerd in New Jersey (2003:330).

63. Kaunaumeek was about twenty miles from Stockbridge, Massachusetts (Edwards 1949:119) where a mission to the Housatonic Indians had been started by John Sergaant in 1734 under English sponsorship. After Sergeant's death, the Stockbridge mission would be led by Edwards from 1751 to 1758 (Marsden 2003: xiv-xv, 173-75).

year (January–December 1743). Spiritual practices that appear in his diary from this period include centering prayer (1949:110), ejaculatory prayers (1949:117), the prayer of God's absence (1949:119), solitude prior to preaching, journaling, fasting (1949:120–21), confession of sin—his disparaging remark about the spirituality of a Yale faculty member (1949:133), and singing the Psalms (1949:37). Brainerd's September 20 entry, during a grave illness, describes recollected prayer, or perhaps a form of *lectio divina* from the Hallel. The words "I shall not die, but ... live" (Ps 118:17) rolled over and over in his mind throughout the day as physical healing occurred (1949:136). Also, spiritual reading appears to have been a regular practice since his conversion (1949:65), and he was apparently involved in a ministry of distributing alms to the poor from a fund he supervised (1949:146). God was preparing him for his most fruitful yearlong ministry among Native Americans in New Jersey, from June 1745 to June 1746.

Journal (June 1745–June 1746): Grace at Crossweeksung

On June 19, 1745, Brainerd arrived in Crossweeksung in New Jersey, where he preached to four women and several children. Like the woman at the well, says Brainerd, they responded enthusiastically, fanning out to invite small enclaves of family and friends from as far as thirty miles away to come hear him (Edwards 1949:203). Centrifugal mission quickly became centripetal. On June 22 Brainerd preached to thirty, and then to forty on June 27. Not a word of opposition was heard from these same Native Americans who had vehemently opposed attempts to evangelize them just months before. On June 28 they requested that Brainerd begin preaching twice daily (1949:204–5). He describes his interaction with them after preaching:

> I spent some considerable time in discoursing with them in a more private way, inquiring of them what they remembered of the great truths that had been taught them from day to day.... It was amazing to see how they had received and retained the instructions given and what manner of knowledge some of them had acquired in a few days. (1949:205–6)[64]

---

64. No doubt grace is a valid explanation for their retention, as Brainerd seems to imply. Another is that retention rates for what is heard among oral cultures is much greater than for text-based cultures. The experiences of gospel communication in oral cultures, especially those employing images, might yield helpful insights for our transi-

The first baptisms were of Brainerd's interpreter and his wife on July 21, and their children on July 26 (Edwards 1949:207, 212). August 7–9 saw unusual visitation of God's Spirit, as many alcoholics came to a deep spiritual and emotional awareness of their impotency, their need of Jesus, and the impossibility of extricating themselves from their condition[65]—this in response to Brainerd's telling of the parable of the banquet (Luke 14:16–23). One notorious alcoholic, who also practiced demonic rites and incantations and had been a murderer, was "brought now to cry for mercy with many tears" (1949:217). Brainerd describes the group's response to the word:

> I stood amazed at the influence that seized the audience almost universally, and could compare it to nothing more aptly than the irresistible force of a mighty torrent, or swelling deluge....
> They were almost universally praying and crying for mercy, in every part of the house, and many out of doors, and numbers could neither go nor stand . . . and so were everyone praying apart, although all together. (1949:216–17)

One cannot but be impressed by Brainerd's emphasis on the heart. Of several Native Americans who had been exposed but not converted to Christ, Brainerd described them as "utter strangers to their own hearts and altogether unacquainted with the power of religion, as well as with the doctrines of grace" (Edwards 1949:226). This sounds much like Ignatius's attentiveness to one's heart in his *Spiritual Exercises*. The emphasis on tears of contrition over sin in Week 1 of the *Exercises* is not unlike what is seen here in Brainerd's work—though built on a very different theological structure. In talking with those described as "utter strangers to their own hearts," Brainerd was

> surprised to see their self-righteous disposition, their strong attachment to the covenant of works for salvation, and the high value they put upon their supposed attainments. Yet after much discourse, one appeared in a measure convinced that "by the

---

tion from a text-based to an image-based culture in postmodernity. Apparently, those in oral cultures who hear a story three times can repeat it without alteration, according to Clyde Cowan (n.d.). Fuller Seminary's *Reel Spirituality* project is examining how story and image communicate the Christian message.

65. Brainerd's work at this point exhibits aspects of Step 1 in the Twelve Steps. Alcoholism was prevalent in the tribe.

deeds of the law no flesh living can be justified," and wept bitterly, inquiring what he must do to be saved. (1949:226)

On August 25, twenty-five Natives were baptized (Edwards 1949:226), and the next day, ninety-five were present to hear the story of the lost sheep (Luke 15:3-7). That day, the community of believers was knit together by the Spirit with a deep love for each other. At Brainerd's request, they stayed together all through that night until daybreak in a watch of prayer for his short term mission to Natives on the Susquehannah River, which he commenced just before dusk. Here we see the solitary prayer of a leader being recapitulated in a corporate, extended waiting upon God of his followers. By November 4, forty-seven had been baptized after a remarkable four and one-half months (1949:243). On March 24, the number reached 130. The response became so great that Brainerd petitioned his superiors at SPCK to pray on the basis of Luke 10:2 that the Lord would send more laborers for the harvest (1949:253).

In addition to God supernaturally freeing people from their addictions was Brainerd's costly incarnational care for the Natives and the deep sense of community that emerged among them. He practiced extensive spiritual direction regularly, spending "hours in private conference with some of my people about their souls' concerns" (Edwards 1949:256). Proclamation was but the instigation and context for the real soul work that Brainerd undertook in listening to whatever was stirring in their hearts. He was highly personal, referring to them as "my people." One gets a keen sense of Brainerd's love for the Native Americans, as well as and their love for him and for each other. After administering the Lord's Supper on April 27, he writes,

> I walked from house to house, and conversed particularly with most of the communicants, and found they had been almost universally refreshed at the Lord's Table, as with new wine. Never did I see such an appearance of Christian love among any people in all my life.... I think there could be no greater tokens of mutual affection among the people of God in the early days of Christianity than what now appeared here. The sight was so desirable, and so well becoming the gospel, that nothing less could be said of it than that it was "the doing of the Lord," the genuine operations of Him who is love. (1949:294)

At the close of his year at Crossweeksung, he wrote to the SPCK these words:

> What amazing things has God wrought in this space of time for these poor people! What a surprising change appears in their tempers and behavior! How are morose and savage pagans in this short space of time transformed into agreeable, affectionate, and humble Christians, and their drunken and pagan howlings turned into devout and fervent prayers and praises to God! They "who were sometimes darkness are now become light in the Lord." ... And now to Him that is of power to establish them according to the gospel, and the preaching of Christ—to God only wise, be glory, through Jesus Christ, for ever and ever. Amen. (Edwards 1949:307)

Conclusion on Brainerd's Rhythms of Spirituality and Mission

What can be said about Brainerd's spirituality and mission, which we have seen in this period and the times of preparation that preceded it? I have summarized my findings in Table 34 below.

1. *Grace Observed.* Perhaps the most remarkable description of prevenient grace in this entire study is given by Brainerd with regards to his mission at Crossweeksung. Before going to the Natives there, he had written that he was totally dejected over his lack of effectiveness and had determined that if, in a year's time, genuine conversions had not occurred, he would resign from the SPCK (Edwards 1949:243–44). Yet on August 16, not two months later, he wrote,

> I never saw the work of God appear so independent of [human] means as at this time. ... God's manner of working upon them appeared so entirely supernatural and above [his own human] means that I could scare believe He used me as an instrument. ... I seemed to do nothing, and indeed to have nothing to do, but to "stand still and see the salvation of God." I found myself obliged and delighted to say, "Not unto us," not unto instruments and means, "but to thy name be glory." God appeared to work entirely alone, and I saw no room to attribute any part of this work to any created arm." (1949:224)

In his journal and diary entries we have cited, Brainerd repeatedly mentions God's transforming grace in connection with both his spiritual practices and his mission practices, especially at Crossweeksung. Stronger hints of accepting grace can be seen in his diary than in any of the writings examined in this study, except for the New Testament. He mentions one woman who had "never before obtained any settled comfort," though Brainerd believes "she had passed a saving change some days before. She now appeared in a heavenly frame of mind, composed and delighted" (Edwards 1949:259). "Comfort" seems to be the term used for assurance of God's acceptance of believers in Christ. He tells of how he answers those who ask, "'But how shall I know whether God has chosen me to everlasting life?'": "By pressing them to come and give up their hearts to Christ, and thereby 'to make their election sure'" (1949:260). Apparently, he taught that believers could in the present be sure of their election to eternal life on the basis of giving their hearts—their whole persons— completely to Jesus Christ. However, a door to ambiguity is left open by Brainerd's seeming view that "a saving change" is a necessary precondition for "comfort" (1949:259-60). One might ask, how much and what kind constitutes a saving change? Luther would have cringed. Nevertheless, Brainerd's and Edward's teaching is far better, in my view, than a notional faith devoid of transformation on one hand, or, on the other hand, the medieval suspension of assurance of salvation until death and notion of the accumulation of virtue over time.

Brainerd's views of grace were central to his vivid descriptions of desolate and consoling experiences. First, grace was the only means available to Brainerd for release from his desperate state, and eventually he came to see desolation itself as a means of grace. Second, grace—the merciful free offer from a suffering Savior on the cross—became the primary means of touching the hearts of the Native Americans without any reference to terror or judgment (Edwards 1949:249). This was as surprising to Brainerd as were the wholly new conceptions of God's glory and character given him at his conversion. The latter echoes the third renunciation of false or inadequate images of God urged by John Cassian in his *Conferences* (*Conf.* 1985:3).[66]

---

66. It should be noted that these new conceptions came to Brainerd not after a lengthy process of renunciations and resolutions regarding the seven deadly sins (which had proven wholly ineffective for him), but at the very onset of his conversion. Cassian would envision such renunciation as accompanying a more advanced stage

2. *Space and Time for God.* Brainerd's spirituality was greatly nurtured in natural settings, which were especially plentiful in Native American lands. He met God in fields, walking alone in a retired place, in a dark thick grove, in a usual solitary place, a house, a cottage, and in the woods. He met God regularly in these places for morning devotion, solitude at noon, and secret devotion in the evening. He often spent an entire day alone with God, and on one occasion was in solitude for three days. "Filling up our time with and for God is the way to rise up and lie down in peace" (Edwards 1949:127). As with Jesus, Geert Groote, and Ignatius, Brainerd's pattern shows that long periods of solitary preparation preceded fruitful engagement in their public ministries.

3. *Spiritual Disciplines Practiced.* In Brainerd we have seen the threefold structure of communion, community, and ministry, as well as the golden thread of fasting, prayer, and almsgiving. In his solitary communion with God, he also practiced spiritual reading, meditation on Scripture, self-examination, confession to God and others, worship, singing psalms, recollected prayer, the prayer of God's absence, prayer of surrender, prayer to forgive enemies, ejaculatory prayer, centering prayer, study of theology and the Scriptures, intercession, and Sabbath.

Communal practices included the Lord's Supper (perhaps weekly), corporate prayer and worship, singing psalms, all-night prayer, family prayer, hospitality, prayer with friends in small groups, private spiritual direction, and dying well. As previously noted, the Native Americans tended to practice spiritual disciplines communally in the same way Brainerd had practiced them in solitude, a typical pattern we have seen between leaders and followers. A final practice was dying well. Beyond the scope of this study were Brainerd's final days in the home of Jonathan Edwards under the care of Edwards's godly daughter, Jerusha. There he died at the age of twenty-nine after a long battle with tuberculosis in an environment of prayer and love.

4. *Mission.* Some aspects of Brainerd's approach to mission among the Native Americans were indigenous. Others were not. Brainerd was moving from a modern text-based culture to a pre-modern oral culture, and from an agrarian society to a hunter-gatherer society with

---

of spiritual development. In fact, Brainerd's language of being "swallowed up in Him" (1949:69) is typical of the third stage of traditional spiritual theology: union.

Table 34: Summary of Brainerd's Rhythms of Spirituality and Mission in His Life and Diary (Adapted from Edwards 1949)

Time and Space/Place	Inner Disciplines Practiced	Grace: Divine Power	Outward Mission Practiced
Time:	*Solitude / Abiding:*	*Empowering Grace:*	*Bearing Witness*
Morning devotion	Silence	Held strongly	Deed:
Noon solitude	Solitude	Connected to spiritual practice	• Almsgiving←
Evening: 1 hour in secret devotion	Secret prayer ("secret duties")	Associated with mission	• Acts of compassionate love→
1 day of solitude	Fasting	*Accepting Grace:*	• Suffering, forgiving love in persecution←
3 days of solitude from Friday morning to Sunday evening	Spiritual reading	Believed in accepting grace, with indications of assurance of salvation in the present	Word:
	Meditation		• Proclamation of the gospel in the Puritan and Reformed traditions
Fill every inch of time	Meditation on Scripture in evening devotions		
All night in prayer	Self-examination	*Prevenient Grace:*	
Space/Place:	Confession to God and others	Strong emphasis on prevenient grace, especially in his journal report to SPCK on his mission to Native Americans in NJ	*Means of Support:*
Fields away from Yale	Worshiping God in contemplating his glory		Vow of poverty, begging for alms (asking for finances for Native Americans)
Walking alone in a very retired place			
Dark thick grove	Study; theological and biblical		
A solitary place as usual	Intercession		*Pilgrim-Separate:*
A day at usual place of retirement	Prayer of surrender		Culture-denying elements stronger than culture-affirming elements
	Prayer to forgive enemies		
A house	Ejaculatory prayer		*Indigenous-Incarnate:*
Cottage a place for solitary prayer in the woods	Centering prayer		Translation into heart language, language learning, and use of interpreters
	Sabbath		
	Dying well		

Community / Loving One Another: Lord's Supper Hospitality Corporate prayer with friends or small groups Corporate singing Family prayer Spiritual direction (private conference) Singing the Psalms All-night prayer		
→Indicates centrifugal mission	←Indicates centripetal mission	

nomadic habits. Brainerd expected the Natives to become agrarian and taught them husbandry (Edwards 1949:286). With the loss of discretionary time this would entail,[67] they needed to become, in his judgment, more "laborious and industrious" (1949:297). He also expected those converted to adopt English culture and custom, and referred to the people as a whole as "poor pagans" (1949:206-8).[68] But Brainerd was also culture-affirming in his mission, using interpreters for his preaching, arranging for prayer in the tribe's native tongue during his services (1949:207-8), and himself learning the languages of tribes he evangelized (1949:252). He also told a plethora of biblical stories and parables, a method especially effective with oral cultures.[69]

67. As noted in chapter 1, those in hunter/gatherer societies have more discretionary time than those in agrarian societies (Lingenfelter 2000).

68. Although this term and others like it, which were common in the literature of Christians at the time, exhibit an ethnocentric view of Native American culture, it should be noted that Brainerd and Edwards are equally derogatory in the terminology they employ to describe their own fallen natures and the deadness of New England religious life.

69. He told many stories with great effect, including: the parable of the great banquet (Edwards 1949:216), the parable of the lost sheep (1949:226), Zacchaeus and the

His ministry not only involved empowered proclamation, but also compassion. He called for just protection of Native American lands when there was threat of it being taken from them (Edwards 1949:271). His mission was at first centrifugal, but became centripetal, as we have seen. An earmark of spiritual awakenings is that centripetal movement occurs as news spreads of new life that God is giving.

Brainerd's Influence on the Great Missionary Century

David Brainerd's short life was far outlived by the influence of his *Diary*. George Marsden calls it "one of the most influential missionary accounts of all time" (2003:333). John Wesley published an abridged version in England, and during the spiritual awakenings in the first half of the nineteenth century the *Diary* became one of the most widely read literary works in North America and overseas (2003:333). Stephen Neill calls it "a classic of devotional life" and says that it lives on in the lives of Henri Martyn (1781–1812) and William Carey (1761–1834), the father of modern missions (1986:192). Timothy George also notes Brainerd's influence on these two, as well as on Adoniah Judson (1788–1850), Hudson Taylor (1832–1905), and David Livingstone (1813–1873). George illustrates Brainerd's powerful legacy from Carey's and Martyn's journals (1991:44–45). For instance, Carey wrote,

> Let us often look at Brainerd in the woods of America, pouring out his very soul before God for people. Prayer, secret, fervent, expectant, lies at the root of all personal godliness. A competent knowledge of the languages current where a missionary lives, a mild and winning temper, and a heart given up to God—these are the attainments, which, more than all other gifts, will fit us to become God's instruments in the great work of human redemption. (George 1991:44)

Of Brainerd, Martyn wrote, "I long to be like him; let me forget the world and be swallowed up in a desire to glorify God" (George 1991:45).

Brainerd also influenced women missionaries, who became a powerful force in the Protestant mission expansion of the nineteenth century. Ann Judson, wife of Adoniah, had an extensive ministry in her own right as a schoolteacher, evangelist of women, and translator. She was

---

transfiguration (1949:255), the parable of the Prodigal Son (1949:271), and Mary and Martha (1949:278), to name a few.

an intellectual, who read theological works and became more proficient at Burmese than her husband, according to Dana L. Robert, author of *American Women in Mission* (1996:6–7, 43–46). Having read the works of Edwards, Ann Judson must have been influenced by Brainerd even as her husband had been. Mary Lyon (1797–1849) founded Mt. Holyoke Women's Seminary in 1837 against formidable odds, many hardships— including her father's death when she was six, and the prevailing attitudes against the education, rights, and influence of women. Women at her school were given an hour of solitude each day for prayer. Lyons held morning and evening worship sessions for prayer as well as days of prayer and fasting. Her institute was referred to as the "Protestant nunnery" (Robert 1996:95–101). A line of influence can be drawn from Brainerd to Mary Lyon and her mentors through one of his converts at Yale, Samuel Hopkins.[70] These and other nineteenth century missionaries patterned their rhythms of spirituality and mission after those of Brainerd.

Summary

In this chapter, I have examined the rhythms of spirituality and mission in the *Devotio Moderna*, Ignatius and the early Jesuits, and David Brainerd. I have found that:

1. Groote, Ignatius, and Brainerd all experienced an eremitic period after their conversions in which they practiced long extended periods of solitude before leading fruitful ministries that attracted significant numbers of followers, whose spiritual practices, in turn, were more communal.

2. Groote's eremitic patterns became embodied in regular one- or two-day silent retreats every several weeks in the second stage of the *Devotio Moderna*'s history, undoubtedly contributing to its growth. Ignatius's eremitic patterns became embedded in the Society of Jesus through its

---

70. Amanda Porterfield traces Brainerd and Edwards's influence on Lyons to her mentor and teacher Joseph Emerson. Emerson was a strong supporter of Edwards's theology through the influence of Nathanael Emmons, who with Emerson and Lyon had acquired the idea of disinterested benevolence as the motivation for ministry from Edwards's primary interpreter, Samuel Hopkins, a key New Divinity leader until his death in 1803. Hopkins had been converted by Brainerd during the Great Awakening at Yale in 1741 (1997:16–17).

thirty-day retreats for taking the *Spiritual Exercises*—a standard feature of Jesuit life for now more than five hundred years, which has surely contributed to its longevity. Brainerd's eremitic patterns were emulated by Protestant mission leaders during the nineteenth century.

3. In all three cases, space and time for God expressed in solitary and communal spiritual practices were inseparably linked to outward mission in deed and word, with priority given to word. All three were called upon to express suffering, forgiving love. Mission was first centrifugal before it was centripetal, and all three developed indigenous expressions of mission in the heart language of the people. Spiritual and mission practices in all three movements expressed communion, community, and ministry, as well as the golden thread of fasting, prayer, and almsgiving.

4. All three expressed the flexible nature of spiritual practices, though Ignatius developed this most explicitly in the organizational culture of the Society, as described in its *Constitutions*. As the Jesuit order abandoned this flexibility and depended upon colonial power it lost vitality and power.

5. Each practiced a subversive spirituality, making spiritual disciplines transformative and available in fresh ways. All practiced spiritualities of the heart, which emanated in transforming mission.

6. All three embodied patterns that connect with the postmodern thirst for spiritual direction and mentoring, soul awareness, and small communities of belonging. The *Devotio Moderna* speaks to the desire for a hands-on, everyday spirituality that is economically viable and strongly communal, and that provides monthly silent one-day retreats away from the pressure of daily life. Ignatian spirituality connects to the postmodern fascination with the imagination, image, and the senses in its affective meditation upon Christ. This spirituality is very suited to recovery, given its strong emphasis on paying attention to one's heart, and its extended eight-day and thirty-day retreats speak powerfully to our contemporary collapse of space and time. Brainerd speaks to a spiritual thirst for recovery, story, and the environment. I will now in the next chapter discuss rhythms of spirituality and mission in the postmodern age.

6

Rhythms of Spirituality and Mission in the Postmodern Age

> Stop at the cross-roads; look for the ancient paths; ask, "Where is that way that leads to what is good?" Then take that way, and you will find rest for yourselves.
>
> —Jer 6:16 (*New English Bible*)

THE ANCIENT PATHS ARE THE HISTORIC SPIRITUAL PRACTICES THAT have been explored in the last three chapters, practices that have been vehicles of grace to transform lives and cultures. According to Jeremiah, they are pathways through which God has promised rest, so needed in the face of the current collapse of space and time. In this chapter, I complete this study's cultural analysis by examining the spiritualities of Generations X and Y, which have emerged within this collapse. I address three research questions: What characterizes the spirituality of the postmodern generations in light of this collapse? How does space and time with God relate to the mission and faith maturity of Generations X and Y? What rhythms of spirituality and mission are needed in these generations?

The Spirituality of the Postmodern Generations and Secularization

To his surprise, sociologist Greg Stanczack found that spirituality was not dying in Generations X and Y as he and many others had expected.[1] Following the fathers of sociology—Marx, Weber, and

---

1. Teresa Watanabe wrote "Once a largely forgotten factor in social research, dismissed by those who believed that society would inevitably secularize and cast spiritu-

Durkeim—Stanczack believed that secularization was pushing religion progressively and irresistibly to the periphery of culture.

> [Stanczack] came to USC to test his hypothesis that religion was disappearing among youth. Almost immediately, he said, he found out he was wrong. "I was looking mostly at Generation X and Generation Y, and saw that religion was giving structure and meaning to their lives," he said. "To these people, religion is the core of what is radically transforming their lives." (Watanabe 2000:28)

Rick Richardson of InterVarsity Christian Fellowship (IVCF) found similar phenomena among college students with whom he worked. In 2001 he reported,

> For just over a dozen years or so, I've asked people if they've ever had an experience of feeling close to God. It used to be that about thirty percent of the folks would respond positively. Now it is up to about sixty percent. And just within the past five years—during which time I have been asking people to rate their desire to know God I've seen the average go up from 6.5 to 8 [apparently out of 10]. (2001:18)

So what happened on the way to a secular society? As many have argued, the Enlightenment's reduction of human life solely to the empirical leaves deep spiritual longings unsatisfied, which have erupted in our culture's spiritual quest. Yet, though the fathers of sociology and theologians like Harvey Cox, author of *The Secular City*, had it wrong (Shenk 2006), the process of secularization still has life. Christopher Kaiser breaks secularization into six distinct progressive processes—one of which, the cultural,[2] includes the standardization of time and its separation from place (1996:88–111), as discussed in chapter 2. On this

---

ality aside, religion is now a hot field of inquiry. Until recently, a long-standing academic bias against religion has blinded many scholars to its powerful role in shaping both private lives and the public culture" (2000:1). Subgroups devoted to the study of faith and religion in the social sciences now represent the largest of such groups within these scholarly disciplines. Factors cited in this turnaround include the spiritual resurgence in North America, increased funding by foundations, and more people studying the phenomena. Many universities now have centers devoted to the study of the impact of faith on social problems—the first of which was the University of Southern California (USC) Center for Religion and Civic Culture (2001:1, 28).

2. Others are sociopolitical, spiritual, sociopsychological, cosmological, and phenomenological.

view, the collapse is an integral factor in the processes of secularization. It infects and affects all we are and do, including our spirituality. As Os Guinness suggests, "'increased religiosity' is actually a new secularity with a religious gloss" (1993:337). As I argue in this section, the spiritualities of Generations X and Y have been shaped by and in reaction to this collapse. Thus, their spiritualities are being secularized on one hand, while on the other they are resisting secularization by subverting its space-time collapse.

Generational Study[3]

One way to study a culture is generationally (Shenk 2003). The characteristic outlook of a generation—an age cohort generally lasting from fifteen to twenty years—can provide a window into cultural developments. Sociologist Richard W. Flory traces one key theoretical concept in the study of generations—an idea called generational imprinting—back to the work of Karl Mannheim in the 1920s (2000:233-34). Howard Schuman and Jacqueline Scott have shown that "generational consciousness" is imprinted through the interaction of macro events (or developments) with the personal experience of them, a process not complete until late adolescence (1989:359-81).

However, as Beaudoin (1998), Clark (1999), and others have noted, generational study poses some challenges. First, it is hard to define generational boundaries. Second, generations often defy characterization— particularly so in the case of Generation X—and any one characteristic is true obviously for only part of that generation. Third, a feature of an age cohort like Generation X may actually be a marker typical of a de-

---

3. My approach in this chapter is fourfold: (1) for Generation X spirituality, I look at Richard W. Flory, Don E. Miller (2000), Colleen Carroll (2002), Tom Beaudoin (1998), William Mahedy and Janet Bernardi (1994), Charles van Engen (1997c), and others. This literature review yields a profile of Generation X spirituality in light of the collapse of space and time. I look to see if resistance communities have been formed by Xers using historic spiritual practices of solitude, community, and ministry. (2) For Millenial spirituality, I review the work of Wendy Murray Zoba (1999, 2001), Mark Yacconilli (2001, 2006), Richard R. Durn (2001), Dean (2004), Chap Clark (1999, 2004), and others. (3) I then summarize Jerry Lee's findings (1995, 1996, 1997) based on data collected on more than 2,700 respondents including Generations X and Y from sixty groups whose leaders participated in the Leadership Institute's *Journey to Reach the Next Generations* Project. (4) I compare the Christian spiritualities emerging in Generations X and Y in relation to the space-time collapse and suggest a discernment process for leadership communities to develop their rhythms of life.

velopmental stage that all generations pass through (Ford and Denney 1995:31). Fourth, some generational characteristics change over time, and so a profile of Generation X in 1990 will differ from one in 2000. Fifth, because imprinting is not complete until late adolescence, the younger a generation, the less we understand it. Finally, spirituality is more difficult to study than are the visible religious institutions of a group (Wuthnow 1998:vii). Even so, studying spiritual practices and time usage provides a look at the more visible aspects of spirituality and helps us get at this issue.

The Spirituality of Generation X and Space-Time

As discussed in chapter 2, Xers between three and twelve years old had fifty-one hours of free time per week in 1981, a figure that dropped to thirty-two hours for Millennials in the same age range in 1997 according to Howe and Strauss (2000:168–74). Seventy-seven percent of the seven hundred Xers interviewed for *Time* magazine in 1990 were attracted to "the easy going life-style" of the sixties (Gross and Scott 1990). Though Xers' pace of life accelerated, and their free time diminished since then, the "whatever whenever" attitude they exhibited towards time persists, as does their view of work as secondary to other life interests. Xers have had more time and space than either Boomers or Millennials to express their spiritual hunger as they have moved into adulthood. Whether this continues will depend largely on whether they capitulate en masse to the consuming pressures of careerism and materialism. Xers' immersion in the temporal-spatial codes of the Internet appears to have had an ambiguous relationship to their spirituality, as we shall see. In spite of the difficulties inherent in characterizing the spirituality of Generation X, I will review what has been written on the issue before looking at the spirituality of Generation Y and examining results of my own field research on both generations.

Open to Unhurried Solitude, Silence, Meditation, and Prayer

In an important book on Gen-X spirituality, *Virtual Faith*, Tom Beaudoin describes his generation's hunger for solitude and silence. "One of the most common spiritual questions I have heard from Xers is 'Where and how can I get away and not see anyone'" (1998:165)? An Xer student of mine who worked as an athletic trainer in Pasadena while attending Fuller Seminary was asked by some of his unbelieving clients what he did at seminary. He described for them his days of solitude, silence, and meditation at a retreat center, which are required assignments for my course. My student's clients expressed strong interest in doing these same practices of spirituality themselves. Xers are open to giving significant time and space to these even without belief in Jesus Christ. Many postmoderns can be introduced to the practices of spirituality while they are still resistant to the gospel. This seems out of sequence from a modern perspective, which necessitates belief before practice and rationality over experience and mystery.[4] One young adult practiced solitude for thirty minutes daily in scriptural meditation with a God he did not believe existed. After a year and a half in a group of Xers practicing this discipline, he became a follower of Jesus. No wonder missiologist Jon L. Dybdahl has said, "For Generation X, spirituality is the mission" (1997).

This remains an underutilized means of mission by those serving Generation X adults, but might be profitably explored with members of this generation. Ben Johnson's idea of evangelism as spiritual direction could be helpful here (1991). A biblical precedent for such a sequence is Lydia and her friends' regular practice of prayer by the river near Philippi, a practice that predated their encounter with Paul's band and their subsequent conversion (Acts 16:11-15).[5] Jesus and Christian spiritual writers may then become spiritual guides and mentors to many postmoderns before their conversion. Biblical texts describing various spiritual practices could be introduced to pre-Christian Xers, as could historical practices such as *lectio divina* and the Ignatian exercises in which journaling, poetry, art, and the imagination are used to place oneself into narrative passages of Scripture.[6] Richard Peace has

---

4. Rick Richardson thinks postmodernity reverses the sequences typical of modernity as follows: (1) "Experience before explanation"; (2) "Belonging before believing"; (3) "Identification before influence"; (4) "Image before word"—by image he means the use of intuition and the imagination typical of poetry and the arts as opposed to cognition and propositions; and finally (5) "Trust before truth" (2001:2, 16, 17).

5. Cf. pp. 123 n.28 and 125 above.

6. *Lectio divina* is a Latin term meaning the divine reading of the word. It has a 1,500-year tradition in the history of the church. The best resource I have seen to teach this method of Bible reading to Xers is Richard Peace's *Contemplative Bible Reading* (1998a), which I have used in my Monday evening group for Xer men. It is designed for small groups and has excellent leader instructions. I have used it to train group par-

suggested that spiritual practices utilizing the imagination and senses, such as Ignatius of Loyola's *Spiritual Exercises*, will resonate deeply with postmoderns (2006b). In a pluralistic culture, where four of the five pillars of Islam are spiritual disciplines (prayer, almsgiving, fasting, and pilgrimage)[7] and Eastern religions are introducing Americans to a plethora of spiritual practices, church and mission institutions face fertile opportunities despite the challenges. The rest experienced in solitude, prayer, and silence is real, even if these are not practiced in the context of faith in Jesus. Xers who hunger for these practices will reverberate with groups that go on retreat to wait on God through various historic practices and spiritual disciplines. Beaudoin writes that Xers are drawn to "John of the Cross, Ignatius, Teresa of Avila, and others from the rich heritage of spirituality. Sometimes, I suggest neglected, somewhat obscure works such as the *Rule* of Saint Benedict for a spiritual challenge on a weekend retreat" (1998:165). Ministries that do not devote much time and space for God in these disciplines betray their own biblical heritage, fail to resonate with the spiritual ethos of the culture, and miss a major missional opportunity. By engaging in these practices, many Xers are resisting the collapse of space and time and thus helping the church to allow God to make room for himself in its life and mission.

Eclectic, Sensate, and in Search of a Heritage

After becoming a Christian through IVCF, a student friend of mine was searching for a church home near his campus. When I asked what he was looking for, he responded without hesitation: "a church with rock-worship that is liturgical and sacramental." When hearing this, older audiences usually react with laughter or surprise. Xers see nothing incongruous about this response, as they piece together spiritualities from various traditions in ways that seem incompatible to previous generations. My friend's answer reflects three characteristics of Generation X

---

ticipants to bring others into the presence of God using this method. For an accessible version of the Ignatian exercises from a Protestant perspective, see James Wakefield's *Sacred Listening* (2006). For a Catholic perspective, see Margaret Silf's *Inner Compass* (1998) and Joseph A. Tetlow's *Spiritual Exercises* (1992).

7. I owe this insight to Jon L. Dybdahl's handouts used in a course on spirituality he taught at Andrews University Theological Seminary in Berrien Springs, Michigan (n.d.).

spirituality: it is eclectic, sensate, and in search of a heritage—each of these relating to space and time and their collapse.

1. *Eclectic.* Christian believers from Generation X want to draw from all parts of the Christian faith. On the positive side, spiritual eclecticism allows them to benefit from the best of Protestant, evangelical, Catholic, charismatic, Orthodox, and other Christian spiritualities (C. Van Engen 1997c). This fosters gratitude for what God has done through each part of the Christian tradition and expresses the unity for which Jesus prayed (John 17), as well as the enrichment that diverse parts of his body contribute to other parts (1 Cor 12). On the negative side, new believers who remain theologically ungrounded for long may combine belief in Jesus with other spiritualities in ways that result in syncretism and compromise their worship of him as the risen Lord. They may follow fellow Xer Jon M. Sweeney, who writes that "we dabble a bit in yoga, we meditate in different traditions, we pray and we move from one spiritual group to another freely" (2001:xiv). As Beaudoin observes, the Internet's compression of space feeds spiritual eclecticism. "When Scripture appears as hypertext format, where does 'real' Scripture begin and end? What if every Scripture were hot?" he asks. "Hypertext, after all, is the most common way of navigating through the Web. People usually travel on the Internet using clickable links—text leading to text leading to images leading to music leading to video leading to text leading to . . . " (1998:125–26). An endless sequence of spiritual sites available in cyberspace can be accessed by simply clicking onto links for terms like "spirit" or "meditation." These can instantly connect the user to myriads of Web sites for a vast array religious, cult, occult, and new age groups anywhere on the globe. The collapse of space brings spiritual pluralism to Xers' fingertips instantaneously.

2. *Sensate.* Generation X spirituality is sensate; that is, it is experiential, involving all the senses, especially the visual. It is a physical spirituality and thus it is open to spiritual disciplines that can only be done in the body (Willard 1998b:353). Xers have embraced sacred dance, spiritual art, religious tattoos, the sacraments, and participatory approaches to faith. When studying the story of the Good Samaritan, IVCF staff person Doug Schaupp takes students to feed the homeless as a part of the study (2001). Beaudoin thinks Xers' "lived theology" is also to be found

in pop culture's vast array of sacred images, which express their many spiritualities (1998:29–36). Xers largely reject modernity's elevation of rationality over experience and it's focus on propositions without life. Richard Flory and Donald E. Miller agree in *Gen X Religion* (2000), the best sociological look at the generation's spirituality. They have collected case studies of Generation X groups and congregations in Southern California—one Jewish, one Gothic, and nine Christian, including African-American, Korean, Latino, and multi-ethnic. Based on his analysis of these case studies, Flory has developed a theoretical construct for Generation X religion comprising five major characteristics,[8] the first of which is its experiential nature (2000:235–37). The cases studied showed that Xers experiencing God through participation in music, dance, art, and the media.

> Technological and pop-cultural literacy, as learned through computers, movies, and MTV ... give Gen Xers the ability to use various technology and art forms to shape their own religious expressions and experience. These are neither text-based nor do they have a traditional linear structure; rather they are malleable, multidimensional narratives. (Flory 2000:245)

Beaudoin thinks this non-linear malleable sense of time in cyberspace gives Xers a transcendent awareness of the "eternal now" (1998:86–87), as well as a sense of time's uncertainty and scarcity.

> This uncertainty about our position in time makes it difficult for us to feel any sense of religious stability, certainty, or confidence. ... our feeling that the present continually escapes us, our sense of being out(side) of time, can keep us from knowing any depth of religious experience.
>
> God—and the mystery of our creation in God—transcends our own out-of-timeness. Being open to experiences of grace can give us a new sense of being at home in time, particularly if we can accept that our anxieties about the parameters of time stem from our own limitations, not God's. (1998:129)

If Beaudoin is correct, "experiences of grace" can bring Xers both a sense of "being at home in time" and "a depth of religious experience" through rhythms of spiritual practices, which, as Chilton has observed,

---

8. Flory's five characteristics of Generation X religion are: (1) experiential; (2) entrepreneurial; (3) identity in community; (4) "race-, ethnic-, and gender-inclusive"; and (5) authentic (2000:235–41).

can address our culture's problem with time being too scarce or vacant (2002:6).

3. *In Search of a Heritage.* The case studies in *Gen X Religion* examine mostly Xer-led conservative, independent groups, as well as several groups affiliated with large organizations that have managed to create their own institutional space free of external control (Flory 2000:247). Donald Miller and Arpi Misha Miller note that these entrepreneurial Generation X groups have few counterparts among mainline Protestant denominations, whose existing churches are attracting relatively few Xers (2000:2). What *Gen X Religion* leaves out are those Xers who attend Catholic, mainline, and Orthodox parishes, which leads to the last point in this section.

As Colleen Carroll has shown in *The New Faithful: Why Young Adults are Embracing Christian Orthodoxy*, many Xers and Millennials are flocking to Orthodox and Catholic churches, which connect them with a rich heritage of religious art, icons, and recitations of historic Christian creeds (2002:25-120).[9] Xers' fascination with this kind of spirituality derives in part from their quest for links to a history beyond their immediate painful past. One of my students from a broken home traveled thousands of miles just to locate the gravestone of a grandfather he had never known and see if he could learn something about him and his other ancestors. He was looking for roots in his family heritage, which his family of origin had failed to provide. In a similar way, liturgical and sacramental churches put us in touch with a long tradition of prayer and spiritual practice. Liturgy roots us in our spiritual history, in its mystery, and in worship and prayer.

Authentic and Transparent

Authenticity is another of the Flory's five characteristics of Generation X religion. Why should a whole generation find hypocrisy so abhorrent and want to tell it like it is? For one, their Boomer parents, who started out to change the world in the sixties, had difficulty spending time with their children or keeping their marriages intact—a glaring discrepancy

---

9. For similar views about Generation X openness to spiritual heritage of historic traditions, see Beaudoin (1998:150-58) and Wendy Zoba's comments about Millennial interest in traditional forms of worship and ritual (2001:84). For a critique of evangelicalism's lack of liturgy, see Simon Chan (2006).

already mentioned. Their hypocrisy hurt Xers deeply. The social revolution started by Boomers bequeathed a devastating legacy for Xers, who were left to pick up the pieces: broken families, economic indebtedness, addictions, powerless churches, leadership failures, political deceit, and moral decline. Xers have experienced the highest rate of divorce among their parents of any previous generation: 40 percent (Gross and Scott 1990:58). As they were growing up, they frequently came home to empty residences, and so they were left to create their own social tribes. They were abandoned.

Still one of the best books on Generation X, *Generation Alone: Xers Making a Place in the World* (1994), describes well this abandonment and the loss of a sense of place. The book is based partially on authors William Mahedy and Xer Janet Bernardi's participation in one of the few Episcopal projects geared for Xers. Prior to becoming a chaplain at San Diego State University, Mahedy had worked with Vietnam veterans suffering from Post Traumatic Stress Disorder (PTSD). To his surprise, he observed the same symptoms among students that he had observed in veterans suffering from PTSD (1994:22–29). Our culture's social fragmentation produced a war zone, and Xers were traumatized in the battle. They were wounded, disillusioned, and suspicious of institutions run by Boomers, the source of so much of their pain. Little wonder they need to be real. Anyone transparent about their scars is deemed to be authentic by Xers, who need unhurried time to be heard as they tell their stories.

Spiritual transparency was evident during the 1995–96 spiritual awakening among young adults and youth, who poured out public confession of sin and vivid descriptions of pain and abuse. That year, Campus Crusade for Christ staff spent three days at its national conference in unplanned public confession of sin. At the conclusion of each confession, other staff spontaneously huddled to lay hands on and pray for the one who had made confession (Dedinger 1997). Christians from Generation X readily practice James 5:16: "Confess your sins to one another, and pray for one another, so that you may be healed." About the same time, Doug Schaupp and his IVCF staff at UCLA began a whole new way of engaging the campus. They discovered the power of sharing their own stories of pain, abuse, and addiction. Their vulnerability not only connected them with pre-Christian students but also allowed them to talk about Jesus subjectively as a man of suffering, who understood and cared for the pain of others. Their InterVarsity chapter became a safe place in which pre-Christians found authentic friendships while taking as much time as they needed to consider Jesus objectively as the risen Lord. Usually it took a year or more before they could respond to him as the world's Savior, to whom they could give trust and allegiance (Schaupp 2000).

Why do they need so much more time than previous generations? Many Xers grew up trying to relate to as many as ten adult figures who were part of their lives, each briefly and only then in an absent manner. As a result, these Xers do not know who they are (Shenk 2000) and were left to fashion social space from among their peers and the media. But as J. Richard Middleton and Brian J. Walsh point out, the blur of successive and disconnected media bites, each with its own reality, echoed the succession of adult figures passing their lives and produced what some fear may be a postmodern identity crisis like "multiple personality disorder" (1995:55–56). Little wonder Xers have fragmented selves, have matured more slowly, and have difficulty trusting or making long-term commitments. Why expect more without more time invested in them? Xers' trust in God and others takes longer to form than previous generations. For them trust is a spiritual discipline (Mahedy and Bernardi 1994:96–97). They would rather not make a decision than make an inauthentic and hypocritical one.

Formed in Suffering, Healing, and Play

Generation X spirituality has been formed by a triad of suffering, healing, and play. Each element of the triad needs the others in this generation's spiritual formation into the image of Christ.

1. *Suffering*. Generation X spirituality has been formed by suffering and pain. Mahedy and Bernardi speak of the need for American Christianity to understand that the soul must endure winter in order for there to be fruitfulness in spring and summer. They argue that Xers have been shaped in spiritual desolation so that they will later bear immense fruit (1994:161–69). Similarly, Alan J. Fadling (2001) teaches that the pruning described in John 15:1–3 is necessary to produce more fruit in the lives of Jesus's followers. Fadling uses this passage to popularize a six-stage model of spiritual formation developed by the late New Testament theologian Robert H. Guelich and social worker Jane O. Hagberg in *The*

Critical Journey (1989). Fadling equates pruning with the spiritual desolation and sense of abandonment in stages four and five of their model. Fadling's teaching has resonated with Xers' experience of the "cloud of unknowing" as well as "the dark night of the soul" about which St. John of the Cross wrote. Some, like Xer Andy Crouch (1996:33) and Kevin G. Ford and Jim Denney (1995:258–59), have thus termed this the generation of the cross.[10]

Tom Beaudoin speaks of Jesus's suffering, the cross, and Generation X pain. In a nuanced theological interpretation of video, movie, and music groups' portrayals of these themes, he argues that suffering provides "a unifying factor in a fragmented world" and creates ambiguity, so necessary for developing mature faith (1998:96–120). Suffering for Crouch is the heart of the gospel.

> Hiding from suffering hides us from the gospel, turning forgiveness, healing, and the Holy Spirit into empty abstractions. The gift I believe my generation can bring to the church is a repentance from our culture's flight from suffering, a turn toward the Cross, and with it, a return to the reality of the good news. ... As we enter into suffering before the Lord, we find the gospel. There our emptiness is mysteriously transfigured into forgiveness, healing, and resurrection. I believe my generation is ready for this gospel. We know, beneath all our activism and busyness, that we do not have the answer. We know that no human institution, program, or ideology can fill the yawning chasm gaping beneath our feet. (1996:33)

Suffering slows the flow of time. It forces us to listen to Jesus's pain, our own pain, and that of others. Xers are receptive to Alister E. McGrath's call to extended time in silent contemplation of the cross. "[The church] might prefer to contemplate something other than the dying Jesus Christ—but her thought about God and the world must be based upon that haunting and deeply disturbing image" (1988b:189). I have observed this among Xers in two ways: (1) they are often drawn to images of the cross during silent retreats—one Fuller student, whose family members expressed little affection, was drawn to embrace

---

10. On the *Cloud of Unknowing*, which was written by an unknown fourteenth century author, see Elizabeth Dreyer (1996:89). St. John of the Cross was a sixteenth century Spanish mystic whose treatise, *The Dark Night of the Soul*, has popularized the idea that God's hiddenness is really his means of grace, forming us more fully into the image of Christ. See Colin P. Thompson (1996:232).

a life-size statue of Jesus suffering on the cross; and (2) they want to celebrate communion reflecting quietly on Christ's suffering more frequently than do older generations. N. T. Wright, who himself celebrated communion daily in his capacity as Chaplain of Worcester College at Oxford, writes:

> Some people are afraid of silence. They fill their world with noise, so they can't hear what they are thinking or feeling deep down. But they then also shut out the quiet whisper of God's love—and the quiet sadness of a world in pain. In prayer, silence can help us to hear all three and to bring them together In an increasingly noisy world, maybe this is one thing we deeply need. (1997b:2–3)

2. *Healing.* This generation's spirituality is integrally related to healing. Xers such as Karen Kuzhan (2005) have experienced inner healing prayer drawing upon the work of Leanne Payne, Charles H. Kraft, and others. This form of prayer involves a supernatural intervention by the Spirit, bringing the presence of Jesus into the painful memories of past wounds. In his presence, past experiences of abuse, sin, and trauma can be healed. According to Payne, Kraft, and others, healing these wounds removes diabolical strongholds of emotional, physical, and spiritual bondage (Payne 1989).[11] Crouch described this approach to prayer with young Harvard Xers in the 1990s.

> Eating disorders, sexual addiction, drug abuse, alcoholism, and compulsive shopping—all these demonstrate that the core experiences of pain and sin are interrelated and, indeed, feed off one another in an escalating cycle of consumption. . . . I have held countless conversations with students about sin and forgiveness, and many of these have ended in prayer for the healing of some deeply rooted experience of pain. . . . The reason our pain retains its power to cripple us is nearly always lack of forgiveness. If someone has hurt us deeply, that person's sin continues to have power over us until we release that person of the debt to us. (1996:33)

---

11. I myself have received inner healing from a deep dread of our son's relapse through prayers of a group of mostly Generation X leaders who anointed me with oil and with and the laying on of hands, according to James 5:13–17.

I have repeatedly observed emotional healing as Xer seminary students and pastors go on extended retreats for solitude, prayer, and silence, which echoes Suedfeld's experience with REST treatment for addictions.[12] Bernardi and Mahedy have observed many Xers seeking help from Twelve Step groups and therapy (1994:82). All modes of healing require quiet unhurried listening to the soul and to the movement of the Holy Spirit. Brief therapies, short pastoral counseling, and hurried meetings simply do not allow the depth of Christ's healing love to be expressed.

3. *Play.* Generation X spirituality is being formed in play. Play provides a means of recovering one's lost childhood, which may explain, in part, why Xers relate differently to time than their parents. Sociologist Peter Berger says that games alter time in profound ways. In joyous play, he says, "the time structure of the playful universe takes on a very specific quality, it becomes eternity.... The outside world has, for the duration of the game, ceased to exist. And, by implication . . . pain and death, which are the law of that world, have also ceased to exist" (1990:66–67). F. Lynn Mallery has argued that because the cultural opposite of play is work and the theological opposite of work is faith, then an analogy between faith and play must exist (1990). Interestingly, an important part of Xers' growth in spiritual formation is their discovery of God's playfulness with them during their extended retreats. One sad effect of the collapse of space and time in the past thirty years is the loss of childhood play.[13] God appears to be redressing this loss in Generation X spirituality.

Redefining the Church

The spiritual stirrings in Generation X contain the seeds of a more sustained spiritual movement of the Holy Spirit than was experienced in the revival of the late 1960s and early 1970s. The Jesus Movement in those years largely dissipated as Boomers became enculturated through their slavery to workaholism and greed as mentioned in chapter 2. However, a crucial threat to the spiritual depth of Xers in the years ahead

---

12. REST treatment of addictions and other pathologies are described in chapter 2.

13. My daughter-in-law, Erin Jensen, teaches second grade in California. As a member of Generation X, she laments the loss of recess and P.E. time because of the sheer amount of information she is required to cover with her students.

is materialism. Xers want to be very well off financially, as consistently shown in studies.[14] Nevertheless, Charles Van Engen and others have argued that at least some Christian believers in this cohort have been redefining the church and its leadership in ways that have not happened in the past millennium of Western church history, except for periods of renewal (1997c). But for such redefinition to become embedded in the life of the church, time and space for God and community will need to be created and protected; the god of mammon must be resisted and biblical illiteracy addressed. Only then can the following redefinitions of radically faithful Xers[15] be preserved:

1. The church is relationships, not institutions (Van Engen 1997c). Generation X spirituality is communal—a key emphasis of emergent church leaders (mostly Xers) such as Doug Pagitt (2004:51) and Dan Kimball (2003:111-17). Having had to form tribes of their own, Xers often distrust institutions and urge replacing institutional forms of church with a communal experience of God.

> The integrity of the church in the West is under siege because of the extent to which institutionalism has overtaken the church. There are observable signs of this condition. One is the sheer proliferation of programs and activities.... This trivialization of the church through preoccupation with activities is like a cancer that destroys the vitality of the body from within. On the surface the church appears to be alive and well Inside, there is another condition.... Our activist culture has gulled us into mistaking activity for spiritual power and focus. This is an important facet of the cultural captivity into which the church has fallen. (Shenk 1995a:73-74)

14. Putnam cites studies showing that materialism among high school seniors and college freshmen steadily rose from the late 1960s to the 1990s, when it has leveled off. In the late 1960s the annual UCLA survey of college freshmen showed about 40 percent thought "being very well off financially" was very important. That figure grew to 75 percent in 1998. Similar trends were reported in a nationwide survey of high school seniors conducted by the University of Michigan (1999:259-61).

15. An example of a radically obedient Xer-led ministry, which is creating space and time for God, for community, and for loving at risk urban children among the poorest of the poor, is the work of David Bayne with a ministry called Word Made Flesh. He is helping the staff of this organization root their compassion in periodic retreat days and daily rhythms of silence, prayer, and solitude (2007). Contemplation and communal living among the poor constitute two of the twelve distinctives of an emerging new monasticism. See Rob Moll (2005:10-41).

2. The church is inclusive, not exclusive, of ethnic and gender diversity. It is heterogeneous not homogeneous. One of Flory's five characteristics of Generation X faith is that it is "race-, ethnic-, and gender-inclusive" (2000:239). Xers form relationships across ethnic and racial boundaries more readily than previous generations. As one of my seminary students shared in class, she and her friends from other ethnic groups were more like each other than like their parents' generation, precisely on the issue of inter-racial and inter-ethnic relationships. All groups in the case studies in *Gen X Religion* saw racial-ethnic inclusion as a moral imperative (Flory 2000:239). On gender, "the more conservative or traditional the ideology and more tied to an existing organization, the fewer opportunities there are for women in the group; the less conservative or traditional the ideology and the more independent the group, the more opportunities there are for women" (2000:239). Even in conservative and less independent groups, however, members of Generation X are breaking these patterns with their strong emphasis on equality before God. "There is no longer Jew or Greek, there is no longer slave or free, there is no longer male and female; for all of you are one in Christ Jesus" (Gal 3:28).

3. Spiritual and personal identity is formed in community. This idea is another of Flory's five characteristics (2000:238). As Flory points out, religious Generation X identity derives from a community far more than for individualistic Boomers (2000:238). Since the identity and character crises facing our society grew out of its loss of community, this is a hopeful sign. In *Community that is Christian* Julie A. Gorman sees individualism as the key threat to small groups patterned after Jesus's example (2002:42–59). Commenting on Jesus and his community, Richard B. Hays writes,

> The community of Jesus' followers is to be characterized by a strong sense of communal life; they are to forgive, to share their goods, to reach across ethnic and national boundaries and, of course, to live as a nonviolent community. This vision cannot be carried out by isolated individuals seeking to cultivate a private spirituality; instead all these practices are essentially relational. ... [It challenges] a church hypnotized by Enlightenment mantras about the rights of the individual and wallowing in postmodern self-indulgence. (1999:153–54)

How might this kind of community form Generation X sense of identity? Flory's case studies showed at least two mechanisms at play: (1) members shared their stories in symbols—art, tattoos, music; and (2) members told their stories in light of the faith community's history— that is, how the community's life and message brought about personal transformation and meaning (Flory 2000:238–39). Thus, God's story, their personal stories and that of the community became integrated. As noted in chapter 3, Wright argues that Jesus constituted his community around stories, symbols, and praxis, in which his disciples eventually came to see that Israel's story, their stories, and God's reign were coming to climatic fulfillment in Jesus's own life and mission. Xers need to have their stories patiently listened to in a community that will lovingly notice and interpret it in light of God's story in Jesus.[16] But such identity formation requires greater time than most institutional settings foster.

4. Worship has become a central means of encountering God in community. Sustained worship lasting a half an hour or more is not uncommon in Generation X expressions of church. Not since the Protestant Reformation has the centrality of the church's proclamation been so challenged (Van Engen 1997c). Though the word is proclaimed and taught, it supports worship, not the other way around. With the emphasis on worship and storytelling, it will be important for Generation X not to overlook its widespread biblical illiteracy, according to former IVCF president Steve Hayner (1989). Many new believers in the generation are quite ignorant of the rich stories found in biblical as well as church history. In the long run, biblical illiteracy poses a threat to Generation X spirituality in the years ahead. Sadly, the structures in the modern church seem ill-fitted for the challenge. The local assembly and seminaries struggle to deeply form the spirituality of Generation X leaders and to teach theology, mission, and history in a reflective, formational, and narrative way.

5. The church is a missional community embodying justice and compassion. There is a group of Generation X leaders and followers who are being deeply formed who comprise a small but growing movement that Jonathan R. Wilson has termed "the new monasticism" (1998:cover). The

---

16. One Fuller student requested that I listen to his entire life story—something another male had never done with him. In four or five sessions he told me his story.

movement's linkage of communion, community, and mission among the poor is described by IVCF's Scott Bessenecker's *The New Friars: The Emerging Movement Serving the World's Poor* (2006:85–134).

Redefining Spiritual Leadership

Not only have members of Generation X redefined the church as relationships not institutions, but they are redefining spiritual leadership as well. Charles Van Engen (1997c) has observed that they tend to view or experience leadership as:

1. Legitimated by spirituality and authenticity; not position or credential
2. Drawing spirituality from Catholic, Protestant, Orthodox, and other sources
3. Occurring primarily in bi-vocational teams, versus professional lone-ranger CEOs
4. Mentored-networked relationships that flow incarnationally before being expressed organizationally

Xers' redefinitions offer hope. More than many expressions of the church, they are drawn towards patterns we have seen in Jesus, the early church, and selected historical leaders. Generation X leaders are entrepreneurial—one of Flory's five characteristics (2000:237). They tend to be creative and initiate their own ministries—an indication of significant future leadership (Clinton 1988:87).

But Generation X redefinitions pose dilemmas. College, youth, and young adult pastors who worked with this age cohort have indicated that the ratio of those giving care to those needing care needs to be about one to four.[17] An important reason for this is because of the mentoring deficit this generation experienced on its way to young adulthood, largely due to the breakdown and fragmentation of the family and other social structures. Thus, groups with one hundred members of this generation necessitate leadership cores of twenty-five to thirty to adequately mentor, disciple, and pastor. This renders most leader-

---

17. This insight became clear to me in a conversation at Voyagers Church in Irvine, CA with Darron Jones, who pastored youth during the mid 1990s when the last of the Xers were in high school. This ratio may also be needed for the Millennials.

ship structures woefully inadequate and requires an unprecedented emergence of volunteer leadership teams. But insufficient space and time has been created in most leadership structures to nurture leaders in the communal disciplines of solitude, meditation, prayer, silence, and intercession needed to refresh and build leaders of character, depth, and power. There exists a leadership gap.

Recent empirical research paints a similar picture. Time conflict was identified as the number one concern of youth leaders in a landmark study of 2,131 youth ministers funded by the Lilly Endowment and the Huston Foundation. The data was collected in 1996 and analyzed by youth ministry authorities Merton Strommen, Karen E. Jones, and Dave Rahn, who reported their findings in *Youth Ministry that Transforms* (2001). The youth workers in the study (mostly Xers) ranked erosion of time for spiritual disciplines as their highest concern out of seventy

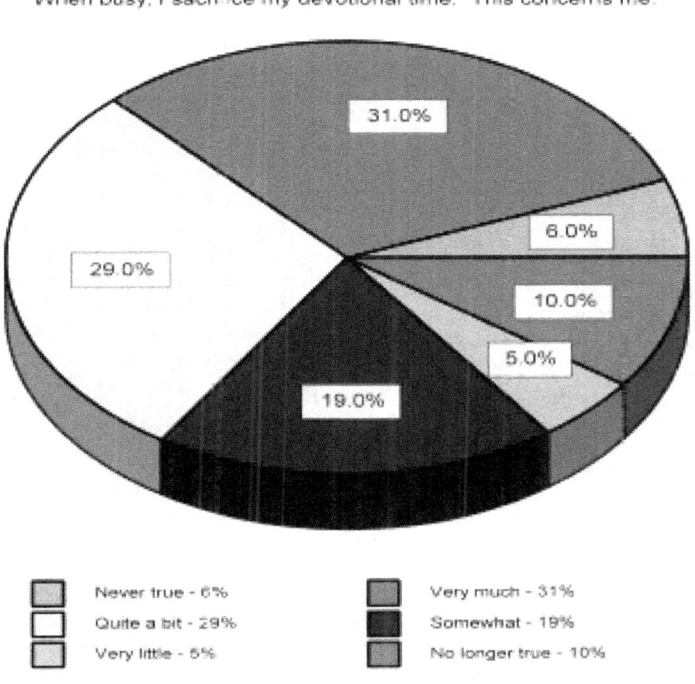

Figure 2: Youth Leaders Concerned over Sacrificing Devotional Time (Stommen, Jones, and Rahn 2001:47)

Table 35: Summary of Generation X Spirituality and Time-Space Collapse

Characteristics of Gen-X Spirituality	Space-Time Collapse	Strengths (+) and Threats (−)
1. Openness to Solitude, Prayer, and Silence	More leisure time growing up Whatever/whenever attitude toward time Cultural thirst for spiritual disciplines and rest	+ Easier to create time with God + Openness to Spirit's agenda − Lack of long-term discipline + Pre-evangelism
2a. Eclectic	Internet space of flows brings pluralism home	+ Best of all Christian spiritualities − Syncretism with other gods
2b. Sensate	Non-linear malleable sense of speed/not at home in time Consuming pop media culture	+ Can give sense of eternal now − Can inhibit depth of spirit − Materialism could take over
2c. In Search of a Heritage	Want to find roots in time prior to their immediate painful past	+ Will be enriched by what God has done in past; his story
3. Authentic/Transparent	Social fragmentation/PTSD	+ Identify with pain of world
4a. Formed in Suffering	Suffering slows time Pruning/the cross	+ Listen to own pain and that of others + Waiting for God; dark night
4b. Formed in Healing	Healing requires time to listen	+ Healing beyond us/only God
4c. Formed in Play	Play suspends time	+ Can recover lost childhood

5. Redefining the Church	Time in inclusive relationships with people, not institutions Identity formation takes time Worship primary over word Express social compassion	+ Activism will not replace God – Relationships can replace God + Storytelling and listening – Biblical illiteracy + New emerging monasticism
6. Redefining Leadership	Leaders have hurry sickness	+ 1/4 ratio requires volunteer leaders

items,[18] while concern over not having enough time with people because of administrative responsibility was ranked fourth (2001:46–53). Time pressures, time urgency, and hurry sickness are undermining youth pastors' spiritual lives and their time with people. Notice in Figure 2 above that 79 percent of the total sample—the three largest pieces of the pie—reported concern over the time squeeze on their devotional practice.

To summarize my discussion on Generation X spirituality, I have said that it is (1) open to solitude, prayer, and silence; (2) eclectic, sensate, and in search of a heritage; (3) authentic and transparent; (4) formed in suffering, healing, and play; (5) redefining the church; and (6) redefining leadership. These are displayed in column one of Table 35 above. I have argued that these characteristics are positively and negatively related to the collapse of space and time, as displayed in the third column of Table 35. The collapse has contributed to the eclectic nature and role of suffering in this generation's spirituality, while the role of play and their redefinitions of church and leadership have resisted the collapse. A counter-cultural sense of time and space will be needed if this generation is to be formed deeply in Christ so that it can reflect his glory and compassion. But I argue that materialism, lack of long-term discipline, and biblical illiteracy threaten the protection, health, and maturation of such communities.

---

18. Indicated by their responses to the question displayed in Figure 2 above..

Millennial Spirituality and Space-Time

How is Millennial spirituality similar to and different from Generation X spirituality, and how does it relate to the collapse of space and time? These are difficult questions.[19] A relatively small portion of Millennials are only now in their early to mid-twenties, which theorists consider to be late adolescence.[20] As mentioned above, generational consciousness is imprinted through an interaction between personal and national histories and is only completed in late adolescence. Therefore, we should be guarded as to what we can conclusively say about Millennial characteristics, especially their spirituality. In 1999, youth ministry authority Chap Clark said, "It is too early to take a stand but not too early to make some observations and take some guesses" (1999:12). But based on two recent landmark studies and a 2005 survey, we can say considerably more about Millennial spirituality and make some provisional comparisons with Generation X spirituality.

Are Millennials Spiritually Hungry?

One would hardly think that Millennials are spiritually hungry when reading *Millennials Rising* by generational theorists Howe and Strauss. The authors do not even mention spirituality in their summary of Millennial characteristics—the main criticism Wendy Zoba levels at their work (2001:83)—except to say that younger Millennials are spending over one hour per week less at church than Xers did at the same age (Howe and Strauss 2000:172). Similarly, a March 1999 *Life* magazine cover story on teens reported only a handful of their interviewees naming religion as an influence in their lives (Adato 1999:42). David Brooks was met with a silent response when he raised the issue of character

---

19. See Zoba (2001:83) on the difficulties surrounding generational studies.

20. Theorists now generally view North American adolescence as being comprised of three stages: early (roughly ages 10–13), mid (14–18), and late adolescence (19–mid 20s). See Chap Clark (2004:11, 26–28, 83, 203 n. 6). Adolescence is limited to societies that have undergone massive urbanization. Sharon Daloz Parks dates the onset of adolescence in the United States to the Civil War (2000:46), while Clark dates its beginning at the dawn of the twentieth century (1999:12). He notes that in the past century adolescence expanded its boundaries, beginning at 14 1/2, while today it starts about 12 and ends at about 22, up from 16 (2004:28). Parks thinks young adulthood has emerged as a new life stage called "twenty-something" (2000:46–47).

with Princeton Millennials (2001:53–54).[21] And so, some might conclude that spirituality is passé with this cohort. Not so, according to Brooks (2001:53). Though he largely agrees with Howe and Strauss's portrait of Millennials as optimistic, trustful of authority, smart, rule followers, team players, and highly supervised (2000:7–11), Brooks sees a spiritual hunger in this generation despite his concerns over its lack of character. This was affirmed in his Princeton interview with Robert Wuthnow, who said, "In the past ten or twelve years students are no longer embarrassed about being interested in religion—or spirituality, as they call it. That's a huge change. People used to feel as if they had acne being raised in a religious home" (Brooks 2001:53). Brooks chimes in,

> I hadn't been on campus more than five minutes before I started hearing about all the students who do community service—tutoring at a charter school in Trenton, working at Habitat for Humanity-style building projects, serving food at soup kitchens. But religion tends to be more private[22] than public with them, and the character of their faith tends to be unrelievedly upbeat. "It's an optimistic view," Wuthnow says. "You just never hear about sin and evil and judgment. It's about love and success and being happy." (2001:53)

Chap Clark, thinks that the optimistic confidence and positive attitudes exhibited by Millennials as noted by Brooks (2000), Zoba (1999, 2001), and Howe and Strauss (2000:3–29)[23] actually cover their underlying pain. "They are not willing to let you see their pain so they may send up a smoke screen. Millennials may appear collected and competent, but inside they are still children. Look beyond the veneer and you will see the cracks" (Clark1999:13). That is, they are more likely to hide what Xers openly shared. This is one of the biggest differences between the two generations—the lack of transparency among Millennials, at least when they are with you in person. Jenny Hall observes that the Millennial college students with whom she works prefer to be vulnera-

---

21. Brooks did witness a new interest in moral questions and the existence of evil on a return visit to Princeton just after 9/11 (Kantrowitz and Naughton 2001:49).

22. Millennials are more open to non-verbal works of compassion or justice than verbal witness.

23. In addition to the Generation Y traits mentioned above, Howe and Strauss have given the following: high birth rate, acceptance of authority, little free time, orientation towards science, and computer literate (2000:3–10).

ble on their blogs (2006). But Clark thinks differences between Xers and Millennials have been exaggerated. "The only difference I see between Gen X and Gen Y is that those in the Y camp have learned to protect themselves better. They may act like they are entitled, but internally, their callused walls are thicker" (1999:14). He is less optimistic than many theorists about Millennials because their families continue to fragment; their parents' divorce rates are similar to that of Xers' parents. Yes, Millennials are spiritual, but Clark wonders how authentic they are in following Jesus given the selfishness he saw expressed in their spirituality (1999:13–14).

A Changing Picture: Hurt and the National Study of Youth and Religion (NSYR)

In a landmark ethnographic study of Millennials, reported in his book *Hurt*, Clark became a participant observer as a substitute teacher in La Crescenta Valley High School, in Los Angeles County, during the 2001–2 school year. His methodology allowed him to get behind mid-adolescents' exterior veneer and layers of defense and become a trusted adult on their turf in whom they could confide (2004:10–11). He discovered more widespread hurt and loneliness than he had imagined and a universal sense of having been abandoned by an adult society too busy to genuinely listen and express care. At the same time, he found a longing to spend more unhurried time just being with adults (2004:54–54). This study was not narrowed to any single question, such as spirituality, but rather sought to develop a comprehensive picture of the generation's inner and often hidden landscape in eight broad categories[24]—one of which was the busyness and stress of mid-adolescents' world. "As a result of the abandonment they have faced throughout their lives, most midadolescents carry inside them a powerful defense mechanism that keeps them running as fast and as hard as they can" (2004:144). So how does this affect their spirituality? Clark does not share Colleen Carroll's assertion that they are responding to abandonment with a return en masse to orthodox Christian spirituality.[25] He and Carroll differ on the size, if not the existence, of this return. He says,

---

24. Other categories were peers, school, family, sports, sex, ethics or morality, and the party scene.

25. In support of Carroll's assertion, her research was focused primarily on

> According to my research, the only evidence related to this assertion was that midadolescents are perhaps more open to the possibility of a transcendent reality beyond the observable universe. This is a far stretch from saying that today's adolescents are [scripturally] spiritual.... Those who are embracing Christian orthodoxy are in search of a more meaningful spiritual experience than the modernistic, rationalistic, cognitive, educational model they grew up on. For the vast majority of this new batch of midadolescents, however, the demands of biblical faith are not on their radar screens. (2004:190)

The concerns that Clark and others have voiced over Millennial spirituality were born out a year later in the largest empirical study ever undertaken on North American teenage spirituality—a more quantitative and narrowly focused study than Clark's.[26] The findings were published in *Soul Searching: The Religious and Spiritual Lives of American Teenagers* (2005) by sociologists Christian Smith with Melinda Lundquist Denton. The research found that: (1) religion and spirituality are important to a majority of American teens; (2) the religion practiced by these teens is heavily influenced by their parents—the single most influential factor; (3) the faith of these teens is compartmentalized, individualistic, is not highly prioritized, and generally lacks transformative power—again reflecting their parents' shallow faith formation; (4) though most teens give lip service to eclecticism in principle, in practice they identify themselves with historic faith traditions, not atheistic, agnostic, or non-Western spiritualities—only two percent of teens identify themselves as seekers (2005:266); (5) they are not well informed about nor educated in their own historic traditions, as evidenced by the widespread biblical illiteracy among Christian teens; (6) the basic goal of religious practice is to be individually successful, do right, and find inner, private happiness; and (7) these teens know little about sin or God's glory, and they view God as uninvolved and seldom intervening in their lives, if at all (2005:259–64). Smith and Denton's term for this vague

---

Generation X. Of the young adults she interviewed, a relatively small percentage were from Generation Y (2002:13).

26. The study was funded by the Lilly Endowment. Data was collected through phone surveys with 3,290 randomly selected teens between 13 and 17 from July 2002 to March 2003. This was followed by in depth interviews in person with 267 of the teens. Methods were partially quatative (2005:6, 292–307).

teenage faith is Moralistic Therapeutic Deism—MTD. In an interview with Kathy Henning, Smith said, "My firm belief is that MTD is the actual, functional, de facto religious faith of the majority of American teenagers from a variety of religious and nonreligious traditions" (Henning 2006:28). However, Smith and Denton found a portion of the sample that did not fit the MTD profile, and that "there are consistent and impressive differences in outcomes between highly religious American teens and nonreligious teens" (2005:257). On the sociological measures of religious vitality, Mormon teens scored the highest, followed by conservative Protestant and black teens. These, in turn, were followed by mainline Protestant, Catholic, Jewish, and nonreligious teenagers (2005:261).

I wish to note several implications of the rich store of NSYR findings. The first is that the home should become a center for spiritual practice and education, as the *Shepherd of Hermas* (*Herm. Vis.* 1999:1.3.1–2), the Protestant Reformers (Bradley 1997), and recent studies have so strongly advocated.[27] Smith, himself the father of three children, said that the research has encouraged him "to be more intentional, purposive, authorized to teach them. . . . As a result, I have talked with them more, discussed theological issues. I put together a year-long introductory course on Christian history and theology for my kids" (Henning 2006:29). Second, the fact that 38 percent of teens in the sample pray at least once a day, while another 27 percent pray at least weekly (Smith and Denton 2005:46) suggests that various prayer practices should play a more central role in ministries and missions to U.S. students. This was the conclusion of one IVCF staff team in discussing implications of the *Soulsearching* findings for their campuses (Tom Allen 2005).[28] Third, a high priority should be placed on fostering safe counter-cultural communities of belonging and listening, where students can be mentored in theological reflection and spiritual practices from historic Christian traditions.

---

27. See Lee, Rice, and Gillespie (1997:372–81) as well as Gary Thomas (2000).

28. IVCF Area Director Tom Allen sent a May 18, 2005 e-mail summation of an Inland Area staff discussion on *Soulsearching* to IVCF staffer Jon Ball, who forwarded it to me on January 9, 2006. I am indebted to Allen for permission to cite his summation.

Examples of Historic Christian Spirituality: Millennial Youth

Anticipating the need for biblical and spiritual depth among teens long before the NSYR project put the spotlight on the issue, the Lilly Foundation began its Theological Programs for High School Youth in the early 1990s. The purpose was to fund programs of spiritual and theological formation among high school seniors and hopefully attract some to a vocation of ministry. The first program, funded in 1992, was the Youth Theology Institute (YTI) at Emory University. Directed by Don C. Richter, YTI showed what was possible for many programs that followed. Richter describes YTI's first decade:

> Our aim is to get these students to see what is at stake when they read the Bible. We have to help them to get beyond reading the Bible as literature—important as that is—and invite them to see how the stories and images make an authority claim on their lives. We ourselves as teachers and mentors, need to trust that the Bible has life-changing stories that we can come back to again and again throughout our lives.... Worship, of course, is the focal practice of life together in a covenant community. We wanted YTI scholars [high school participants] to experience life-giving worship ... We found that many teens came to our academy experience-rich but reflection-poor. That's because in much youth work around the country today there is an emphasis on chalking up experiences without reflecting on them theologically. At YTI, we ... hold head and heart together. (Schier 2001)

From 1998 to 2002 the Lilly Endowment spent $57.3 million on programs developed by thirty-three schools of theology and Christian colleges. Recapping the results of these programs, Craig Dykstra, the Endowment's Vice President for Religion, said that reports from parents, pastors, educators and students themselves indicated that the purposes of the initiative were materializing and that former participants have begun to appear in seminaries. In 2002, $25.3 million was awarded to another sixteen schools, bringing the total to forty-nine institutions representing a wide diversity of Christian traditions from across the theological spectrum (Lilly 2002, 2006).[29]

29. This program funded initiatives started by schools including such diverse institutions as Calvin Theological Seminary, Azusa Pacific University, St. Mary's Seminary, Claremont, Multnomah Bible College, Andover Newton Theological Seminary, and Associated Mennonite Biblical Seminary (Lilly 2002).

What about Millennials in churches? At the Princeton Forum on Youth Ministry, homiletics professor Jana Childers cited seventh graders who voted *lectio divina* the most important part of their confirmation process at a United Methodist church in Indiana, and teens who participated in labyrinth prayer walks in Redondo Beach, California.[30] She also mentioned the multiplication of Millennial hits on one church Web site when a rendition of the Jesus Prayer was posted,[31] and Sister Patricia McCullah's report of passionate teen response to the Ignatian meditation exercises she teaches (Childers 1999). From an evangelical vantage point, Wendy Zoba also sees Millennial interest in ancient forms of prayer. "In the course of writing two books on teen issues and in researching a third, I have found that many are being drawn to traditional forms of worship, particularly its tactile expressions in ritual and liturgy" (2001:84). She thinks ancient forms of prayer may be more common among Millennials than Xers. One day, while she was researching youth spirituality, her seventeen-year-old son interrupted her to tell her about a book he ordered for the small group study he was leading (2001:84). It was Bonhoeffer's *Cost of Discipleship* (1959). Zoba also pointed to Mark Yaconelli's work with the Youth Ministry and Spirituality Project at San Francisco Theological Seminary as an example of this trend. The Project, funded by the Lilly Endowment from 1998 to 2004, tested a contemplative, multi-generational approach to youth ministry in sixteen churches (Yaconelli 2006:14). This approach subverts the dominant youth ministry models, which had left Yaconelli burnt out and seriously considering leaving ministry (2001). The models he critiques are the:

1. Entertainment model; revolving around programs to retains kids

---

30. The labyrinth has a long history as an aid to prayer. A person begins at the circumference of the labyrinth—a large circular area that contains concentric circles and pathways resembling a maze that lead the one praying progressively towards the center where he/she shares whatever is at the center of her/his heart with God. After meeting God there, discerning his presence and heart, the person moves back towards the circumference and the world. The focus in prayer leading outward is intercession for the world. Labyrinths have been used in non-Christian spiritualities. Group magazine and many others have developed Christ-centered labyrinths.

31. The Jesus Prayer is, "Lord Jesus Christ, Son of God, have mercy on me, a sinner," or simply, "Jesus, mercy" (Muto 2000:104).

2. Charismatic leader model; centered in a personality freeing adults of their responsibility

3. Information model; dispensing ideas—for example, confirmation classes (Yaconelli 2001)

According to Yaconelli, what these models share in common are the very same forms used by secular consumer culture—professionals and products. None of these models captures "the spirit that gave rise to Christianity," says Yaconelli (2001). Instead, in his model "lay" adults replace professionals and the presence of God replaces products. Paying attention to God's presence—what he might be saying or doing—becomes the focus for both adults and youth. Ancient practices helped participants in the Youth Ministry and Spirituality Project be attentive to God's presence and their own hearts. Thus they discerned how God was calling them to companion with youth. Contemplative action furnished the basis for theological reflection. Participating teens, adults, and sometimes entire congregations have been renewed (2001, 2006:241).

Richard Dunn notes that this kind of paying attention requires a change in tempo or "pacing." "The need for speed and volume and sensation increases with each new wave of youth-culture media," he writes (2001:39). Those ministering to youth need to slow down so they can focus attention. "Pacing requires me to listen to the heart of an adolescent, seeing beyond words and behaviors. Pacing therefore demands time, the time it takes to go beyond the surface in a conversation or to enter the social turf of the student.... Pacing is costly" (2001:16). Dunn suggests that pacing is essential for youth ministry to be a God-bearing vocation (2001:156)—an idea popularized by Kenda Creasy Dean and Ron Foster, who teach youth ministry at Princeton Theological Seminary. In *The Godbearing Life: The Art of Soul Tending for Youth Ministry* (1998), they argue that youth ministry is:

1. *A Spiritual Discipline.* Youth ministry is a spiritual practice of bearing Jesus Christ to others, even as Mary (a youth) bore the Son of God, ushering him into the world (Dean and Foster 1998:41–54). But to be God-bearers we must be space-makers—first in our own lives and then in the lives of youth. This changes our relationship to time.

Godbearers seek sacred space, and we try to help create it for youth. Our firsthand familiarity with sacred space equips us to draw others into the *kairos* experience of sacred space. *Kairos* time refers to those moments in space and time when we no longer measure time *chronologically* (in minutes and hours) but *qualitatively*. In *kairos* time an individual or community experiences the spirit of God filling up the time to its fullest measure. *Kairos* time is full of God-consciousness, not bound by clock-consciousness. (1998:185)

2. *A Missional Task.* Youth workers should be trained to function cross-culturally. Dean and Foster have brought together the worlds of spirituality and mission (1998:35–36). Some evangelical youth leaders have done the same. Jeff King reports on a Seattle area youth ministry that grew to six hundred through fasting, prayer, worship, and ministries of compassion and evangelism (1997:48). Dunn (2001), Bass and Richter (2002), Dean (2004), Clark and Kara E. Powell (2006), Mike King (2006), and Yaconelli (2006) have all written about spiritual practices as the heart and center of youth ministry. In these examples, historic Christian spiritualities are springing up in the spiritual desert of society's continued abandonment of yet another generation (Clark 2004). Fanning the fires of divine passion are those subversive and deeply incarnational approaches that bring adults, youth, and mentors together in covenant communities to lavish time on God, each other, and for quiet reflection.[32]

Examples of Historic Christian Spirituality: College Millennials

Around 2000, Generation Y began arriving on college campuses. What has since characterized Christian spiritualities that have developed

---

32. Dean's most recent book, *Practicing Passion* (2004), is the most theologically sophisticated book on youth spirituality I have seen. She also draws heavily on the social sciences and the history of spirituality. Among others, she quotes Ignatius of Antioch: "Leave me to imitate the passion of my God" (*Ign. Rom.* 1999:6.3). She argues that only the passion of Christ can truly ignite the passion youth are seeking. "Adolescents do not want to suffer, but they do desperately want to love something *worthy* of suffering, and to be so loved. The Christian story both authenticates adolescent passion and turns it inside out, redeeming, redirecting, and redefining it with a more profound Passion still: the suffering love of Jesus Christ" (2004:2).

among this generation on campus amidst the collapse of space and time? Campus ministries from historic Christian traditions can help answer the question. Every two years since 2001, the Ivy Jungle Network has surveyed staff members of para-church, denominational, and local church-based college student ministries. The most recent survey, conducted with 463 respondents in 2005,[33] yielded several findings germane to this study (Ivy Jungle Network 2005).

The report reflects several strengths: (1) the spiritual formation of college ministry staff is deepening—84 percent indicate spiritual growth in the past year; (2) community is developing—almost 90 percent of students participate in small group fellowships—up from 2003; and (3) mission is increasing—70 percent of the ministries conduct short-term missions, and a similar percentage have local service projects among the poor—also up from 2003 (Ivy Jungle network 2005). However, the report also reflects some challenges:

1. *Challenges Facing Students.* Not surprisingly, college ministry staff reported stress, busyness, and time scarcity as the most common challenge by far facing their students in the last two surveys. "The heat seems turned up and the pace has increased." The next most frequently cited challenge was a cluster of discipleship issues—integrating faith with life, developing passion for God, and growing in an intimate walk with God (Ivy Jungle Network 2005).

---

33. "The State of College and University Ministry" 2005 survey sample consisted of the following: (1) theological traditions— 69 evangelical, 14 percent in mainline Protestant denominations, 8 percent other; 4.1 percent liberal, and .4 percent Catholic; (2) type of campus minister—20 percent parachurch staff, 28 percent local church college ministry staff, 31 percent denominational campus ministry staff, and 15 percent campus chaplain or faculty or staff of a college; (3) type of college campus being served—59.7 percent state college/university, 17.8 percent private Christian college, 9.5 percent private secular college, 7.4 percent other, 5.4 percent commuter, and .2 percent military; (4) generation—9 percent Generation Y, 47 percent Generation X, 40 percent Boomers and 3.7 percent pre-Boomers. Though ethnic minority campus ministries were under-represented, nevertheless, the ministries represented reported 3 percent Native American, 7 percent Hispanic, 8 percent Asian, 10 percent African-American and 72 percent Caucasian. Though only about 50 percent of the groups reported doing evangelism, still 32 percent of the students participating in the campus ministries represented were new believers or not yet followers of Jesus (The Ivy Jungle Network 2005).

2. *Challenges Facing Ministries.* The most commonly reported challenge was finding student leaders. Since 2001, the percentage of student leaders devoting ten or more hours per week in ministry leadership roles decreased from 14.4 percent to 10.2 percent over this period, while the percentage spending five to ten hours per week in leadership roles dropped from 42.6 percent to 10 percent (Ivy Jungle Network 2005). IVCF staffer Jon Ball identifies time and relationships as the two greatest challenges in student ministry on the campuses of the division he helps oversee.[34] In reference to relationships, he means students' lack of capacity and maturity to form and nurture relationships and carry on conversations. In place of real relationships and communication, Ball said students substitute virtual ones that lack depth and meaning (2007). He finds it difficult to get face time with students and to encourage them in deeper relationships with peers. This undoubtedly reflects Millennials' defensive layers, which Clark's research so clearly exposed. Ball affirms Clark's view that abandonment created this generation's central need for safe places of unconditional acceptance.

Field Research Findings on Spirituality and Mission in Generations X and Y

This section deals with my fourth research question introduced in chapter 1: How does space and time with God relate to mission and faith maturity in the postmodern generations? In 1993, The Leadership Institute, the organization I founded and lead, began the *Journey to Reach the Next Generations* project for pastors and other leaders interested in engaging in fresh ways the generations that represent the church's future. Research was an important component in the project design. From 1996 to 1997 The Leadership Institute conducted descriptive field research on a sample of 1,598 people drawn from 34 groups whose leaders participated in the *Journey*. Members of Generations X and Y represented a sizeable percentage of the sample, which came from 5 states, 18 churches, 6 denominations, and 2 parachurch organizations.[35] Jerry Lee, of Loma Linda University School of Public Health,

---

34. Ball is Associate Divisional Director for the Greater Los Angeles Division of IVCF.

35. This field research did not seek to show causal relationships between variables in the research question addressed in this section—space and time for God, mission,

was the research consultant who analyzed the data collected through a questionnaire administered by *Journey* participants.³⁶ The questionnaire is displayed in Appendix I. Lee summarized his findings and analysis of data collected from this sample (1997). He also analyzed data collected through a nearly identical questionnaire administered 2 years earlier to 1,197 people from 15 Seventh-day Adventist churches and subgroups in Southern California, whose leaders comprised the first group of *Journey* participants (1995a). The questionnaires measured the respondents' self-perceptions concerning:

1. *Spiritual and Missional Practices in Relation to Time*. The questionnaires asked about the frequency and duration of seven spiritual and mission practices, including solitude, prayer, meditation, Bible reading, verbal witness—talking about the work of God in ones life, and acts of compassion and mercy.³⁷ Social scientists refer to these as religious behaviors.

2. *Faith Maturity*. One of the most often used scales for measuring faith maturity is the intrinsic/extrinsic (*I/E*) scale developed by Gordon W. Allport and J. M. Ross (1967:423–43). The *I/E* scale measures the motivation and attitudes associated with faith in adults, as well as the ex-

---

and faith maturity among the postmodern generations. Rather it sought only to show correlations wherever they exist. A correlation between two variables does not necessarily mean that a casual relationship exists between the two variables in either direction. Other conditions besides the correlation must be present (Lee 2001:6–7). I abandoned my original quasi-scientific research design that had pre- and post-tests in favor of a simpler descriptive design. The more I read research projects utilizing quasi-scientific designs to test the efficacy of a spiritual practice, the less convinced I became of the intricate causal pathways shown between the practice—the independent variable—and some change in the dependent variables. Jerry Lee explained that to use a quasi-scientific design assumes a causal hypothesis, which is then tested (2002). I am only willing to hypothesize a primary cause to grace not to a practice. But, grace is not a variable that can be directly tested and causal relationships in social research are tricky to pin down. Chap Clark has voiced reservations about causal relationships being attributed to certain practices by Christian Smith in recent research being conducted at University of North Carolina—Chapel Hill (2004:215 n. 3).

36. Richard L. Gorsuch explains why questionnaires have been used successfully to study religiosity, but he suggests several limitations to them and urges openness to other methodologies (1984:228–36).

37. See Appendix I. In the section "Practicing your Faith" of the questionnaire, items one through five ask about solitude, prayer or meditation, Bible reading, verbal witness, and acts of mercy or compassion.

tent to which adult faith is integrated with everyday life (Lee 1995a:2). Intrinsic motivation is based upon "religion as end" (1995a:9). Persons with intrinsic motivation relate to God primarily on the basis of God's intrinsic worth, rather than the benefits gained by such a relationship. On the other hand, extrinsic motivation is based upon "religion as means" (1995a:10).[38] By contrast, persons with extrinsic motivation relate to God primarily because of benefits derived from God (1995a:2). Since Allport's and Ross's scale was designed with adults in mind, children and adolescents often found it unintelligible; so Gorsuch and G. Daniel Venable developed an age universal I/E scale that could be understood at a sixth grade level and above (1983:181–87). The age universal I/E scale was used in the questionnaire (see Appendix I). Later, Gorsuch and Susan E. McPherson, using the Gorsuch and Venable scale, found that extrinsic motivation had two distinct dimensions or subcategories: social comfort and personal comfort (1989:348–54). We used this scale, which distinguishes between these two dimensions of extrinsic motivation.[39]

3. *Volunteer Leadership Roles.* Three types of volunteer leaders were compared with each other and with followers: those in governance roles, those in pastoral care roles, and those in missional or outreach roles.[40]

4. *Church or Group Climate.* The questionnaire also includes nine items measuring the warmth of a church or group as well as its thinking climate.[41] Items dealing with the warmth measure the respondents' perceptions of how friendly, welcoming of strangers, accepting of dif-

---

38. For a summary report of his 1985 survey of the first fifteen years of some seventy published I/E research papers, see Michael J. Donahue (1985:418–23). As Lee points out, the concept of "religion as means and ends" is not original to him (2007), but he thinks may be traced to C. Daniel Batson. In particular, Lee cites the article "Religious Prosocial Motivation: Is It Altruistic or Egoistic?" by Batson et al. (1989:873–84).

39. Extrinsic and intrinsic motivation are measured by the fourteen items in the section of the questionnaire entitled "Motivation." See Appendix I.

40. Item four of the demographic section of the questionnaire deals with leadership roles. See Appendix I.

41. Items one through four of the questionnaire's "Church Climate" section deal with how warm the respondent perceives his or her church or group, while items five through nine of this section deal with the thinking climate of the church or group. See Appendix I.

ferences, and caring and warm their group is. Items dealing with thinking climate involve the respondents' perceptions of the degree to which their group challenges their thinking, encourages them to ask questions, expects them to learn and think, and is an environment in which they actually learn a lot.[42] See the "Church Climate" section of the questionnaire in Appendix I. What were the findings to my research question with churches and groups whose leaders participated in the *Journey to Reach the Next Generations* project? Both the inter-church and Adventist samples showed a clear linkage between spirituality and mission. Lee's analyses revealed:

1. *Correlations of Frequency and Duration of Spiritual Practice with Frequency of Mission*. In both samples, frequency in talking about the work of God in one's life correlated strongly with time with God, prayer, and Bible reading; a weaker correlation was found between frequency of compassion and time with God in the Adventist sample, but not in the inter-church sample (Lee 1995a:2; 1997:1–2). Many charts could be used to illustrate these correlations from both samples. The one I chose, displayed in Figure 3 below, shows a strong relationship in the Adventist sample between verbal witness and time with God and Bible reading. As Lee wrote, "Notice that Bible reading and time alone with God seem to be additive. The more Bible reading or time alone with God the more witnessing" (1995b:1). Figure 3 shows that the frequency of talking about the work of God in one's life increases with both the frequency and duration of time alone with God and reading Scripture. In fact, a major jump in verbal witness occurs as one moves from under thirty minutes alone with God on an average day to more than thirty minutes, especially if Bible reading is daily.

---

42. These items are from the *Valuegenesis* questionnaire administered in the early 1990s to 14,748 North American Adventist youth in field research conducted by the Search Institute in Minneapolis in conjunction with a team of denominational administrators, youth ministry practitioners, and researchers from Andrews University, Loma Linda University, La Sierra University, and Oakwood College (Dudley and Gillespie 1992:vii–ix, 301). Climate items in the *Valuegenesis* survey came from research questions developed by the Search Institute in studying fifty thousand youth in six denominations: Disciples of Christ, Evangelical Lutheran, Presbyterian Church, United Methodist, United Church of Christ, and U.S. Southern Baptist (1992:41, 169–73).

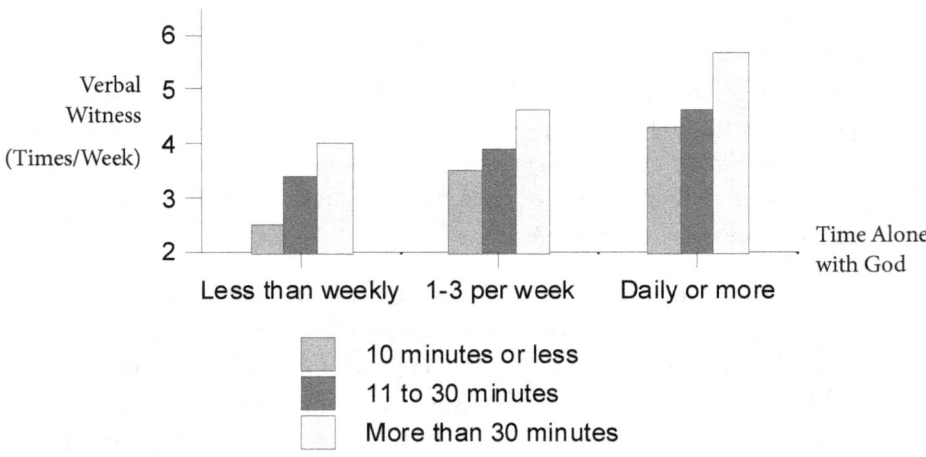

Figure 3: Correlation of Verbal Witness with Frequency and Duration of Solitude and Duration of Solitude and Bible Reading (Adapted from Lee 1995b)

In this same sample, Lee found significant differences between the time Millennials and Xers devoted to spiritual and missional practices. On average, Xers reported more frequent solitude, prayer, meditation, and Bible reading than did Millennials. They also told others about the work of God in their lives more frequently than did Millennials (2006:1). No other significant difference between Xers' and Millenials' practices were found. These differences are most likely related to age, as I will discuss next.

2. *Correlations of Faith Maturity with Spiritual Practice, Mission, and Age up to Fifty.* In the inter-church sample, fairly strong positive correlations were reported between intrinsic motivation (the measure of faith maturity we used) and each of the following: verbal witness, reading the Bible, and prayer (Lee 1997:1). In the same sample, intrinsic motivation increased with age until about ages fifty to sixty, and decreased after age seventy—a finding that echoed patterns found in the earlier Adventist

sample.[43] Extrinsic motivation was high among the young and the old, and was lowest among middle-aged individuals (Lee 1997:2). As might be expected, intrinsic and extrinsic motivation are negatively correlated to each other, though, as Lee observed, "the associations are not strong" (1997:1).[44] These patterns were born out when Lee compared the intrinsic and extrinsic motivations of Xers directly with those of the Millennials in the Adventist sample. As we would expect, the Generation X part of the sample scored significantly higher on the intrinsic scale and significantly lower on the extrinsic scale than did Generation Y (2006:2).[45] In other words, Xers in this sample were more mature in their faith than Millennials, which seems logical. I would guess that these differences are more developmental or age-related than they are indicative of generational distinctives. However, this hunch should be tested by further research on these generations.

3. *A Volunteer Leadership Logjam.* In the Adventist sample, Lee found that "[Volunteer or lay] leaders reported fewer acts of mercy, less witnessing, praying, and reading their Bible and had lower intrinsic religious motivation and higher extrinsic (personal benefit) religious [sic] motivation than members" (1996:2). Further study should be done to see if such self-reporting by leaders is indeed accurate or due to some factor such as a possible "humility effect" (Lee 1996:9).[46] Similarly, in the inter-church sample, volunteer leaders generally had no higher levels of

43. To Lee's knowledge, this finding has not been reported in the literature (1994). I have started to write an article (with Lee as co-author) for submission to journals, which will report more extensively on these field research projects than the more narrowly defined focus of this study allows. Another round of data collection may be conducted with future *Journey* participants. We would compare the findings of such a study with the baseline established by our research in the 1990s and with recent research reported in this chapter.

44. In the Adventist sample, groups with higher extrinsic scores reported lower scores in time alone with God in prayer, frequency of Bible reading, and frequency in mission practices (1995a:22).

45. Xers in the Adventist sample scored an average of 3.97 and Millennials 3.63 on the intrinsic scale. On the extrinsic scale, Xers scored 3.09 while Millennials scored 3.33. A five-point scale was used to measure responses to the intrinsic and extrinsic items in the Adventist sample in contrast to a nine-point scale in the inter-church sample. The scale in the Adventist sample is: 1 = Strongly Disagree, 2 = Disagree, 3 = Not Sure, 4 = Agree, 5 = Strongly Agree.

46. Lee wonders if leaders tend to possess a greater degree of humility than followers, which is manifested in under-reporting of their practices.

spiritual and missional practices than non-leaders. They only reported higher levels if they had outreach roles or if they engaged in all three kinds of leadership roles: outreach or mission, pastoral care, and governance (1997:2). Leaders with roles in mission, then, had greater faith maturity, time with God, and frequency of witness than those they led. Thus, the volunteer leaders who scored the highest in faith maturity were those whose abiding was strong, who expressed care for others in the group, and who reached out in mission. The field research on this sample shows a strong linkage between spirituality and mission and strongly suggests the efficacy of abiding, loving one another, and bearing witness as described in John 15. This may be one of the most important findings of the field research, and seems to have major implications on how volunteer leadership is developed.

4. *Further Research Is Needed on Possible Time Thresholds for Spiritual Practice.* As already mentioned, thirty minutes of solitude and Bible reading on a average day appeared to be a threshold above which verbal witness jumped significantly in the Adventist sample. There also seemed to be a threshold in the same sample regarding frequency of compassionate mission. "It seems to show that meeting alone with God is *not* associated with any increased acts of mercy" unless Bible reading occurs at least weekly (Lee 1995b:1). More study is needed to see if these or other thresholds can be generalized. One place to look for time thresholds for spiritual practices is in the relationships between church or group climate and these practices. For a Christian community to be missional with the postmodern generations (or with any generation), it must be relationally warm and open in its thinking, as has been discussed in this chapter. In the Adventist sample, there was no correlated increase in spiritual and mission practices when the group moved from low to moderate warmth. However, an increase of group warmth from average to high was associated with an increase in spiritual practices. "Groups which evaluated their church as a thinking church showed a similar pattern except for how often they read their Bible" (1995a). In terms of average individual alone time with God, at what point in a group does the correlation between a warmer climate and increased time spent in solitude and other spiritual practices commence? Twenty minutes per day? Thirty minutes per day? Which disciplines fell into this pattern and which did not? Do these patterns show up in other

research samples? These are the questions to be addressed in future research. A final caution in pursuing these questions is that we not assume nor imply a causal relation in any correlation that may be found. This has been the constant intention throughout this study.

Comparisons between Spiritualities of Generations X and Y in Relation to Space-Time

I have looked at how the space-time collapse of the past fifty years has related positively and negatively to the spiritualities of the postmodern generations. I have reviewed our findings concerning the relationships between spirituality, mission, faith maturity, and time in two field research samples with sizeable representations of Generations X and Y. At this point, we can conclude that Millennial patterns of Christian spirituality are similar to those of Xers, with notable differences. Here are some comparisons:

1. Xers were left alone more than were Millennials. Susan Van Riesen noted that, because her generation was abandoned, Xers especially need the Spirit's presence and to know that God hears them (1998). The Millennials, on the other hand, were supervised in an endless round of activity. Yet, as Chap Clark's study has shown, their sense of abandonment and loneliness is just as deep, just different and more hidden—they are less open about it (2004). Both generations need to know that "nothing can separate them from the love of God" (Rom 8:39), that Jesus stays closer than a sibling and that God can and will re-parent them (Hayner 1989). Both need mature guides to embody such love and to mentor them into kingdom adulthood, not socialize them into U.S. society's corrosive norms.

2. Because it had less free time and far more supervision while growing up than Generation X, Generation Y generally exhibits greater time urgency; thus, creating space for God may be a greater challenge for Millennials. As fifteen-year-old Martha Schewhn said, "Teenagers often have strict schedules. In a society that is constantly telling us to do so many things, it is often hard to find time for God and for the rest we need" (Bass and Richter 2002:139). This may be one factor that accounts for the finding in our Adventist field research sample that Millennials spend less time alone with God than Xers. Extended times of solitude

and silence with God (without "productivity") will be important as Millennials discover they are embraced by God as they are. Periodically slowing and stopping the addictive pace of this generation so it can rest will be impossible without divine intervention and support of a caring community. Both generations, in similar but different ways, need the grace of God to make them at home in time—quality time, *kairos* time—with him and others. This will take a major infusion of God's power over the gods of this age. He will come to them—both Xers and Millennials—and do for them what they cannot do for themselves— making room for himself in space and time.

3. Those in both generations need safe environments where they will be listened to and loved unconditionally. In time, embracing grace as the fundamental ethos of such environments will dissolve their mistrust of God and others—a precondition for healthy development into young adulthood and for experiencing transforming grace, which attends spiritual practice. The challenge for both generations will be to develop patterns (a rule or rhythm of life) for the long haul when God seems absent and to practice these with the support of Christian communities in which the virus of space-time compression is being continuously debugged and resisted. The burning question facing college and youth ministries in the current time crunch is "How?" How might God do the impossible?

4. The answer, at least in part, lies in our past—in the ancient paths mentioned at the beginning of this chapter (Jer 6:16). Millennials who are embracing orthodox Christian faith appear to make up a smaller percentage of their age cohort than do Xers of the same ilk. Yet these faithful Millennials may be even more oriented to ancient forms of prayer and liturgy than Xers, as the experiences of Yaconelli, Zoba, and others have suggested. These young adults can and do connect to stories from the past like those in this study—stories of inner loneliness, depression, and abandonment by the death of parents or in being sent away (Geert Groote at age ten, Ignatius at fifteen, Brainerd at eight, and Mary Lyon at six), and of young adult conversions (Brainerd at twenty, Lyon in her twenties, Ignatius at thirty, and Groote at thirty-four). These and other stories from the past can motivate a fresh appropriation of ancient spiritual and missional practices that were at the heart of the passionate

responses to God of these men and women. Their obedient, subversive efforts to overcome the marginalization they faced from prevailing societal and religious groups might further ignite the imagination of these two marginalized generations to follow suit in our own day.

One example illustrating how this can work is the story of Chris and Tammi Jehele, who live in the most violent inner city neighborhood of Kansas City, where thirty fatal shootings have occurred in the past eight years. The Jehele's direct a multi-ethnic team of eight staff and a number of adult volunteers leaders (mostly Xers and Millennials) in a program called The Hope Center, which mentors and re-parents kids at risk who live in the eight-square-block area where the staff reside. They work with children of drug addicts, prostitutes, and absent or dead parents with the mission of developing them into world-class Christian leaders. Jehele found that he and his staff were suffering burnout from the intense demands of their work until they met seasoned spiritual director Craig Babb.[47] Babb introduced them to the rhythms of praying the hours liturgically, which they do in community three times daily, and taking one-day silent retreats monthly in the pattern of the *Devotio Moderna* (Jehele 2007a). The center's program of training and tutoring youth—not unlike the urban youth outreaches ran by the New Devout—emphasizes spirituality, education, character, justice, leadership, interpersonal relationships, and life skills. It also stresses ecological care and recreation. Kids enter this intensive process by a minimum of one year's participation in the worship and Bible study outreach and by exhibiting some of the fruit of the Spirit (Jehele 2007a; The Hope Center 2007). Another potential parallel might borrow from how the *Devotio Moderna* developed an economic structure that allowed its members to earn financial resources for their houses and for the poor in the community—a model from which The Hope Center and other communities in the new monasticism might profitably learn.

47. Craig Babb is a certified spiritual director having been trained at the Benedictine Abbey in Pecos, New Mexico. He is the Midwest staff representative of The Leadership Institute and founder and director of Rhythm of Grace.

Generations X and Y Discerning Fresh Rhythms of Spirituality and Mission

As mentioned earlier, 70 percent of college ministries conduct local service projects. The growth of these projects and the emergence of the new monasticism, with its focus on contemplation and compassion, reflects an awakening desire among college ministries for deeper, more sustained spiritual practice.[48] As IVCF director of global projects Scott A. Bessenecker says, "Like earlier movements, the ones today attract mostly 20-somethings who long for community, intimacy with Jesus, and to love those on the margins of society" (Moll 2005:40). These earlier movements are those such as the Franciscans and Celtic orders. In *After Heaven*, Wuthnow's seminal study of changes in North American spirituality since 1950, he writes, "Among the people we talked to, spending time cultivating their relationship with God seemed more often to free them from material concerns and other self-interested pursuits so that they could focus on the needs of others" (1998:192). Among the most effective mission strategies for a community that follows Jesus is to create space and time for its people to simply be in God's presence, resting in Jesus's care for themselves and for his world.[49]

So how do we proceed from here? Jeremiah's description of being at a crossroads seems apt in the face of our culture's captivity to hurry sickness and the other gods of our age. They have produced a diminished spirituality across the generations—what Wuthnow calls a "spirituality of seeking"—driven people who only catch God on the run in an ever-increasing pace of life (1998:1–18). What hope is there of developing healthy rhythms of spiritual life on a broad scale for the long haul—a "spirituality of practice," as Wuthnow urges (1998:168–98)? Absolutely none, apart from grace! All of us, whatever our generation, would do well to heed Jeremiah's instructions given to a generation who inherited from previous generations a devastating legacy of spiritual, social, and economic decay and who faced the prospect of impending exile. The rule and power of the false gods to which Judah had given herself had

---

48. See two leaders in the new monasticism: Bessenecker (2006) and Shane Claiborne (2006).

49. See Appendix J for suggestions on spending time in extended personal communion with God.

reaped their destruction and had robbed them of God's *shalom*. So how do we proceed?

The prophet said, "Stop at the crossroads; ask 'Where is that way that leads to what is good?'" (Jer 6:16). I believe the current situation calls for a suspension of life as usual, a stopping. In place of our usual patterns, we might set aside unhurried periods for solitary and communal worship, repentance, prayer, and spiritual discernment on questions to which we have few or no answers—similar to what occurs in an Ignatian retreat. As we saw, when Ignatius of Loyola faced the urgent question of how his fledgling order would support itself, he sought the Lord in what he called "making an election" (1991c:*Sp. Ex.*[169–89]). I suggest that many college and youth leaders, along with their adult mentors, may be led to do something similar in retreat settings.[50] Calling a moratorium on activity as usual among the volunteer leaders and staff might allow us to let that which breaks God's heart—our sin and that of our culture—begin to break our hearts. We may weep as God shows us how our society's systematic abandonment of its young has wounded him on the cross. This may not be easy, but it will be cleansing and freeing, even as tears of repentance often were for Brainerd, Ignatius, and the New Devout. In particular, we may confess the sins of our society to the Lord as though they are our own, like Daniel's confession (Dan 9:8) in his great prayer of intercession (9:3–19). I suggest we who are leaders take the lead in transparency concerning our sin and brokenness. The Holy Spirit might also lead us to ask forgiveness for our generation's abandonment of theirs. After a period of *examen*, examination, worship, and meditation on Matthew 28:16–20, I offer these discernment questions:

1. Over the next several months, how are we sensing God calling us as student volunteers and mentors to be with Jesus in community and solitude—to see him, worship him, and experience his grace and presence amidst our doubts and inner struggle (Matt 28:16–18a)?

---

50. See Yaconelli on a "liturgy of discernment" and a very helpful process for facilitating a one-day youth ministry retreat geared for both youth and adult volunteers (2006:243–48). For help in developing a rule of life you may visit http://www.theleadershipinstitute.org/rol/.

2. To what daily, weekly, monthly, and occasional rhythms of withdrawal and re-engagement do we sense God drawing us? What elements of a rhythm of life are becoming clear?

3. What are we hearing from Jesus regarding his commission of us? Specifically, what are we hearing about living compassionately among our families, peers, and the poor (Matt 28:18b–20)?

4. What constitutes appropriate leadership roles in our context? What doesn't?

After discerning the Spirit's leading through our questions, we may use the prophet's words as a basis for a leadership community covenant: "Take that way, and you will find rest for yourselves" (Jer 6:16b *NEB*).

Summary

I have now completed the second half of the cultural analysis of this study, which was begun in chapter 2. In this chapter I analyzed the spiritualities of Generations X and Y (primarily in their historic Christian expressions), which I argued were shaped in reaction to and because of the collapse of space and time. The analysis here was based on a literature review and field research data collected on the spiritualities of both generations. I developed a profile of Generation X spirituality from my survey of respected theorists and a case study of Generation X religious groups. I then did the same for Millennials, focusing on two landmark studies and a 2005 survey of Christian college ministries. These showed stress and time pressures to be universal challenges among Millennial students. Findings from my field research showed a strong relationship between spirituality and mission among Millennials and Xers:

1. Time with God was linked with the frequency of verbal witness in both field research samples. Millennials in one sample practiced solitude and verbal witness less frequently than Xers.

2. Faith maturity increased with age until about fifty to sixty, and decreased after age seventy, in both field research samples. Faith immaturity was high among the young and the old and lowest among the middle-aged. As we would expect, Xers in one sample scored significantly higher in faith maturity and lower in faith immaturity than Millennials.

3. A leadership challenge was found in that volunteer leaders were no more mature in their faith, and in general were doing no more about it in terms of spiritual and mission practices, than those they led, with one exception—volunteers with mission roles. These volunteers scored higher in their faith maturity and their spiritual practices than other volunteers. Thus, healthy volunteers were those who were abiding, loving one another, and bearing witness more (John 15).

4. More research is needed to determine minimum time thresholds for the frequency and duration of solitude, prayer, meditation, and Bible reading as they relate to mission and church climate. However, some of the data suggests that twenty to thirty minutes per day may be a threshold that should be examined in other samples.

I compared the spiritualities of the two generations and found more resistance to space-time compression in Generation X spirituality than among the Millennials. However, orthodox Millennials (a smaller percentage of their cohort than Xers) may be more open to ancient practices such as those illustrated in the historical part of this study. The new monasticism may be a means to help develop contemplation in both generations. I closed by suggesting a discernment process for student ministry leadership communities to develop rhythms of life.

This ends the body of this study. So what has it established regarding its two-fold thesis? I now draw together my findings in light of my thesis and make recommendations in the conclusion.

7

Conclusion

> This study relates the theme of spirituality in a fundamental way to modernity/postmodernity; and it locates spiritual practices theologically and historically as the background for considering the kind of response needed in the culture we now inhabit.
>
> —Wilbert Shenk (2008)

IN THIS CONCLUDING CHAPTER, I EXTRACT THIS STUDY'S KEY FINDINGS from which I synthesize a model for spirituality and mission. Based on these, I make some recommendations. The reader should remember that the findings, model, and recommendations reflect the limitations of the study, which I identified in the introduction and throughout.[1] Though mountains of important material are absent from my selections—such as the Pauline corpus in the biblical analysis, and Augustine's writings in the historical analysis[2]—still, the diversity of my selections tends to strengthen the study. The more my thesis is supported by findings from

---

1. In short, the cultural analysis was limited to examining the mechanisms and manifestations of the space-time collapse in America since 1950 and the characteristics of the spiritualities of Generations X and Y that emerged in this collapse. Part of the cultural analysis was field research on respondents to a questionnaire (not randomly selected) from about sixty groups representing six denominations and several independent and parachurch groups in six states. The theological analysis was limited to reflection on and analysis of selected synoptic accounts of Jesus's withdrawals from the crowds, his teachings on spirituality and mission in Matthew 5–7 and 28:16–20, and John 15, and then fourteen withdrawals for prayer in Acts. My historical analysis was limited to selected texts from the apostolic fathers, Origen, the *Devotio Moderna*, Ignatius of Loyola, and David Brainerd's *Diary*.

2. Finding grace in spiritualities or missions outside of Paul or Augustine, argues for its centrality.

a variety of sources, methodologies, and disciplines, the greater tends to be its validity.

Argument. Findings reported in each of the analyses of this study strongly supported one or both parts of my thesis: (1) empowered inward spirituality—expressed in creating time-space for God through solitary and communal spiritual practices—correlates with transforming outward mission, expressed in word and deed; and (2) the collapse of space and time in the postmodern age requires the church devote more plentiful space-time to spiritual practices in her structures of mission, church, and leadership development. I should note that the first part of my thesis was tested only on periods and groups in which mission expansion occurred. Also, I am not arguing for a causal relationship between space and time with God and outward mission, only that a positive correlation exists between the two.

Questions Addressed in This Study. My two-fold thesis was tested by examining the cultural, theological, historical, and field questions (and their subsidiaries) addressed in this study, and I reported my findings as indicated:

1. *Cultural.* What characterizes the collapse of space and time and the spirituality of the postmodern generations? (Chapters 2 and 6, pertaining to my second thesis).

2. *Theological.* How does space and time with God relate to mission in selected texts from the New Testament? (Chapters 3 and 4; first thesis).

3. *Historical.* How does space and time with God relate to mission in selected first and second millennium spiritual classics and their authors' movements? (Chapters 4 and 5; first thesis).

4. *Field.* How does space and time with God relate to the mission and faith maturity of the postmodern generations? (Chapter 6; both theses).

In the following two sections I review the most important findings of the study. Some of them are drawn from a single research question (and its subsidiaries), while others are drawn from two or more research questions (and subsidiaries). From these findings I draw my main conclusions.

Key Findings from Jesus, Historical Classic Texts, and My Field Study

From my study of Jesus, selected historical spiritual texts, and my field study, I have formed six strongly held conclusions: (1) spirituality and mission are inseparably linked in grace; (2) only participation in God's grace enables imitation of him; (3) spirituality subverts the status quo with fresh rhythms in space-time; (4) both solitude and community are essential—the eremitic and cenobitic traditions; (5) there are normative practices for subversive spirituality and transforming mission; and (6) we need radical flexibility to keep practices from supplanting God.

Spirituality and Mission Are Inseparably Linked in Grace

The case for the first part of my thesis—that empowered inward spirituality is correlated with transforming outward mission in the texts I selected—is based on the following:

1. *Jesus's Life and Ministry.* I found that Jesus repeatedly withdrew from the crowds for rest or communion with his Father (more often alone, but also in the community of his disciples), followed by re-engagement in mission. Mark's Gospel portrays Jesus's withdrawals from the crowds as being intimately associated with his doing mission in deed and word, with power, authority, healing, attracting of followers, and suffering love. The same was true for Luke's Gospel. In both gospels, some aspect of grace attends each withdrawal or subsequent mission.

2. *The Early Church.* I found that the apostles' withdrawals for prayer in Acts were closely tied to subsequent mission, just as with Jesus's rhythms in Luke. Connected with each of the apostles' fourteen withdrawals in Acts (three solitary and eleven communal), mission happens usually by proclamation. Grace attends each withdrawal or subsequent mission. The apostolic fathers were saturated with spiritual and mission practices. The spiritual practices they taught were, whether explicitly or implicitly, associated with outward mission—usually in deed. This is not seen primarily in withdrawal episodes that require narrative texts (of which there is only *The Martyrdom of Polycarp*), but in the proximity of mission and spiritual practices to each other in didactic texts or letters. Prevenient and transforming grace were present, but accepting

grace disappeared—replaced by merit and penance. Origen also taught transforming grace in relation to mission and prayer.

3. *Second Millennium Leaders*. For Geert Groote, Ignatius of Loyola, and David Brainerd, space and time for God in solitary and communal spiritual practices were linked to their empowered missions in deed and word, with the priority given to the latter. All three connected transforming grace to spirituality and mission, though only Brainerd moved toward accepting grace.

4. *My Field Research*. I found a positive relationship between spirituality and mission. Time with God was linked with the frequency of verbal witness, and an increase in spiritual practice from moderate to high correlated to an increase of group warmth and accepting grace in one field research sample. Further research is needed to establish whether this is a generalized pattern and whether a time threshold exists above which this association is true.

Only Participation in God's Grace Enables Imitation of Him

In the Sermon on the Mount, Jesus teaches that virtue is a gift flowing from participation in and imitation of God. The virtues Jesus commended and the vices he condemned in the Sermon are key to obeying the great commandment and provided the basis for the seven deadly sins and some of the virtues of later spiritual theology. So, imitation of Christ is not just copying his inward virtues, nor his outward behavior (his death, his spiritual practices, his rhythms of spirituality, and his mission), but requires God's grace (his initiation, power, and love) in the individual human person and in the body of Christ. As Kenda Creasy Dean observes, the Greek word for imitation (*mimesis*) implies participating, while the Latin term (*imitatio*) implies copying. "Christians do not 'ape' Jesus' life, death, and resurrection; by God's grace, we are incorporated into them. We become part of them, and in so doing they begin to define us" (Dean 2004:47).

Spirituality Subverts the Status Quo with Fresh Rhythms in Space-Time

God-given spiritual practices over time inevitably lose their divine purpose and empowerment and become barriers to grace and to God himself. Yet Jesus drew from Israel's daily, weekly, monthly, and annual spiritual practices, which had actually become a means of supplanting God, keeping others at bay, and truncating Israel's mission. He subverted these symbolically and prophetically by practicing them in powerful new ways and by teaching his disciples the same.

According to the Synoptic Gospels, Jesus's frequent retreats from the crowds constituted a departure from the customary religious practices of the day in terms of time and space. These retreats lasted an hour, part of a night, all night, and approximately fifty days in places including wilderness, a lonely place, a hillside, a mountain, a room, and a garden—most of which were not typical places for spiritual practice like the temple, synagogues, and homes. Also, Jesus apprenticed his disciples as an itinerant, rather than in schools at fixed locations as was typical of Jewish rabbis.

1. *Early Church*. What Jesus practiced primarily in solitude during his withdrawals from the crowds in Luke, the church practiced in Acts, but with a notable contrast: the church withdrew primarily for communal prayer. These withdrawals lasted one hour, for a period of hours, three days, and ten days. They occurred daily, weekly, late into the night, and at midnight. These happened in an upstairs room of a house where they stayed, in private homes, at the temple, in synagogues, at regular gathering places of congregations, in prisons, on ships, on a rooftop, and by the Jordan River. Jesus, as portrayed by Luke, prayed more frequently in lonely desert places and less in community than did the church in Acts.

2. *Second Millennium*. Geert Groote subverted the monastic disciplines of his day by revising them in new ways so they would be available to the masses in the common vernacular. Spirituality was no longer accessible only for those who made fixed monastic vows and joined a religious community in some remote rural area. Groote formed open communities in towns and urban areas, making spiritual practices available to the common people in their heart language based on voluntary resolutions. Ignatius of Loyola made the *Spiritual Exercises* both portable and adapt-

able; they could be done anytime anywhere, not restricted to monasteries nor to the church's calendar. This departure from prevailing patterns served the early Jesuits well in their educational and mission work, which took them throughout the world. Brainerd adapted his spiritual practices indigenously for Native Americans, though he also sought to make them more industrious and agrarian. All three leaders practiced spiritualities of the heart emanating in missions, which transformed followers and developed leaders to help expand their missions.

The spiritualities of Groote, Ignatius, and Brainerd connect with postmodern thirsts for spiritual direction and mentoring, for soul care and for small communities of belonging. The *Devotio Moderna* speaks to the growing desire for a hands-on everyday spirituality that is economically viable and strongly communal. Its patterns of monthly one-day silent retreats away from the pressure of daily life speaks to the stress of our culture. The Jesuits connect to postmodern fascination with the imagination, image, and the senses in its affective meditation upon Christ and the need for extended multi-day retreats, and in recovery from addictions. Brainerd also connects to spiritual thirsts for recovery, for story, and for solitude in natural settings.

Both Solitude and Community Are Essential—the Eremitic and Cenobitic Traditions

This conclusion is based on the following. Jesus commanded secret solitude—the crux of his critique of Jewish spirituality. Corporate spiritual practices without solitude can easily devolve into means of obtaining human approval and notice, which Jesus said precludes divine reward altogether (Matt 6:5-7). On the other hand, solitude without community devolves into a self-centered spirituality that fails to serve others with suffering love, which Jesus commanded his followers to show to one another (John 15:12). He modeled both serving in community and solitude. In each part of this study, both solitude and community were present to varying degrees.

1. *Solitude and Community in the Early Church.* Whereas in Luke's Gospel Jesus's early mission was sustained primarily by solitary prayer, in Acts the initial phase of the church's mission was sustained primarily by corporate prayer. But it was not long before solitary prayer became a crucial

means in the early church for emphatically removing the exclusion of Gentiles from the church's mission. Divine intervention came to Peter and Paul in their solitude to change the fledgling church's worldview and the course of her subsequent mission. Though communal spiritual practices predominate in the Apostolic Fathers, solitary spiritual practices were found throughout. The best known expression of the eremitic tradition involved the desert fathers and mothers, who were influenced by Jesus's forty day sojourn in the desert and his frequent sojourns to deserted places, by John the Baptist, and by Origen's mystical theology. In time, even the most secluded hermits found they needed the fellowship of peers. Origen also played a key role in the development of the cenobitic tradition through his influence via John Cassian on St. Benedict, a key figure in the development of Western monasticism. In this tradition daily solitude was embedded in the rhythms of set hours.

2. *Solitude and Community in the Second Millennium.* After their conversions, Groote, Ignatius, and Brainerd all experienced an eremitic period in which they practiced long periods of extended solitude, before they led fruitful ministries that attracted many followers, whose spiritual practices, in turn, were more communal. Groote's eremitic patterns became embodied in regular one- or two-day silent retreats every several weeks during the second stage of the *Devotio Moderna*'s history, which may well have contributed to its growth. Ignatius's eremitic patterns became embedded in the Jesuits' thirty-day retreats associated with the *Spiritual Exercises*—a standard feature of Jesuit life for more than five hundred years, which has surely contributed to its longevity. Finally, Brainerd's eremitic patterns were emulated by Protestant mission leaders during the nineteenth century.

There Are Normative Practices for Subversive Spirituality and Transforming Mission

The spiritual practices observed in all parts of this study—the theological, historical, cultural and field analyses—were: solitude/abiding; community/loving one another; and ministry/bearing witness. Thus, I call them kingdom constants. Scripture (meditation, reflection, and theological study), worship, prayer, and the Lord's Supper[3] also appeared in

---

3. Simon Chan (2006) argues that until the church discovers who she is corporately, she is unable to know what she is to do without lapsing into Pelagianism or individual-

all my selected scriptural and historical texts, and so I consider these constants also.[4] Through my theological and historical analyses, I also found the golden thread of fasting, prayer, and giving alms, in Jesus's teaching as well as in the teaching and experience of the apostolic fathers, Origen, and the three second millennium leaders. In both the golden thread and the three priorities of the kingdom, two practices are inward and one is outward. Thus, embedded in each of these triads is a built-in rhythm in which inward spirituality supports outward mission. When outward mission is accompanied by compassion, healing, and transformation, people are drawn, often in crowds, to the missionary. At this point, the mission's greatest danger lies in its potential to consume the missionary with busyness, exhaustion, and prayerlessness unless adequate inner rhythms are created, protected, and honored. Jesus and other leaders examined in this study felt the need for periodic escape from the crowds with their needs so they could move inward for solitary or communal prayer.

Certain constants in mission were also clearly seen in the theological and historical analyses. To a lesser extent they also appeared in the cultural and field analyses. These include:

1. *Proclaiming the Word–Performing Compassionate Deeds.* Starting with Jesus, those in this study proclaimed the good news of the kingdom of God (the gospel) and performed compassionate deeds of healing and justice. Proclamation appears more prominently than compassionate deeds in Acts, Geert Groote, Ignatius of Loyola, and Brainerd. Others,

---

ism, which has plagued the evangelical church in the West. Chan holds that in worship, the church discovers who she is. In the weekly rhythms of liturgical worship—shaped by the church's long history of theological reflection and prayer—Scripture, theology, prayer, the Eucharist, and mission are brought together in deeply mysterious ways, which spiritually form the people of God corporately and individually. In liturgical worship, inward and outward movements are merged. For the missiological dimension of liturgy and the Eucharist, see Chan (2006:82–84) and Wright (2007).

4. Had I included Quaker and other non-sacramental groups in my study, neither the Lord's Supper nor baptism, which I identify as constants, would have appeared. Quakers have engaged in some of the most profound mission work involving social justice in modern history. Most noteworthy are their contributions to the anti-slavery movement in seventeenth and eighteenth centuries in England and America. They exerted major influence upon John Newton, William Wilberforce, and the successful efforts of the Clapham Sect (see L. Paul Jensen 1998).

such as the apostolic fathers, gave greater prominence to deeds of mercy and compassion than to proclamation.

2. *Indigenous and Culture-affirming–Pilgrim and Culture-denying.* To varying degrees, the expressions of mission we have studied were both indigenous—culture affirming—as well as pilgrim—culture denying. Jesus's use of parables was an example of the indigenous principle, which was also seen in the Jesuits' mission in China, Groote's use of Middle Dutch rather than Latin, and Brainerd's efforts among the Native Americans. The pilgrim principle was seen in Jesus's critique of pagan prayer practices and by his acceptance of allegiance generally reserved for either Yahweh or Caesar. It was also seen in Groote's and Ignatius's work against injustice and critique of the practice of concubinage.

3. *Prophetic–Forgiving, Suffering Love.* Taking a prophetic stance by subverting the status quo invites opposition, which we are to endure with forgiving, suffering love. Jesus's prayer for the forgiveness of his executioners is echoed in the dying prayer of Stephen for those stoning him. Such suffering love for one's persecutors manifests authentic spirituality. For the early church, imitating Christ meant imitating his death. Polycarp, Ignatius of Antioch, and Origen expected to be martyred. Groote, Ignatius of Loyola, and Brainerd were also called upon to express suffering, forgiving love.

4. *Centrifugal–Centripetal.* Jesus's ministry was first centrifugal before it became centripetal, when healing and transformation occurred. This pattern was reversed on the Day of Pentecost but was observed again later in Acts as well as in the ministries of Groote, Ignatius, and Brainerd.

We Need Radical Flexibility to Keep Practices from Supplanting God

Matthew gives us among the most important means in all Scripture for keeping spiritual practices free of anything that would divert attention or allegiance from the center—Jesus himself. When Jesus commissioned the eleven, Matthew portrays the place, time, and agenda of the eleven's encounter of him as totally subject to his initiative and authority. Matthew lays out a radically flexible inner commission (Matt

28:16–18a), which precedes the Great Commission (Matt 28:18–20) and helps to keep practices fluid under Jesus's initiative, guidance, power, and control, so that contemplation and worship of him are realized. This prevents new forms and practices from devolving into a spirituality of our initiative, our guidance, and our power, which focuses on the disciplines themselves rather than on him—the rightful object of our contemplation and worship. It also keeps mission firmly rooted in spirituality. Sadly, my study found no scholars who bring out the inner commission; most start discussing the Great Commission at verse 18, not 16.

Groote and Ignatius of Loyola each wrote eloquent statements concerning the flexible nature of spiritual practices as means, not ends. "A man should let every external religious exercise go" unless they foster the fruit of the Spirit, wrote Groote (1988b:92). Stated conversely, Ignatius argued for more rigorous spiritual exercise only at the point when the "the spirit will grow cold . . . and lower passions grow warm" (*Const.* 1991d: [502]). This contrasts to the fixity of spiritual disciplines associated with monastic vows of their days. Ignatius developed this fluidity most explicitly in the organizational culture of the Society, as described in their *Constitutions*. As the Jesuits abandoned this flexibility and depended upon colonial power, they lost vitality and power. In our current cultural context, then, how much time is needed for spiritual practice, and in what spaces?

Key Findings Regarding the Collapse of Space and Time

In the cultural analysis, I discovered theorists lamenting different aspects of the collapse of space and time, their demands for resistance to its spatial temporal codes, communities utilizing various spiritualities to heal conditions associated with the collapse, and both hunger and cries for the practice of spiritual disciplines rooted in historic traditions. From these and the previous findings follow the second part of my thesis: we need more plentiful time and space for God in solitary and communal spiritual practice in our structures of church, mission, and leadership development.

Lament, Resistance, Healing, and Spirituality

1. *Lament.* Since 1950, devastating social decay has accompanied a new round of space-time compression. These include the disappearance of neighborhood places that serve as hubs for pleasurable association (third places), the loss of social capital, the rise of hurry sickness (workaholism) and other addictions, the loss of duration, and the corrosion of character. The loss of discretionary time (true for many but not all segments of the population) and the erosion of the sense of place have helped to loosen social bonds, weaken community, and increase stress and a sense of drivenness. The Internet has encouraged multi-tasking and produced a new temporal experience in which time is instantaneous, segmented, and reversible, further accelerating our pace of life, which becomes harmful without respite. In short, the collapse has addictive and isolating qualities. Its addictive quality functions like a computer virus, which freezes the operating systems of organizations and communities. In many Christian contexts, the Holy Spirit gets frozen out of organizational environments without periodic time and space devoted to waiting upon God. The collapse's isolating quality has been deeply felt by two abandoned generations, who have been left with a keen sense of loneliness, pain, PTSD symptoms, and too few spiritual mentors to guide them into adult community and identity. Theorists in various disciplines have been lamenting these developments.[5]

2. *Resistance, Subversion, and Healing.* My study found a chorus of cries for change. Especially prophetic has been the call for resistance communities to subvert both the spatial temporal codes and the influence of the elite power brokers of "the networked society" (Castells 1996) and "liquid modernity" (Bauman 2000). The environmental movement has called for a return to the land and a slower pace—glacial time. Mushrooming coffee shops like Starbucks now identify themselves as third places where people hang out for hours on end. Other efforts to

---

5. Solely negative responses have come from geographer David Harvey (1990, 2001), economist Juliet B. Schor (1992), and sociologists Bauman (2000), Oldenburg (1997), and Sennett (1998). Those whose responses are more mixed—lamenting while seeing some positives—include sociologists Giddens (1990), Castells (1996, 1997, 1998), and Wuthnow (1998), social psychologist Levine (1997), cardiac psycologists Ulmer and Schwartburd (1996), and public policy expert Robert Putnam (1999, 2002). Ulmer, Schwartzburd, and Levine showed that a fast pace of life is not always harmful if periodic respite is given from it.

resist these temporal spatial codes involve proven means of healing. The medical and therapeutic communities have developed treatment processes utilizing solitude, transparent community, and spirituality. The Twelve Steps use small groups, mutual confession, meditation, and total dependence on a higher power in the fight against addiction. Those with severe nicotine addiction had more than twice the rate of recovery one and two years after a single twenty-four-hour period of total solitude and silence using a method called REST. Hurry sickness has been found to be a risk factor for heart disease and survivors of cardiac episodes have been successfully treated for time pathologies using meditation and small groups that meet bi-monthly for at least a year. Not only was spirituality found in effective treatments for addictions and time pathologies, but also in treatments given by psychologists and training offered by secular ethicists to develop compassion, love, and character. Expressions of mission to better society were associated with some of these spiritualities.

3. *Hunger for Spirituality from a Historical Tradition*. The cultural analysis found hunger for historic spiritual practices among orthodox Christian believers in Generations X and Y. This hunger, often fed in liturgical worship, is partly rooted in a desire for personal connection with a history prior to their family's painful abandonment of them in their recent past. Previous generations are also expressing this hunger, as seen in Wuthnow's study of spirituality in North America (1998:171–98). He and others call for a sustained disciplined "spirituality of practice" rooted in historic traditions.

We Need Increased Space and Time with God until He Fills Us with Love

This conclusion is a variation or restatement of the second part of my thesis, which follows from the seven previous conclusions and the findings on which they were based. The argument is very simple. If A, B, C, and D have been shown in this study, then E must follow. So the flow of the argument for my final conclusion—the thesis's second part is as follows:

A. Solitary and communal rhythms of daily, weekly, annual or occasional (and sometimes monthly)[6] prayer, scriptural meditation, and other spiritual practices accompanied empowered mission in all periods of mission expansion examined in this study.[7]

B. The collapse of space and time has diminished unhurried time with God and people in organizational structures of church, mission, and leadership, just when virtue is low, mentoring is weak, and workaholism and addictions are prevalent among U.S. Christians. The cultural belief that time is money has infected our organizations, eroding the kingdom value that time is love.

C. Spiritual practices including extended solitude, meditation, and community have proven effective in healing addictions, broken relationships, and other harmful effects of the collapse.

D. The mission of the church in Western culture is impotent at a time when hunger for spirituality, relationships, and healing is rampant.

E. Because A, B, C, and D have been demonstrated in this study, then my thesis follows: we need more plentiful time and space for God in solitary and communal spiritual practices in our structures of church, mission, and leadership development if we are to have a passionate spirituality adequate for a mission that transforms and heals lives, relationships, structures, and cultures.

A Model for Christian Spirituality and Mission

Based on my findings and conclusions, I am now ready to propose a model for spirituality and mission, displayed in Figure 4 below. The model is comprised of three elements: (1) shapes—two intersecting circles, a bell-shaped curve, and a rectangle; (2) halves—upper and lower, left and right; and (3) practices—normative practices, practices in polarity, and optional practices.

---

6. Monthly spiritual practices were not observed in the calendar of the first and second century church—the period of the early church, which I studied. However, the *Devotio Moderna* observed silent retreats before seventeen annual feast days commemorating various saints, which occurred every several weeks or so.

7. The field study did not measure weekly and annual/occasional retreat practices.

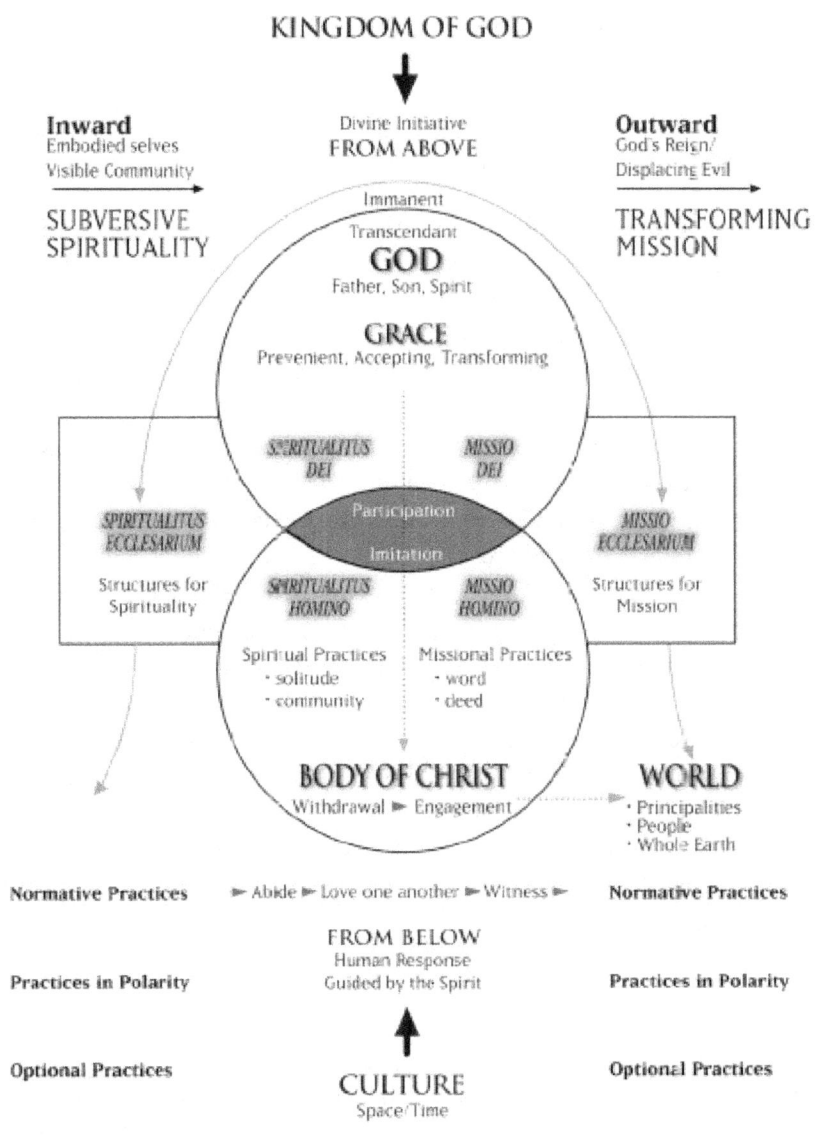

Figure 4: A Model for Christian Spirituality and Mission

1. *Shapes*. There are two are circles: the upper represents the transcendent triune God of grace and the lower represents the body of Christ. The intersection between the two portrays believers' participation in God's life and imitation of him.[8] The bell-shaped curve represents God's immanence—his presence in his creation and his world. The rectangle signifies organizational structures developed to foster spirituality (on the left) and mission (on the right).

2. *Halves*. The upper half represents the kingdom of God—divine initiative from above.[9] The lower half symbolizes human response guided by the Spirit in the cultural context of space and time. In the upper half, inside the upper circle, are *spiritualitus Dei* and *missio Dei*. *Spiritualitus Dei* is a Latin term for the spirituality of God—his communion with repentant human beings who have participated in the death, burial, and resurrection of Jesus. *Missio Dei* is the mission of God, who is seeking relationship with all who have been separated from him by sin and who is working for justice and new creation in his world to reverse the death, decay, and slavery of evil's reign.

In the lower half, within the lower circle, are the human practices of spirituality and mission—*spiritualitus homino* and *missio homino*. Also, in the lower half within the rectangle are the church's organizational structures of spirituality and mission—*spiritualitus ecclesarium* and *missio ecclesarium*. The idea for terms using *spiritualitus* was sparked by the parallel terms used in the field of missiology that differentiate between mission from below and mission from above. This is something the field of spirituality has not yet developed in its own nomenclature, a move that could help keep Christian spirituality from lapsing into Pelagianism.

---

8. Wright talks about this intersection as the overlapping and interlocking of heaven and earth, which are only separated by a thin veil (2006:58–66). God is not a deist God—distant from the world and uninvolved in it (typical of post-Enlightenment Christianity in its liberal and conservative forms), nor is God identical with creation as in pantheism (typical of Eastern mysticism, which has no critique of evil). No, God is apart from but active in the world—especially via Scripture, worship, prayer, sacrament, and mission.

9. I have defined the kingdom of God as God coming to his people doing for them what they cannot do for themselves in order that he might establish his loving and holy rule in all creation (L. Paul Jensen 1999:29–32).

Conclusion 273

The left half of the model represents inward spirituality and the right half represents mission. God's reign usually begins with the inward and moves outward, and so the horizontal arrows on the page point from left to right.

3. *Practices.* First, normative practices for both spirituality (on the left) and mission (on the right) are shown in the bottom half just below the lower circle (see top of Table 36 below). At the bottom of the figure are normative practices. Jesus's rhythms of spirituality and mission, which drew from and reformulated first century Jewish practices, strongly influenced subsequent church and mission leaders selected for this study. A path of influence was drawn from Jesus through Acts and the apostolic fathers to Origen regarding Jesus's teaching on fasting, prayer, and almsgiving, which became normative (Matt 6:5–7). Origen also taught the practices of communion (solitude), community, and ministry, which Jesus modeled (Luke 6) and taught (John 15). These three disciplines subsume all other practices. Also normative were the scriptural practices of theological study, meditation, prayer, worship, and the Lord's Supper, as well as the missional practices of proclaiming God's reign accomplished in the cross and resurrection of Jesus, healing, compassionate justice, and baptism.

Table 36: Classifications of Three Kinds of Practices in a Model for Spirituality and Mission[10]

Spiritual Practices	*Missional Practices*
Normative Practices: Abide, love one another, bear witness	
Scripture/Theology	Proclamation
Worship	Cross/Resurrection
Prayer/Contemplation	Compassion/Healing
Fasting	Justice/Almsgiving
Sacrament: Lord's Supper	Sacrament: Baptism

10. See the graphics of the model of spirituality and mission in Figure 4 above and Figure 5 below.

Practices in Polarity	Practices in Polarity[11]
Continuum of: • Solitary–Communal • Eremitic–Cenobitic • Listening–Speaking • Consolation–Desolation • Spontaneous–Liturgical • Culture affirming–Culture denying	Continuum of: • Kerygmatic Word–Compassionate Deeds • Prophetic–Forgiving, Suffering Love • Centrifugal–Centripetal • Indigenous–Pilgrim • Culture-affirming–Culture-denying
Optional Practices	*Optional Practices*
Many examples, such as: • Journaling • Pilgrimage • Spiritual direction	Many examples, such as: • Mass evangelism • Environmental action • Literacy work

Second are practices in polarity (see middle of Table 36 above). Innovation in spiritual and mission practices occurred as Christianity spread from Palestine into new cultures, which shaped these innovations, such as Origen's use of neoplatonic ideas in contemplation and evangelism. So, spiritualities and missions were indigenous and culture-affirming. Yet they were also prophetic and culture-denying, expressing the pilgrim principle. These are practices in polarity. Opposites were both present, but in each case one pole was more in focus than the other as conditions in church and culture changed. Great fluidity between poles occurred. Polarities for subversive spirituality (middle left of Table 36 above) include: solitary–communal;[12] eremitic–cenobitic;

---

11. Practices in polarity are discussed in this section explaining the model of spirituality and mission I proposed in Figure 4. Practices in polarity are pairs of practices that are on opposite ends of a continuum or spectrum. When one is in solitude with God, he or she is not in community with others. These are two opposite spiritual practices in polarity. When one speaks and acts prophetically against evil and injustice she or he invites hostility or persecution from the powers in charge at which point the response that Jesus calls for is patience, meekness, and suffering love that does not revile in return and often remains silent in the face of accusation. Suffering love and the prophetic stance against evil are two mission practices in polarity.

12. Though solitude and community are polarities that are both needed, I accept

listening–speaking;[13] consolation–desolation; culture-affirming–culture-denying; and spontaneous–liturgical.[14] Polarities for transforming mission (middle right of Table 36) include: kerygmatic word–deed; suffering love–prophetic; centrifugal–centripetal; indigenous–pilgrim; and culture-affirming–culture-denying.

Third are optional practices, which are taken up or discarded as needed (see bottom of Table 36). A plethora of optional practices includes journaling, pilgrimage, and inner-healing prayer. But even normative practices exhibit great variety in how they are expressed. Scripture reading and meditation, for example, have had a great many forms. *Lectio divina*, which has a fifteen-hundred-year history, has gone through a variety of adaptations, having first a twofold and later a fourfold sequence. So whether practices are normative, optional, or function in opposite polarities, flexibility and fluidity remain at the fore. In light of the above, the prime question before us, then, is how much time, what spaces, and to which practices is the Spirit calling us in order to fill us with a passionate love that would fulfill the great commandment in our current situation? The short answer is whatever it takes. I will make specific recommendations in the next section.

The effects of the collapse of space and time are depicted in Figure 5 below. Notice that God, his grace, and his initiative fade into the background. What is left is a focus on our practices and structures of spirituality and mission. God is greatly diminished as are our worship and contemplation of him. We need enough time to get refocused on him and what the Spirit is doing within our hearts personally and corporately to

---

Henri Nouwen's and C. Miller's argument for a priority or sequence of solitude before community as modeled and taught by Jesus. Nouwen says, "If we do not know we are the beloved sons and daughters of God, we're going to expect someone in the community to make us feel special and worthy. Ultimately, they cannot. If we start with trying to create community, we'll expect someone to give us the perfect, unconditional love. But true community is not loneliness grabbing onto loneliness.... Many relationships begin out of a fear of being alone, but they can't ultimately satisfy a need that only solitude with God can fulfill. *Community is solitude greeting solitude.* 'I am the beloved; you are the beloved; together we can build a home or place of welcome together'" (Nouwen et al. 2006:114). Chan uses the term "*a community of solitaries*" to express the same idea (1998:119–120).

13. Prayer is a conversation involving both listening and speaking to God.

14. Both spontaneous prayer and set prayer can be either a living response to grace or a dead ritual. For liturgy as a gift and means of grace, see Wright (2006:166–67), Chan (2006:87), and Foster (1992:110).

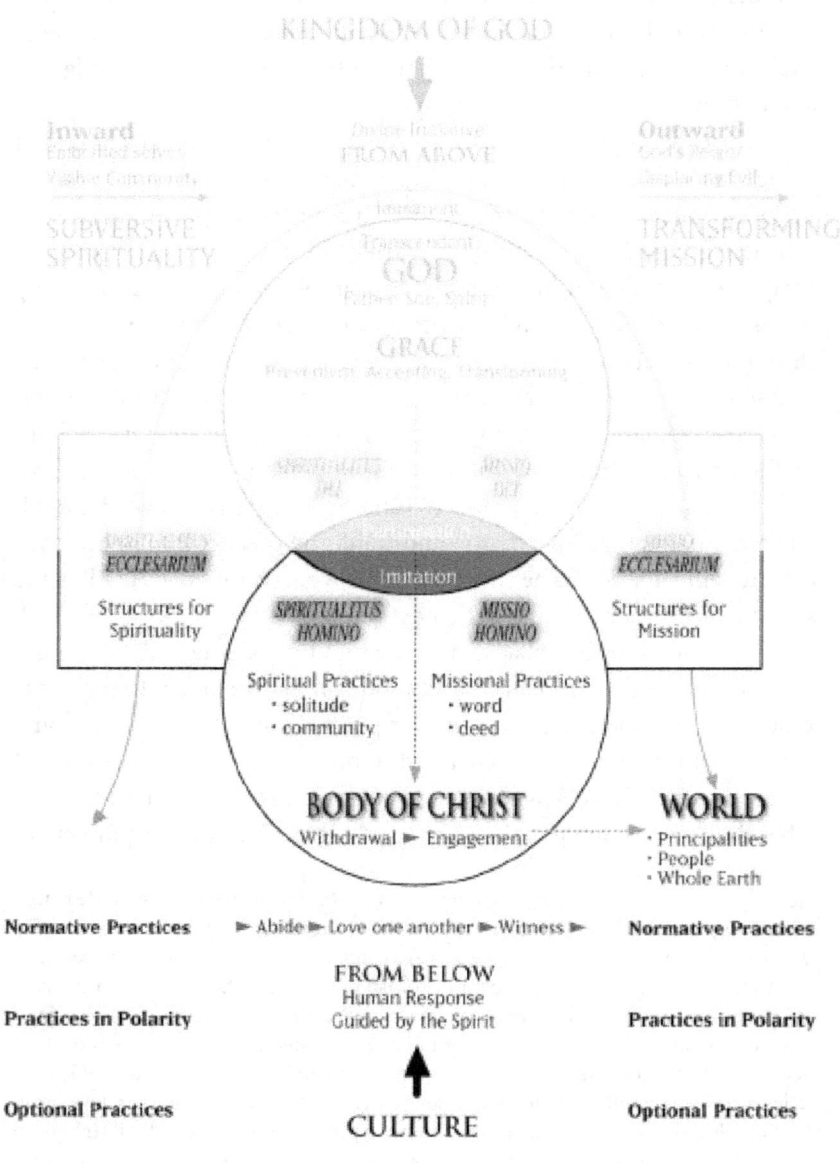

Figure 5: Effects of the Collapse of Space and Time

fill us with love for himself, one another, ourselves and the world he loves: its people, its structures, and its environment. To do so, we will need his power to resist the temporal-spatial codes so deeply embedded in our environments and to follow his leading in creating unhurried time and open space for as long and as often as necessary. We will become culture-denying in the most fundamental and challenging ways.

Recommendations

In this section I will make recommendations based on this study in four areas: (1) making spirituality the ethos of mission and ministry structures, (2) mission practices in contemporary culture, (3) further study and research, and (4) studying and teaching spirituality in the academy.

Making Spirituality the Ethos of Our Mission and Ministry Structures

If, by the Spirit's direction and power, we are to create more time and space for God so that passionate Christian spirituality might saturate the ethos of our ministry structures and cultures, what specific recommendations do I have as to how this might occur?

Discernment Retreats

Leaders who feel this need—personally, organizationally, and culturally—might consider a moratorium on ministry as usual. This would involve withdrawing from as much normal activity as possible for a period of discernment in which a series of retreats would be taken in order to become more deeply aware of God's heart for and movement in our lives, our families, our ministries, and our culture. My suggestion for college ministry leaders at the end of chapter 6 could serve as one way to implement this recommendation.[15]

---

15. Larry Winger, vice president of Provision Ministries, was instrumental in developing a Sabbath week in which half of the hundred or so employees were given a paid week off to seek rest and greater intimacy with God, and the next week the other half were given the same. The first day of each week the employees were required to spend the day in a directed silent one-day retreat led by The Leadership Institute staff.

Rhythms of Life

Leaders, preferably in their leadership teams,[16] should, as part of such a discernment process, discern and establish rhythms of life both personally and organizationally. Discernment of daily, weekly, monthly, annual/occasional spiritual and missional practices, and how these will be embodied personally and organizationally, should be addressed. These will vary greatly according to (1) an individual's personality and calling, as well as current stages and roles in life, including vocation; and (2) an organization's or movement's life cycle (Table 27; Clinton 1992:4.32–53), its size, and the unstated beliefs and assumptions that have been embedded by its leaders previously.[17] How much time? What space? My research suggests a minimum for daily, weekly, monthly, and annual/occasional rhythms.

1. *Daily*. I recommend that twenty to thirty minutes per day alone with God be the starting place,[18] which would ideally be divided between morning and evening times for solitary prayer, worship, Scripture reading, meditation, *examen*, and other disciplines. Many are being led to pray at set hours, often as communities. All leadership gatherings should begin their times together with a period of listening to God and Scripture, out of which space be given for responses of prayer to God (in silence or out loud), for ourselves, for one another, and for people being served in the church and in the culture. Such prayer should occur before moving to structural and functional issues. The presence or absence of this pattern will embed either the assumption that God is present and active in our organizational cultures or the assumption that he is not.

2. *Weekly*. Establish weekly corporate worship. Consider a weekly Sabbath[19] and weekly time with people among whom the community is called to incarnate themselves in mission.

16. This is particularly problematic if the entire team is not on the same page regarding their own need for deeper formation and the need to transform their organizational culture so spirituality is the center.

17. See Edgar H. Schein (2004:211–53).

18. Thirty minutes was the minimum suggested by my field research sample. "A commonly agreed upon length is every day for at least twenty minutes," writes Susan Muto of spiritual reading (2000:156).

19. InterVarsity Christian Fellowship in Southern California has developed in the past decade a staff culture with an embedded rhythm of weekly Sabbath, which has

3. *Monthly.* Consider individual or corporate days away in silent retreat.

4. *Annual and Occasional.* Consider an annual individual or corporate multi-day retreat away (not a conference) for prayer, silence, meditation, self-examination, and hearing God's renewed call in ministry and mission.

Establishing a rhythm of life takes time for it to become spiritually and missionally transforming. It will evolve and needs to be periodically renewed. If its practice is not becoming transformational at the heart level over time, ask God what more or what less is needed (see Tables 2 and 3 in chapter 1 for practices/disciplines). Leaders often need a mentor or spiritual director in such a process.[20]

The Lord's Supper and Affective Contemplation of the Cross

Make the Lord's Supper central in the life of the body of Christ, for both scriptural and historic reasons. The pain of Generations X and Y resonates deeply with the passion of our Lord, as do the tactile elements of bread and wine.

Spiritual Mentors for the Next Generations

Nothing is more urgent than to seek the Lord, petitioning him to raise up mature spiritual mentors (Luke 10:2) from among parents, grandparents, retirees, and other adults who can become "spiritual formators" (Doherty 2003) for the next generations. This will require spiritual transformation on the part of these mentors and their costly personal commitment for as long as it takes to see passionate Christian spirituality develop in the lives of children, youth, and young adults until there is overflow into God's mission. From these generations may come a future

---

been created and protected. See Eugene Peterson on the weekly rhythms built into creation week and Sabbath's role in those rhythms (2005:65–74).

20. Organizations providing this kind help include: Leadership Transformations in Boston, online: http://www.leadershiptransformations.org; Transforming Center in Wheaton, IL, online: http://www.thetransformingcenter.org; be-ing in San Diego, online: http://www.be-ing.com; *ImagoChristi* in Denver, online: http://www.imagochristi.org; and my organization, The Leadership Institute in Orange, CA, online: http://www.tli.cc/.

Origen, Geert Groote, Salome Sticken, Ignatius, Brainerd, Ann Judson, or Mary Lyon, not to speak of the countless whose faithful following of Jesus will never be widely known.

Spiritual Reading, Biblical Story, Meditation, and Theological Reflection

Spiritual reading of scriptural texts narrating Jesus's withdrawals for communion with his Father and his subsequent mission practices, as well as those of the apostles in Acts, should be encouraged in the process of developing a rhythm of life.[21] This will keep our spiritual practices continually shaped by Scripture. Amazingly, no list of spiritual practices of which I am aware includes Jesus's command in Luke 10:2 to pray that the Lord of the harvest send forth laborers. Reading classics that integrate the inward and the outward should also be encouraged. Finally, immerse the next generations in biblical story, Scripture memorization (probably with images and icons), and theological reflection.

Mission Practices to Engage Contemporary Culture

Here I recommend mission practices that extend Jesus's new creation. I note whether they express Walls's indigenous or pilgrim principles (1996:53–54) and which of Bosch's six necessary elements for Western missiology they embody—ecological, counter-cultural, ecumenical, contextualized, lay-focused, and centered in a worshiping community (1995:55–61). I recommend collaborative mission initiatives in four urgent areas, starting with mission in deed and then word.

Justice and Compassion for the Marginalized

The church can and should create partnerships with organizations and communities that serve the marginalized living in areas of urban decay—the poor, oppressed, and children at risk. Millennial children raised in poor inner city neighborhoods have plenty of time, unlike the Millennials from the suburbs (Jehele 2007b). The church in suburbia can commit financial and material support, as well as short-term missions to those serving Christ among the poorest of the poor in urban America. This would express the heart of Jesus and challenge the

---

21. See withdrawals of Jesus in Table 14 and of the apostles in Tables 21 and 22.

captivity of opulent Christians to the gods of materialism, greed, and careerism. It would also provide a slower pace for time-compressed Millennials from suburbia who are eager for social action. The leaders of the new monasticism who practice healthy spiritual rhythms of life might thus be an important means of deeper formation for the wider church, whose resources could, in turn, help extend Christ's compassion among the disenfranchised. Such efforts would express Walls's pilgrim principle and provide a worship-centered, ecumenical, lay-focused, counter-cultural response to this great need in our culture, which could help renew the church and form her more fully in the image of Christ. Thus these efforts would embody four of the six elements in Bosch's missiology for Western culture (1995:55–61).

Contemplative Evangelism

Richard Peace has coined the term "contemplative evangelism," by which he means evangelism that "springs from an encounter with God" and careful listening to him (2004:12). Listening to God helps one engage in a two-way conversation rather than just a monologue with God.[22] This is what I term spirituality as a means of mission. But "spirituality is the mission" as well (Dybdahl 1997), in that the spiritual disciplines or practices themselves have drawing power and can be practiced even before belief in Jesus as Lord—a notion Peace includes in his term "contemplative evangelism." This can also be understood as pre-evangelism—a step towards encountering Jesus as Lord and Savior that is an underused form of mission. I recommend that a number of Christian organizations collaborate together in a contemplative evangelism pilot project to see what can be learned about using prayer labyrinths and other spiritual practices as a form of mission, especially on college campuses that are building meditative spaces for time-compressed Millennials. Such an initiative would be indigenous in that it draws upon widespread spiritual hunger; but it would also express the pilgrim principle by resisting our culture's compressed spatial-temporal codes. It would express four of Bosch's essential elements for Western missiology; being contextual-

---

22. Listening to God prepares one to truly listen to one who is not yet a follower of Jesus, not just conduct a monologue. Peace's latest book *Holy Conversations* (2006b) is aimed at helping small groups of believers actually enter into two-way conversation about the gospel with unbelievers over a twelve-week span.

ized, counter-cultural, ecumenical, and open to contemplative worship (1995:55-61).

Ecological Engagement

The relational view of space and the doctrine of the Incarnation, as articulated by Torrance (1969) and Lilburne (1989), have provided a theological foundation for ecological concern. In entering space via the Incarnation, Jesus sacralized it. As believers gather in particular places and spaces, they also sacralize them by turning them into places of intimacy with the one who created them, furnishing a basis for resisting the forces that threaten the environment. This is a major opportunity in view of secular theorists pleading for the church to engage environmentally. Castells and Putnam think that religious groups and especially churches, with their built-in social networks, are best positioned to increase social capital (Putnam 1999) and provide needed resistance (Castells 1997:67) through environmental action. If such efforts were cooperative and interdenominational in nature, and had embedded within them space and time for God through the disciplines of meditation on God and his creation, postmodern people would respond. Generations X and Y have already expressed considerable ecological concern, presenting an important missiological bridge to our culture. Such ecological efforts would express the indigenous principle among large numbers in our society who are concerned about what we are doing to our world, and would express three elements of Bosch's missiology for the West; being ecological, ecumenical, and contextualized (Bosch 1995:55-58).

Recovery: the Twelve Steps

The counter-cultural, lay-led recovery movement presents the church with immense opportunities for mission and renewal. Addicts who are not following Jesus are joining Christ-centered Twelve Step programs, where they practice mutual confession (Jas 5:15), intimate community (Gal 6:1, 2), and other spiritual disciplines—with many coming to Jesus. Another approach some Christian addicts have adopted is to join non-Christian recovery groups where they gradually introduce pre-Christians to Jesus Christ as the highest power; the one true God and Savior. Ignatian affective meditation on the life and death of Jesus provides similar spiritual and emotional dynamics for recovery. Also, based on Seudfeld's studies, extended solitude and silence appears to be an underutilized resource that Christians could introduce to Twelve Step programs and groups in order to improve rates of recovery. These efforts would express both the indigenous and pilgrim principles. Furthermore, mission initiatives in recovery are both counter-cultural and contextualized, as well as ecumenical and focused on the laity, as Bosch's missiology strongly advocates (1995:56–59).

Further Study and Research

This study has highlighted the need for further research and study in the following areas:

1. *Paul.* Study Paul's teachings and practices of spirituality and mission compared with those of Jesus. Heated debate has occurred as to Paul's spirituality and his mission and how and to what extent these related to Jesus. Much research could be fruitfully done here.

2. *Biblical Survey of Spiritual Practices.* Create a biblical catalogue of various spiritual disciplines and exercises in their historical, cultural, and theological context. Descriptions of each practice and how they functioned in the story of God's people could be included.

3. *Origen.* Explore further the relationship between Origen's mission and his spirituality in what he taught and practiced. An entire dissertation could and should be done on Origen, as he is a pivotal figure in the histories of both spirituality and mission. Compare findings on Origen's spirituality and his mission to those of Jesus and the apostles.

4. *The Influence of Ludolf of Saxony.* Ludolf's *Life of Christ*, a massive and influential work, might be fruitfully plumbed for his methods of affective meditation, which so influenced late medieval renewal movements, including the *Devotio Moderna* and especially Ignatius of Loyola a century and a half later. Study how Ludolf understood the spiritual and missional practices of Jesus.

5. *Influence of the* Devotio Moderna *on Protestantism.* Study how this movement influenced the spirituality and mission of Puritanism, John Newton, William Wilberforce, and others.

6. *Comparison of Edwards's and Brainerd's writings to those of Ignatius of Loyola.* Explore Edwards's and Ignatius's similarities on sanctification in light of their differing views on justification.

7. *Puritanism.* Examine how Puritan families functioned as the center of spiritual formation and mission. To what extent did they accomplish what late medieval monasticism did?

8. *Field Research.* Update our research with ministries of current *Journey* participants. Compare our current findings with our research of a decade ago and with recent and current research on the faith development of Millennials. Also, compare our findings with current research being funded by the Lilly Foundation on how college affects the religious life of youth as they pass through their college years.

Studying and Teaching Spirituality in the Academy

During the course of my PhD program, I developed an integrated model for studying and teaching spirituality in the academy, which I have endeavored to implement as I progressed throughout my program (see Figure 6 below). The seed thought for this model came from Sandra Schneiders, whose three approaches to studying spirituality are theological, historical, and anthropological (1995:213–15). The model communicates two sides of my PhD program, which I tried to keep in balance: the cognitive and formative.

Six elements comprise the model:

1. *Upper Circle—Spiritual Theology.* This is the same as Schneiders's theological approach and is positioned just under the arrow at top in Figure 6. This suggests a controlling role for grace, God's self-disclosure in Jesus, the coming of the kingdom, and a normative role for Scripture and theology. Spiritual theology can be done with a systematic approach (Chan 1998), a dogmatic, biblical studies or biblical theology approach (Doherty 2003), or some hybrid of these (Allen 1997).

2. *Lower Circle—Spiritual Anthropology.* This is the same as Schneider's anthropological approach, positioned above the arrow at the bottom of Figure 6. Anthropology, psychology, sociology, and intercultural studies are a few of the many academic disciplines in this circle. The circles in-

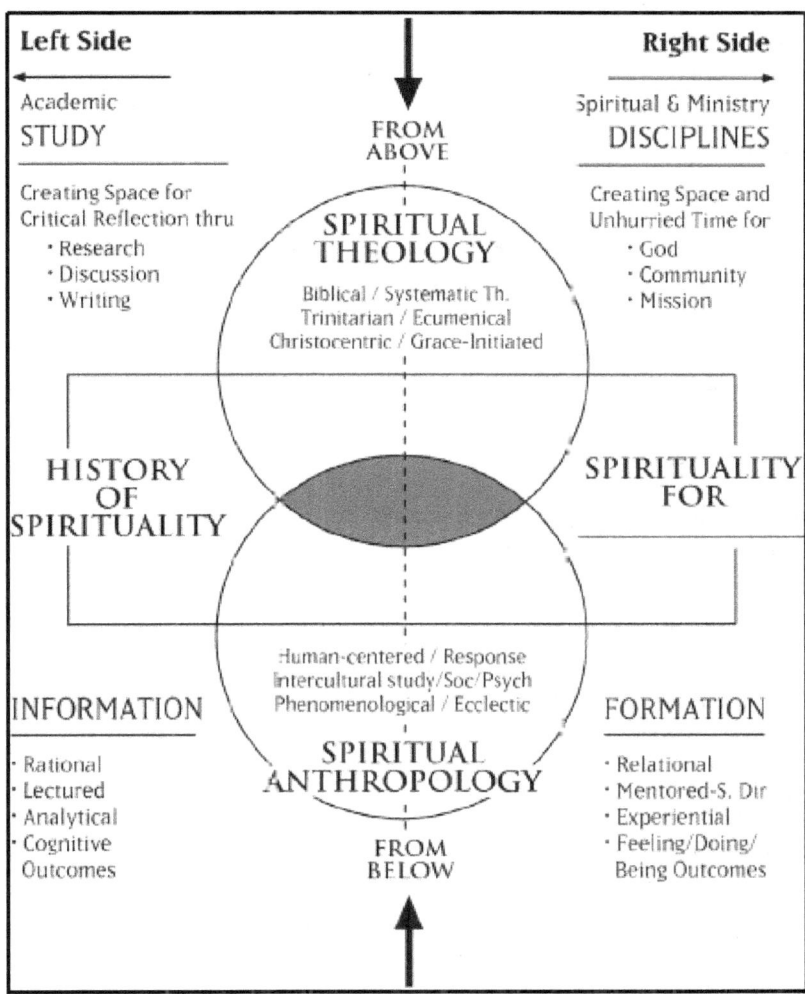

Figure 6: Jensen's Integrative Model for Studying Spirituality in the Academy

tersect in the shape of a football, which represents a holistic approach to the study of spirituality that comes both from above and from below.

3. *Left Side of Rectangle—History of Spirituality*. This is the same as Schneiders's historical approach and is positioned to intersect both the upper and lower circles. This suggests that historical studies in spirituality should be integrated with both circles, as this PhD program has tried to do.

4. *Right Side of Rectangle—Spirituality of* ____. This represents the spirituality of the student and the field she or he may wish to integrate with the field of spirituality—in my case missiology.

5. *Left Side*. This represents traditional academic study—creating space for critical reflections through reading, research, discussion, and writing. The focus is on information, which is rational, lectured, analytical, and involves cognitive outcomes.

6. *Right Side*. This represents spiritual and ministry disciplines—creating space and unhurried time for God, community, and mission. The focus is on formation, which is relational, mentored, experiential, and involves feeling, doing, and being outcomes.

I have implemented this model in the course design of a ten-week course I teach at Fuller Theological Seminary, entitled "Spiritual Formation in College and Young Adult Settings." I devote a third of the total course time—40 of the 120 hours—to spiritual formation. This is what I call the one-third rule. The forty hours are divided between solitary spiritual practices and some communal practices. Three one-day silent retreats are required in which students practice a total of eighteen hours of extended personal communion with God.[23] Four weeks of spiritual journals are required, reflecting sixteen hours of daily time alone with God and in Scripture. Also required is a contemplative exercise of intercession in which students listen to the Lord for what he is doing in a group in which they have leadership responsibility. I want students to experience leadership and ministry flowing out of prayer and discernment. They also engage in a ministry of compas-

---

23. For suggestions I give students for these silent retreats lasting six hours each, see Appendix J. I have found that if two retreats are done together as a class, the students will have enough experience to do the third retreat meaningfully on their own.

sion or justice with unbelievers. The formational parts of the class are given a credit or no credit grade based on whether they did the assigned practices. The remainder of the course is devoted to the cognitive and critical thinking aspects of the class. These assignments are graded on the typical A–F scale.

Over a thousand students have taken this course since I began teaching it in 1990. The transformation has been deep and profound among hundreds of the students and in many of their ministries. I believe this has been in part because space and time was created and protected for God alone and he has filled it with himself. He has chosen to honor the covenant I made with him: as long as he allowed me to teach, I would do everything I could to keep the many good things about academic learning—great content, stimulating reading, excellent theory—from impinging on the space reserved for him alone.

I long for at least one of the more than 120 graduate schools of theology in North America to require students in each of their programs to spend at least three hundred hours of solitary time alone with God—not to speak of the time needed in communal spiritual practices—in order to be awarded a masters-level degree. I know of no such school. Yet, in many of these same schools, students seeking graduate degrees in the field of marriage and family therapy are required to provide up to three thousand hours of supervised therapy to clients in order to receive a state license to practice professionally. This remarkable discrepancy illustrates the secularization of the pastoral formation process in the academy. Rigorous critical thinking and theological reflection is not antithetical to prayer and spiritual formation. The two need each other. At Fuller, students are now required to take two spirituality courses, which is about all we can rightfully expect. So how might we get to the three-hundred-hour target?

Based on this model, I have a proposal for seminaries and graduate schools of theology. In order to graduate, all masters-level students would eventually be required to complete three hundred hours of solitude. These hours with the Lord would be divided between daily solitude and monthly one-day silent retreats, with one or two overnight retreats also required before they complete their programs. These hours would be integrated into required MA or MDiv courses taught by professors who want to make their course work more formational. To accomplish this, they would develop spiritual practices and exercises germane to the course content. For example, students taking the required course in medieval and Reformation history would have the option of using it to fulfill their formational requirements for the quarter. If they elected to do so, they would draw from whatever practices were worked out to do their daily and extended monthly exercises. For example, they might imitate Luther's or Calvin's practices, or those of the *Devotio Moderna*. This would add up to thirty-three hours of formational work. Students would write reflections on these exercises and relate it to the cognitive dimension of the course. A student would be encouraged to use one course per quarter in this way, but not more than one. Thus, the formational load would be spread out evenly over nine courses, ideally spanning three years. This would result in a total of three hundred hours of required solitude.

Obviously, in any required course in which the professor allowed students this option, those using the course for formational credit would be doing a third less cognitive work than the others. I suggest some kind of arrangement by which students who miss part of the reading have the content summarized for them by other students who have covered it. This is called jigsaw reading. Likewise, those who have missed out on the formational side can learn vicariously from those who did the formational exercises. I suggest a trial period during which a few interested professors at a time could experiment with this model in their courses to see if it can be done without lowering the cognitive outcomes among students who elect to use the course for their formational requirements.

A Concluding Metaphor: Sailing

I began the preface with the metaphor of an automobile with trouble under the hood. In the cultural analysis, I have looked under the hood and examined an immense problem in the Western church: the disconnect between the transmission (mission) and the engine (spirituality). However, the picture of an automobile is not what is needed for the current situation, so I will conclude here using a different metaphor.

Zaugmett Bauman describes the postmodern period as being fluid. In fact, he holds that this era is not postmodern at all, but rather a new phase of modernity: what he calls "liquid modernity," in contrast to "solid modernity," which characterized the modern age up to the mid-twentieth century. In this liquid phase of modernity, the stability of the family has dissolved (2000:91–129) character has been corroded (Sennett 1998:31), and virtue has given way to image (Covey 1989:18–21). The large factories and solid organizations of the industrial age, built on institutional loyalty and lifetime careers, are being replaced by lighter organizations and the unencumbered networks of the information age. The instantaneous time, timeless time, and reversible time in the Internet's space of information flows (Castells 1997:126; Beaudoin 1998:127–29) have further changed our relationship to space and time during the last fifty years. We have become a non-reflective culture with information overload and with scarcely time to think, in what Charles Jencks calls "space-time implosion" (1996:56).

Everything from the solid phase of modernity has changed, much like ground liquefying under our feet in an earthquake. We might cry out like the psalmist, "Save me, O God, for the waters have come up to my neck. I sink in deep mire, where there is no foothold; I have come into deep waters, and the flood sweeps over me" (Ps 69:1-2). Liquid modernity implies that since the ground beneath our feet has given way, we are now swimming to a point of exhaustion, and as most theorists agree, many are drowning. This is true of Christians and pre-Christians alike. The image suggests countless biblical allusions to the dangers of water such as the flood (Gen 7:1—8:19), threatening waters and rivers (Isa 43:2), and the storm that overtook the disciples and Jesus (Mark 4:35–5:1). What we need in this context is a ship in which we can rest and a voyage that will move us intentionally toward our destinations. The human heart cries out for this kind of purpose and direction in spite of postmodern protestations that no such things exist.

I would like to suggest that the ship we envision for our voyage through postmodern waters be a sailing vessel. Sailors have navigated the world's oceans, seas and lakes for millennia and the accumulated wisdom of the vocation has been passed down from one generation of sailors to the next—symbolizing Wuthnow's spirituality of practice (1998:14–18). Sailors live aboard ships, not on land, though they do make stops at ports of call, and they do have connection with the land—representing Wuthnow's spirituality of dwelling typical of America before 1950 (1998:3–4). They may also choose to go overboard for a dip in the surrounding waters—symbolizing Wuthnow's spirituality of seeking, which arose after 1950 (1998:3–4). But they are neither landlocked nor trapped in the waters because they have a place on board to rest, eat, sleep, play, and practice their vocation. As they learn the disciplines of sailing, they cannot and do not supply the vessel's power. That is the role of the wind. The disciplines practiced do not cause the wind nor determine its direction. Utilizing the practices of their vocation, sailors can only place the sails of their vessel in a position to catch the wind when it comes so that it may receive as much of the wind's power as possible.[24]

In our time, the church has only begun to recover its vocation of sailing so that it can navigate the realities of liquid modernity. Deep and profound changes lie ahead if it is to become seaworthy in these waters. This will continue to require building sailing vessels, training communities of sailors to recover lost practices that have fallen into disuse because of the collapse of space and time, and a willingness not to usurp the role of the Holy Spirit and grace in the inbreaking of God's reign. The church needs to apprentice the future generations in these disciplines, realizing that the disciplines will never cause grace or produce God's reign. They will simply create open space for God to be active, and for us to notice where God is active and to have our sails up so that when the winds of the Spirit move, they will move us towards God's destination.

---

24. I first saw sailing used as a powerful metaphor in ministry during the mid 1990s. It became a controlling image in the work of Clarence Schilt and Ken Curtis and their church leaders at the Calimesa Adventist Church as they began to apply the spiritual disciplines of abiding, community, and bearing witness (C. R. Miller 2007:77–95) learned through The Leadership Institute's *Journey to Reach the Next Generations*. More recently, sailing has been used to illustrate the relationship between grace (the power and action of the wind) and the disciplines (the practices of the sailing vocation) by Marjorie Thompson (2001). Understanding grace as "God's enabling power" was first made clear to me through Wayne Anderson's message on grace in the early 1990s (see Anderson (2006). In this connection, Alister McGrath cautions that spiritual disciplines can never be conceived as the cause of grace (1999:45–46). He follows the late medieval preacher Johann Geiler in the use of sailing as an analogy to illustrate the relationship between grace and discipline. McGrath writes, "He [the sailor] can do nothing to cause the wind to blow; that lies outside his control." He continues, "However, he can do certain things which allow him to take advantage of the wind when it does blow—such as unfurl the sail, or turn the sail directly into the wind. In the same way, Geiler argues, believers cannot cause God's grace; they can nevertheless dispose themselves in such a way as to make the most of it, in terms of spiritual growth and personal development" (1999:46).

Appendix A

Some Contemporary Definitions of Spirituality

Simon Chan	A. Spirituality is "the human subjective response to whatever is regarded as the 'real'" (1998:15).
	B. "Christian spirituality is to be understood in terms of personal (but not individualistic or private, since the Christian life is always defined by a person's concrete existence within a community) relationship with God" (1998:15).
John Macquarrie	"The word 'spirituality' is used in a broad way, and includes prayer, worship and whatever other practices are associated with the development of the spiritual life.... I believe that fundamentally spirituality has to do with *becoming a person in the fullest sense* ..." (2000:63).
Walter Principe	A. "Spirituality, in this author's opinion, points to those aspects of a person's living a faith or commitment that concern his or her striving to attain the highest ideal or goal" (1983:139).
	B. "For a Christian this would mean his or her striving for an ever more intense union with the Father through Jesus Christ by living in the Spirit" (1983:139).
Sandra Schneiders	Spirituality refers to "(1) a fundamental dimension of the human being, (2) the lived experience which actualizes that dimension, and (3) the academic discipline which studies that experience" (2000:250).
Philip Sheldrake	Spirituality is "the conscious human response to God that is both personal and ecclesial. In short, 'life in the Spirit'" (1992:37).

Marjorie Thompson	A. "Spirituality is how we live our faith with integrity in this world. The spiritual life is the growing vitality and energy of God's Spirit in us. The choreography of the Holy Spirit in the human spirit" (2001).
	B. "Christian spirituality means the way in which our relationship with God is lived and understood in the person of Jesus Christ. We are intended to be formed in the image of Christ–the notion of spiritual formation rooted in grace" (2001).
Geoffrey Wainwright	Spirituality is "the combination of praying and living" (1986:592).
Gordon Wakefield	Spirituality is "those attitudes, beliefs, practices which animate people's lives and help them to reach out towards super-sensible realities" (1983:361).

Appendix B

What Is a Spiritual Discipline?

> In the first century, the Greek term Askein (to practice something) referred to disciplined athletic training, which the Apostle Paul applied to the spiritual training and practice of Christian believers (1 Cor 9:24–25, 1 Tim 1:7b–8). Such is the meaning of the term "spiritual discipline."

Eugene Peterson	"We begin by insisting that *askesis* is not a spiritual technology at our beck and call but is rather immersion in an environment in which our capacities are reduced to nothing or nearly nothing and we are at the mercy of God to shape his will in us" (1992:90).
Dallas Willard	"A discipline is any activity within our power that we engage in to enable us to do what we cannot do by direct effort.... Somewhat ironically, perhaps *all* of the 'spiritual' disciplines are, or essentially involve, bodily behaviors" (1998b:353).
Richard Foster	"The disciplines are God's way of getting us into the ground, they can only get us to the place where something can be done. They are God's means of grace. The inner righteousness we seek is not something that is poured on our heads. God has ordained the disciplines of the spiritual life as the means by which we place ourselves where he can bless us" (1988:7).
Henri Nouwen	"A spiritual discipline is human effort to create open space to listen to the voice of the one who calls us the beloved" (1993).

Marjorie Thompson	"A rule of life is a pattern of spiritual disciplines that provides structure and direction for growth in holiness. When we speak of *patterns* in our life, we mean attitudes, behaviors, or elements that are routine, repeated, regular.... A rule of life, like a trellis, curbs our tendency to wander and supports our frail efforts to grow spiritually" (1995:138).

Appendix C

Physical Symptoms, Psychological Signs, and Underlying Beliefs of Time Pathologies

(Adapted from Ulmer and Schwartzbburd 1996:336–37, 352)

Physical Symptoms	1. Rapid behaviors (e.g., walking, talking, and eating fast; speech is often dysrhythmic).
	2. Shallow upper-chest breathing. Often accompanied by sucking in air while speaking, expiratory sighing, and slightly elevated shoulders.
	3. Tics eyebrow, shoulders; rapid eye blinking is sometimes seen.
	4. Nervous repetitive movements (e.g., knee jiggling, finger tapping, nail biting, teeth grinding).
	5. Smacking or clicking sound as mouth opens to speak, due to tense jaw muscles.
	6. Hurrying the speech of others; interrupting.
	7. Head nodding while speaking; excessive head nodding while listening.
	8. Facial tautness; expressing tension and anxiety.
	9. Tuneless humming.
	10. Periorbital pigmentation, due to excessive ACTH production from chronic struggle.

Psychological Symptoms	1. Impatience with the rate at which things happen; irritable when kept waiting.
2. Difficulty relaxing—feels guilty or restless.
3. Experiences a "racing mind"; may report sleep disturbances because of it.
4. Reports frequent attempts to do more than one thing at a time; difficulty listening without thinking of other things.
5. Makes a fetish out of being on time; or is chronically late.
6. Reports chronic feelings of time pressure.
7. Reports feeling overburdened or overwhelmed with all that needs to be done; may report often being overtired.
8. May admit to poor relationships; lack of close friends.
Underlying Beliefs	1. If I'm late, I'm a failure.
2. Other people's opinions of me are of crucial importance.
3. I am what I do. If I am not doing anything, I am nothing.
4. I'm a good person if I get everything done. If I don't, I'm a bad person.
5. If I do something wrong or don't get something done, I'm a bad person.
6. I'm not permitted to relax until I'm finished or exhausted.
7. Wasting time is a sin.
8. If I make a mistake, something bad will always happen.

Appendix D

Luke's Gospel, Part A

Jesus's Rhythms of Spirituality and Mission

Event	Time and Space/Place	Inner Discipline Practiced/ Taught	Grace: Divine Initiative/ Power	Outward Mission Practiced
Jesus's baptism and temptation (3:21–22; 4:1–13) In solitude	*Time*: 40+ days *Place*: Jordan; the wilderness	Prayer Listening to God's voice Baptism Fasting Prayer of authority Scripture quoted from memory to resist temptation Meditation Worship	The Father's voice Spirit descending in the form of a dove Fullness of the Holy Spirit	Begins ministry (4:14–41) *Word*: Teaches in the synagogue in Nazareth, reads Scripture, opposition→ *Deed*: Teaches in Capernaum synagogue, heals demon-possessed, news spreads← *Deed*: Heals Simon's mother-in-law, heals all sick brought to him←
Jesus's early morning retreat (4:42) In solitude	*Time*: When day broke *Place*: A lonely spot	Solitude Silence Saying no to wishes of crowd for him to stay Saying yes to the Spirit's leading to Judea		(4:43—5:15) *Word*: Proclaims the gospel in the synagogues of Judea, teaches the crowds→ *Deed*: Miracle of the haul of fish, heals the leper and paralytic←

297

Appendix D

Event	Time and Space/Place	Inner Discipline Practiced/ Taught	Grace: Divine Initiative/ Power	Outward Mission Practiced
Jesus's pattern of withdrawal (5:16) In solitude	*Time*: From time to time *Space*: Lonely places	Prayer Solitude		(5:17–39) *Deed*: Heals lame man, opposition *Word*: Calls Levi *Deed*: Heals on Sabbath, opposition
Choosing the Twelve (6:12–16) In solitude and community	*Time*: All night *Place*: The hills	Prayer Solitude Discerning selection of apprentices	Jesus initiated the commissioning of the Twelve after prayer	(6:17–49) *Word*: Teaches disciples and those who came from Judea, Jerusalem, Tyre/ Sidon← *Deed*: Heals all who touch him← *Word*: Sermon on the Plain←

→*Indicates centrifugal mission*   ←*Indicates centripetal mission*

Appendix E

Luke's Gospel, Part B
Jesus's Rhythms of Spirituality and Mission

Event	Time and Space/Place	Inner Discipline Practiced/ Taught	Grace: Divine Initiative/ Power	Outward Mission Practiced
Transfiguration (9:28–36) In community	*Time*: After 8 days *Place*: The mountain	Prayer Silence Worship Community Sleep and rest	Jesus's face and clothes dazzle Moses and Elijah appear	(9:43—10:12) *Deed*: Heals boy with demon, sets face to Jerusalem *Word*: On mission / Cost of discipleship / Mission instructions to the 70
Jesus's model of prayer (11:1) In solitude	*Time*: Once; until he ceased prayer *Place*: In a certain place	Prayer Solitude Community		(11:2–26) *Word*: Teaches the Lord's Prayer and importance of persistent prayer *Deed*: Heals a mute demonized man, conflict *Word*: Teaches about spiritual conflict

Event	Time and Space/Place	Inner Discipline Practiced/Taught	Grace: Divine Initiative/Power	Outward Mission Practiced
Last Supper (22:14–39) In community	*Time*: Passover supper on the Day of Unleavened Bread *Place*: An upstairs room	Reciting and singing the Hallel Eucharist and blessing Intercession for Peter	Jesus sends Peter and John to make preparations Miraculous guidance and provision	(22:47—24:11) *Deed*: Jesus's trial, death, and resurrection *Word*: Witness to thief on the cross, prayer for forgiveness of his executioners, prayer committing his spirit to God
Jesus's prayer on Maundy Thursday (22:39–46) In solitude and community	*Time*: An hour of testing *Place*: Mount of Olives	Solitude Community Prayer of relinquishment and surrender Prayer of anguish	An angel from heaven appears bringing strength	
Jesus's commission: appearance of the resurrected Jesus among the eleven and the rest of the company (24:33–53) In community	*Time*: When Cleopas and his companion came and announced they'd seen Jesus *Place*: Where disciples were assembled in Jerusalem, perhaps the upper room	Listening to Jesus open Scriptures: law of Moses, Psalms, prophets Study: Jesus gives interpretation of Scriptures Prayer of *examen*: letting Jesus surface doubt	Jesus's miraculous and sudden appearance	(Luke 24:47–49) *Word*: Jesus says to proclaim repentance and forgiveness to all nations in his name; they were to start in Jerusalem→ Disciples to stay in the city until armed with power

→*Indicates centrifugal mission*   ←*Indicates centripetal mission*

Appendix F

Three Branches of Spiritual Theology

(Adapted from Allen 1997:7-20)

Stage 1	Stage 2	Stage 3
Catholic: Purgation	Catholic: Illumination	Catholic: Union
Protestant: Justification and sanctification	Protestant: Sanctification	Protestant: Sanctification and glorification
		Orthodox: Deification
Ascetical/Moral Theology: The Active Life—*Praktike*	*Mystical Theology:* The Contemplative Life—*Theoretike*	
Goal: Martha—serving others	Goal: Mary—sitting at the Lord's feet (Luke 10)	
Means: The Spirit's power and meditation on the Scriptures to bring freedom from the eight deadly thoughts[1]	Means: Indirect Communion: *Physike* Cataphatic tradition: Discursive meditation	Means: Direct Communion: *Theoria* Apophatic tradition: Non-discursive meditation
Repentance or Conversion Developing virtue,[2] revamping passions Love of neighbor	Through nature Physical nature Human nature Through Scripture	Without images Through audible or thought words

1. The eight (or seven) deadly thoughts or sins are appetite, lust, avarice, sadness, anger, sloth, vainglory, and pride (Allen 1997:10).

2. The main virtues associated with ascetical branch of classical spiritual theology are divided into two categories: (1) the theological virtues, which derive from Scripture: love, faith, and hope; and (2) the cardinal virtues, which derive from Plato: prudence, temperance, courage, and justice. The cardinal virtues were incorporated into spiritual theology by St. Ambrose and his convert St. Augustine (Fadling 2007). Robert Wilkins notes that one biblical virtue, which was also considered such by ancients, is patience (Gal 5:22). He writes that the very first Christian treatise on a virtue was written by Tertullian and that on patience (2003:275-290). Ancient philosophers like Seneca and Cicero understood patience as fortitude in adversity whereas Tertullian understood the virtue to mean longsuffering and merciful love (2003:284-285).

Appendix G

Summary of Rhythms of Spirituality and Mission in the *Devotio Moderna*

(Adapted from J. Van Engen 1988)

Time and Space/Place	*Inner Disciplines Practiced*	*Grace: Divine Power*	*Outward Mission Practiced*
Time:	*Abiding (Solitude):*	*Empowering Grace:*	*Bearing Witness:*
Daily:	Silence	Held strongly	Mission in Deed:
• Eucharist: early morning	Fasting	Connected to spiritual practice	• Hospitality providing homes for the poor←
• Praying the hours:	Prayer:	Associated with mission	• Entering economic life of community by copying texts or in textile←
• In community: matins (3–4 a.m.), prime (6 a.m.), vespers (6 p.m.), compline (8 p.m.)	• Prayer of surrender and relinquishment	*Accepting Grace:*	
	• Recollected prayer	Not taught	
	• Centering prayer	*Prevenient Grace:*	• Giving excess goods and money to poor
	• Prayer of examen	Eclipsed by emphasis on human will	
• In solitude: terce (9 a.m.), sext (Noon), none (3 p.m.)	• Prayer of lament	Only faintly seen and rarely found	Mission in Word:
	• Lord's Prayer		• Lay preaching of Geert Grote→
• Spiritual reading: 1 hour	• Ejaculatory prayers		• Weekly collations←
• Manual labor: 6–8 hours	• Praying or singing the Psalms		• Schools and dorms for youth←
• Mutual confession			

Summary of Rhythms of Spirituality and Mission in the Devotio Moderna

Time and Space/Place	Inner Disciplines Practiced	Grace: Divine Power	Outward Mission Practiced
Weekly: • Sunday mass: all houses • Kessler's exercises • Collations: Sunday eve Monthly: • 17 2-day retreats alone with God before feast days *Space/Place:* Houses in cities and towns	Thanksgiving, praise Obedience: imitating Christ and his virtues Memorizing Scripture Meditation on Scripture Meditation on the life and passion of Christ Spiritual reading Journaling in notebooks Saying yes, saying no Sacrifice Simplicity: no ownership Rest, sleep, manual labor Retreat: EPC Slowing, interiority *Loving One Another (Community):* Living in communal houses Property in common Small group Praying the hours together		*Means of Support:* Tent-making *Pilgrim-Separate:* Culture-denying was dominant Living in common *Indigenous-Incarnate:* Culture-affirming practiced at certain points Use of vernacular
→Indicates centrifugal mission		←Indicates centripetal mission	

Appendix H

Summary of Rhythms of Spirituality and Mission in Ignatius and the Early Jesuits

(Adapted from Ignatius of Loyola 1991a–d; Ganss et al. 1991)

Time and Space/Place	Inner Disciplines Practiced	Grace: Divine Power	Outward Mission Practiced
Time:	*Abiding (Solitude):*	*Empowering Grace:*	*Bearing Witness:*
6 months in solitary recovery	Silence	Held strongly	Mission in Deed:
3 days confession	Frequent long times of solitude in nature	Connected to spiritual practice	Giving alms ←
1 hour	Vigils	Associated with mission	Acts of compassionate love →
1 day	Affective meditation	*Accepting Grace:*	Suffering, forgiving love in persecution ←
3 days	Spiritual reading	Not taught	
2 or 3 times per day	Taking notes, journaling	*Prevenient Grace:*	Establishing free colleges for youth ←
2-year pilgrimage	Discernment of spirits	Seen most frequently in Diary with infused contemplation	Mission in Word:
30-day retreats	Spiritual direction		Preaching of Ignatius and followers →
40 days of prayer	Making an election		
Whenever possible	Simplicity, poverty		Giving the Spiritual Exercises ←
Daily or weekly	Praying the hours		Cross-cultural mission →
	Recollected prayer		
	Examen		
	Pilgrimage		
	Mass		

Summary of Rhythms of Spirituality and Mission

Time and Space/Place	Inner Disciplines Practiced	Grace: Divine Power	Outward Mission Practiced
Space/Place:	*Spiritual Exercises:*		*Means of Support:*
Private rooms or houses anywhere	Fasting when possible		Vow of poverty/ begging for alms
Houses outside of cities	Finding God in all things, praying without ceasing		*Pilgrim-Separate:*
By a river	Vow of poverty		Culture affirming stronger than culture denying elements
Under the sky	Vow of chastity		
Churches and cathedrals	Vow of obedience (submission)		*Indigenous-Incarnate:*
On ships when traveling	Study theology and Bible		Culture affirming more dominant in later mission
	Dying well		
	Loving One Another:		Translation into heart language
	communion, confession		
	small group		
	sung vespers, compline		
	begging alms, poverty		
	selecting leaders		

→Indicates centrifugal mission   ←Indicates centripetal mission

Appendix I

Journey to Reach the Next Generations
Project Questionnaire

For each question, please give the one response that best describes you.

1. I am: __ male   __ female

2. My age is _____

3. I describe myself as:

    __ American Indian   __ Latino or Hispanic
    __ Black or Afro-American   __ White
    __ Asian or Pacific Islander   __ Other _____

4. Do you participate in a leadership body:

    __ making decisions/planning for your group/church (church board, mission board, student ministry council, etc.)
    __ giving care/nurture to those in your group/church (elders, volunteer youth staff, etc.)
    __ doing outreach to those not in our group/church (outreach events, prison/campus ministry, friendship evangelism, etc.)

5. Have you filled out this questionnaire during the past month? ____

6. Where are you filling this out?

    __ leadership gathering   __ worship service
    __ fellowship gathering   __ midweek gathering
    __ home Bible study/   __ Sunday school
        fellowship

In the statements below, "religion" and "religious" refer to your beliefs about God and the experience/practice of your faith whether or not you have membership in an organized church or religious body. The term "church" refers to any group of believers with or without formal membership. For each statement, give one of the following responses:

Agree Totally	Agree Strongly	Agree Moderately	Agree Somewhat	Not Sure	Disagree Somewhat	Disagree Moderately	Disagree Strongly	Disagree Totally
1	2	3	4	5	6	7	8	9

Church Climate: Think about the local church or group you attend. To what extent do you agree with the following statements as they relate to your church or group?

- ___ It feels warm.
- ___ It accepts people who are different.
- ___ It is friendly.
- ___ Strangers feel welcome
- ___ I learn a lot.
- ___ Most members want to be challenged to think about religious issues and ideas.
- ___ It challenges my thinking.
- ___ It encourages me to ask questions.
- ___ It expects people to learn and think.

Motivation: What motivates your religious life?

- ___ I enjoy reading about my religion.
- ___ I go to church because it helps me make friends.
- ___ It doesn't much matter what I believe as long as I am good.
- ___ It is important to spend time in private thought and prayer.
- ___ I pray mainly to gain relief and protection.
- ___ I try hard to live out all my religious beliefs.
- ___ What religion offers me most is comfort in times of trouble and sorrow.
- ___ Prayer is for peace and happiness.
- ___ Although I am religious, I don't let it affect my daily life.
- ___ I go to church mostly to spend time with my friends.
- ___ My whole life is based on my religion.

___ I go to church mainly because I enjoy seeing people I know there.

___ Although I believe in my religion, many other things are more important in my life.

Practicing Your Faith: What are you doing?

On an average day in the past week, I met alone with God:

___ 0 min.
___ 1–10 min.
___ 11–20 min.
___ 21–30 min.
___ 31–40 min
___ 41–50 min.
___ 51–60 min.
___ 1 hour or more

For the following questions, choose one: 1=never; 2=less than once a month; 3=about once a month; 4=2 or 3 times a month; 5=once a week; 6=several times a week; 7=once a day; 8=more than once a day

How often do you:

___ Pray or meditate, other than at church or before meal?
___ Read the Bible on your own?
___ Tell someone about the work of God in your life?
___ Do acts of mercy and compassion for others?
___ Teach a class or group in church/ministry?

Appendix J

Suggestions for Extended Personal Communion with God

Thank you for your participation in CF554. As to the requirements for those who cannot make this Friday's retreat, here are suggestions for how you might use the 6 hours of extended personal communion (EPC) with the Lord:

1. If possible, complete your EPC by the Monday after the Friday retreat, so as to not get behind on the formational assignments (it is difficult, if not impossible, to play catch up with formational exercises and still receive the full formational impact of them).

2. Find a time and place in which you will experience the fewest interruptions (away from phones, cell phones, media, etc.), so you can focus on God.

3. The purpose of the EPC is to spend the time with the Lord in whatever way he knows that you need. Therefore, begin your time by identifying your expectations and agendas for your EPC and releasing them to God and the leading of the Holy Spirit. God may wish to bring you refreshment, challenge, encouragement, conviction, joy, grieving, play, etc. God may lead you to any or none of the above.

4. The problem of distractions is universal. You will find your mind wandering or racing to many things other than God. Two ways to deal with them: (1) let your mind wander to each distraction and offer up the "distraction" to God—not one of them that comes to mind is unimportant to him; and (2) resist each distraction and then return your attention to God.

5. Bring to your EPC whatever helps you to spend time with God. Examples might include worship CDs, personal journal, Bible, lunch or meal if you prefer not to fast, an instrument if you play one, appropriate clothing if you wish to spend time outdoors, a blanket or lounge chair, etc.

6. If you want to go out-of-doors, try to go to an area that is secure or ask someone to go with you, assuming they won't interrupt your time.

7. Use some of your time with God for silence—for the purpose of listening to what God may be saying or not saying. If he says nothing, remember it is ok to just be in his presence without communication. If you are an active personality, you may find walking or hiking to help you be attentive to God. Find whatever helps you to be attentive to him based on the way you are wired.

8. If you become drowsy, let God give you a nap. Is there not an analogy between a child falling asleep on her/his parent's lap and doing the same with God? Often, students wake up from their nap refreshed, able to be much more attentive and aware of God's voice.

9. Remember:

> "Prayer is companionship with God"
> —Clement of Alexandria.

> "Prayer is someone you are with, not something you do"
> —Chuck Miller.

References Cited

Adams, Henry B.
1980 "Effects of Reduced Stimulation on Institutionalized Adult Patients." In *Restricted Environmental Stimulation: Research and Clinical Applications*. By Peter Suedfeld with contributions by Henry B. Adams et al. Pp. 320–64. New York: Wiley and Sons.

Adato, Allison
1999 "The Secret Lives of Teens." *Life*, March: 38–45.

Allen, Diogenes
1997 *Spiritual Theology: The Theology of Yesterday for Spiritual Help Today*. Boston, MA: Cowley.

Allen, Tom
2005 E-mail to Jon Ball forwarded to author. January 9, 2006.

Allport, Gordon W., and J. M. Ross
1967 "Personal Religious Orientation and Prejudice." *Journal of Personality and Social Psychology* 5 (4): 432–43.

Anderson, Wayne
2006 "Grace." CF554 class presentation, Fuller Theological Seminary, School of Theology. April 7.

Asami, Shin
2004 Personal conversation with retreatants. Riverside, CA. May.

Athanasius
1980 "The Life of Antony." In *Athanasius: The Life of Antony and the Letter to Marcellinus*. Robert C. Gregg, trans. Pp. 29–99. Classics of Western Spirituality. Mahwah, NJ: Paulist.

Ball, John
2006 "Spirituality and Discipleship in College and Young Adult Settings." CF554 class presentation. Fuller Theological Seminary, School of Theology. May.
2007 Telephone conversation with author. February.

Bamberger, John Eudes, trans.
1981 "Introduction." In *Evagrius Ponticus: The Praktikos and Chapters on Prayer*. Pp. xxiii–xciv. Cistercian Studies Series, 4. Kalamazoo, MI: Cisterian.

Banks, Robert, and Julia Banks
1989 *The Church Comes Home: A New Base for Community and Mission*. Rev. ed. Claremont, CA: Albatross.

Barbour, Julian
1999 *The End of Time: The Next Revolution in Physics*. New York: Oxford University Press.

Letter of Barnabas.
In Holmes, *Apostolic Fathers*. Pp. 270–327.

Barta, Karen A.
1988 *The Gospel of Mark*. Message of Biblical Spirituality, 9. Wilmington, DE: Glazier.

Barth, Karl
1961 "An Exegetical Study of Matthew 28:16–20." In *The Theology of the Christian Mission*. Gerald H. Anderson, ed. Pp. 55–71. New York: McGraw-Hill.

Bass, Dorothy C.
1997 *Practicing Our Faith: A Way of Life for a Searching People*. The Practices of Faith Series. San Francisco: Jossey-Bass.
2000 *Receiving the Day: Christian Practices for Opening the Gift of Time*. San Francisco: Jossey-Bass.
2003 Practicing Our Faith Web site. Valparaiso Project on the Education and Formation of People in Faith. Valparaiso University. Online: http//:www.practicingourfaith.org.

Bass, Dorothy C., and Don C. Richter
2002 *Way to Live: Christian Practices for Teens*. Nashville, TN: Upper Room.

Batson, C. Daniel, et al.
1989 "Religious Prosocial Motivation: Is It Altruistic or Egoistic?" *Journal of Personality and Social Psychology* 57 (5): 873–84.

Bauman, Zygmunt
2000 *Liquid Modernity*. Malden, MA: Blackwell.

Bayne, David
2007 E-mail to author. January 20.

Beattie, Melody
1987   *Codependent No More: How to Stop Controlling Others and Start Caring for Yourself.* The Hazelden Meditation Series. San Francisco: Harper & Row.

Beaudoin, Tom
1998   *Virtual Faith: The Irreverent Spiritual Quest of Generation X.* San Francisco: Jossey-Bass.

Benedict of Nursia
1975   *The Rule of Saint Benedict.* Anthony C. Meisel and M. L. del Mastro, trans. New York: Doubleday.

Berger, Peter
1990   *A Rumor of Angels: Modern Society and the Rediscovery of the Supernatural.* New York: Doubleday.

Bessenecker, Scott
2006   *The New Friars: The Emerging Movement Serving the World's Poor.* Downers Grove, IL: InterVarsity.

Bockmuehl, Markus
1992   "How Did Jesus Pray? The Spirituality of Jesus in the Apostolic Church." In *Alive to God: Studies in Spirituality Presented to James Houston.* J. I. Packer and Loren Wilkinson, eds. Pp. 56–71. Downers Grove, IL: InterVarsity.

Bolger, Ryan
2000   "Introduction to Modern/Postmodern Culture." MP 520 class presentation. Fuller Theological Seminary, School of World Mission. October.

Boman, Thorleif
1960   *Hebrew Thought Compared with Greek.* Jules L. Moreau, trans. London: SCM.

Bonhoeffer, Dietrich
1995   *The Cost of Discipleship.* New York: Touchstone.

Borg, Marcus, and N. T. Wright
1999   *The Meaning of Jesus: Two Visions.* San Francisco: Harper.

Bosch, David J.
1978   "The Why and How of a True Biblical Foundation for Mission." In *Zending Op Weg Naar De Toekomst: Essays aangeboden aan Prof. Dr. J. Verkuyl ter gelegenheid van zijn afscheid als hoogleraar in de missiologie en evangelisistiek aan de Faculteit der Godgeleerdheid van de Vrije Universiteit te Amsterdam.* J. D. Gort, ed. Pp. 33–44. Kampen, Neth.: Kok.

314 References Cited

(1979) 2000 *Spirituality for the Road.* Eugene, OR: Wipf and Stock.
(1991) 1997 *Transforming Mission: Paradigm Shifts in Theology of Mission.* Maryknoll, NY: Orbis.
1995 *Believing in the Future: Toward a Missiology of Western Culture.* Valley Forge, PA: Trinity.

Bouyer, Louis
1963 *The Spirituality of the New Testament and the Fathers.* Mary P. Ryan, trans. History of Christian Spirituality, 1. New York: Seabury.

Bradley, James
1997 "Tertullian and the Foundations of Western Spirituality." CH517 class lecture. Fuller Theological Seminary, School of Theology. Audio Technology Center, audiocassette no. 2.
2006 E-mail to author. October 2.

Bradshaw, Paul F.
1992 *The Search for the Origins of Christian Worship: Sources and Methods for the Study of Early Liturgy.* New York: Oxford University Press.
1999 "The Origins of Easter." In *Passover and Easter: Origin and History to Modern Times.* Pp. 1–7. Two Liturgical Traditions Series, 5. Notre Dame: University of Notre Dame Press.

Brandon, S. G. F.
1951 *Time and Mankind: An Historical and Philosophical Study of Mankind's Attitude to the Phenomena of Change.* London: Hutchinson.

Brooks, David
2001 "The Organizational Kid." *Atlantic Monthly* 287 (4): 40–54.

Brown, Colin
1979 "Vine, Wine." In *New International Dictionary of New Testament Theology.* Colin Brown, ed. Vol. 3, pp. 918–23. Grand Rapids: Zondervan.
1990 *Christianity and Western Thought: A History of Philosophers, Ideas, and Movements.* Downers Grove, IL: InterVarsity.

Brueggemann, Walter
1977 *The Land: Place as Gift, Promise, and Challenge in Biblical Faith.* Philadelphia: Fortress.

Bunge, Gabriel
2002 *Earthen Vessels: The Practice of Personal Prayer.* Michael J. Milner, trans. San Francisco: Ignatius.

Campbell, Jonathan
1996 "A Postmodern Challenge: The Gospel and Church in Changing Culture." Unpublished MS. Fuller Theological Seminary, School of World Missions.

Carroll, Colleen
2002   *The New Faithful: Why Young Adults are Embracing Christian Orthodoxy*. Chicago: Loyola.

Carson, D. A.
1984   *Matthew*. Vol. 8 of *The Expositor's Bible Commentary*. Frank E. Gaebelein, ed. Grand Rapids, MI: Zondervan.

Cassian, John
1985   *Conferences*. Colm Luibheid, trans. The Classics of Western Spirituality. New York: Paulist.
2000   *The Institutes*. Boniface Ramsey, trans. Ancient Christian Writers, 58. New York: Newman.

Cassidy, Scotty
N.d.   "Tools of Personal Change: The Twelve Steps." In *Second Chance*. Pp. 15–17. Unpublished Christian adaptation of the Twelve Steps of Alcoholics Anonymous. Memphis, TN: Second Chance Ministries.

Cassidy, Scotty, and Jean Cassidy
1995   Group therapy session.

Castells, Manuel
1996   *The Rise of the Network Society*. Vol 1. of *The Information Age: Economy, Society, and Culture*. Malden, MA: Blackwell.
1997   *The Power of Identity*. Vol 2 of *The Information Age: Economy, Society, and Culture*. Malden, MA: Blackwell.
1998   *The End of the Millennium*. Vol. 3 of *The Information Age: Economy, Society, and Culture*. Malden, MA: Blackwell.

Catherall, Gordon A.
1978   "Jesuits (Society of Jesus)." In *The New International Dictionary of the Christian Church*. J. D. Douglas, ed. P. 531. Rev. ed. Grand Rapids, MI: Zondervan.

Chadwick, Henry
1990   "The Early Christian Community." In *The Oxford Illustrated History of Christianity*. John McManners, ed. Pp. 20–61. New York: Oxford University Press.

Chan, Simon
1998   *Spiritual Theology: A Systematic Study of the Christian Life*. Downers Grove, IL: InterVarsity.
2006   *Liturgical Theology: The Church as Worshiping Community*. Downers Grove, IL: IVP Academic.
2007   E-mail to author's dissertation committee. April 17.

Childers, Jana
1999 "The Shameless Path." Track 4 of *Spirituality*, vol. 2 of *Cloud of Witnesses*. Audio journal on CD. Princeton Theological Seminary, Institute for Youth Ministry. Online: http://www.ptsem.edu/iym/cow/mp3/vol2/04.mp3.

Chilton, Bruce
2002 *Redeeming Time: The Wisdom of Ancient Jewish and Christian Festal Calendars*. Peabody, MA: Hendrickson.

Chittister, Joan
1990 *Wisdom Distilled from the Daily: Living the Rule of St. Benedict Today*. San Francisco: HarperCollins.

Claiborne, Shane
2006 *The Irresistible Revolution: Living as an Ordinary Radical*. Grand Rapids, MI: Zondervan.

Clark, Chap
1999 "The Needs of the Class of 2004: An Interview with Dr. Chap Clark, Ph.D." *The Ivy Jungle Report* 7 (Summer): 1, 12–15.
2004 *Hurt: Inside the World of Today's Teenagers*. Grand Rapids, MI: Baker Academic.

Clark, Chap and Kara E. Powell
2006 *Deep Ministry in a Shallow World: Not-So-Secret Findings about Youth Ministry*. Grand Rapids, MI: Zondervan.

Clebsch, William A.
1980 "Preface." In *Athanasius: The Life of Antony and the Letter to Marcellinus*. Robert C. Gregg, trans. Pp. xiii–xxi. The Classics of Western Spirituality. Mahwah, NJ: Paulist.

1, 2 Clement.
In Holmes, *Apostolic Fathers*. Pp. 22–127.

Clinton, J. Robert
1988 *The Making of a Leader*. Colorado Springs, CO: NavPress.
1992 *Bridging Strategies: Leadership Perspectives for Introducing Change*. Altadena, CA: Barnabas.

Collett, Barry
2002 "Organizing Time for Secular and Religious Purposes: The *Contemplation of Sinners* (1499) and the Translation of the Benedictine Rule for Women (1517) of Richard Fox, Bishop of Winchester." In *The Use and Abuse of Time in Christian History: Papers Read at the 1999 Summer Meeting and the 2000 Winter Meeting of the Ecclesiastical History Society*. R. N.

Swanson, ed. Pp. 145–60. Studies in Church History, 37. Woodbridge, UK: Boydell and Brewer.

Collins, Kenneth J., ed.
2000 *Exploring Christian Spirituality: An Ecumenical Reader*. Grand Rapids, MI: Baker.

Conforti, Joseph A.
1995 *Jonathan Edwards, Religious Tradition, and American Culture*. Chapel Hill: University of North Carolina Press.

Countryman, L. William
1987 *The Mystical Way in the Fourth Gospel: Crossing over into God*. Philadelphia: Fortress.

Cousins, Ewert
1987 "The Humanity and Passion of Christ." In *Christian Spirituality: High Middle Ages and Reformation*. Jill Raitt, Bernard McGinn, and John Meyendorff, eds. Pp. 375–91. World Spirituality: An Encyclopedic History of the Religious Quest, 17. New York: Crossroad.

Cowan, Clyde
2003 Personal conversation with author.

Cox, Harvey
1965 *The Secular City: Secularization and Urbanization in Theological Perspective*. London: SCM.

Crouch, Andy
1996 "A Generation of Debtors: A Gen-Xer Reflects on the Deficits Bequeathed to His Generation and on Its Fear of Redemption." *Christianity Today*, November 11: 31–33.

Crump, David Michael
1999 *Jesus the Intercessor: Prayer and Christology in Luke-Acts*. Biblical Studies Library. Grand Rapids, MI: Baker.

Cullman, Oscar
1961 "Eschatology and Missions in the New Testament." Olive Wyon, trans. In *The Theology of the Christian Mission*. Gerald H. Anderson, ed. Pp. 42–54. New York: McGraw-Hill.
1964 *Christ and Time: The Primitive Christian Conception of Time and History*. Floyd V. Filson, trans. Rev. ed. Philadelphia: Westminster.

Curtis, Brent, and John Eldredge
1997 *The Sacred Romance: Drawing Closer to the Heart of God*. Rev. ed. Nashville, TN: Nelson.

Dalmases, Candido de
1985 *Ignatius Loyola, Founder of the Jesuits: His Life and Work.* Jerome Aixala, trans. St. Louis, MO: Institute of Jesuit Sources.

Davies, W. D.
1974 *The Gospel and the Land: Early Christianity and Jewish Territorial Doctrine.* Sheffield, UK: Sheffield Academic.

Davis, Kenneth Ronald
1974 *Anabaptism and Asceticism: A Study in Intellectual Origins.* Scottdale, PA: Herald.

Dean, Kenda Creasy
2004 *Practicinng Passion: Youth and the Quest for a Passionate Church.* Grand Rapids, MI: Eerdmans.

Dean, Kenda Creasy, and Ron Foster
1998 *The Godbearing Life: The Art of Soul Tending for Youth Ministry.* Nashville, TN: Upper Room.

Dedinger, Jerry
1997 Personal conversation with author.

Didache
In Holmes, *Apostolic Fathers.* Pp. 246–69.

Dieburg, Peter
1988 "Rector Peter Dieburg of Hildesheim on the Schism of 1443." In *Devotio Moderna: Basic Writings.* John Van Engen, trans. Pp. 235–41. The Classics of Western Spirituality. New York: Paulist.

Doherty, Robert
2003 "Spiritual Formation and Spiritual Direction." Notes presented at a conference on *Spiritual Formation: An Ignatian Approach to Spirituality.* Vanguard University, Institute for Leadership Studies. March 6–8, 10–11.

Donahue, Michael J.
1985 "Intrinsic and Extrinsic Religousness: The Empirical Research." *Journal for the Scientific Study of Religion* 24 (4): 418–23.

Donin, Hayim Halevy
1980 *To Pray as a Jew: A Guide to the Prayer Book and the Synagogue Service.* New York: Basic Books.

Doohan, Leonard
1985 *Luke: The Perennial Spirituality.* Santa Fe, NM: Bear.

Dowd, Sharyn E.
1989 "New Testament Theology and Spirituality of Early Christianity: Relationships and Implications." *Lexington Theological Quarterly* 24 (3): 69–80.

Dreyer, Elizabeth
1996 "The Cloud of Unknowing." In *A Dictionary of Christian Spirituality*. Gordon S. Wakefield, ed. Pp. 89–91. London: SCM.

Dudley, Roger L., and V. Bailey Gillespie
1992 *Valuegenesis: Faith in the Balance*. Riverside, CA: La Sierra University Press.

Dunn, Richard D.
2001 *Shaping the Spiritual Life of Students: A Guide for Youth Workers, Pastors, Teachers, and Campus Ministers*. Downers Grove, IL: InterVarsity.

Dupre, Louis, and Wiseman, Jonathan A.
2001 "Jonathan Edwards 17-3-58; Commentary." In *Light from Light: An Anthology of Christian Mysticism*. Louis Dupre and James A. Wiseman, eds. Pp. 382–89. New York: Paulist.

Dybdahl, Jon L.
1997 Personal conversation with author. Riverside, CA: La Sierra University. April.

Edwards, Jonathan, ed.
(1949) 2005 *The Life and Diary of David Brainerd*. Grand Rapids, MI: Baker.
2001 *Personal Narrative* and *A Treatise Concerning Religious Affections*. In *Light from Light: An Anthology of Christian Mysticism*. Louis Dupre and James A. Wiseman, eds. Pp. 390–411. New York: Paulist.

Erkel, R. Todd
1995 "Time Shifting." *Family Therapy Networker*, January–February: 33–39.

Evans, Craig A.
1999 "Jesus and the Continuing Exile of Israel." In *Jesus and the Restoration of Israel: A Critical Assessment of N. T. Wright's Jesus and the Victory of God*. Carey C. Newman, ed. Pp. 77–100. Downers Grove, IL: InterVarsity.

Fadling, Alan J.
2001 "The Critical Journey." "Spirituality and Discipleship in College and Young Adult Settings." CF554 class presentation. Fuller Theological Seminary, School of Theology. November 15.
2007 Phone conversation with author. March 26.

Faulkner, Barbara L.
1978   "Eastern Orthodox Church." In *The New International Dictionary of the Christian Church*. J. D. Douglas, ed. Pp. 322–25. Rev. ed. Grand Rapids, MI: Zondervan.

Feuerherd, Peter
2001   "Quiet Revolution: Pollster Sees the Bible as a Key to Transformation." *Record* 146 (4): 7–9.

Fleming, David L.
1996   *Draw Me into Your Friendship: The Spiritual Exercises, A Literal Translation and a Contemporary Reading*. St. Louis, MO: Institute of Jesuit Sources.

Flory, Richard W.
2000   "Conclusion: Toward a Theory of Generation X Religion." In *Gen X Religion*. Donald E. Miller and Richard W. Flory, eds. Pp. 233–249. New York: Routledge.

Folger, Tim
2000   "From Here to Eternity." *Discovery*, December: 54–61.

Ford, Kevin G. and Jim Denney
1995   *Jesus for a New Generation: Putting the Gospel into the Language of Xers*. Downers Grove, IL: InterVarsity.

Foster, Richard J.
1988   *Celebration of Discipline: The Path to Spiritual Growth*. Rev. ed. San Francisco: Harper & Row.
1992   *Prayer: Finding the Heart's True Home*. New York: HarperCollins.

Foulkes, Francis
1989   *The Letter of Paul to the Ephesians: An Introduction and Commentary*. Rev. ed. The Tyndale New Testament Commentaries. Grand Rapids, MI: Eerdmans.

Funk, Mary Margaret
2002   *Thoughts Matter: The Practice of the Spiritual Life*. New York: Continuum.

Galinsky, Ellen, Stacy S. Kim, and James T. Bond
2001   "Executive Summary." In "Feeling Overworked: When Work Becomes Too Much." Pp. 5–14. New York: Families and Work Institute. Online: http://familiesandwork.org/summary/overwork.pdf.

Ganss, George E., et al., ed. and trans.
1991   *Ignatius of Loyola: The Spiritual Exercises and Selected Works*. With introductions and notes, pp. 1–63, 67–68, 117–20, 217–24, 229–34, 369–480. The Classics of Western Spirituality. Mahwah, NJ: Paulist.

Gardner, Christine J.
2001   "Tangled in the Worst of the Web." *Christianity Today*, March 5: 42–47.

George, Timothy
1991   *Faithful Witness: The Life and Mission of William Carey*. Birmingham, AL: New Hope.

Giddens, Anthony
1990   *The Consequences of Modernity*. Stanford: Stanford University Press.

Glasser, Arthur F., Charles E. van Engen, Dean S. Gilliland, and Shawn B. Redford
2003   *Kingdom and Mission*. Pasadena, CA: Fuller Theological Seminary.

Gorman, Julie A.
2002   *Community That Is Christian: A Handbook on Small Groups*. Grand Rapids, MI: Baker.

Gorsuch, Richard L.
1984   "Measurement: The Boon and Bane of Investigating Religion." *American Psychologist* 39 (3): 228–36.

Gorsuch, Richard L., and Susan E. McPherson
1989   "Intrinsic/Extrinsic Measurement: I/E-Revised and Single-Item Scales. *Journal for the Scientific Study of Religion* 28 (3): 348–54.

Gorsuch, Richard L., and G. Daniel Venable
1983   "Development of an Age Universal' I-E Scale." *Journal for the Scientific Study of Religion* 22 (2): 181–87.

Gort, Jerald
1979   "The Contours of the Reformed Understanding of Christian Mission." In *Mission Focus* 7 (3): 37–41. Wilbert Shenk, ed.

Green, Lee
2002   "The Indisputable Mr. Scruples." *Los Angeles Times Magazine*, March 10: 1.

Green, Michael
1995   *Evangelism in the Early Church*. Updated ed. Guildford Surrey, UK: Eagle.

Gregg, Robert C.
1980 "Introduction." In *Athanasius: The Life of Antony and the Letter to Marcellinus*. Richard J. Payne, ed. Pp. 1–26. The Classics of Western Spirituality. New York: Paulist.

Groote, Geert
1988a "Resolutions and Intentions, But Not Vows: Written Out by Master Geert in the Name of the Lord." In *Devotio Moderna: Basic Writings*. John Van Engen, trans. Pp 65–75. The Classics of Western Spirituality. New York: Paulist.
1988b "A Sermon Addressed to the Laity." In *Devotio Moderna: Basic Writings*. John Van Engen, trans. Pp. 92–97. The Classics of Western Spirituality. New York: Paulist.
1988c "Noteworthy Sayings of Master Geert." In *Devotio Moderna: Basic Writings*. John Van Engen, trans. Pp. 76–77. The Classics of Western Spirituality. New York: Paulist.
1988d "Letter [62]: On Patience and the Imitation of Christ." In *Devotio Moderna: Basic Writings*. John Van Engen, trans. Pp. 84–91. The Classics of Western Spirituality. New York: Paulist.
1988e "Letter 29." In *Devotio Moderna: Basic Writings*. John Van Engen, trans. Pp. 78–83. The Classics of Western Spirituality. New York: Paulist.

Gross, David M., and Sophfronia Scott
1990 "Proceeding with Caution." *Time*, July 16: 56–62.

Guinness, Os
1993 *The American Hour: A Time of Reckoning and the Once and Future Role of Faith*. New York: Free Press.

Gundry, Robert H.
1993 *Mark: A Commentary on His Apology for the Cross*. Grand Rapids, MI: Eerdmans.

Hagberg, Janet O., and Robert A. Guelich
1989 *The Critical Journey: Stages in the Life of Faith*. Dallas: Word.

Hahn, H. C.
1980 "Chronos." In *Dictionary of New Testament Theology*. Vol 3, pp. 839–45. Colin Brown, ed. Grand Rapids, MI: Zondervan.

Hall, Jenny
2006 "Spiritual Formation in College and Young Adult Settings." CF554 class presentation. Fuller Theological Seminary, School of Theology. May.

Harding, Mark
1994   "The Lord's Prayer and Other Prayer Texts of the Greco-Roman Era: A Bibliography." In *The Lord's Prayer and Other Prayer Texts from the Greco-Roman Era*. James H. Charlesworth, Mark Harding, and Mark Kiley, eds. Pp. 101–257. Valley Forge, PA: Trinity.

Harrison, Everett F.
1985   *The Apostolic Church*. Grand Rapids, MI: Eerdmans.

Harvey, David
1990   *The Condition of Postmodernity: An Inquiry into the Origins of Cultural Change*. Oxford: Blackwell.
2001   *The Spaces of Capital: Towards a Critical Geography*. New York: Routledge.

Hayner, Stephen A.
1989   Personal conversation with author. Chicago. March.

Hays, Richard B.
1999   "Victory over Violence: The Significance of N. T. Wright's Jesus for New Testament Ethics." In *Jesus and the Restoration of Israel*. Carey C. Newman, ed. Pp. 142–79. Downers Grove, IL: InterVarsity.

Henning, Kathy
2006   "The Faith of the Next Generation." *Response* 29 (1): 26–29.

Shepherd of Hermas
       Mandates. In Holmes, *Apostolic Fathers*. Pp. 375–417.
       Similitudes. In Holmes, *Apostolic Fathers*. Pp. 418–527.
       Visions. In Holmes, *Apostolic Fathers*. Pp. 334–73.

Hernandez, Willy
2006   *Henri Nouwen: A Spirituality of Imperfection*. New York: Paulist.

Herxen, Dirk
1988   *A Customary for Brothers*. In *Devotio Moderna: Basic Writings*. John Van Engen, trans. Pp. 155–75. The Classics of Western Spirituality. New York: Paulist.

Hesselgrave, David J.
2000   "Great Commission." In *The Evangelical Dictionary of World Missions*. A. Scott Moreau, Harold Netland, and Charles E. van Engen, eds. Pp. 412–14. A. Grand Rapids, MI: Baker.

Hinson, E. Glenn
1996   *The Early Church: Origins to the Dawn of the Middle Ages*. Nashville: Abingdon.

Hofferth, Sandra L., and John F. Sandberg
2000   "Changes in American Children's Time: 1981–1997." Pp. 1–48. Working paper for the Center for the Ethnograpy of Everyday Life, Universtity of Michigan. Online: http://ceel.psc.isr.umich.edu/pubs/papers/ceel013-00.pdf.

Holmes, Michael W., ed.
1999   *The Apostolic Fathers: Greek Texts and English Translations*. Updated ed. Grand Rapids: Baker.

The Hope Center
2007   The Hope Center Web site. Online: http://www.hopecenterkc.org/.

Hornblower, Margot
1997   "Great Xpectations." *Time*, June 9: 58–68.

Houston, James
1989   *The Transforming Friendship: A Guide to Prayer*. Oxford: Lion.

Howard, Philip E.
(1949)   2005   "Prefatory Note" and "Biographical Sketch of the Life and Work of Jonathan Edwards." In *The Life and Diary of David Brainerd*. Jonathan Edwards, ed. Pp. 7–8, 11–39. Grand Rapids, MI: Baker.

Howe, Neil, and Bill Strauss
1993   *13th Gen: Abort, Retry, Ignore, Fail?* New York: Vintage.
2000   *Millenials Rising: The Next Great Generation*. New York: Vintage.

Hurtado, Larry W.
1999   *At the Origins of Christian Worship: The Context and Character of Earliest Christian Devotion*. Grand Rapids, MI: Eerdmans.

Hyma, Albert
1924   *The Christian Renaissance: A History of the "Devotio Moderna."* New York: Century.

Ignatius of Antioch
   To the Ephesians. In Holmes, *Apostolic Fathers*. Pp. 136–149.
   To Polycarp. In Holmes, *Apostolic Fathers*. Pp. 194–201.
   To the Smyrnaeans. In Holmes, *Apostolic Fathers*. Pp. 184–93.
   To the Trallians. In Holmes, *Apostolic Fathers*. Pp. 158–65.

Ignatius of Loyola
1991a   *Autobiography*. Parmananda R. Diviarkar, trans. In Ganss, *Ignatius of Loyola*. Pp. 65–111.

1991b	*The Spiritual Diary*. Edward J. Malatesta and George E. Ganss, trans. In Ganss, *Ignatius of Loyola*. Pp. 238–70.
1991c	*The Spiritual Exercises*. George E. Ganss, trans. In Ganss, *Ignatius of Loyola*. Pp. 113–214.
1991d	*Constitutions of the Society of Jesus*. George E. Ganss, trans. In Ganss, *Ignatius of Loyola*. Pp. 271–321.
1991e	*Selected Letters*. Martin E. Palmer, trans. In Ganss, *Ignatius of Loyola*. Pp. 323–65.

Irenaeus
1956   *Against Heresies*. In *The Ante-Nicene Fathers*. Alexander Roberts and James Donaldson, eds. Rev. by A. Cleveland Coxe. Vol. 1, Pp. 309–568. Grand Rapids, MI: Eerdmans.

Ivens, Michael
1986   "Ignatius of Loyola." In *The Study of Spirituality*. Cheslyn Jones, Geoffrey Wainwright, and Edward Yarnold, eds. Pp. 357–62. Oxford: Oxford University Press.

The Ivy Jungle Network
2003   "The State of College and University Ministry." Online: http://www.ivyjungle.org, accessed February 24, 2007.
2005   "2005 Survey Results: The State of College and University Ministry November 2005." Online: http://www.ivyjungle.org, accessed February 24, 2007.
2006   "Campus Ministry Update November 2006." Online http://www.ivyjungle.org, accessed February 24, 2007.

Jackson, J. B.
1979   "The Order of a Landscape: Reason and Religion in Newtonian America." In *The Interpretation of Ordinary Landscape: Geographical Essays*. D. W. Meinigg, ed. Pp. 153–63. Oxford: Oxford University Press.

Jacob, E. F.
1952   "Gerard Groote and the Beginnings of the 'New Devotion' in the Low Countries" *Journal of Ecclesiastical History* 3: 41–57.

Jefford, Clayton N.
1995   Review of *The Apostolic Fathers*. *Journal of Early Christian Studies* 3 (1): 81–83.Jefford, Clayton N., Kenneth J. Harder, and Louis D. Amezaga Jr.
1996   *Reading the Apostolic Fathers: An Introduction*. Peabody, MA: Hendrickson.

Jehele, Chris
2007a   Personal conversation with author. Forest Falls, CA. February.
2007b   Personal conversation with author. Mountain Center CA. October.

Jencks, Charles
1996 *What Is Postmodernism?* 4th ed. London: Academy Editions.

Jensen, L. Paul
1997 "Journey to Reach the Next Generations: Research Findings." Unpublished MS.
1998 "The Spirituality and Mission of William Wilberforce and the Clapham Sect." Unpublished MS.
1999 "A Pioneer Kingdom Builder: A Leadership Study on Paul Jensen from 1985-99—The Leadership Institute Story." Unpublished MS.
2003 "Historical Methods for Studying Spirituality and Mission in Selected Spiritual Classics." Unpublished MS.

Jensen, Lyle H.
2000 "Then and Now: Reflections on a Mature Discipline." *American Crystallographic Newsletter* (Winter): 18-19.

Johnson, Ben Campbell
1991 *Speaking of God: Evangelism as Initial Spiritual Guidance.* Louisville, KY: Westminster John Knox.

Jones, Darron
1996 Personal conversation with author. Irvine, CA.

Junkin, E. Dixon
1996 "Up from the Grassroots: The Church in Transition." In *Church between Gospel and Culture: The Emerging Mission in North America.* George R. Huntsberger and Craig Van Gelder, eds. Pp. 308-18. Grand Rapids, MI: Eerdmans.

Kaiser, Christopher B.
1996 "From Biblical Secularity to Modern Secularism: Historical Aspects and Stages." In *The Church between Gospel and Culture: The Emerging Mission in North America.* George R. Huntsberger and Craig Van Gelder, eds. Pp. 79-112. Grand Rapids, MI: Eerdmans.

Kantrowitz, Barbara, and Keith Naughton
2001 "Generation 9-11." *Newsweek* 138 (20): 47-56.

Kempis, Thomas, à
1982 *The Imitation of Christ.* Paraphrased by Donald E. Demaray, ed. Grand Rapids: Baker.

Kern, Stephen
1983 *The Culture of Time and Space 1880-1918.* Cambridge: Harvard University Press.

Kidder, Rushworth M.
1994   *Shared Values for a Troubled World: Conversations with Men and Women of Conscience.* San Francisco: Jossey-Bass.

Kimball, Dan
2003   *The Emerging Church: Vintage Christianity for New Generations.* Grand Rapids, MI: Zondervan.

King, Jeff
1997   "Church in Action: Getting Teens Hungry for the Gospel." *Christianity Today*, January 6: 48-49.

King, Mike
2006   *Presence-Centered Youth Ministry: Guiding Students into Spiritual Formation.* Downers Grove, IL: InterVarsity.

Kinnert, Edward
1981   "Toward a Method for the Study of Spirituality." *Review for Religious* 40 (1): 3-19.

Koenig, John
1992   *Rediscovering New Testament Prayer: Boldness and Blessing in the Name of Jesus.* Harrisburg, PA: Morehouse.

Kuchan, Karen L.
2005   *Visio Divina: A New Prayer Practice for Healing and Growth.* New York: Crossroad.

Ladd, George Eldon
1959   *The Gospel of the Kingdom: Scriptural Studies in the Kingdom of God.* Grand Rapids, MI: Eerdmans.

Landeen, William M.
1951   "Gabriel and the Brethren of the Common Life." *Church History* 20 (1): 23-36.
1964   "The *Devotio Moderna* in Trier." *Andrews University Seminary Studies* 1: 62-78.
1984   "Martin Luther's Intervention in Behalf of the Brethren of the Common Life in Herford." *Andrews University Seminary Studies* 22 (1): 81-97.

Lane, William L.
1974   *The Gospel According to Mark: The English Text with Introduction, Exposition and Notes.* The New International Commentary on the New Testament. F. F. Bruce, ed. Grand Rapids, MI: Eerdmans.

Lasch, Christopher
1978   *The Culture of Narcissism: American Life in an Age of Diminishing Expectations.* New York: Norton.

Lash, Scott, and John Urry
1994   *Economies of Signs and Space.* London: Sage. Quoted in Castells, *The Power of Identity.* Pp. 125–26.

Latourette, Kenneth Scott
1975   *A History of Christianity,* vol. 1: *Beginnings to 1500.* New York: Harper & Row.

Le Goff, Jacques
1980   *Time, Work, and Culture in the Middle Ages.* Arthur Goldhammer, trans. Chicago: University of Chicago Press.

Lears, T. J. Jackson
1981   *No Place of Grace: Antimodernism and the Transformation of American Culture, 1880–1920.* New York: Pantheon.

Leclercq, Jean
1981   "Preface." In *Evagrius Ponticus: The Practicos and Chapters on Prayer.* Pp.vii–xii. Cistercian Studies Series, 4. Kalamazoo, MI: Cisterian.
1985   "Monasticism and Asceticism II: Western Christianity." In *Christian Spirituality: Origins to the Twelfth Century.* Jill Raitt, Bernard McGinn, and John Meyendorff, eds. Pp. 113–31. World Spirituality: An Encyclopedic History of the Religious Quest, 16. New York: Crossroad.

Lee, Jerry W.
1994   Personal conversation with author. Loma Linda, CA: Loma Linda University. December.
1995a   *Next Generation Project Study: Report on Initial Survey.* Report on initial survey conducted for the Southeastern California Conference of Seventh-Day Adventists and The Leadership Institute. Loma Linda, CA. January 3.
1995b   Memorandum sent to author as fax transmission, with two charts illustrating the joint association of reading the Bible and meeting alone with God with witnessing and acts of mercy. February 9.
1996   *The Next Generation Project: Comparison of Year 1 and Year 2.* Report on second survey conducted for the Southeastern California Conference of Seventh-Day Adventists and The Leadership Institute. Loma Linda, CA. June 21.
1997   Letter to author. October 22.
        N.d. Phone conversation with author.
2001   *Research Methods: A Syllabus for SHCJ 534.* Loma Linda University, School of Public Health.

2002   Personal conversation with author. Loma Linda, CA. June.
2006   "Comparisons of different age groups." Document sent to author as e-mail attachment, reporting on new correlations computed on Adventist sample. November 13.
2007   E-mail to author. October 14.

Lee, Jerry W., Gail T. Rice, and V. Bailey Gillespie
1997   "Family Worship Patterns and the Correlation with Adolescent Behavior and Beliefs." *Journal for the Scientific Study of Religion* (36) 3: 372–81.

Levine, Robert
1997   *A Geography of Time: The Temporal Misadventures of a Social Psychologist, or How Every Culture Keeps Time Just a Little Bit Differently.* New York: Basic Books.

Lilburne, Geoffrey R.
1989   *A Sense of Place: A Christian Theology of the Land.* Nashville: Abingdon.

Lilly Endowment
2002   "Lilly Endowment invests $25.3 million to expand theological school programs for young people." News release, June 20. Online: http://www.lillyendowment.org/pdf/TheologicalExofVoc2002Winners.youngpeople.pdf.
2006   "Theological School Program for High School Youth." Online: http://www.lillyendowment.org/religion_tpfhsy.html.

Lingenfelter, Sherwood
2000   Personal conversation with author. Pasadena, CA. August 29.

Longenecker, Richard N.
1981   *Acts.* Vol. 9 of *The Expositor's Bible Commentary.* Frank E. Gaebelein, ed. Grand Rapids, MI: Zondervan.

Lonsdale, David
2000   *Eyes to See, Ears to Hear: An Introduction to Ignatian Spirituality.* Rev. ed. Traditions of Christian Spirituality. Maryknoll, NY: Orbis.

Lovelace, Richard
1975   *The Dynamics of Spiritual Life.* Downers Grove, IL: InterVarsity.

Luzbetak, Louis J.
1995   *The Church and Cultures: New Perspectives in Missiological Anthropology.* Maryknoll, NY: Orbis.

MacIntyre, Alasdair
1984   *After Virtue: A Study in Moral Theory.* Notre Dame: University of Notre Dame Press.

Macquarrie, John
2000   "Spirit and Spirituality." In *Exploring Christian Spirituality: An Ecumenical Reader*. Kenneth J. Collins, ed. Pp. 63–73. Grand Rapids, MI: Baker.

Mahedy, William, and Janet Bernardi
1994   *A Generation Alone: Xers Making a Place in the World*. Downers Grove, IL: InterVarsity.

Maier, Paul L., trans.
1999   *Eusebius—The Church History: A New Translation and Commentary*. Grand Rapids, MI: Kregel.

Mallery, Lynn
1990.   Unpublished presentation. Riverside, CA.

Marsden, George M.
2003   *Jonathan Edwards: A Life*. New Haven, CT: Yale University Press.

Marshall, I. Howard
1980   *The Acts of the Apostles*. The Tyndale New Testament Commentaries. Grand Rapids, MI: Eerdmans.

Martyrdom of Polycarp
        In Holmes, *Apostolic Fathers*. Pp. 222–45.

McCue, James F.
1997   "Liturgy and Eucharist II: West." In *Christian Spirituality: High Middle Ages and Reformation*. Jill Raitt, Bernard McGinn, and John Meyendorff, eds. Pp. 427–38. World Spirituality: An Encyclopedic History of the Religious Quest, 17. New York: Crossroad.

McGinn, Bernard
1993   "The Letter and the Spirit: Spirituality as an Academic Discipline." *Christian Spirituality Bulletin* 1 (2): 1–10.

McGrath, Alister
1988a   *Justification by Faith: What It Means for Us Today*. Basingstoke, UK: Pickering.
1988b   *The Mystery of the Cross*. Grand Rapids, MI: Zondervan.
1999   *Christian Spirituality: An Introduction*. Oxford: Blackwell.

McGuckin, John A.
2001   "The Early Church Fathers (1st to 6th Centuries)." In *The Story of Christian Spirituality: Two Thousand Years, from East to West*. Gordon Mursell, gen. ed. Pp. 31–72. Minneapolis: Fortress.

McIntire, C. T.
1978   "The Great Schism." In *The New International Dictionary of the Christian Church*. J. D. Douglas, ed. P. 429. Rev. ed. Grand Rapids, MI: Zondervan.

Meisel, Anthony C., and M. L. Del Mastro, trans.
1975   "Introduction." In *The Rule of Saint Benedict*. Pp. 9–41. New York: Doubleday.

Meredith, Anthony
1986   "Origen." In *The Study of Spirituality*. Cheslyn Jones, Geoffrey Wainwright, Edward Yarnold, eds. Pp. 115–19. New York: Oxford University Press.

Meye, Robert P.
1993   "To Grace a Debtor." *Theology News & Notes* 40 (2) 8–11.

Meyendorff, John
1987   "East and West on the Eve of Modern Times." In *Christian Spirituality: High Middle Ages and Reformation*. Jill Raitt, Bernard McGinn, and John Meyendorff, eds. Pp. 439–53. World Spirituality: An Encyclopedic History of the Religious Quest, 17. New York: Crossroad.

Middleton, J. Richard, and Brian J. Walsh
1995   *Truth Is Stranger than It Used to Be: Biblical Faith in a Postmodern Age*. Downers Grove, IL: InterVarsity.

Middleton-Stewart, Judith
2002   "Time and the Testator, 1370–1540." In *The Use and Abuse of Time in Christian History: Papers Read at the 1999 Summer Meeting and the 2000 Winter Meeting of the Ecclesiastical History Society*. R. N. Swanson, ed. Pp. 133–44. Studies in Church History, 37. Woodbridge, UK: Boydell and Brewer.

Miller, Charles, R.
2007   *The Spiritual Formation of Leaders: Integrating Spiritual Formation and Leadership Development*. Fairfax, VA: Xulon.

Miller, Donald E., and Richard W. Flory, eds.
2000   *Gen X Religion*. New York: Routledge.

Miller, Donald E., and Arpi Misha Miller
2000   "Introduction: Understanding Generation X. Values, Politics, and Religious Commitments." In *Gen X Religion*. Donald E. Miller and Richard W. Flory, eds. Pp. 1–12. New York: Routledge.

Miller, J. Keith
1991   *A Hunger for Healing: The Twelve Steps as a Classic Model for Christian Spiritual Growth*. San Francisco: HarperCollins.

Minor, Mitzi
1996   *The Spirituality of Mark: Responding to God*. Louisville: Westminster John Knox.

Miramax
2001   *Kate & Leopold*. James Mangold, director. Burbank, CA: Miramax.

Mitchell, Christopher W.
2003   "Jonathan Edwards Scottish Connection." In *Jonathan Edwards at Home and Abroad: Historical Memories, Cultural Movements, Global Horizons*. David W. Kling and Douglas A. Sweeney, eds. Pp. 222–47. Columbia: University of South Carolina Press.

Moll, Rob
2005   "The New Monasticism: A Fresh Crop of Christian Communities Is Blossoming in Blighted Urban Settings All over America." *Christianity Today*, September: 38–46.

Moreau, A. Scott
2000   "Mission and Missions." In *The Evangelical Dictionary of World Missions*. A. Scott Moreau, Harold Netland, and Charles E. van Engen, eds. Pp. 636–38. Grand Rapids, MI: Baker.

Mosbarger, Joy
2004a   "New Testament Spirituality: A Definition and Methodology." Unpublished MS.
2004b   Telephone conversation with author. December 12.

Moule, C. F. D.
1961   *Worship in the New Testament*. Ecumenical Studies in Worship, 9. London: Lutterworth.

Muto, Susan
2000   "Carthusian Spirituality." In *Catholic Spirituality from A to Z*. Pp. 35–36. Ann Arbor, MI: Servant Pub.

Myers, Ched, Marie Dennis, Joseph Nangle, Cynthia Moe-Lobeda, and Stuart Taylor
1997   *Say to This Mountain: Mark's Story of Discipleship*. Maryknoll, NY: Orbis.

Neely, Alan J.
2000   "Missiology." In *The Evangelical Dictionary of World Missions*. A. Scott Moreau, Harold Netland, and Charles E. van Engen, eds. Pp. 633–35. Grand Rapids, MI: Baker.

Neill, Stephen
1986 *A History of Christian Missions*. Rev. ed. The Penguin History of the Church, 6. London: Penguin.Newbigin, Leslie
1989 *The Gospel in a Pluralistic Society*. Grand Rapids, MI: Eerdmans.

Nixon, R. E.
1978 "Pentecost." In *The New International Dictionary of the Christian Church*. J. D. Douglas, ed. P. 763. Rev. ed. Grand Rapids, MI: Zondervan.

Noll, Mark A.
2000 *Turning Points: Decisive Moments in the History of Christianity*. Grand Rapids, MI: Baker Academic.

Noonan, David
2001 "Stop Stressing Me." *Newsweek* 137 (5): 54–55.

Norris, Norris
2000 "Origen." In *The Early Christian World*. Philip F. Esler, ed. Vol. 2, pp. 1005–26. New York: Routledge.

Nouwen, Henri J. M.
1986 *Lifesigns: Intimacy, Fecundity, and Ecstasy in Christian Perspective*. New York: Image Books.
1993a "Being the Beloved." *Robert Schuller with the Hour of Power*. Episode 1177. Garden Grove, CA: The Crystal Cathedral.
1993b "The Disciplines of the Beloved." *Robert Schuller with the Hour of Power*. Episode 1179. Garden Grove, CA: Hour of Power.

Nouwen, Henri J. M., Michael J. Christensen, and Rebecca Laird
2006 *Spiritual Direction: Wisdom for the Long Walk of Faith*. San Francisco: Harper.

Obermann, Heiko A
1988 "Preface." In *Devotio Moderna: Basic Writings*. John Van Engen, trans. Pp. 1–3. The Classics of Western Spirituality. New York: Paulist.

Oldenburg, Ray
1997 *The Great Good Place*. New York: Marlowe.

O'Malley, John W.
1993 *The First Jesuits*. Cambridge: Harvard University Press.

O'Meara, John J., trans.
1954 "Introduction" and "Notes." In *Prayer. Exhortation to Martyrdom*. Pp. 3–14, 199–240. Ancient Christian Writers: The Works of the Fathers in Translation, 19. New York: Newman.

Origen
1954a   Prayer. In *Prayer. Exhortation to Martyrdom*. John J. O'Meara, trans. Pp. 15–140. Ancient Christian Writers: The Works of the Fathers in Translation 19. New York: Newman.
1954b   Exhortation to Martyrdom. In *Prayer. Exhortation to Martyrdom*. John J. O'Meara, trans. Pp. 141–98. Ancient Christian Writers: The Works of the Fathers in Translation 19. New York: Newman.

Pagitt, Doug
2004   *Reimagining Spiritual Formation: A Week in the Life of an Experimental Church*. Grand Rapids, MI: Zondervan.

Parks, Sharon Daloz
2000   *Big Questions, Worthy Dreams: Mentoring Young Adults in Their Search for Meaning, Purpose, and Faith*. San Francisco: Jossey-Bass.

Payne, Leanne
1989   *The Healing Presence: How God's Grace Can Work in You to Bring Healing in Your Broken Places and the Joy of Living in His Love*. Westchester, IL: Good News.

Peace, Richard V.
1998a   *Contemplative Bible Reading: Experiencing God through Scripture*. Colorado Springs, CO: NavPress.
1998b   *Spiritual Autobiography: Discovering and Sharing Your Spiritual Story*. Colorado Springs, CO: NavPress.
1998c   *Meditative Prayer: Entering God's Presence*. Colorado Springs, CO: NavPress.
1999   *Conversion in the New Testament: Paul and the Twelve*. Grand Rapids, MI: Eerdmans.
2002   Personal conversation with author. Pasadena, CA. February 19.
2004   "Evangelism and Spiritual Formation." *Theology News & Notes* 51 (3): 10–12, 23.
2006a   Personal conversation with author. Pasadena, CA. January.
2006b   *Holy Conversations: Talking about God in Everyday Life*. Downers Grove, IL: InterVarsity.

Peterson, Eugene H.
1980   *A Long Obedience in the Same Direction: Discipleship in an Instant Society*. Downers Grove, IL: InterVarsity.
1987   *Working the Angles: The Shape of Pastoral Integrity*. Grand Rapids, MI: Eerdmans.
1989   *The Contemplative Pastor: Returning to the Art of Spiritual Direction*. The Leadership Library, 17. Carol Stream, IL: Christianity Today.

1992 *Under the Unpredictable Plant: An Exploration in Vocational Holiness.* Grand Rapids, MI: Eerdmans.
2002 "Saint Mark: The Basic Text for Christian Spirituality." In *Exploring Christian Spirituality: An Ecumenical Reader.* Kenneth J. Collins, ed. Pp. 327–38. Grand Rapids, MI: Baker.
2005 *Christ Plays in Ten Thousand Places: A Conversation in Spiritual Theology.* Grand Rapids, MI: Eerdmans.

Pierson, Paul E.
1998 "Historical Development of the Christian Movement." MH520 course syllabus. Fuller Theological Seminary, School of World Mission.

Piggin, Stuart
2003 "The Expanding Knowledge of God: Jonathan Edwards's Influence on Missionary Thinking and Promotion." In *Jonathan Edwards at Home and Abroad: Historical Memories, Cultural Movements, Global Horizons.* Pp. 266–96. David W. Kling and Douglas A. Sweeney, eds. Columbia: University of South Carolina Press.

Plantinga, Cornelius Jr.
1995 *Not the Way It's Supposed to Be: A Breviary of Sin.* Grand Rapids, MI: Eerdmans.

Pohl, Christine D.
1999 *Making Room: Recovering Hospitality as a Christian Tradition.* Grand Rapids, MI: Eerdmans.

Porterfield, Amanda
1997 *Mary Lyon and the Mount Holyoke Missionaries.* Religion in America Series. Oxford: Oxford University Press.

Post, Regnerus, R.
1968 *The Modern Devotion: Confrontation with Reformation and Humanism, Studies in Medieval and Reformation Thought.* Heiko A. Oberman, ed. Studies in Medieval and Reformation Traditions, 3. Leiden: Brill.

Principe, Walter H.
1983 "Toward Defining Spirituality." *Studies in Religion* 12 (2): 127–41.

Putnam, Robert D.
2000 *Bowling Alone: The Collapse and Revival of American Community.* New York: Simon & Schuster.
2002 *Bowling Alone* Web site. Online: http://www.bowlingalone.com.

Quindlen, Anna
2002   "Doing Nothing Is Something: The Overscheduled Children of 21st Century America, Deprived of the Gift of Boredom." *Newsweek* 139 (19): 76.

Radewijns, Florentius
1988   "On the Life and Passion of Our Lord Jesus Christ, and Other Devotional Exercises." In *Devotio Moderna: Basic Writings*. John Van Engen, trans. Pp. 187–204. The Classics of Western Spirituality. New York: Paulist.

Reid, Barbara E.
1994   "Prayer and the Face of the Transfigured Jesus." In *The Lord's Prayer and Other Prayer Texts from the Greco-Roman Era*. James H. Charlesworth, Mark Harding, and Mark Kiley, eds. Pp. 39–53. Valley Forge, PA: Trinity.

Reilly, Michael Collins
1978   *Spirituality for Mission: Historical, Theological, and Cultural Factors for a Present-Day Missionary Spirituality*. Maryknoll, NY: Orbis.

Richardson, Don
1975   *Peace Child: An Unforgettable Story of Primitive Jungle Treachery in the 20th Century*. Ventura, CA: Regal.
2000   "Redemptive Analogies." In *The Evangelical Dictionary of World Missions*. A. Scott Moreau, Harold Netland, and Charles E. van Engen, eds. Pp. 812–23. Grand Rapids, MI: Baker.

Richardson, Rick
2001   "Evangelism Outside of the Box: An Interview with Rick Richardson." *The Ivy Jungle Report* 8 (Spring): 1–2, 16–19.

Ritterman, Michele
1995   "Stopping the Clock: Can Therapy Still Be an Oasis in a Time-Obsessed World?" *Family Therapy Networker*, January–February: 45–51.

Robert, Dana L.
1996   *American Women in Mission: A Social History of Their Thought and Practice*. Macon, GA: Mercer University Press.

Robinson, John P., and Geoffrey Godbey
1999   *Time for Life: The Surprising Ways Americans Use Their Time*. University Park: Pennsylvania State University Press.

Rolheiser, Ronald
1999   *The Holy Longing: The Search for a Christian Spirituality*. New York: Doubleday.

Rosenfeld, Alvin, and Nicole Wise, with Robert Coles
2001   *The Over-Scheduled Child: Avoiding the Hyper-Parenting Trap.* New York: St. Martin's.

Sack, Robert D.
1988   "The Consumer's World: Place as Context." *Annals of the Association of American Geographers* 78 (4): 642–64.

Schaef, Anne Wilson, and Diane Fassel
1990   *The Addictive Organization: Why We Overwork, Cover Up, Pick up the Pieces, Please the Boss, and Perpetuate Sick Organizations.* San Francisco: Harper-Collins.

Schaupp, Doug
2000   "Introduction to Modern/Postmodern Culture." Notes for MP520 class presentation. Fuller Theological Seminary, School of World Mission.
2001   "Spirituality and Discipleship in College and Young Adult Settings." CF554 class presentation. Fuller Theological Seminary, School of Theology.

Scheepsma, Wybren
1995   "'For Hereby I Hope to Rouse Some to Piety': Books of Sisters from Covenants and Sister-Houses Associated with the *Devotio Moderna* in the Low Countries." In *Women, the Book and the Godly Selected Proceedings of the St. Hilda's Conference, 1993.* Lesley Smith and Jane H. M. Taylor, eds. Vol. 1. Cambridge, UK: Brewer.

Schein, Edgar H.
2004   *Organizational Culture and Leadership.* San Francisco: Jossey-Bass.

Schier, Tracy
2001   "Don Richter on the Spiritual Formation of Young People." Interview with Don Richter, Resources for American Christianity Web site, June 14. Online: http://www.resourcingchristianity.org/Interview.aspx?ID=92.

Schneiders, Sandra M.
1986   "Theology and Spirituality: Strangers, Rivals, or Partners." *Horizons* 13 (2): 253–74.
1995   "Spirituality as an Academic Experience: Reflections from Experience." In *Broken and Whole: Essays on Religion and the Body.* Maureen A. Tilley and Susan A. Ross, eds. Pp. 208–18. The Annual Publication of the College Theology Society, 39: Lanham, MD: University Press of America.
2000   "Spirituality in the Academy." In *Exploring Christian Spirituality: An Ecumenical Reader,* Kenneth J. Collings, ed. Pp. 249–69. Grand Rapids, MI: Baker.

Schor, Juliet B.
1992   *The Overworked American: The Unexpected Decline of Leisure*. New York: Basic Books.

Schuman, Howard and Jacqueline Scott
1989   "Generations and Collective Memories." *American Sociological Review* 54 (3): 359–81.

Sennett, Richard
1998   *The Corrosion of Character: The Consequences of Work in the New Capitalism*. London: Norton.

Shank, David A.
1980   Review of *Spirituality for Mission: Historical, Theological, and Cultural Factors for a Present-Day Missionary Spirituality*. *International Review of Mission* 69 (274): 231–33.

Sheldrake, Philip
1992   *Spirituality and History: Questions of Interpretation and Method*. New York: Crossway.
2007   *A Brief History of Spirituality*. Malden, MA: Blackwell Publishing.

Shenk, Wilbert R.
1995a   *Write the Vision: The Church Renewed*. Harrisburg, PA: Trinity.
1995b   "Forward." In *Believing in the Future: Toward a Missiology of Western Culture*. By David J. Bosch. Pp. ix–x. Valley Forge, PA: Trinity.
2000   "Introduction to Modern/Postmodern Culture." MP 520 class lectures. Fuller Theological Seminary, School of World Mission.
2003   Personal conversation with author. Pasadena, CA.
2006   Telephone conversation with author. November 17.
2008   E-mail to author. January 1.

Silf, Margaret
1998   *Inner Compass: An Invitation to Ignatian Spirituality*. Chicago: Loyola.

Smith, Christian, and Melinda Lundquist Denton
2005   *Soul Searching: The Religious and Spiritual Lives of American Teenagers*. New York: Oxford University Press.

Stafford, Tim
1991   "The Hidden Gospel of the Twelve Steps: Understanding the Origins of the Recovery Movement Can Help Christians Know How to Relate to It Today." *Christianity Today*, July 22: 14–19.

Stanley, David M.
1980   *Jesus in Gethsemane: The Early Church Reflects on the Suffering of Jesus*. New York: Paulist.

Steinsaltz, Adin
2000 *A Guide to Jewish Prayer*. New York: Schocken.

Stewart, R. A.
1982 "Passover." In *New Bible Dictionary*. Pp. 881–83. 2nd ed. Wheaton, IL: Tyndale.Stewart-Sykes, Alistair, trans.
2004 [Tertullian, Cyprian, Origen] *On The Lord's Prayer*. Popular Patristics Series. Crestwood, NY: St. Vladimir's Seminary Press.

Stone, Michael
N.d. "Addiction Disease." Unpublished MS. Tustin, CA.

Strand, Kenneth A.
1969 "The Brethren of the Common Life: A Review Article of R. R. Posts's *The Modern Devotion*." *Andrews University Seminary Studies* 7: 65–76.
1984 "Highlights of the Academic Career of William M. Landeen." *Andrews University Seminary Studies* 22 (1): 97.

Stricken, Salome
1988 "Salome Sticken: A Way of Life for Sisters." In *Devotio Moderna: Basic Writings*. John Van Engen, trans. Pp. 176–86. The Classics of Western Spirituality. New York: Paulist.

Strommen, Merton, Karen E. Jones, and Dave Rahn
2001 *Youth Ministry that Transforms: A Comprehensive Analysis of the Hopes, Frustrations, and Effectiveness of Today's Youth Workers*. Grand Rapids, MI: Zondervan.

Suedfeld, Peter
1980 *Restricted Environmental Stimulation: Research and Clinical Applications*. New York: Wiley.

Sweeney, Jon M., ed.
2001 *God Within: Our Spiritual Future—As Told by Today's New Adults*. Woodstock, VT: SkyLight Paths.

Talbert, Charles H.
1982 "The Way of the Lukan Jesus: Dimensions of Lukan Spirituality." *Perspectives in Religious Studies* 9 (3): 237–49.

Tetlow, Joseph A.
1992 *Ignatius Loyola: Spiritual Exercises*. The Crossroad Spiritual Legacy Series. New York: Crossroad

Thatcher, Adrian
1993 "Spirituality without Inwardness." *Scottish Journal of Theology* 46 (2): 213–28.

Thomas, Gary
2000 *Sacred Marriage: What if God Designed Marriage to Make Us Holy More than to Make Us Happy?* Grand Rapids, MI: Zondervan.

Thompson, Colin P.
(1983) 1996 "St. John of the Cross." In *A Dictionary of Christian Spirituality*. Gordon S. Wakefield, ed. P. 232. London: SCM.

Thompson, Marjorie J.
1995 *Soul Feast: An Invitation to the Christian Spiritual Life.* Louisville: Westminster John Knox.
2001 "Marjorie Thompson on Christian Spirituality." Track 8 of *Spirituality*, vol. 2 of *Cloud of Witnesses*. Audio journal on CD. Princeton Theological Seminary, Institute for Youth Ministry. Online: http://www.ptsem.edu/iym/cow/mp3/vol2/08.mp3.

Throckmorton, Burton H., Jr., ed.
1992 *Gospel Parallels: A Comparison of the Synoptic Gospels.* 5th ed. Nashville: Nelson.

Thurston, Bonnie
1993 *Spiritual Life in the Early Church: The Witness of Acts and Ephesians.* Minneapolis: Fortress.

Tickle, Phyllis
2001 *The Divine Hours: Prayers for Springtime.* New York: Doubleday.

Toffler, Alvin
1970 *Future Shock.* New York: Random House.Toffler, Alvin, and Heidi Toffler
1995 *Creating a New Civilization: The Politics of the Third Wave.* Atlanta: Turner.

Toon, A. S.
1978 "Carthusians." In *The New International Dictionary of the Christian Church*. J. D. Douglas, ed. Pp. 196–97. Rev. ed. Grand Rapids, MI: Zondervan.

Toon, Peter
1978 "Augustinan Canons" and "Augustinian Hermits (Friars)." In *The New International Dictionary of the Christian Church*. J. D. Douglas, ed. P. 88. Rev. ed. Grand Rapids, MI: Zondervan.

Torrance, Thomas F.
1969 *Space, Time, and Incarnation.* London: Oxford University Press.

Trueblood, Elton
1964   *The Humor of Christ: A Bold Challenge to the Traditional Stereotype of a Somber, Gloomy Christ.* San Francisco: Harper.

Tugwell, Simon
1984   *Ways of Imperfection: An Exploration of Christian Spirituality.* London: Darton Longman & Todd.

Ulmer, D. K., and L. Schwartzburd
1996   "Treatment of Time Pathologies." In *Heart and Mind: The Practice of Cardiac Psychology.* Robert Allan and Stephen Scheidt, eds. Pp. 329–62. Washington, DC: American Psychological Association.

Underwood, T. L.
1978   "Mendicant Orders." In *The New International Dictionary of the Christian Church.* J. D. Douglas, ed P. 649. Rev. ed. Grand Rapids, MI: Zondervan.

Van Engen, Charles Edward
1997a   "Biblical Foundations of Mission." MT520 course syllabus material. Fuller Theological Seminary, School of World Mission.
1997b   "Biblical Foundations of Mission." MT520 course packet. Fuller Theological Seminary, School of World Mission. Pp. 1–86.
1997c   Consultation on Generation X. Pasadena, CA. April.
2000a   "Theology of Mission." In *The Evangelical Dictionary of World Missions.* Scott Moreau, Harold Netland, and Charles E. van Engen, eds. Pp. 949–51. Grand Rapids, MI: Baker.
2000b   Personal conversation with author. Pasadena, CA. October.

Van Engen, John H., trans.
1988   "Introduction" and "Notes." In *Devotio Moderna: Basic Writings.* Pp. 7–61, 316–28. The Classics of Western Spirituality. New York: Paulist.

Van Riesen, Susan
1998   Personal conversation with author. Mountain Center, CA. May.

Ventura, Michael
1995   "Prisoners of Time: The Age of Interruption." *Family Therapy Networker,* January–February: 19–31.

Verkuyl, J.
1978   *Contemporary Missiology: An Introduction.* Dale Cooper, trans. and ed. Grand Rapids, MI: Eerdmans.

Wainwright, Geoffrey
1986   "Types of Spirituality." In *The Study of Spirituality.* Cheslyn Jones, Geoffrey Wainwright, and Edward Yarnold, eds. Pp. 592–605. New York: Oxford University Press.

Wakefield, Gordon S., ed.
1983   "Spirituality." In *A Dictionary of Christian Spirituality*. Pp. 361–63. London: SCM.

Wakefield, James L.
2006   *Sacred Listening: Discovering the Spiritual Exercises of Ignatius of Loyola*. Grand Rapids, MI: Baker.

Walls, Andrew F.
1996   *The Missionary Movement in Christian History: Studies in the Transmission of the Faith*. Edinburgh, UK: Orbis.

Watanabe, Teresa
2000   "The New Gospel of Academia." *Los Angeles Times*, October 18: A1, A28.

Webber, Robert E.
2003   *Ancient Future Evangelism: Making Your Church a Faith-Forming Community*. Grand Rapids, MI: Baker.

Webster's Ninth New Collegiate Dictionary
1987   Springfield, MA: Merriam-Webster.

Whitrow, G. J.
1980   *The Natural Philosophy of Time*. 2nd ed. Oxford: Clarendon.

White, Ann C.
2002   Telephone conversation with author. July 9.

Wilken, Robert Louis
2003   *The Spirit of Early Christian Thought: Seeking the Face of God*. New Haven: Yale University Press.

Willard, Dallas
1988   *The Spirit of the Disciplines: Understanding How God Changes Lives*. San Francisco: Harper & Row.
1998a   Personal conversation with author. Mountain Center, CA. May.
1998b   *The Divine Conspiracy: Rediscovering Our Hidden Life in God*. San Francisco: Harper.
2001   Personal conversation with author. Chatsworth, CA. August 15.

Williams, Eric
1996   Tribute to Josh Turville given at his memorial service. Santa Ana, CA. September.

Williams, Rowan
1980   *Christian Spirituality: A Theological History from the New Testament to Luther and St. John of the Cross*. Atlanta: John Knox.

Wilson, Jonathan R.
1998   *Living Faithfully in a Fragmented World: Lessons for the Church from MacIntyre's After Virtue*. Christian Mission and Modern Culture. Harrisburg, PA: Trinity.

Wimmer, Joseph F.
1982   *Fasting in the New Testament: A Study in Biblical Theology*. New York: Paulist.

Witherington, Ben III
2004   *The Acts of the Apostles: A Socio-Rhetorical Commentary*. Grand Rapids, MI: Eerdmans.

Wright, N. T.
1992   *The New Testament and the People of God*. Vol. 1 of *Christian Origins and the Question of God*. London: SPCK.
1996   *Jesus and the Victory of God*. Vol. 2 of *Christian Origins and the Question of God*. Minneapolis: Fortress.
1997a   *What St. Paul Really Said: Was Paul of Tarsus the Real Founder of Christianity?* Grand Rapids, MI: Eerdmans.
1997b   *A Moment of Quiet*. Colorado Springs, CO: Lion.
1998   *Reflecting the Glory: Meditations for Living Christ's Life in the World*. Minneapolis: Augsburg.
1999   *The Way of the Lord: Christian Pilgrimage Today*. London: SPCK.
2000   Telephone conversation with author. June 26.
2001   *Mark for Everyone*. London: SPCK.
2002   *Paul for Everyone: Galatians and Thessalonians*. London: SPCK.
2003   *The Resurrection of the Son of God*. Vol. 3 of *Christian Origins and the Question of God*. Minneapolis: Fortress.
2004a   *Matthew for Everyone*. Vol. 1. 2nd ed. London: SPCK.
2004b   *Matthew for Everyone*. Vol. 2. 2nd ed. London: SPCK. 2004c *John for Everyone*. Vol. 2. 2nd ed. London: SPCK.
2005   "The Challenge of Following Jesus in the 21st Century." Frank Pack Lectures delivered at Pepperdine University, Seaver College. January 9–11. Online: http://seaver.pepperdine.edu/dean/lectureseries/pages/20050111.htm.
2006   *Simply Christian: Why Christianity Makes Sense*. New York: HarperCollins.
2007   "Space, Time, and Sacraments." Seminar on the Lord's Supper and baptism, Calvin College, January 6. Online: http://www.calvin.edu/worship/idis/theology/ntwright_sacraments.php.

Wuthnow, Robert
1998   *After Heaven: Spirituality in America since the 1950s*. Berkeley: University of California Press.

Yaconelli, Mark
2001 "Mark Yaconelli on Making Space for God in Youth Ministry." Track 2 of *Spirituality*, vol. 2 of *Cloud of Witnesses*. Audio journal on CD. Princeton Theological Seminary, Institute for Youth Ministry. Online: http://www.ptsem.edu/iym/cow/mp3/vol2/02.mp3.
2006 *Contemplative Youth Ministry: Practicing the Presence of Jesus*. Grand Rapids, MI: Zondervan.

York, John V.
2001 *Missions in the Age of the Spirit*. Springfield, MO: Logion.

Zerbolt, Gerard
1988 *The Spiritual Ascents*. In *Devotio Moderna: Basic Writings*. John Van Engen, trans. Pp 243–315. The Classics of Western Spirituality. New York: Paulist.

Zoba, Wendy Murray
1999 *Generation 2K: What Parents and Others Need to Know about the Millennials*. Downers Grove, IL: InterVarsity.
2001 "The CT Review: Decoding Generations." *Christianity Today*, April 2: 83–84.

Scripture Index

Old Testament

Genesis
7:1—8:19	289

Exodus
32:19	79

Deuteronomy
6:4–5	75
6:16	91
8:3b	91

2 Kings
25:25	79

Psalm
22	81
55:17	75
69:1–2	289
80:8–9	103
91:11–12	91
113–18	81, 83
116–18	81
118:17	202
120–34	81, 83

Isaiah
5:4–6b	103
6:13	99
42:6	99
43:2	289
49:6	99
65:22	99

Jeremiah
6:16	213, 253, 255

Daniel
6:10	75
9:8	255
9:3–19	255

Zechariah
8:18–19	82
8:19	79

New Testament

Matthew
3:13–17	86
4:1–11	86
4:2	91
4:3, 7	91
4:6	91
5:48	99
5:1	86
5–7	70, 72, 73, 90, 98, 102, 106, 107, 134, 258
5:3–8	102
5:3–11	99
5:7	102
5:8	148
5:9	102
5:13	102
5:13–16	99
5:14–16	102
5:11	99
5:20	99

Matthew (cont.)

5:21–30	99, 102
5:27–42	99
5:38–48	99, 102
5:44	100, 102
6:1–18	134, 137
6:2–4	102
6:2–6	102
6:2, 5, 16	101
6:5	100, 134
6:5–6	102
6:5–7	273
6:6	100, 134
6:7	102
6:8–15	93
6:9–15	100, 102
6:9–13	134
6:16	82
6:16–18	79, 100, 102, 134
6:19–21	99, 102
6:20	134
6:33	100
6:24–34	99, 102
7:1–5	99, 102
7:7–11	100, 102
7:15–20	99, 102
7:21–22	101
7:23	101
9:2–6	77
9:38	91
10:1	93
11:28	70
14:13	86
14:22–33	86
17:1–13	86
24:13	172
26:17	80
26:17–30	86
26:36–46	88
27:46	97
28:16–18a	108, 255, 267
28:16–19	105
28:16–20	70, 86, 95, 98, 105, 107, 111
28:18–20	105, 113, 267

Mark

1:1–13	90
1:2–3	71
1:9–11	86, 87, 95
1:11–13	86, 87, 95
1:12	91
1:14–34	87, 96
1:16—4:34	96
1:35	78, 86, 88, 90, 96, 146
1:35–38	96
1:36—3:6	88
1:39	96
2:5	77
2:23–26	78
2:27	78
2:28	78
3:1–6	78
3:13–19	86, 88, 96
3:20	96
3:20—6:6	96
4:35—5:1	289
4:35—6:30	96
6:7–13	96
6:30–33	88
6:30–34	90
6:31	93, 96
6:31—8:30	96
6:32	90
6:33–44	88
6:45–52	86, 89, 90, 95
6:47–48	90
6:53–56	89
8:7	68???
8:31—10:45	96
9:2–13	86, 89, 90, 95
9:2–50	97
9:8b	93
9:14–50	89
9:34	71
10:32, 52	71

Scripture Index 347

10:46—14:1	96
12:28–31	82
12:29–31	75
14:1—15:39	96
14:12	80
14:12–26	86, 89, 90
14:32–42	78, 86, 89, 90
14:26	81, 83
14:32–42	78, 86, 89, 90
14:53—16:8	89
15:34	81, 97
16:8	89, 105
16:9–20	105

Luke

2:41	80
3:21–22	86, 119, 127, 297
4:1–13	86, 119, 127, 297
4:3, 4	91
4:10–11	91
4:14–41	119, 127, 297
4:42	86, 120, 127, 297
4:43—5:14	120
5:16	78, 83, 86, 120, 127, 298
5:17–39	120, 298
5:20	77
6:12	93, 146
6:12–19	121
6:12–17	94
7:12	78
9:1–10	121
9:22—24:51	128
9:28	78, 86, 128, 299
9:28–36	86, 128, 299
9:32	70, 93
10:1	93
10:2	91, 204, 279, 280
10:12	259
10:25–37	75
11:1	146, 299
14:16–23	203
15:3–7	204
19:1–10	77
22:8	80
22:14–39	86
22:39–46	86, 300
22:40	90
24:33–49	94
22:43	95
23:34	97, 126
23:40–43	97
23:46	97
24:36–39	86, 105
24:45–49	95
24:49	119

John

1:14	18
2:23	80
7:2–37	80
11:41–42	146
15	29, 70, 72, 73, 98, 101, 104, 106, 107, 223, 250, 257, 258, 263
15:2	103, 104
15:4	101
15:5	103
15:7	104, 104
15:7, 10	104
15:8	103
15:9	104
15:10	103
15:11	104
15:12	103, 104, 263
15:12–13	103
15:13	13
15:16	104
15:18–19	103
15:19–21	104
15:26–27	104
15:27	103, 104
17	219

Acts

1:1–2	115
1:3	113
1:4–5, 8	117

Acts (cont.)

1:6	117
1:6—2:4	117
1:7	113
1:8	113, 119
1:13–14	119
1:15	120
1:12—2:4	127
2:1–4	119
2:5–41	117, 127
2:14–42	119
2:42–47	117, 120, 127
2:47	117, 127
3:1–10	118, 127
3:6—4:23	118, 127
4:24–30	115, 121
4:24–32	118, 127
4:33	118
6:7	127
7:60	126
8:26–39	122
9:1–19	123, 124, 128
9:9–22	124
9:15	125
9:20—16:40	128
10:2–3, 9	124
10:1–23	123, 128
12:1–19	123
12:24	123
13:1–3	123, 127
13:4–5	123
13:14–41	122
14:21–28	121, 123
14:25	123
14:26	123
14:44–52	122
15	126
15:35	124
16:6–34	124
16:11–15	122, 217
16:11–34	124
16:13–15	122
17:1–9	122
18:1–6	122
18:9	124
18:11	124
20:3, 5–6	119
20:6	119
20:16	119, 120
22:22	125
24	117
24:24–27	122
27:9–44	122
28	117
28:1–15	122
28:16–31	122

Romans

8:21	113
8:37–38	144
8:39	251
12:2	18

1 Corinthians

9:19–26	18
12	219

2 Corinthians

4:10	20

Galatians

1:17	125, 128
5:22–23	162
3:28	228
6:1, 2	282

Ephesians

1:10	114
3:17	22
4:22	58, 114
4:22–24	114
6:12	58

Philippians

2:10–11	113

Colossians

2:8, 14–15, 20	22

James

5:15	282

1 Peter

2:9	18

1 John

4:13	173
4:16–18	144
4:19	173
5:11–13	144

Index

abandoned, 45, 50–52, 212, 222, 236, 246, 251, 267, 268
Abraham, 75, 77
absentee parents, 50
absolution, 77, 82, 93
Adams, Henry B., 60
Adato, Allison, 234
addiction, 13, 55–59, 64, 65, 184, 222, 225, 269
   denial, 57, 58, 115
   disease, 32, 56, 58, 62, 64–66, 269
   organizational, 58, 129, 155, 212, 267, 268, 270, 272, 278
   sexual, 56, 225
   stages of, 58, 126, 163, 177, 193
   theological treatment of, 56
Adventist research sample, 247, 249, 250
   faith maturity of Generations X compared with Millennials, 248
   spiritual practice correlated to mission, 247, 248
   church and group climate, 250, 251
   volunteer leaders compared to followers, volunteer leadership logjam, 249
Alexander the Great, 72
Alexandria in Egypt, 112, 130, 140, 144, 146
Alexandrian Catechetical School, 148
Allen, Diogenes, 5, 148, 155
Allen, Tom, 238
Allport, Gordon W., 245
altruism, 47
American Bowling Congress, 46
American Heart Association, 68
Amezaga, Louis D., Jr., 128
amidah, 76
Amsterdam, 160
Anabaptists, 158
Anderson, Wayne, 290
Andover Newton Theological Seminary, 239
Andrews University, 218, 247
Andrews University Theological Seminary, 218
annihilation of time, 2
Antioch, 112, 121, 123, 124, 127, 135, 141, 151, 242, 266
Antony, St., 27, 90, 148, 149
apostle John, 173
apostolic fathers, 27, 30, 112, 131, 134, 139–41, 143–47, 151, 152, 258, 260, 265, 266, 273
apostolic order, 186, 195
Arabia, 125, 128
Arius, 34, 149
Asami, Shin, 116
ascetic theology, 148
askesis, 7, 293
Associated Mennonite Biblical Seminary, 239
assurance, 144, 146, 172–74, 185, 206, 208
Athanasius, 130, 149
attendance, North American decline in
   church, 48, 51

club, 46, 47
Augustine, 108, 258, 301
Augustinian Canons Regular, 157
Augustinian Hermits, 157
authority
  under civil, not religious law, *Devotio Moderna*, 159, 161. *See also* middle way.
  Xers' trust of figures in, 223
  Jesuit submission to, 195, 195
  of elders, deacons, and bishops increased from 90–155 CE, 129
  of Jesus, 11, 82, 87, 88, 91, 119, 122, 260, 266
  of Roman empire being subverted, 148, 152
  prayer of, 96
  positions in Worldcom and Enron
    those in them with little time for ethical reflection, 68
Azusa Pacific University, 239

Baby Boomers, 3, 42, 50–52, 216, 222, 226, 228, 243
Ball, Jon, 238, 244
Bamberger, John Eudes, 150
Banks, Julia, 120
Banks, Robert, 120
baptism, practice of, 84, 86, 87, 91, 92, 95, 114, 119, 120, 122, 136, 142, 145, 265, 273, 297
baptism of the Spirit, 119
Barbour, Julian, 31
Barnabas, The Epistle of, 130, 139, 140, 142
Barta, Karen A., 84
Barth, Karl, 11, 105
Bassano, 185
Bauman, Zygmunt, 2, 3, 39, 42, 44, 54, 57, 268, 288

liquid modernity, 3, 42, 268, 288, 290
nomadic habits, 44, 209
solid state of modernity, 44
Bayne, David, 227
Beatitudes, 99
Beattie, Melody, 57
Beaudoin, Tom, 42, 215, 216, 224, 289
Bede, 173
be-ing (a spiritual formation organization based in San Diego), 279
Benedict of Nursia, 150
Benedictine monasticism, 150
berakah, 76
Berger, Peter, 226
Bernardi, Janet, 13, 215, 223, 226
Beschi, Constantine Josephus, 196
Bessenecker, Scott, 230, 254
Bockmuehl, Markus, 72, 75, 81, 97, 103
body of Christ, 261, 272, 279
Boman, Thorleif, 32, 33
Bond, James T., 55
Bonhoeffer, Dietrich, 240
Boniface, 26
Borg, Marcus, 74, 84
Bosch, David J., 15, 19, 23, 105, 282
Boston, Massachusetts, 66
Bouyer, Louis, 71
Bradley, James, 1, 28, 36, 144, 145, 198, 238
Bradshaw, Paul F., 119, 139, 141
Brainerd, David, 28, 154, 197–207, 209–12, 252, 255, 261, 263–66, 280
Brandon, S. G. F., 74
Brazil, 186, 187
Brooks, David, 52, 234
Brown, Colin, 36, 103
Brueggemann, Walter, 35
Buffalo, New York, 39
Bunge, Gabriel, 112

busyness and stress, 64, 98, 224, 236, 243, 265
Caesar, 133, 145, 266
Calimesa Adventist Church, 290
call of Jesus' twelve apostles, 94
Calvin, John, 157, 158, 239
　Institutes of, 158
Calvin Theological Seminary, 239
Campbell, Jonathan, 14, 16
Campus Crusade for Christ, 222
Capernaum, 87, 96, 297
capital accumulation, 43
capitalism, 42, 43, 67
cardinal virtues, 110, 148, 301
Cardoner River, 179
Carey, William, 26, 28, 105, 210
Carroll, Colleen, 215, 221, 236
Carson, D. A., 105
Carthusians, 155
Cassian, St. John, 150, 206, 264
Cassidy, Jean, 56, 57
Cassidy, Scotty, 56, 59
Castells, Manuel, 2, 3, 42, 49, 52–54, 268, 282, 289
Catherall, Gordon, A., 194, 197
Catholic missiology, 19
Catholic Reformation, 30, 158, 194
causal relationships between variables, 244, 245
Celtic monasticism, 26
Celtic orders, 254
cenobitic tradition of spirituality, 90, 152, 260, 264, 274
Center for Religion and Civic Culture, USC, 214
centralization of power and authority from 10th–14th centuries, 155
Chadwick, Henry, 148
Chan, Simon, 12, 182, 221, 264, 291
Character Counts curriculum, 68
Charlesworth, James H., 68, 72, 74–76, 80, 81
Childers, Jana, 240

Chilton, Bruce, 32, 33, 74, 79, 84, 120, 220
China, 266
Chittister, Joan, 56
Christian mission, 19–21, 23, 24
　Orthodox focus on the glory of God and the sacraments as mission, 19
　post Vatican II Roman Catholic perspecive on, 19
　Reformed perspective on, 20
Christian spirituality, 10–12, 21, 27, 71, 84, 114, 139, 236, 251, 272, 277, 279, 291, 292
Christology, 34
chronos, 114
church climate
　measurement and importance of, 246, 250
CIA, 68
circumcision, 77, 124
Cisterian order (Trappists), 155
Claiborne, Shane, 254
Clapham Sect, 265
Claremont, 239
Clark, Chap, 215, 234–37, 242, 245,
Clebsch, William A., 149
Clement of Alexandria, 130, 144, 310
Clement of Rome, 131, 136, 143
Clinton, J. Robert, 230, 278
Cluny, the monastery at, 155
co-dependency, 57
coffee shops, 45, 268
Coles, Robert, 52
Collett, Barry, 38
Collins, Kenneth J., 10, 71
colloquies, 169, 171
co-mingling, 155
commercialization of time, 41
compression of space-time, 2, 4, 14, 41–43, 49, 53, 252, 257, 268
computerization, 43

concubinage, 160, 188, 266
Conforti, Joseph A., 198
Connecticut, 198, 201
conquest of land promised to
    Abraham, 77
Constantine, Emperor of Rome, 26,
    72, 155
Constantinople, 148, 156
container notion of space, 34
contemplation
    infused, 189, 304
    Greek, 147
contemplative life
    vision of God, 148
contextualization, 195, 196
conversion, 23, 85, 96, 122, 123,
    127, 159, 163, 166, 173, 177,
    178, 199, 200, 202, 206, 217
Corinth, 124, 128, 129
Cornelius, 119, 123, 124
Corpus Christi College, Oxford
    University, 38
Crouch, Andy, 13, 224, 225
counter-temple movement, 77, 90
Countryman, L. William, 124
Cousins, Ewert, 156
Cowan, Clyde, 203
Cox, Harvey, 35, 214
critique of capitalism, 43, 67
cross, 81, 84, 89, 93, 95, 97, 142,
    167, 170, 183, 206, 224, 225,
    232, 255, 273, 300
Crossweeksung, 198, 202, 205, 206
crucifixion of Jesus, 128
Crump, David, 116
Crusades, 155
Cullman, Oscar, 20, 33
Curtis, Brent, 2
customaries for houses of the
    Devotio Moderna,163, 168,
    171

Damascus in Syria, 85, 119, 123–25
dark night of the soul, 224

Davies, W. D., 35
Davis, Kenneth Ronald, 158
Day of Atonement, 79, 80, 83
de Dalmases, Candido, 177
de Foucauld, Charles, 26
de Nobili, Robert, 196
de Voragine, Jacobus, 178
Dean, Kenda Creasy, 7–9, 215, 241,
    242, 261
Dedinger, Jerry, 222
Denney, Jim, 216, 224
Denton, Melinda Lundquist, 237,
    238
desacrelized space, 35
desert fathers and mothers,
    148–50, 154, 264
devaluation of the body, 146
Deventer, 159–61, 166
Diaspora, Jewish, 120
didache, the 82, 96, 129, 130, 133,
    134, 137, 139, 142
didaskale (teacher), 96
Dieburg, Peter, 173
diocese of Utrecht, 160
discernment
    questions for, 256
Disciples of Christ, 247
disciplines, spiritual
    celebration, 33, 79, 120, 121
    celibacy, 154, 166
    confession, 56, 69, 74, 121, 139,
        140, 142, 169, 170, 173, 178,
        183, 192, 193, 195, 202, 207,
        222, 255, 269, 282, 302, 304,
        305
    journaling, 178, 194, 202, 217,
        275, 304
    pilgrimage, 79–81, 126, 127,
        178, 179, 185, 195, 218, 275
    praying the Psalms 6, 94
    recollected prayer, 93, 202, 207
    sacrifice, 78, 94, 97, 123, 166
    secrecy, 100, 102, 106, 166
    simplicity, 8, 120, 156, 166, 178

disciplines, spiritual (cont.),
    small groups, 46, 47, 76, 117,
        167, 170, 171, 207, 209, 217,
        228, 269, 281
    spiritual reading, 166, 167, 202,
        207, 278
    study, 76, 94, 148, 170, 181, 191,
        192, 207, 208, 253, 264, 273
    submission, 168, 172, 191, 194,
        249, 305
    watching, 89, 90, 93, 123
disciplines of the Beloved, 94
discursive meditation, 148
disease
    addiction as a disease of the
        feelings, 56
    coronary artery, 62
    heart disease, 32, 64, 269
disorders
    multiple personality, 223
    post traumatic stress, 222
distorted images of God, 150
diversity
    ethnic and gender, 228
divorce, 99, 222, 236
Dixon, Junkin, E., 24
Doherty, Robert, 84, 100, 104, 279, 284
Dominicans, 156, 161
Donahue, Michael J., 246
Donin, Hayim Halevy, 33, 75
Doohan, Leonard, 116
Dowd, Sharyn E., 101
Dreyer, Elizabeth, 224
Dudley, Roger L., 247
Dunn, Richard D., 215, 241, 242
Dupre, Louis, 199
Dybdahl, Jon L., 217, 281
dying well, 171, 172, 207

Easter, 94, 105, 114, 119, 120, 169
Eastern mysticism, 272
Edict of Toleration, 148
Edwards, Jerusha, 207

Edwards, Jonathan, 28, 154, 197, 207
Egypt, 77, 129, 133
Eighteen Benedictions, 75, 76, 82, 120
Eldredge, John, 2
Elijah, 89, 93, 95, 108, 125, 128, 299
emergent church leaders, 227
    Doug Pagitt, 227
    Dan Kimball, 227
Emory University, 239
emotional burnout, 57
emphasis on the heart, 203
empty tomb, 105
Enlightenment, 2, 23, 228, 272
    rationalism, 2, 155
entertaining in homes
    decline in North America, 46, 48
environment, 35, 212, 277, 282
environmentalism, 54
    grassroots, 54
    movement, 54, 268
eremitic tradition of spirituality, 30, 90, 152, 155, 159, 163, 170, 179, 211, 212, 260, 264, 270
Erkel, R. Todd, 61
eschatological
    focus of mission, 20
    focus of early Christian spirituality, 113
    imagination, 113
    kingdom, 113
eschaton, 114
Eucharist, 8, 81, 83, 142, 149 166, 170, 171, 183, 265, 300, 302.
    See also Lord's Supper.
Euclid, 32
Eusebius, 130, 147
euthyos, 91
Evagrius Ponticus, 150
evangelical activism
    recent growth of, 47, 54
Evangelical Lutheran, 247

evangelism, 23–25, 85, 96, 139, 140, 143, 161, 217, 232, 242, 243, 272, 281, 306
  process of, 85, 96
Evans, Craig A., 79
Exercises of Ignatius of Loyola and the Twelve Steps, 184
Exodus, 33, 75, 77
exorcism, 96, 101
experience and mystery, 217
extrinsic motivation, 246, 249
  personal comfort, 246
  social comfort, 246

faceless experts, 68
factory, 3, 39, 40
  routinization of factory work, 3
Fadling, Alan J., 223
faith maturity, 25, 213, 244, 245, 248, 250, 251, 256
fall of Jerusalem, 105
false gods, 239
Families and Work Institute, 52
Far East, 174, 180
Fassel, Diane, 55
faster pace
  higher coronary death rates, 62
Faulkner, Barbara L., 146
fear of
  silence, 209
feast days of the Christian church, 158, 162, 165, 255, 257, 259
Felix, 117, 122
Ferdinand, King of Spain, 177
festivals in ancient Judaism
  Feast of Tabernacles, 80, 83
  Feast of Unleavened Bread, 119, 300
  Hanukkah, 80
  Passover, 80, 81, 83, 90, 97, 104, 119, 120, 128, 300
  Pentecost, 80, 83, 112, 117, 119, 120, 126, 169, 266
  Purim, 80, 83

feudalism, 154, 194
Feuerherd, Peter, 14
five pillars of Islam, 218
fixed vows in monasticism, 154, 160, 194
Fleming, David L., 177, 181
flexible timekeeping
  agricultural rhythms, 36
  seasonal changes, 32, 36
Flory, Richard W., 215, 219, 220, 221, 228, 229
Folger, Tim, 31
Ford, Kevin G., 216, 224
Foster, Richard J., 7, 8, 91, 97, 275, 293
Foster, Ron, 7–9, 241, 242
Foulkes, Francis, 114
Fourth Crusade, 156
Fox, Richard, 37, 38
fragmented selves, 223
France, 196, 196
Franciscans, 156, 157, 168, 254
fraternal correction in the *Devotio Moderna*, 169, 171
Friars, 156, 230
Funk, Mary Margaret, 150
future shock, 2
Future Workaholics of America, 52

Galilee, 24, 78, 83, 89, 93, 95–97, 105, 109, 127
Galinsky, Ellen, 55
Gangites River, 122
Ganss, George E., 158, 176–79, 181, 184–87, 189, 190, 192–94, 304
Garden of Gethsemane, 78, 90, 97
Gardner, Christine J., 56
Geiler, Johann, 290
Generation X traits, 50, 51, 216–33, 251–53
Generation Y traits, 50, 51, 234–39, 251–53
generational change, 49

Gentile mission, 123, 128
George, Timothy, 210
Gese Broekelants, 167
Giddens, Anthony, 2–4, 36, 42–44, 54, 68, 268
    deconstructionists, 43
    dis-embedding mechanisms, 43
    high modernity, 3, 43
    institutional analysis of modernity, 43
    radicalized modernity, 43
    reflexive appropriation knowledge, 43, 44
Gillespie, V. Bailey, 238, 247
Glasser, Arthur F., 122, 125
Global Ethics, 68
glory of the Son of God, 199
Gnosticism, 129, 141
Goa, 186, 193, 196
God-fearers, 122
golden thread of fasting, prayer, and almsgiving, 101, 106, 110, 133, 137, 140, 152, 166, 182, 207, 212, 265
Good Friday, 114
good fruit, 99, 102
good tree, 99, 102
Gorman, Julie A., 228
Gorsuch, Richard L., 245, 246
Gort, Jerald, 20
grace
    accepting grace, 12, 69, 144–46, 152, 172–74, 189, 206, 208, 261
    embracing grace, 12, 252
    empowering grace, 143, 173, 189
    initiating grace, 18
    prevenient grace, 12, 18, 173, 174, 189, 205, 208
    transforming grace, 12, 18, 143, 145, 152, 190, 206, 252, 260, 261
Great Awakening, the first, 154, 200, 211

great commandment, 82, 110, 261, 275
Great Commission, 24, 82, 105, 111, 267,
Great Schism, 156
greatest challenges in student ministry, 244
Greece, 32
Green, Lee, 68
Green, Michael, 112
Gregg, Robert C., 148
Gregory the Great, 173
Gregory of Nyssa, 150
Gross, David M., 51, 216, 222
Groote, Geert, 27, 153, 157, 159, 160, 162, 163, 166, 167, 170–72, 177, 182, 207, 211, 252, 261–67, 280
Guelich, Robert A., 223
Guinness, Os, 215
Gundry, Robert H., 84

Hagberg, Janet O., 223
Hahn, H. C., 32
Hall, Jenny, 235
Hallel, 81, 83, 202, 300
Harder, Kenneth J., 128
Harding, Mark, 72, 80
Harnack, Adolf, 147
Harrison, Everett F., 121
Harvard, 46, 49, 201, 224
Harvey, David, 2, 31, 42, 43, 53, 54, 268
Hayner, Stephen A., 229, 251
Hays, Richard B., 79, 228
hearing the Father's voice call him "The beloved"
    Jesus at his baptism, 87, 91
heart righteousness, 100
Hellenization, 147
Henning, Kathy, 238
Hermas, Shepherd of, 129–31, 136–39, 141, 143, 144, 173, 238

Herxen, Dirk, 160, 163, 167, 169, 170, 172, 173
Hesselgrave, David J., 105
Hinson, E. Glenn, 134
historical reconstruction, 72, 74, 76, 128
Hofferth, Sandra L., 51
Holmes, Michael W., 129, 131–37, 139–41, 144
Holy Spirit, the
　in definition of Christian spirituality, 10–12
　in postmodernity, 17
　in mission, 21–23
　in doctrine of *perichoresis*, 34, 35
　in Jesus's life and mission, 95, 104
　in promise of Jesus for his followers, 113
　in Polycarp's martyrdom, 133
　in John Calvin's view of sanctification as portrayed in his Institutes, 158
　in *Devotio Moderna* texts, 162, 168
　in Jonathan Edwards, 199
　in Generation X, 224, 226
　frozen out of organizations, 58, 268
　role of in asking forgiveness for abandoning the postmodern generations, 224, 225, 255
　in grace and the inbreaking of God's reign, 290
homemakers, 47
Hope Center in Kansas City, 253
Hornblower, Margot, 13, 51
House of St. Martha, 187
Howard, Philip E., 198
Howe, Neil, 13, 42, 50–52, 216, 234, 235
hurry, 2, 32, 55, 62–64, 120, 233, 254, 268
　not necessarily harmful, 65

Hurtado, Larry W., 72
Huston Foundation, 232
Houston, James, 55
Hyma, Albert, 158–61, 170
hypertext, 219
hypocrites, 100, 134

I/E scale
　age universal, 246
Iconium, 123
identity formation, 229, 232
Ignatius of Antioch, 129, 130, 135, 136, 140–44, 151, 242, 266
Ignatius of Loyola, 27, 153, 158, 169, 176, 177–80, 182–90, 193, 195–97, 199, 207, 211, 212, 218, 242, 252, 255, 258, 261–67, 280, 283, 284, 304
　exercises, 27, 176, 177, 181, 193, 218
　use of imagination, 170, 184
ImagoChristi in Denver, 279
imitation of Christ, 11, 12, 84, 100, 101, 166, 168, 261
implosion
　space-time, 3, 4, 69, 289
incarnation, 2, 24, 33–35, 141, 282
India, 22, 187, 196
Indians at Kaunaumeek, 201
indigenizing principle, 18
Industrial Revolution, 2–4, 39, 41
informal connecting activities, 46
information revolution, 3, 52, 289
inner commission, 107, 108, 266, 267
inner healing, 225, 275
inner rhythms, 94, 98, 141, 265
Inquisition, 155, 180
Institute for Social Research, 50, 65
Institute of Ethics, 68
inter-church sample, 245, 247–51
　faith maturity of Generations X compared with Millennials, 248, 249

358 Index

inter-church sample (cont.),
   spiritual practice correlated to mission, 247, 248
   church and group climate, 250, 261
   volunteer leaders compared to followers,
   volunteer leadership logjam, 249, 250
International Society for the Study of Time, 32
Internet, 42, 47, 53, 54, 56, 216, 219, 232, 268
   addictive and isolating, 42, 53, 268
   pornography, 56
   spiritual pluralism available instantaneously, 219
   virtual community, 53
InterVarsity Christian Fellowship (IVCF), 214, 218, 219, 222, 229, 238, 244, 254
intrinsic motivation, 246, 248
intrinsic-extrinsic (I/E) scale, 245
invention, 3, 39
   airplane, 40
   automobile, 40
   light bulb, 40
   radio, 40
   telegraph, 39, 40
   telephone, 40
Irenaeus, 130, 131
Italy, 187
itinerant apprenticeships, 96
Ivens, Michael, 194
Ivy Jungle Network, 243, 244

Jackson, J. B., 36, 40
Jacob, E. F., 159, 160, 170
Jefford, Clayton N., 128–34, 136, 144
Jehele, Chris, 253, 280
Jencks, Charles, 3, 153, 289
Jensen, Erin, 226
Jensen, L. Paul, 265, 272, 285
Jensen, Lyle H., 2
Jerusalem Council, 128
Jesuit missionaries, 26, 176, 177, 181, 185–87, 190, 191, 195–97, 211, 263, 264, 266, 304
Jesus
   his prayer, 81, 86, 88–91, 93, 95–97, 100, 106, 110, 240
   his reformulation of Jewish prayer, 72–78, 80–83
   his withdrawals
      early morning prayer, 86, 88, 96
      from the crowds, 70, 83, 86, 93, 98, 110, 116, 151, 258, 260, 262, 265
      Gethsemane, 76, 86, 89, 90, 93, 95, 97
      Last Supper, 81, 86, 89, 128, 300
      night in prayer, 86, 89, 90, 127, 208
      Sermon on the Mount, 29, 72, 86, 98, 100, 102, 104, 106–8, 134, 261
      taking disciples away for rest, 86
      temptation, 82, 86, 87, 91, 129, 174, 297
      Transfiguration, 86, 89, 93, 95, 97, 128, 299
      two synoptic commissions, 86
John of the Cross, 218, 224
John the Baptist, 76, 95, 149, 264
Johnson, Ben Campbell, 217
Jones, Darron, 230
Jones, Karen E., 231
Joppa, 123
Jordan, 81, 83, 87, 90–93, 95, 123, 126, 127, 151, 262, 297
Josephson, Joseph and Edna, 68

journaling, 178, 194, 202, 217, 275, 304
Judaism in the 1st century
　exclusion of sinners, 75
　festal calendars, 74. See also festivals in ancient Judaism
　spiritual practices, 70, 72, 74, 81, 83, 90, 100, 101, 108, 110
　synagogues, 24, 78, 82, 83, 96, 100, 120–22, 126, 151, 262, 297
Judson, Adoniah, 28, 210
Judson, Ann, 210, 211, 280

kairos time, 114, 242, 252
Kaiser, Christopher B., 38, 41, 214
Kantrowitz, Barbara, 235
Kate and Leopold, 1–2
Kern, Stephen, 39–41
Kidder, Rushworth M., 68
Kiley, Mark, 72
Kim, Stacy S., 55
Kimball, Dan, 227
King, Jeff, 242
King, Mike, 242
kingdom of God, 13, 19–21, 27, 100, 265, 272
kingdom of self, 13
Kinnert, Edward, 71
Koenig, John, 116, 120, 121,
Kuchan, Karen L., 225
Küng, Hans, 23

La Crescenta Valley High School, 236
La Sierra University, 247
labor time, 38, 39
labyrinth, 240
Ladd, George Eldon, 100
ladder of progressive purity, 148
lament, 81, 93–95, 97, 268, 302
Landeen, William M., 153
Lane, William L., 79
Lasch, Christopher, 42, 50
Lash, Scott, 54

last days, 114, 115
Last Supper, 81, 86, 89, 128, 300
latchkey kids, 50
late adolescence, 215, 216, 234
late capitalism, 42, 67
Latourette, Kenneth Scott, 164
laying on of hands, 121, 225
Le Goff, Jacques, 37, 38
The Leadership Institute, 14, 244, 253, 277, 279
Leadership Transformations, Boston, 279
Lears, T. J. Jackson, 40
Leclercq, Jean, 150
lectio divina, 202, 217, 240
Lee, Jerry W., 238, 244, 245, 247–50
Levine, Robert, 31–33, 37–41, 65, 66, 258
light, 40, 79, 99, 139, 205
Lilburne, Geoffrey R., 34, 35, 282
Lilly Endowment, 231, 237, 239, 240
Lingenfelter, Sherwood, 3, 41, 209
lived theology, 219
livings, 159
Livingstone, David, 210
Loma Linda University School of Public Health, 244
Longenecker, Richard N., 115, 116, 119, 122
Lonsdale, David, 177
Lord's Supper, 78, 81, 83, 93, 103, 104, 106, 114, 120, 200, 201, 204, 207, 209, 265, 273, 279
　See also Eucharist.
loss
　childhood play, 226
　community, 69, 228
Lovelace, Richard, 5
Ludolf of Saxony, 283
Luzbetak, Louis J., 19
Lydia, 122, 124, 217
Lyon, Mary, 28, 211, 252, 280
Lystra, 123

MacIntyre, Alasdair, 69
Macquarrie, John, 9, 291
Mahedy, William, 13, 215, 222, 223, 226
Maier, Paul L., 147
making an election, 183, 184, 186, 255
Malatesta, Edward J., 176, 149, 163
Mallery, Lynn, 226
Malta, 117, 122
Manresa, 158, 178, 179, 185
Mark
    rhythms of spirituality and mission, 30, 112, 113, 115, 151, 153, 211–13, 272
Mark, John, 123
Marsden, George M., 198, 201, 210
Marshall, I. Howard, 119
Martha
    metaphor for active life, 148
Martyn, Henri, 210
martyrdom, 84, 97, 113, 126–29, 131, 132, 134, 135, 140, 143, 144, 146, 149, 154, 185
Mary
    metaphor for contemplative life, 148
materialism, 216, 227, 233, 281
Matteo Ricci, 196
McCue, James F., 155
McGinn, Bernard, 9
McGrath, Alister, 108, 224, 290
McGuckin, John A., 148
McIntire, C.T., 156
McPherson, Susan E., 246
medieval mission, 26
Meisel, Anthony C., 148
men over fifty-five, 49
mendicant orders, 156, 157, 160
mendicare (to beg), 156
mentoring deficit, 50, 230
merchant time, 37
merit, 144–46, 152, 158, 164, 172, 173, 189, 261

meritocratic elite, 52
Message Bible, 70
Meye, Robert P., 11, 12
Meyendorff, John, 155
middle way, 161
Middleton, J. Richard, 223
Middleton-Stewart, Judith, 37
Milan, 37
Millennials, 31, 42, 50–52, 69, 216, 221, 230, 234–36, 240, 242, 244, 248, 249, 251–53, 256, 257, 280, 281, 284
    enthographic study, 236
    hectic pace, 52
    lack of transparency, 235
    time press, 52
Miller, Arpi Misha, 221
Miller, Charles, R., 6, 7, 104, 170, 194, 290, 310
Miller, Donald E., 13, 215, 220, 221
Miller, J. Keith, 56, 57
Minor, Mitzi, 71, 84
Miramax, 1, 2
missio Dei, 21–24, 272
missio ecclesiarum, 21, 22, 272
missio homino, 272
missio hominum, 21, 22
mission
    from above, 21, 272
    from below, 21, 272
missional practices, 30, 113, 115, 248, 250, 252, 273, 278, 283
    compassionate acts, 182
    verbal witness, 139, 173, 235, 245, 247, 248, 250, 256, 261
missiones ecclesiae, 21
Mitchell, Christopher W., 198
Model for Christian Spirituality, 15, 30, 258, 270, 271
modern age, 1, 3, 30, 41, 43, 44, 152, 153, 288
modern era, 3, 26, 44, 153
modernity, 3, 29, 36, 38, 43, 44, 49, 258, 268, 288–290

Moe-Lobeda, Cynthia, 83
Moll, Rob, 227, 254
monthly new moons, 33
Moody Bible Institute, 198
moratorium
　activity as ususal, 255, 277
Moreau, A. Scott, 24
Mosbarger, Joy, 70–72
Moses, 74, 89, 93, 95, 108, 128, 135, 142, 299, 300
Moule, C. F. D., 71, 72, 74, 78, 116
Mount of Olives, 89, 93, 108, 300
MTV, 220
multi-disciplinary, 28
multi-tasking, 268
multitemporality, 66
Multnomah School of the Bible, 239
Muslim conquests, 154
Muto, Susan, 155, 240, 278
mutual confession, 69, 169, 269, 282
My Space, 53
Myers, Ched, 83, 94, 96
mystical theology, 5, 148, 264
mysticism
　infused, 189, 304

Nangle, Joseph, 83
narcissistic self absorption, 50
Naughton, Keith, 235
Nazareth, 87
Neely, Alan J., 18
Neill, Stephen, 193, 196, 210
neoplatonic, 146, 147, 154, 274
Netherlands, 157
networked society, 3, 54, 69, 268
New English Bible, 213
new Exodus, 81
New Jersey, 201, 202
new legalism, 22, 108
New Light Presbyterians, 201
new modes of transportation, 37

new monasticism, 227, 229, 253, 254, 257, 281
New Moon festivals, 79, 82
New Revised Standard Version, 27
New York, 1, 39, 40
New York City, 1
Newbigin, Lesslie, 20–22, 108
Newton, John, 265, 283
Newton, Sir Isaac, 36
Newtonian physics, 34
Nicene Creed, 35
Nicene Fathers, 35
Nineteenth Annotation of *The Spiritual Exercises* of Ignatius of Loyola, 181
Nixon, R. E., 120
Noll, Mark A., 112
Noonan, David, 52
Nouwen, Henri J. M., 5–7, 91, 94, 104, 109, 149, 275, 293

Oakwood College, 247
Obermann, Heiko A., 157
Oldenburg, Ray, 42, 45, 268
oppression, 23, 76, 83, 97
oratories
　private prayer spaces in homes, 146
Origen, 27, 30, 112, 130, 145–48, 150, 151, 258, 261, 264–66, 273, 280, 283
orphans, 137–39, 142
outer commission, 108
out-of-timeness, 220
Oxford, 38 159, 225
Oxford Group, 55
Oxford Movement, 55

pace of life, 3, 43, 62, 65–67, 69, 216, 254, 268
　accelerating, 2, 3, 43, 69, 268
　rapid, 40, 62, 63, 65, 66
Pacific Bell, 68
pacing, 241

paganism, 72, 114, 148
Pagitt, Doug, 227
papal suppression of Jesuits, 195
papal supremacy, 155
Parable of the Banquet, 114, 203, 209
Paris, 159, 179, 180, 181, 185, 186
Parks, Sharon Daloz, 234
Parousia, 114
Payne, Leanne, 225
Peace, Richard V., 5-7, 50, 76, 85, 96, 217, 281
peacemaking, 138, 171
Pelagianism, 108, 264, 272
penance, 144-46, 152, 164, 172, 173, 179, 189, 261
per capita free time, 49
perichoresis, doctrine of, 35
persecution, 84, 85, 97, 99, 107, 127, 128, 134, 144, 145, 146, 148, 180, 181, 208, 274, 304
    Nero's persecution, 84, 128
    Pliny's persecution in Bithynia, 128
    Severus' persecution, 146
Peterson, Eugene H., 6-8, 13, 70, 80, 81, 84, 149, 162, 279, 293
Pharisees, 99
Philip, 119, 122, 123
Philippi, 119, 122
physics, 31, 32, 34, 36
Pierson, Paul E., 112, 113, 154-57
pilgrim principle, 18, 25, 27, 197, 266, 274, 281
Plantinga, Cornelius Jr., 56
Plato, 138, 146, 147, 301
Pohl, Christine D., 26
Polanco, 186
poorer working class, 49
pop culture, 220
poreuthentes (as you go), 105
Porphyr
    opponent of Oigen, 147
Porterfield, Amanda, 211

Post, Regnerus, R., 161
post-enlightenment Christianity, 272
post-industrialist economy, 42
postmodern era, 3, 14, 31, 41, 43, 65
postmodernity
    experience before explanation, 217
    identification before influence, 217
    information age, 35, 42, 53, 57, 289
    liquid modernity, 3, 268, 288, 290
    loss of social capital, 42, 46, 47, 49, 69, 268
    loss of third places, 45, 268
    love of story, 2
    hunger for spirituality, 9, 15, 254, 270
    radical critique of capitalism, 43
    spirituality of the postmodern generations, 25, 30, 213, 259
    suspicion of meta-narratives, 2
    words less powerful than images, 217
Powell, Kara E., 242
powers of evil, 90, 97
prayer
    as mission, 122
    as preparation for mission, 122
    of abandon, 94
    of blessing, 76, 78, 94,
    centering, 93, 170, 202, 207
    in community, 123, 126, 128
    daily prayer, 75, 78, 120, 155
    ejaculatory, 167, 170, 202, 207
    of forsaken, 93, 97
    of lament, 93-95, 302
    personal, 116
    recollected, 93, 202, 207
    ritual or set, 116
    spontaneous, 116, 121, 128, 275

of surrender, 93, 94, 201, 207, 208, 302
  unceasing, 136, 139, 140, 166, 170
prayerlessness, 98, 265
praying the Psalms, 6, 94
pre-existence of the soul, Origen's belief in, 148
pre-modern era, 3, 26
Presbyterian Church, 247
Princeton College, 201
Princeton Forum on Youth Ministry, 240
Princeton University, 52
Princeton Theological Seminary, 241
principalities of darkness, 13
Principe, Walter H., 9, 10, 291
printing press, 3, 153, 160
prolonged sensory deprivation, 58
Protestant missions, 28, 154
Psalms of Ascent, 81, 83
PTSD, 222, 232, 268
purgation, 148
Puritanism, 176, 197, 283, 284
purity laws, 77
Putnam, Robert D., 31, 42, 46, 47, 49, 50, 54, 55, 64, 227, 268, 282,

Quakers, 265
quantum physics, 31
Queen Isabella of Spain, 177
Quindlen, Anna, 61
Qumran community, 76

Radewijns, Florentius, 168
radical flexibility, 111, 193, 260
Rahn, Dave, 231
railroad expansion, 39
railroad schedules, 3, 39–41
rapiaria, 156
rationality
  modernity's elevation of, 220
  rationalization in late medieval Europe, 155
recommendations, 15, 30, 49, 257, 258, 275, 277
  further study and research, 30, 249, 277, 283
  making spirituality the ethos, 30, 277
  mission practices, 18, 30, 72, 131, 134, 141, 151, 152, 175, 177, 182, 190, 196, 206, 212, 245, 249, 250, 257, 260, 274, 277, 280
  studying and teaching spirituality in the academy, 277, 284, 287
recovery groups, 47, 282
redemptive analogies, 18
Reid, Barbara E., 116
Reilly, Michael Collins, 26, 27, 113, 176, 196, 198
relation of Jesuits to colonial power, 212, 267
relationality in our experience of God, 22, 71
relationship between word and deed, 24
religion as end, 246. *See also* intrinsic motivation.
religion as means, 246. *See also* extrinsic motivation.
repentance after baptism, 136
resistance community, 65
rest, 70, 83, 86, 88, 90, 93, 167, 213, 218, 232, 251, 252, 256, 260, 277, 289, 290, 299
Restricted Environmental Stimulation Technique, 59
resurrection, 11, 76, 77, 83, 89, 105, 113, 114, 118, 121, 127, 128, 144, 183, 184, 224, 261, 272, 273, 300
return from exile, 333, 77, 79

rhythms
    slower, 54
rhythm of life, 162, 252, 256, 279, 280. *See also* rule of life.
Rice, Gail T., 238
Richardson, Don, 18
Richardson, Rick, 214, 217
Richter, Don C., 239, 242, 251
righteousness of God, 145
Ritterman, Michele, 61, 62
ritual perpetuation of the past, 74
Robert, Dana L., 211
Robinson, John P., 49
Rolheiser, Ronald, 14
Rome, 84, 112, 117, 122, 128, 129, 135–37, 143, 144, 149, 178, 185, 186, 188
Rosenfeld, Alvin, 52
Ross, J. M., 245
rule of life, 162, 163, 255, 294. *See also* rhythm of life.
Ruusbroec, Jan, 159

Sabbath, 6, 7, 77, 78, 82, 121, 122, 124, 199, 207, 208, 277, 278, 298
Sack, Robert D., 2
sacred images, 220
sacred romance, 2
sacrifice, 78, 94, 97, 123, 166
Sadducees, 114
salt, 99
Salt Lake City, 65, 66
Samaria, 123
Samuel Hopkins, 211
Sandberg, John F., 51
San Diego State University, 222
San Francisco, 39, 240
San Francisco Theological Seminary, 240
satisfaction, 173, 187–89. *See also* merit and pennance.
Saul of Tarsus, 121, 125
Schaef, Anne Wilson, 58

Schaupp, Doug, 219, 222, 223
Schein, Edgar H., 278
Schier, Tracy, 239
Schneiders, Sandra M., 5, 9, 10, 26, 284, 291
scholasticism, 155
Schor, Juliet B., 49, 268
Schuman, Howard, 215
Schwartzburd, L., 2, 31, 63, 64, 65, 268
Scott, Jacqueline, 215
Scott, Sophfronia, 51, 216, 222
Search Institute in Minneapolis, 247
Second Chance Ministries in Memphis, 56
Second Temple Jews, 114
secrecy, 100, 102, 106, 166
secularization, 214, 215, 287
secularized church, 23
self-help, 47
self-worth, 64
Sennett, Richard, 67, 268, 289
sense of self, 50, 63
separation of
    senses from intelligible, 146
    theology from prayer, 155
    time from place, 3
    time from space, 2, 36, 37, 43, 68, 69, 153
separatist church, 23
sequences typical of modernity, 217
seven deadly sins, 148, 206, 261
Seventh-day Adventist churches, 245
Shank, David A., 27
sharing meals, 53
Sheepsma, Wybren, 167
Sheldrake, Philip, 9, 28, 29, 155, 156, 158, 163, 164, 170, 194, 196, 291
Shema, 74, 75, 82, 120

Shenk, Wilbert R., 2, 15, 214, 215, 223, 227, 258
Sider, Ron, 24
signs of the kingdom, 98, 101
Silas, 124, 127
silence of the heart, 101
silent contemplation of the cross, 224
Silf, Margaret, 218
Simon Rodrigues, 181
Sinai, 125, 128
Sister Patricia McCullah, 240
Sisters of the Common Life, 157, 159, 160, 161, 167
sleep, 6, 52, 63, 93, 124, 135, 290, 296, 303
small groups, 46, 47, 76, 117, 167, 170, 171, 207, 209, 217, 228, 269, 281
Smith, Christian, 237, 238, 245,
Smyrna, 131, 132
soccer parents, 52
social fragmentation, 222, 232
social psychology, 31, 55
social relationships
  disembedding of, 35
Society of Biblical Literature (SBL), 71
Society of Jesus, 28, 153, 176, 177, 181, 186, 189, 211
solitary spiritual practice 122 131, 149, 152
solitude
  frequency of, 247, 257
Southern Baptist, U.S., 247
Spain, 177, 187, 195, 197
spiritual awakening, 13, 198, 210, 222
spiritual direction, 91, 93, 149, 179, 204, 207, 212, 217, 263
spiritual disciplines (see disciplines), 7, 8, 11, 12, 21, 22, 29, 70, 83, 98, 106, 109, 118, 154, 162, 173, 181, 207, 212, 218, 219, 231, 232, 267, 281, 282, 283, 290, 293, 294
spiritual formation
  in North American campus ministers
  in the early Jesuits, 197
  in the family as urged by the *Shepherd of Hermas*, 137
  in Generation X, 223, 224, 226
  in Puritan families, 284
  in seminaries and academic settings, 284–88
spiritual practice
  communal, 4, 25, 29, 30, 69, 90, 100, 118, 126, 127, 131, 132, 142, 143, 146, 152, 157, 193, 201, 211, 212, 227, 231, 255, 259–55, 267, 270, 274, 286, 287
  solitary, 4, 8, 12, 25, 29, 30, 78, 90, 96, 97, 100, 118–22, 124, 126, 131–39, 143, 146, 149, 151, 152, 159, 167, 168, 179, 181, 185, 193, 195, 199, 204, 207, 212, 255, 260, 261, 263, 264, 265, 267, 270, 274, 278, 286, 287
spiritual theology, 5, 29, 110, 148, 207, 261, 284, 301
spiritualitus dei, 272, 276
spiritualitus ecclesiarium, 272, 276
spiritualitus homino, 272, 276
spirituality
  academic discipline, 5, 9, 277
  Christian, 10–12, 21, 27, 71, 84, 114, 129, 236, 251, 272, 277, 279, 291, 292
  definition of, 9, 11, 71, 291, 292
  of dwelling, 289
  of practice, 254, 269, 289
  of seeking, 254, 289
  from above, 12, 21, 109, 272, 286
  from below, 9, 10, 12, 21, 109, 286

spirituality (cont.),
  as lived experience, 10
  as means of mission, 281
spirituality and mission
  metaphor, 99
  model for, 15, 30, 258, 270
  rhythms of, 30, 112, 113, 115,
    151, 153, 211–13, 273
St. Benedict, 27, 38, 112, 150, 155,
  264
Stafford, Tim, 55
standard time zones, 3
standardization of time, 40, 214
Stanley, David M., 7, 90, 113
Starbucks, 45, 268
State of College and University
  Ministry Report
  The Ivy Junle, 243, 244
status quo, 12, 13, 27, 83, 260, 266
Steinsaltz, Adin, 33, 75
Stephen, the apostle
  martyrdom of, 126, 127, 151,
    266
Stewart, R. A., 80
Stewart-Sykes, Alistair, 145
Stockbridge, Massachusetts, 201
stoichei, 22
Stone, Michael, 56
Strand, Kenneth A., 157, 158, 161
strangers to our own hearts, 203
Strauss, Bill, 13, 42, 50, 51, 52, 216,
  234, 235
stress hormones, 64
Stricken, Salome, 167–69, 172, 173
Strommen, Merton, 231
study of
  history of spirituality, 25, 26,
    147, 242
  New Testament spirituality, 70,
    152
  Scriptures, 93, 122, 125, 207,
    300, 301
  space, 32–37
    mission, 19–24, 286

spirituality, 5, 10, 26, 27, 269,
  286
  in North America, 10, 269
spiritual theology, 5, 29, 110,
  148, 207, 261, 301
  time, 32–41
Suedfeld, Peter, 58, 61, 226
surveys
  DDB Needham Lifestyle, 46
  The Leadership Institute's
    surveys of Generations X
    and Y, 244, 251
  Mossbarger's survey of approaches to the study
    of spirituality by New
    Testament scholars, 70–72
  Nickelodeon/Yankelovich Youth
    Monitor, 52
  Putnam's survey studying social
    capital, 46–49
  Roper Social and Politial Trends
    survey, 46
  Smith and Denton's National
    Study of Youth and Religion,
    237, 238
  State of College and University
    Ministry report produced
    by the Ivy Jungle Network in
    2003, 2005, 243
  UCLA's annual survey of college
    freshman, 227
  University of Michigan's survey
    of high school seniors, 227
  Valuegenesis survey of Adventist
    youth, 247
Susquehannah River, 204
sustained narratives, lack of
  in workplaces of late capitalism,
    67
Sweeney, Jon M., 219
Synge, J. L., 32
Syria, 129, 133

Talbert, Charles H., 116

Taylor, Hudson, 26, 210
Taylor, Stuart, 83
tears of contrition, 203
telecommunications, 43
Temple, 75–83, 90, 91, 114, 117, 118, 120, 121, 126, 127, 151, 262
　worship, 80
temporal codes, 42, 54, 65, 267, 268, 281
temporal spaciousness, 62
Ten Commandments, 193
Tephillah, 75, 78, 82
Teresa of Avila, 218
Tertullian, 130, 144, 145, 302
Tetlow, Joseph A., 180, 181, 185
Thatcher, Adrian, 12
the wilderness, 79–81, 83, 90–92, 95, 96, 297
theologia gloriae, 199
Theological Seminary, 218, 239–41, 286
theory of relativity, 31, 36
Third Quest scholars, 74
Thomas, Gary, 238
Thompson, Marjorie J., 162, 290, 292, 294
Throckmorton, Burton H., Jr., 84, 86
Thurston, Bonnie, 75, 76, 78, 80, 116
Tickle, Phyllis, 120
time
　non-linear malleable sense of time for Generation X, 220
　scientific study of, 32
　spent commuting, 48
　thresholds for spiritual practice, 250
　warps, 1
　zones, 3, 39, 40
time pathologies, 64, 65, 69, 269
time spent commuting and social capital, 48

time-keeping devices
　Chinese incense clocks, 33, 41
　mechanical clock, 3, 32, 39
　sand hour glasses, 33
　shadow clocks, 32
　sun dials, 32
　water clocks, 32
Toffler, Alvin and Heidi, 2–3
Tomkins-Ikard Smoking Scale, 59
Toon, A. S., 155
Toon, Peter, 157
torah, 33, 76, 77, 80, 99
Torrance, Thomas F., 32–36, 57, 114, 126, 282
Transforming Center in Wheaton, 279
transport containerization
　late 20th century, 43
transportation revolution
　late 19th century, 41
Trueblood, Elton, 79
trust in systems
　typical of modernity, 68
Tubingen school, 115
Tugwell, Simon, 129, 138
TV, 48, 51
Twelve Steps, 55–57, 184, 203, 269, 282
　Step One, 56
　Step Eleven, 57
types of places or spaces
　desacrilized space, 35
　lonely places, 90, 93, 116, 127, 298
　first places, 45
　fixed undifferentiated space
　　Newton's concept of, 36
　second places, 45
　space of flows, 52–54, 232
　third places, 45, 268
types of time
　clock time, 3, 38, 45, 54, 61
　cyber-time, 61

types of time, cyber-time (cont.),
  instantaneous, 3, 53, 54, 268, 289
  segmented, 4, 53, 54, 268
  reversible, 4, 53, 268, 289
  timeless, 54, 289
  discretionary time, 3, 41, 209, 268
  downtime, 61
  free time, 41, 42, 48, 49–52, 216, 235, 251
  glacial time, 54, 268
  instantaneous time, 289
  labor time, 38, 39
  leisure time, 38, 41, 48, 67, 69, 232
  merchant time, 37
  reversible time, 289
  time is love, 13, 270
  time is money, 39, 270
  uniform public time, 39
  unsegmented time, 62

Ulmer, D. K., 2, 31, 62–65, 268, 295,
underlying pain, 235
Underwood, T. L, 156
unhurried discernment, 184
union with God, 26, 148
United Church of Christ, 247
United Methodist, 240, 247
University of Maryland, 49
University of Michigan, 49, 65, 227
University of Paris, 159, 181
University of Southern California, 214
Urry, John, 54

Van Engen, Charles, 19–21, 219, 227, 229, 230
Van Engen, John, 157–63, 167–70, 172–74, 176, 302
Van Riesen, Susan, 251
Venable, G. Daniel, 246
Venice, 185

Ventura, Michael, 39–41, 53
verbal witness
  frequency of, 248, 256, 261
Verbiest, Ferdinand, 196
Verkuyl, J., 21, 22
vernacular of the populace and indigenous people
  heart language, 159, 171, 208, 212, 262, 305
  language translation and cultural adaptation, 147, 148, 193, 196, 209
Vicenza, 185
view of space, 32, 34–36, 282
  receptacle or container view, 32, 34, 35
  relational view, 34, 36, 282
view of time
  cyclical, 4, 33, 34, 74,
  linear, 4, 33, 74
  teleological, 33, 74
Viking invasions, 154
virtual community, 53
virtual reality, 53
  culture of real virtuality, 55
virtue, 7, 68, 99, 102, 110, 144, 150, 154, 158, 168, 172, 173, 175, 180, 206, 261, 270, 289, 301
visiting friends, 46, 51
voluntary resolutions, 160, 262
volunteer leaders, 233, 246, 249, 250, 255, 257
  governance roles, 246
  misional roles, 246, 250, 257
  pastoral care roles, 246
volunteering, 47
youth, 47
Vox de Heusden, John, 162
Voyagers Church, 230

Wainwright, Geoffrey, 9, 292
Wakefield, Gordon S., 9, 292
Wakefield, James L., 179, 183
Walls, Andrew F., 18, 113, 280, 281

Walsh, Brian J., 223
Watanabe, Teresa, 213, 214
Webber, Robert E., 69
Wesley, John, 210
White, Ann C., 64
Whitrow, G. J., 32, 33, 41
widows, 137-39, 142
Wilberforce, William, 265, 283
Wilken, Robert Louis, 147
Willard, Dallas, 6-8, 14, 70, 149, 219, 293
Williams, Eric, 13
Williams, Rowan, 147
Wilson, Jonathan R., 229
Wimmer, Joseph F., 71, 101
Windesheim, 157
Wise, Nicole, 52
Wiseman, Jonathan A., 199
women who work
  full time, 47
  part time, 47
Worcester College at Oxford, 225
Word Made Flesh, 227
work to live, 51
workaholism, 56, 58, 64, 226, 268, 270
World Health Organization, 66
World War II, 3, 41
worldview, 3, 50, 72, 76, 114, 115, 264
  eschatological, 115
  worldview changes, 3
Wright, N. T., 28, 72, 74-81, 85, 91, 94, 99, 104, 105, 107, 108, 114-16, 122, 125, 128, 131, 145, 225, 229, 265, 272, 275
Wuthnow, Robert, 7-9, 69, 216, 235, 254, 268, 269, 289

Xavier, Francis, 26, 186, 187, 193, 195
Xers, 31, 42, 50-52, 69, 215-31, 234-36, 240, 248, 249, 251-53, 256, 257

Yaconelli, Mark, 240-42, 252, 255
Yale College, 200, 201
yoga, 219
York, 37
York, John V., 125
youth ministry
  a God-bearing vocation, 241
  contemplative, multi-generational, 240
Youth Ministry and Spirituality Project, at San Francisco Theological Seminary 240, 241
Youth Theology Institute (YTI), 239

Zerbolt, Gerard, 160, 173, 175
Zoba, Wendy Murray, 42, 52, 53, 215, 234, 235, 240, 252
Zwolle, 160, 161, 163, 169, 172, 177

www.ingramcontent.com/pod-product-compliance
Lightning Source LLC
Chambersburg PA
CBHW071239300426
44116CB00008B/1096